GROUPS THAT WORK

(and Those That Don't)

J. Richard Hackman
Editor

GROUPS
THAT
W O R K

(and Those
That Don't)

Creating
Conditions
for Effective
Teamwork

 Jossey-Bass Publishers

San Francisco • Oxford • 1991

GROUPS THAT WORK (AND THOSE THAT DON'T)
Creating Conditions for Effective Teamwork
by J. Richard Hackman, Editor

Copyright © 1990 by: Jossey-Bass Inc., Publishers
350 Sansome Street
San Francisco, California 94104
&
Jossey-Bass Limited
Headington Hill Hall
Oxford OX3 0BW

Library of Congress Cataloging-in-Publication Data

Groups that work (and those that don't) : creating conditions for
effective teamwork / J. Richard Hackman, editor.
p.   cm. — (The Jossey-Bass management series)
ISBN 1-55542-187-3
1. Work groups. I. Hackman, J. Richard. II. Series.
HD66.G76   1989
658.4'02—dc20   89-45597
                                                            CIP

Manufactured in the United States of America

The paper in this book meets the guidelines for
permanence and durability of the Committee on
Production Guidelines for Book Longevity of the
Council on Library Resources.

JACKET DESIGN BY WILLI BAUM

FIRST EDITION
First printing: January 1990
Second printing: May 1990
Third printing: December 1990
Fourth printing: May 1991
Code 8964

The Jossey-Bass Management Series

Contents

Preface

This is a book about groups that was itself created by a group. That rather straightforward statement is worthy of a moment of reflection: it is, in some ways, remarkable that a group created a book.

Some tasks, including several discussed here, cannot be done if there is not a group to perform them. Examples include performing a string quartet, safely flying a Boeing 727, and playing a baseball game. Other tasks, however, are almost always accomplished by an individual rather than by a group. No great poem has ever been written by a team; few paradigm-shattering scientific theories are group products; and there are not many group-composed symphonic scores. Successful accomplishment of these tasks requires a kind of focused intelligence and emotional engagement that is far more characteristic of individual human beings than of social systems.

The task of writing a book clearly has more in common with the latter examples than with the former. Typically, books are either written by one person or they are "assembled" products—chapters written by individuals that are collected by an editor and placed between two covers. Even when a book has multiple authors, the authors usually divide up the work among themselves and then splice together their individual products, or one of the authors takes prime responsibility for the writing and is helped in significant ways by the others.

Writing is just not something that a team does easily or, in most cases, well. Yet there are some real potential benefits to be derived from group work on scholarly tasks such as conducting research and presenting the findings. For one thing, there are more resources available, which means that a larger or more interesting project can be undertaken than could be accomplished by an individual working alone. There also are more minds applied to the work and a greater diversity of perspectives brought to bear on it, which can result in observations or insights that might escape the notice of any one individual. And, of course, group members can stimulate each other, cover for one another, and try out ideas on each other—all activities that can boost the quality of the final product.

Thus, a paradox. Both common sense and empirical evidence suggest that groups do not write books, cannot write books, yet group work has great potential advantages. *Groups That Work (and Those That Don't)*, which reports what was learned from an intensive study of twenty-seven diverse task-performing teams, is the product of one group's attempt to benefit from teamwork without falling victim to the problems and frustrations of group writing.

The strategy we evolved to manage this paradox had four main features. First, we attempted to build ourselves into a bounded team—that is, one with real interdependencies among members and a clear leadership structure. We needed to know clearly who "we" were, to define roles so that members had to collaborate to accomplish the work, and to minimize ambiguity about who had the right to decide what. Second, we recognized that many parts of our overall project—such as conducting field observations of teams and actually writing chapters—are done far better by individuals than by groups, so we made such subtasks the specific responsibility of individual members (or, in some cases, of pairs). Third, we acknowledged that both field-work and writing would divert members' attention from our collective task and risk diluting the common thrust we sought, so we decided to have a number of full-group workshops in which we could discuss problems we were encountering, reflect together on findings that were emerging, and begin to identify overall interpretations and conclusions. Finally, once all the chapters had been drafted—including both those that analyze specific teams and the summary chapters that draw together findings about all teams of a given type—the project leader had the task of going through the manuscript from beginning to end: rewriting, cutting, adding, and doing whatever else he could to try to create a book that, for all its diversity, would speak with one voice.

While our strategy seemed reasonable (and, in retrospect, still does), there were major obstacles to overcome in executing it. Our group encountered and suffered from many of the same difficulties as did the groups we studied. For one thing, there were too many of us: a sixteen-person group is too large to do virtually any truly collaborative task, let alone create a book. All of the members (except for the project leader) were doctoral students when the research began, and they had widely varying experience in group theory and in field research methods. Moreover, this project was but one of several being done by each member: at various times, everyone in the group had other work to do that had higher priority. There was also the potential for intergroup conflict within our team: half of the researchers were from the University of Michigan and half were from Yale University, and these two institutions had different research values and traditions.

In contrast to the members, the project leader had considerable previous experience studying and theorizing about group performance—which meant that he also held some preformed ideas about how groups work and how they should be studied. Because the project leader was also the highest-status member of the group, its formal leader, and the academic advisor to some of the members, there was a real risk that his views would carry more weight than they should and that the freshness of perspective brought by the members would be overlooked or suppressed.

Aside from the financial support supplied by the Office of Naval Research and the National Aeronautics and Space Administration, and the usual collegial and staff assistance present in a university setting, the group had little formal organizational support.[1] There were no senior colleagues or administrators around to inquire how the project was going or to offer their help, nor were there specialized support staff available to lend a hand if needed. The group operated on its own.

Finally, and perhaps most troublesome of all, both the

composition of the group and the characteristics of the product
it was creating initially were quite unclear. We only gradually
discovered, as the project unfolded, just who we were and what
it was we were trying to do. For example, the composition of
the research group changed several times in the early months as
new members came on board and as some people who thought
they wanted to participate discovered that they did not. Also,
the concept for this book did not exist until we invented it at a
workshop midway through the project—well after our data had
been collected.

Our theories and findings would suggest that any group
facing these obstacles surely would have problems—and problems we indeed had. Morale swung from euphoria (typically at
the workshops, when our collaboration sometimes generated exciting insights about how groups work), to despair (typically in
the long between-workshop periods when nothing at all seemed
to be happening), and then back again (when we began to see
that the book actually was going to be completed). Members
sometimes were late meeting their commitments and, on occasion, got the work off their desks and consciences by doing less
than the best they could do. Particularly troublesome was getting closure on the end-of-part summary chapters, for which we
occasionally violated our own rules and relied to some extent
on "group writing." When work was late or writing was sloppy,
the leader tended to become frustrated or angry and sometimes
doubted that a high-quality book would ever be finished. On
these occasions, he tended to turn his attention to other activities. This behavior, of course, slowed the project even more and
further diminished members' motivation to make personal sacri-
fices to complete their own parts of the work or to undertake
yet another revision to boost the quality of their chapters one
more notch. We came close to falling into the kind of self-fueling
downward spiral that characterized several of the groups we
studied.

But we made it. How that happened is a lesson in leadership for the team leader—who, ironically, thought he already
knew about such things. His gloom about the prospects of ever
receiving from group members a full set of manuscripts high

enough in quality that he could do a reasonable job of editing them hit an all-time low just before Christmas 1988. At that point, he decided just to get the thing *done*, in hopes that Bill Hicks, our patient Jossey-Bass editor, would go ahead and publish the book even though its quality would likely fall below his usual high standards. So the leader started plowing through the manuscript, chapter by agonizing chapter—and discovered, to his surprise, that perhaps things were not as awful as he had believed. Moreover, as members saw that the leader was now immersed in the book—sending them rewritten chapters, calling to ask for additional data about various teams, and trying to find out who actually had possession of a missing summary chapter— they also began to reengage. In a flurry of activity over the next three months, the book was finished. By finally modeling in his own behavior what he expected from others, the leader was able to rescue what many members were beginning to feel was a doomed project. That the leader should have recognized much earlier the unintended impact of his own behavior is a significant professional embarrassment to him—compensated for, however, by the fact that the book seems to have turned out well. We hope readers agree.

About the Book

Groups That Work (and Those That Don't) seeks to provide insights into how work groups function, insights that will be helpful to those who design such groups, lead them, serve in them, or conduct research on them. Neither a casebook nor an abstract academic monograph, the book links detailed descriptive accounts of specific work groups with theoretical concepts to generate action implications for research and practice.

We have grouped the twenty-seven diverse teams we studied into seven categories. This structure allows readers to identify special issues and opportunities for each of the seven types of groups: (1) top management groups, (2) task forces, (3) professional support groups, (4) performing groups, (5) human service teams, (6) customer service teams, and (7) production teams. Each part of the book is devoted to an analysis of three or four different teams of a given type and includes a summary chapter that points out the distinctive features of that type of group. The concluding chapter of the book explores the overall implications of our findings for the design and leadership of work groups in organizations.

Part One deals with *top management groups.* These are groups consisting of senior managers who, collectively, have responsibility for setting organizational directions and making those decisions that are of greatest consequence to the organization as a whole. The purest form of a top management team, presumably, would be an "Office of the President" in which members equally share senior management authority. Such teams are quite rare. More typical, and the focus of our research, are top management teams with a clear internal authority structure: one member is ultimately in charge, even though he or she may meet frequently with the team or rely heavily upon it to get the work accomplished.

Part Two examines *task forces.* These groups are formed specifically to solve a particular problem or perform a specific task. Task forces and project teams are distinctive in several ways. First, members do not normally work closely together in the organization; instead, they come together from different jobs (or even different organizational units) specifically to perform the team task. Members may perform their regular jobs concurrently with their work on the team, or they may take temporary leaves from normal duties until the team's task is accomplished. Second, the work of the team is nonroutine: the team task is a special one that requires creation of a one-of-a-kind or one-time-only group product. Third, task forces and project teams have an unusual mix of autonomy and dependence. On one hand, they typically are free, within broad limits, to proceed with the work in whatever way members find appropriate. On the other hand, they do their work at the behest of some other person or group, and therefore members are considerably dependent on their client's preferences. Finally, task forces and project teams are temporary groups; typically, they are given a specific deadline for accomplishing the work. Yet even when there is no firm deadline, or when the deadline is fuzzy, everyone knows that the group is temporary and will disband when the task is accomplished or the project completed.

Part Three deals with *professional support groups.* These groups serve their organizations indirectly, by providing expert assistance to those who directly generate the organization's primary task or service. Perhaps the most distinctive feature of such groups is that they typically are in a reactive mode vis-a-vis the rest of the organization. The work is defined, and the objectives are specified, by those who are served—typically individuals or teams with line responsibilities. Moreover, because support teams operate at the pleasure of others (that is, their internal organizational clients), members may, on occasion, find themselves all prepared for work but, in the absence of a specific request for assistance, with no work to do.

Part Four examines *performing groups.* The "product" of these teams' work is an actual performance, be it musical, theatrical, or athletic. The client of the work typically is an audience—although in some cases the audience may be the team itself, as when members "play for the fun of it." The idea of play, whether done for money or for fun, is key to the life and work of performing teams. Also distinctive is their relatively unusual organizational context: the audience for which the performance is done typically is far more salient to and consequential for the team than is the formal organization within which the team operates. In performing groups, finally, leadership generally has more to do with creating and coaching than it does with supervising and managing.

The last three parts of the book examine teams that directly serve an organization's primary clients or customers. The parts differ in who those customers are and in the kind of product or service provided. The teams in Part Five provide human services to clients who are in need of some kind of therapy or rehabilitation. *Human service teams* are distinctive in that people, rather than ideas or things, are processed. The performance of these teams ultimately depends on the degree to which their clients are better off for having experienced members' ministrations. The organizations within which such teams operate typically are institutions such as hospitals or prisons.

The teams examined in Part Six also provide services, but here the clients are customers. *Customer service teams* do not seek mainly to improve the physical or psychological well-being of their clients, as do human service teams. Instead, their objective is to provide service of sufficient quality that customers, who have a choice of providers, will continue to do business with the team and its organization. Whether or not such teams are called "sales teams," selling is a large part of what they do, and therefore members must be especially attentive to and concerned with customers' felt satisfaction with the service provided.

Finally, the teams discussed in Part Seven directly produce whatever is the main business of the organization. In contrast with task forces, members of *production teams* perform their work routinely and more or less continuously. Because they are not one-shot teams, members may get to know one another quite well and come to rely on standardized programs or strategies for turning out the work. And, in contrast with human and customer service teams, production teams typically are more involved with the technology of production than they are with the customers or clients who will receive or use the product. Because of their heavy involvement with technology and their relative insulation from clients, production teams risk losing track of the bigger picture into which their work fits, including how their activities ultimately affect end users of the organization's products.

Cambridge, Massachusetts   J. Richard Hackman
September 1989

Note

1. The early stages of the work were supported by the Psychological Sciences Division of the Office of Naval Research under Contract N00014-80-C-0555 (NR 170-912) to Yale University. The later stages were supported by Cooperative Agreement NCC 2-457 between the Ames Research Center of NASA and Harvard University. We also thank Erin Lehman and Leslie Grubb, whose efforts were invaluable in the final preparation of the manuscript, and Beth Hackman, who prepared the index.

The Contributors

David J. Abramis is assistant professor of management and human resources management at California State University, Long Beach. He received his B.A. degree in psychology from the University of California, Santa Cruz, in 1979, and his Ph.D. degree in organizational psychology from the University of Michigan in 1985.

Tory Butterworth is senior research associate at the Western Psychiatric Institute and Clinic. She received her S.B. degree in management from the Massachusetts Institute of Technology in 1985, and her Ph.D. degree in organizational psychology from the University of Michigan in 1987.

Susan G. Cohen is research scientist at the Center for Effective Organizations, University of Southern California. She received her B.A. degree in psychology from the State University of New York, Buffalo, in 1972, and her Ph.D. degree in organizational behavior from Yale University in 1988.

Mary Lou Davis-Sacks is assistant professor at the school of social work, University of Michigan. She received her B.G.S. degree in general studies from the University of Michigan in 1976, and her Ph.D. degree in social work and social sciences (organizational behavior) from the University of Michigan in 1982.

Daniel R. Denison is assistant professor of organizational behavior at the school of business, University of Michigan. He received his B.A. degree in sociology from Albion College in 1973, and his Ph.D. degree in organizational psychology from the University of Michigan in 1982.

Russell A. Eisenstat is assistant professor of organizational behavior at the Harvard Graduate School of Business. He received his B.A. degree in social studies from Harvard College in 1977, and his Ph.D. degree in clinical and organizational psychology from Yale University in 1984.

Stewart D. Friedman is assistant professor of organizational behavior in the department of management at the Wharton School, University of Pennsylvania. He received his B.A. degree in psychology from the State University of New York, Binghamton, in 1974, and his Ph.D. degree in organizational psychology from the University of Michigan in 1984.

Connie J. G. Gersick is assistant professor of organizational behavior at the Anderson Graduate School of Management at the University of California, Los Angeles. She received her B.A. degree in social psychology from Brandeis University in 1971, and her Ph.D. degree in organizational behavior from Yale University in 1984.

Robert C. Ginnett is associate professor of behavioral sciences and leadership at the U.S. Air Force Academy. He received his B.A. degree in psychology from the University of Maryland, College Park, in 1970, his M.B.A. degree from the University of Utah in 1976, and his Ph.D. degree in organizational behavior from Yale University in 1987.

J. Richard Hackman is Cahners-Rabb Professor of Social and Organizational Psychology at Harvard University. He received his B.A. degree in mathematics from MacMurray College in 1962, and his Ph.D. degree in social psychology from the University of Illinois in 1966. He taught at Yale University until 1986, when he moved to Harvard.

William A. Kahn is assistant professor of organizational behavior at Boston University. He received his B.A. degree in psychology from Clark University in 1981, and his Ph.D. degree in psychology from Yale University in 1987.

Addie L. Perkins is manager of executive and organizational development at Pepsi-Cola Company. She received her B.A. degree in psychology from Morgan State University in 1978, and her Ph.D. degree in organizational psychology from the University of Michigan in 1983.

Richard Saavedra is assistant professor of strategic management and organization at the Carlson School of Management,

University of Minnesota. He received his B.S. degree in psychology from the University of Texas, El Paso, in 1977, and his Ph.D. degree in organizational psychology from the University of Michigan in 1987.

Robert Bruce Shaw is director of research at Delta Consulting Group, New York City. He received his B.A. degree in psychology from the University of California, Santa Cruz, in 1982, and his Ph.D. degree in organizational behavior from Yale University in 1989.

Robert I. Sutton is associate professor of organizational behavior in the department of industrial engineering and engineering management at Stanford University. He is also associate director of the Stanford Center for Organizations Research. He received his B.A. degree in psychology from the University of California, Berkeley, in 1977, and his Ph.D. degree in organizational psychology from the University of Michigan in 1984.

Jack Denfeld Wood is visiting professor at the International Institute of Management Development in Lausanne-Ouchy, Switzerland. He received his B.A. degree in government from Colby College in 1970, his M.A. degree in social psychology from Syracuse University in 1978, and his Ph.D. degree in organizational behavior from Yale University in 1987.

GROUPS
THAT
WORK

(and Those
That Don't)

Introduction

Work Teams in Organizations: An Orienting Framework

- In a young, fast-growing high-technology firm, a group of senior executives has responsibility for redesigning the corporation's structure—and then recommending who will occupy which positions in the new structure.
- In a federal prison, an interdisciplinary group is responsible for the custody and rehabilitation of some one hundred convicted felons, each with a history of drug abuse, who reside in the group's dormitory.
- In a beer distributorship, a group has responsibility for all sales and service to bars, clubs, and retail outlets in one section of a medium-sized city.
- In an agency of the federal government, a group prepares a series of reports to guide the thinking of senior executive branch officials about federal credit policy.
- In a symphony orchestra, a group of musicians form themselves into an independent string quartet and play together professionally for more than fifteen years.
- In an airline cockpit, a group is responsible for transporting passengers from one place to another safely, efficiently, and comfortably.
- In a bank, a group designs a new financial product in response to a regulatory change and plans implementation of the product so it can be offered to customers the first day it becomes legal.

1

Work groups pervade organizations. They are found in the executive suite, on the front line with customers and clients, and on the shop floor. They operate in organizations that provide services, that make things, and that create entertainments. Virtually everyone who has worked in an organization has been a member of a task-performing group at one time or another.

Twenty-seven work groups are described and analyzed in this book. As the sample listed above suggests, they are a diverse lot. The work they do ranges from the routine to the esoteric. Some are richly entwined with other people and groups in their organizations, while others operate mostly on their own. Some have short and finite life spans, while others continue indefinitely into the future. Some are spectacularly successful, and others are dismal failures. Yet each one offers some special insight into the factors that most powerfully shape the development, the dynamics, and the performance of work groups. The lessons these groups have to teach, we believe, can help generate answers to a number of difficult and consequential questions about groups that work:

What can leaders do to help groups be more productive and satisfying?

Why do groups that appear to be similar often vary so much in effectiveness?

Why do things that happen the first time a group meets so strongly affect how the group operates throughout its life?

Why is the way a group relates to *other* groups sometimes more important to its effectiveness than the way members relate to each other?

How does the type of work a group has to perform affect the way members interact and the kinds of problems they typically encounter?

Why do people so often have love-hate reactions to groups of which they are members?

Over the last few years, we have attempted to generate answers to questions such as these by analyzing in detail a diverse set of work groups. We spent considerable time with each group (several months with some of them) and supplemented our observations with data from questionnaires, interviews, and archival records. In this book, we put the groups rather than our theories and methods at center stage. Our intent has been to understand each group in its own terms and to present what we learned in narrative form. While we drew on our full set of data in preparing the book, there are no numbers or tests of theoretical hypotheses here; theories and methods are kept in the background so that the accounts of the groups can be as uncluttered as possible.

Nonetheless, we must address three matters before turning to the groups themselves. First is the domain of the research—what we mean by a *work group* and how we selected those that we studied. Second is our conception of *group effectiveness.* Because we set out to generate findings that could be used to help improve group effectiveness, we must be clear about just what we mean by the term. Third is our orienting conceptual framework. We tried hard to listen carefully to what the groups had to tell us, even when what we heard was contrary to our expectations. Yet we did not approach our groups tabula rasa: we started the research with an orienting framework that led us to look especially carefully at certain features of the groups and their contexts. Knowledge of that framework should help readers interpret what we found, speculate about what we may have missed, and understand why some of what turned up was surprising.

What Is a Work Group?

One problem in doing research on work groups is that the label *group* is casually and commonly used to refer to an enormous variety of social and organizational forms. This practice creates confusion. Consider, for example, the difference between a professional hockey team and the central states group of sales representatives for an insurance company. Members of the hockey team are highly interdependent in real time to accomplish their task. How well they manage their interdependence can spell the difference between winning and losing games. Members of the output can be timed or counted, such measures rarely tell the whole story about their effectiveness. If, for example, an on-going group burns itself up performing one of its tasks, it surely should not be counted as effective even if that specific task was done well. The same thinking would apply if a group alienated or de-skilled its members in the course of carrying out its work.

These considerations suggest a three-dimensional concep-tion of group effectiveness. How effective a group is, in our view, depends on its standing on the following dimensions.

First is the degree to which the group's productive output (that is, its product, service, or decision) meets the standards of quantity, quality, and timeliness of the people who receive, re-view, and/or use that output. If, for example, a group generated a product that was wholly unacceptable to its legitimate client, it would be hard to argue that the group was effective—no mat-ter what the group's own evaluation of its product was or how the product scored on some objective performance index. While it is uncommon for group researchers to rely on system-defined (rather than objective) performance assessments, the fact is that reliable, objective performance measures are rare in work orga-nizations. Even when they do exist, what happens to a team usually depends far more on others' assessments of its output than on any objective performance measure. Thus, it was neces-sary for us to identify the legitimate clients of the groups we studied and to obtain performance assessments from them.

The second dimension is the degree to which the process of carrying out the work enhances the capability of members to work together interdependently in the future. Some groups operate in ways that make it impossible for members to work together again; for example, mutual antagonism could become so high that members would choose to accept collective failure rather than to share knowledge and information with one an-other. In other groups, members become highly skilled at work-ing together, resulting in a performing unit that becomes in-creasingly capable over time; for example, members of a musical ensemble or athletic team sometimes become able to anticipate one another's next moves and to initiate appropriate responses to those moves even as they occur. Even if a group was temporary (such as a one-shot task force), we examined whether its capability as a performing unit increased or decreased over its life.

The third dimension is the degree to which the group experience contributes to the growth and personal well-being of team members. Some groups operate in ways that block the development of individual members and frustrate satisfaction of their personal needs. Other groups provide their members with many opportunities for learning and need satisfaction. Even when the official purpose of a group had nothing to do with personal development, we still examined the impact of the group experience on individual members when we assessed the group's effectiveness.

The relative weights that should be assigned to the three criterion dimensions vary across circumstances. For example, if a temporary team were created to perform a single task of extraordinary importance, then the second and third dimensions would be of little relevance in judging that team's effectiveness. On the other hand, teams sometimes are formed primarily to help members gain experience, learn some things, and become competent as performing units. Because the tasks of such groups may be more an excuse than a reason for their existence, assessments of their effectiveness should depend more on the second and third dimensions than on the first.

In sum, determining how well our teams performed always involved much more than simply counting outputs. Not only was it necessary to consider social and personal criteria, but even assessments of task performance turned out to be complex—because they depended on standards specified by members of the group's social system rather than on those chosen by the researchers.

Orienting Framework

Even though our research strategy had a substantial inductive component, we did not start from scratch. There is a large existing body of research on group dynamics and performance, and we were familiar with that literature (see, for example, McGrath,

1984). Moreover, our own previous research generated some leads about the factors that contribute to the effectiveness of work groups. Thus, we approached the teams that we studied with glasses already on. They were, we hoped, glasses that would not distort what we saw—but they were, in fact, tinted by what we already knew (or thought we knew) about group performance. In the paragraphs to follow, we lay out briefly some of the assumptions we held as we began the research, and we describe the outlines of the conceptual framework that guided our data collection.

Assumptions

Influences on group effectiveness do not come in separate, easily distinguishable packages. They come, instead, in complex tangles that often are as hard to straighten out as a backlash on a fishing reel. To try to sort out the effects of each possible determinant of team effectiveness can lead to the conclusion that no single factor has a very powerful effect—a conclusion reached by more than one reviewer of the group performance literature. Each possible cause loses its potency when examined in isolation from other conditions also in place for the groups under study. In fact, the performance effectiveness of groups in organizations usually is overdetermined—that is, it is the product of multiple, nonindependent factors whose influence depends in part on the fact that they *are* redundant.

Moreover, there are many different ways a group can behave and still perform work well, and even more ways for it to be nonproductive. Systems theorists call this aspect of organized endeavor *equifinality* (Katz & Kahn, 1978, p. 30). According to this principle, a group can reach the same outcome from various initial conditions and by a variety of means. There is no single performance strategy that will work equally well for different groups—even groups that have identical official tasks.

Finally, groups (like any social system) develop and enact their own versions of reality—and then behave in accord with the environments they have helped create. A team's redefinition of reality, which cannot be prevented, can either blunt or enhance the impact of specific actions intended to influence the group. This suggests that understanding the process by which groups create and redefine reality may be critical to any research that aspires to advance understanding about the determinants of group effectiveness.

Together, these assumptions invite reconsideration of traditional ways of managing and studying work teams in organizations. They imply, for example, that those who create and lead work groups might most appropriately focus their efforts on the *creation of conditions* that support effective team performance. Rather than attempting to manage group behavior in real time, leaders might better spend their energies creating contexts that increase the likelihood (but cannot guarantee) that teams will prosper—taking care to leave ample room for groups to develop their own unique behavioral styles and performance strategies. For researchers, these assumptions challenge traditional models of group effectiveness in which specific causes are tightly linked to performance outcomes. They invite an alternative kind of theorizing—one that is more congruent with the facts of life in social systems. The research reported in this book is one attempt to begin to move toward such an alternative paradigm.

Enabling Conditions

To perform well, a group must surmount three hurdles. It must (1) exert sufficient effort to accomplish the task at an acceptable level of performance, (2) bring adequate knowledge and skill to bear on the task work, and (3) employ task performance strategies that are appropriate to the work and to the setting in which it is being performed.[2]

We refer to these three hurdles as the *process criteria* of effectiveness. They are not the ultimate test of how well a group has performed (see above for our views about that), but they turn out to be of great use both for assessing how a group is doing as it proceeds with its work and for diagnosing the nature of the problem if things are not going well. One can readily ask, for example, whether a group is having difficulties because of an effort problem, a talent problem, or a strategy problem.

A high standing on the process criteria cannot be achieved

through exhortation or by instructions to group members. Instead, there appear to be a number of organizational conditions which, when in place, increase the likelihood that a group's work will be characterized by sufficient effort, ample task-relevant knowledge and skill, and task-appropriate performance strategies. The research reported in this book seeks to identify and to illuminate those organizational conditions. We looked especially carefully at three aspects of the performance situation: the structure of the group itself, the organizational context in which the group operates, and the availability of team-oriented coaching and process assistance.

A Group Structure That Promotes Competent Work on the Task. Some groups have difficulty getting anything done because they were not set up right in the first place. Our research explores the role of the following three structural features:

Task structure. Is the team task clear, consistent with a group's purpose, and high on what Hackman and Oldham (1980) call *motivating potential?* Does the team have a meaningful piece of work to do for which members share responsibility and accountability and that provides opportunities for the team to learn how well it is doing?

Group composition. Is the group well staffed? Is it the right size, given the work to be done? Do members have the expertise required to perform the task well? Do they have sufficient interpersonal skill to function well in a team? Is the mix of members appropriate? Are there signs that members are so similar that there is little for them to learn from one another? Or are there signs that they are so heterogeneous that they risk having difficulty communicating and coordinating with one another?

Core norms that regulate member behavior. While it is perhaps unusual to include group norms as an aspect of structure, expectations about acceptable behavior tend either to be "imported" to the group by members or established very early in its life. Moreover, core norms tend to remain in place until and unless something fairly dramatic occurs to force a rethinking about what behaviors are and are not appropriate. Are group norms clear and strong enough to regulate group behavior efficiently, thereby making coordinated action possible? Do they actively promote continuous scanning of the performance situation and proactive planning of group performance strategies?[3]

An Organizational Context That Supports and Reinforces Excellence. While organizational supports may strike some readers as mundane and relatively uninteresting, existing evidence suggests that their presence (or absence) can dramatically foster (or limit) team effectiveness. Specific features of the organizational context that appear significant in creating conditions for team effectiveness include the following:

The reward system. Does it provide recognition and reinforcement contingent on performance? Are rewards administered to the group as a whole or to individuals within the group? Do the rewards provide incentives for task-oriented collaboration, or do they encourage individuals to differentiate themselves from the team effort?

The educational system. Is training or technical assistance available to the group for any aspects of the work for which members do not already have adequate knowledge, skill, or experience? Is such assistance provided at the group's initiative, or do organizational representatives determine when the group should receive it?

The information system. Does the group have ready access to the data and forecasts members need to invent or to select a task- and situation-appropriate strategy for proceeding with the work?

Available, Expert Coaching and Process Assistance. It is not always easy for a team to take advantage of positive performance conditions, particularly if members have relatively little (and relatively negative) experience working collaboratively. A leader or consultant can do much to promote team effectiveness by helping team members learn how to work interdependently—although this is probably a hopeless task if the group has an unsupportive organizational context or if it was poorly structured in the first place.

The role of the help provider is not, of course, to dictate to group members the "one right way" to go about their collaborative work. It is, instead, to help members learn how to minimize the "process losses" that invariably occur in groups (Steiner, 1972) and to consider how they might work together to generate synergistic process gains. Specific kinds of help that might be provided include the following:

Regarding effort. Do members receive assistance in minimizing coordination and motivation decrements (process losses that can waste effort) and in building commitment to the group and its task (a process gain that can build effort)?

Regarding knowledge and skill. Do members receive assistance in avoiding inappropriate "weighting" of different individuals' ideas and contributions (a process loss) and in learning how to share their expertise to build the group's repertory of skills (a process gain)?

Regarding performance strategies. Do members receive assistance in avoiding flawed implementation of performance plans (a process loss) and in developing creative new ways of proceeding with the work (a process gain)?

Summary. Table 1 summarizes our discussion of the enabling performance conditions. It relates the three process criteria of effectiveness—the hurdles that must be surmounted if a group is to perform well—to the conditions that may help a group score well on them. For each of the process criteria, some aspect of the group structure, some feature of the organizational context, and some type of process assistance are identified as worthy of study.

For effort-related issues, one would give special attention to the motivational structure of the group task, to the reward system of the organization, and to group dynamics having to do with coordination, motivation, and commitment. For talent-related issues, one would consider group composition, the educational system of the organization, and group dynamics having to do with how members weight each other's contributions and how they learn from one another. For strategy-related issues, one would consider group norms relevant to the management of

Table 1. Points of Leverage for Creating Conditions That
Enhance Group Task Performance.

| Process Criteria of Effectiveness | Points of Leverage | | |
	Group Structure	Organizational Context	Coaching and Consultation
Ample effort	Motivational structure of group task	Organizational reward system	Remedying co-ordination problems and building group commitment
Sufficient knowledge and skill	Group composition	Organizational education system	Remedying inappropriate "weighting" of member inputs and fostering cross-training
Task-appropriate performance strategies	Group norms that regulate member behavior and foster scanning and planning	Organizational information system	Remedying implementation problems and fostering creativity in strategy development

performance processes, the information system of the organization (that is, whether the group gets the data it needs to design and implement an appropriate strategy), and group dynamics having to do with the invention and implementation of new ways of proceeding with the work.

The framework in Table 1 summarizes where we began the research. As mentioned earlier, we also sought to identify factors that are consequential for group effectiveness but that we had not considered at the outset. As will be seen, a number of such factors did emerge—such as the temporal pace and rhythm of groups' work, authority dynamics between groups and their managers, the substantive and emotional content of the people and things worked with, and the labels applied to groups by others in their organizations.

We discovered that while some portions of our initial framework held up relatively well, the data required us to revise or to elaborate our thinking about other parts of the framework. In a phrase, we learned some things in carrying out the research. We hope that by specifying here the assumptions and suppositions that were in our minds as we conducted our studies, we may have aided readers in harvesting their own lessons from the groups we studied.

Notes

1. Although we were insistent about the boundaries of our domain (and dropped some interesting groups from our research because they did not fall within it), we are relaxed about terminology. Throughout this book, we use the terms *group* and *team* completely interchangeably; we intend no distinction whatever between them.
2. For a more detailed discussion of the ideas in this section, see Hackman (1987) and Hackman and Walton (1986).
3. Norms regulate many aspects of group life, not just the management of performance strategies. We emphasize norms about strategy because they are critical to the task appropriateness of a group's way of proceeding with the work. Norms about other matters (for example, how members relate to one another or how much effort they expend on the task) tend to develop as a function of other aspects of the performance situation, such as the design of the task or the composition of the group.

Part One

TOP MANAGEMENT GROUPS: SETTING ORGANIZATIONAL DIRECTIONS

When we think about the top management of an organization, we usually have in mind a single individual, such as the president or the chief executive officer. This person has responsibility for setting organizational directions and for making the decisions that are of greatest consequence for the organization as a whole. Sometimes, however, top management tasks are performed by *teams* of senior managers who collectively take actions that shape a whole organization. The chapters in this part are about such teams.

The purest form of a top management team, presumably, would be an "Office of the President" in which members equally share senior management authority. Such teams are quite rare in the United States. More typical, and the focus of our research, are top management teams with a clear internal authority structure: one member is ultimately in charge, even though he or she may meet frequently with the team and/or rely heavily upon it.

As will be seen in the groups we studied, top management groups can have considerable difficulty operating as teams. This is surprising, because such teams invariably are composed of seasoned managers who, presumably, have extensive experience in collaborative work. If anyone in an organization should know

15

what it takes for a group to work well, these people should. Yet the groups described in this part have real problems managing their boundaries, their internal processes, and their relations with other people and groups—more problems, on the whole, than any other type of group we studied.

How is this to be understood? Does it have to do with the special challenges posed by work at the top of an organization? Are top management tasks inherently unsuitable for performance by a team? Is it because these management teams, perched at the very top of social systems, do not enjoy the kinds of contextual supports available to most other work teams in organizations? Or is it that the authority dynamics between a chief executive and the rest of his or her team make real collaboration especially difficult? The chapters in this part, by detailing the dynamics of three very different top management teams, offer some leads for answering questions such as these.

The first team, described in Chapter One, is the Fairfield Coordinating Group. This team had responsibility for managing the start-up of a plant that was to produce parts for air conditioners. The special challenge for this team was to create from scratch a new organization in which both technical and human resource systems would be state of the art, a step beyond what was in place at any of the corporation's existing plants. The team's attempt to accomplish those objectives, challenging enough in themselves, was complicated by a change of plant managers part way through the start-up.

Chapter Two examines the Omega Systems organizational restructuring team. This team was created by the chairman of a fast-growing and innovative high-technology firm about two years after the firm was founded. The organization had successfully used a flat organizational structure early in its life, but the chairman believed that the organization had become so large that its management structure should be reviewed. He created the structure team to do that. This team worked mostly by itself during its early deliberations and came up with a plan that everyone agreed had great promise. But as the chairman and senior management colleagues became increasingly involved with the team in planning for implementation of the new structure, the team literally fell apart.

The final chapter in the part, Chapter Three, describes the top management team at Hilltop Hospital, an inpatient facility for disturbed teenagers. The hospital recently had been through some extremely difficult times, including loss of state accreditation, that could have resulted in the facility being closed. Under the leadership of its superintendent, the team had succeeded in weathering that crisis. It was then in a position to engage in proactive rather than reactive management—to take steps to further improve both the quality of services provided and the efficiency of organizational operations. Yet this work, which presumably should have been both easier and more rewarding, turned out to be quite difficult. The reasons for this difficulty provide insight into some of the general problems and dynamics of top management teams.

1

Russell A. Eisenstat

꤮꤮꤮꤮꤮꤮꤮꤮꤮꤮꤮꤮꤮꤮꤮꤮꤮꤮

Fairfield Coordinating Group

It was 1:00 P.M. and the meeting of the Fairfield Coordinating Group (FCG) should have been starting. The FCG was the plant operating committee for an air conditioner components plant built by the Ashland Corporation in Fairfield, Iowa. The group consisted of the plant manager and the directors of the functional areas in the plant. I already had spent a few weeks collecting data at the Fairfield Components Plant (FCP) and had been told that the plant manager and his staff placed great importance on punctuality. I arrived ten minutes early, yet at 1:00 the room was still empty. At 1:10, I glanced at my appointment book to make sure that I was in the right place on the right day. At 1:20, I checked with the plant manager's secretary and found out that he and the members of his staff were not yet back from lunch.

The meeting finally began at 2:30. Al Rasky, the plant manager, began by laying out a tentative agenda, but most of the early part of the meeting was spent discussing an item not on the agenda—rumors from corporate headquarters about the future of the plant. Although the plant was still in its start-up phase, the Ashland Corporation recently had experienced a major decrease in business and there were rumors that the plant might be closed. At 2:45, one of the key members of the plant operating staff, the direc-

19

tor of manufacturing, arrived and took a seat next to the plant manager. No one seemed to notice that he was late. The group met that afternoon until 5:00 and again the next morning from 8:45 until noon.

When I looked over my notes from the meeting, I was perplexed. A substantial amount of work had been accomplished. The FCG discussed a number of issues, some on its agenda and some not. For about one-fifth of the meeting, group members shared information about how things were going in various parts of the plant. The FCG engaged in an extended discussion about how to respond to concerns expressed by the plant's middle management group at a previous meeting. Members worked out an organization plan that would allow the plant to function if corporate headquarters decided to decrease the plant's originally planned expansion rate. Finally, the FCG decided to put together a report for corporate headquarters that described the unique advantages of the Fairfield plant and explained why it should remain open despite the corporate downturn.

Still I wondered why, given the importance of this group for the plant, members were so lax about the starting time for the meeting, about following an agenda, and about confronting the group member who had arrived so late. Did the group really need to spend almost six hours on this work? While the tone of the meeting was generally informal and there were no overt expressions of conflict or hostility between group members, I wondered why some group members often seemed to "tune out" when other members were speaking.

Even though my initial meeting with the FCG left me feeling slightly uneasy about the group, I was unprepared for the outpouring of anger and frustration I heard during my first interview with one of its members. The interview had been scheduled to last an hour, but it continued for more than three. During our conversation, the FCG member accused other members of the group of incompetence and of undermining each other outside of group meetings. He suggested that the reason group meetings were so placid was the group members' fear of speaking openly in meetings about what was really on their minds.

This interview was not an aberration. In later discussions, other group members repeated these sentiments and went on to argue that the FCG came up with worse solutions as a group than did its individual members. Even when the group seemingly came to a consensus on a decision, the group's unanimity fragmented during implementation with "five people doing five different things."

The members of the FCG completed a questionnaire evaluating aspects of their group's organizational context, design, and internal process. The FCG's responses were compared to those of three other groups in the Fairfield Components Plant—a computer systems staff support team and two manufacturing teams—as well as to those of twenty-four other work groups functioning in a variety of organizational contexts. Results showed that the FCG rated the acceptability of the work it produced, as well as the quality of relationships within the group, lower than any of the other three teams studied at the Fairfield Components Plant—and also below the mean of teams from the other organizations surveyed. The team also rated itself below the average on its ability to bring the efforts and expertise of its members to bear on the group task. It rated itself least effective of all in developing appropriate strategies to perform the work. Other plant members were equally harsh in their assessment of the FCG. They complained that they were not quite sure what the FCG did in its seemingly interminable meetings, but what it absolutely did not do was to provide the plant with a clear sense of direction.

A Contradiction?

Yet despite all these criticisms, the group cannot be described as a failure. The FCG's key objective was to manage the start-up of the Fairfield Components Plant, and there was abundant evidence that the start-up had been an overwhelming success. The first manufacturing team in the plant had been approved for production after receiving a highly favorable evaluation by a group of corporate auditors, and the plant had developed training programs, compensation systems, and quality assurance programs that were models for the corporation. Most of the employees in the plant were well satisfied with their jobs and highly committed to making the FCP the finest plant in the Ashland Corporation.

It also was difficult to reconcile the negative evaluations I had heard of the group as a whole with what I knew about the individual group members. Fairfield's first plant manager had carefully chosen each member of the team because of his or her high potential, and the top management of the corporation had ratified each of his choices. Further, the FCG members were motivated as well as talented; they routinely worked long hours and many of them described their work at the Fairfield Components Plant as the most significant assignment of their careers. In fact, the FCG had one of the highest levels of measured internal motivation of any of the teams studied in the overall research project.

How could a group of such individually talented and motivated managers have so much trouble working together as a team? And how, given these difficulties, did they nonetheless manage to create such a successful organization? The answers to these questions have their roots deep in the history of the Fairfield organization.

History of the FCG

Group Formation: Summer 1980. The roots of the Fairfield Coordinating Group extend back to the summer of 1980 when Peter Michaels, Ashland's vice president for domestic operations, chose Barry Mackay to be the plant manager of a new manufacturing facility in Fairfield, Iowa. Mackay formerly had been the head of a planning team coordinating the financial, marketing, engineering, manufacturing, and purchasing work necessary to bring a new line of energy-efficient air conditioners, code named Q-15, into worldwide production. An empty plant was purchased to provide the floor space for production of components for these air conditioners.

Mackay selected the management staff for the FCG from two very different parts of Ashland: from the Q-15 planning team and from two of Ashland's outlying plants—Ridgeway,

Pennsylvania, and Jacksonville, Florida. The members of the Q-15 planning team had spent their years with Ashland working primarily in and around the company's corporate headquarters in Joplin, Missouri. The bulk of Ashland's manufacturing also took place in the Joplin area in large, unionized facilities. Work was organized traditionally in these factories, with hourly employees working within defined job classifications, supervised by a multilayered management hierarchy.

In contrast, Ridgeway and Jacksonville were smaller, non-union facilities. These plants organized employees into teams and emphasized the importance of employee participation and communication across teams and functions. Employees were trained to perform multiple jobs, and status differences were kept to a minimum.

FCG members from Joplin were primarily responsible for the technical areas of the plant, including facilities, manufacturing, computer systems, and the first manufacturing team. Members from the Ridgeway and Jacksonville plants principally managed plant administration, including organizational development and training, finance, and materials.

Two sets of corporate expectations guided the FCG during these early months. First, Ashland's top management expected the Fairfield Components Plant to meet the cost and production standards set for the overall Q-15 project as it produced compressors, gear assemblies, and fans for the new air conditioners. And second, management expected Fairfield to be an "innovative work system" in the tradition of Ashland's Jacksonville and Ridgeway plants.

The FCG Splits: Fall 1980. In the early fall, most of the Fairfield Coordinating Group's meetings were in Joplin. This meant that the personnel from the outlying plants, Ridgeway and Jacksonville, became virtually weekly long-distance commuters to Joplin. To minimize these commutes, most of the personnel from the outlying plants moved their families to Fairfield by the end of the year, and they began to argue that all meetings should be held in the new plant. This created tension with those from Joplin who had an interest in a more extended transition to Fairfield; many of these managers had lived near Joplin all their lives and were trying to convince their families to move to a new part of the country for the first time.

This geographical conflict exacerbated other differences between the two groups—differences in their priorities for the new plant and in their relative understanding of organizational design issues. Because of their technical responsibilities, those from Joplin were most concerned with seeing that the production systems in Fairfield were completed satisfactorily and on time. Many of their jobs also required them to spend a substantial portion of their time away from the plant working with the manufacturers of the plant's machinery. This created tension with those from Ridgeway and Jacksonville, who placed a higher priority on completing the organizational design work in Fairfield. Even when the whole FCG was able to meet to work on design issues, things did not always go smoothly. Because of their greater previous exposure to participative work systems, those from Ridgeway and Jacksonville tended to be frustrated by the naivete of the Joplin group about organizational design issues. Conversely, FCG members from Joplin tended to view those from the outlying plants as intolerant.

The Start-Up Falters: Spring 1981. The FCG's work during the first half of 1981 was complicated by difficulties in permanently filling key positions in the Fairfield organization. As of May, the plant still had not hired directors of personnel and product quality. In addition, Alan Goldin, who had been serving as director of manufacturing, announced in March that for personal reasons he had decided not to move to Fairfield.

The problems created by these unfilled management positions became particularly acute as the FCG prepared for the anticipated summer hiring of the nonexempt personnel who would run the machine lines. Nonexempt hiring could occur only after the necessary personnel and pay systems were in place—and they were not. Further, the FCG began receiving criticism from headquarters that team members "weren't putting things together quickly enough and in a quality manner." By May, the FCG had roughed out a consensus on a range of issues—from

plant philosophy to compensation objectives to team job design. However, none of these systems was completely finalized
or approved. During this period, the group began to vacillate between trying to create a unique organizational design for the
FCP and trying to make up for lost time by adapting policies
and procedures from other Ashland plants.

FCG members reported increased stress levels and decreased satisfaction during this period. The person placed under
the most strain was the plant manager, Barry Mackay. Even
though Barry was still nominally living in Joplin, he was working
ninety-hour weeks in Fairfield. On July 1, stating that he was
acting because of concerns about Barry's health, Peter Michaels
announced that he was changing Barry's position from plant
manager to director of technical services. The new plant manager would be Alan Rasky, previously director of manufacturing
for the Jacksonville plant.

The Second Year: July 1981 to August 1982. During the second half of 1981, the FCG devoted its attention primarily to
developing the plant systems and policies necessary to allow
production to begin in 1982. The group concentrated its work
in four major areas: developing a compensation plan, creating a
plant orientation and training program, developing a system to
manage the delegation of authority from central functional
groups to manufacturing teams, and finalizing the architectural
plans for a major facilities upgrade. The first three of these projects were completed primarily by subgroups of the FCG and
then reviewed, modified, and approved by the group as a whole.
The one exception was the facilities upgrade, which followed a
highly structured group process led by an architectural design
firm.

The continuing split between the members of the group
from Joplin and those from the outlying plants complicated the
FCG's work on these tasks. This split was exacerbated by another decision made during this period. Because of increases in
the size of the work force, the technical functions—manufacturing engineering and systems—were moved to the back of the
plant, or, as it quickly became known, the "outback." In con-

trast, the administrative functions—finance, personnel, and training—remained "up front." In practice, this meant that informal communication was greatly limited between those FCG members—primarily from Joplin—who were located in the back of the plant and those—primarily from Ridgeway and Jacksonville—who remained in the front. As one FCG member whose office was moved to the outback explained, "There is a certain paranoia of not being able to see people all the time. I think it works better [for those up front] because they are able to see each other every day. They are in closer proximity."

By the end of 1981, the FCG was finally able to complete the plant's organizational design. A number of its elements, including the compensation system and the facilities development plan, were presented to Ashland's top management and enthusiastically approved.

Two themes dominated the first eight months of 1982: first, a shift in focus from the development of plant systems to the development of manufacturing teams and, second, the increasingly serious impact of the national economic recession on Ashland as a corporation and on Fairfield as a plant. Both of these factors had substantial effects on the FCG's activities.

While the rest of the plant worked through the spring and summer to prepare the compressor team for production, the FCG increasingly was forced to deal with the consequences of the drastic reduction in demand for air conditioners. Group meetings were spent discussing ways to cut the plant budget as well as the ramifications of other corporate decisions. The FCG's major effort over the summer was a make-buy study to show that manufacturing certain components at the Fairfield plant would be less expensive than buying them from outside Ashland.

Unfortunately, Ashland's business did not improve soon enough to benefit the Fairfield Components Plant. In October 1982, a corporate decision was made to move the Q-15 fan line to Ridgeway and to operate the Fairfield plant with two lines, one producing compressors and the other producing Q-15 gear assemblies. Then, in May 1983, Ashland announced the permanent closure of the Fairfield Components Plant.

What Went Wrong?

A number of problems compromised the effectiveness of the Fairfield Components Group. These problems included unclear management direction, the complexity of the group's task, relatively inexperienced team members, large group size, members' unwillingness to deal explicitly with conflict, and the absence of clear and consistently respected norms about appropriate member behavior.

Unclear Direction. The FCG never received clear and compelling direction either from its leaders (the two plant managers) or from corporate management. During the group's early history, corporate expectations were stated quite broadly—the FCG was supposed to create an organizational design to improve on previous accomplishments in Ridgeway and Jacksonville. The FCG knew it was supposed to be "innovative," but members were often not quite sure exactly what that meant. According to one FCG member, "One of the issues that I pushed back and forth a lot at that time was were they trying to tell us that better meant more innovative, or were they trying to tell us that better meant more efficient and productive?"

Fairfield's first plant manager, Barry Mackay, also hesitated to provide the FCG with direction. Mackay felt that part of managing a participative plant was allowing his staff great freedom to decide on direction for themselves. As Mackay explained, "One of the strategic errors I made was the democratic concept. Every book I read kept spelling out, 'Regardless of how heavy the pressure gets,' it said, 'don't give in and go back to being supposedly autocratic, supposedly directive, supposedly the things that professional managers are supposed to be when they don't come from an innovative work system.' So I hung on to that concept, way too long, where I tried to have the group determine what they wanted to do."

The FCG's second leader, Alan Rasky, did try to provide the team with clearer and more compelling direction. One member described it this way: "Alan . . . points at the mountain and says charge. And a lot of the other FCG [members] wanted to know which footpath are we going to take, and where are we going to rest. And Alan says . . . 'We will figure that out as we go. I know which mountain we want to take and that is the most important thing. We are going to take that mountain, and we will figure out the details as we go.' "

By the end of the second year of the start-up, as the demand for air conditioners diminished and the future of the plant became uncertain, it became evident that the major objective for the FCG was simply ensuring the Fairfield plant's survival. However, it was still unclear to most FCG members exactly how they could positively affect this outcome—the ultimate fate of the plant appeared to be dependent on economic forces almost entirely outside of the group's control. The threat to the plant did lead the FCG to engage in some proactive efforts—such as conducting the make-buy study that showed corporate headquarters the economic value of the Fairfield plant. However, Ashland's economic difficulties ultimately forced the FCG into a reactive stance; ever-larger proportions of members' time were spent responding to changing corporate demands for information.

Task Complexity and Inexperienced Team Members. The lack of clear and compelling direction for the team was compounded by the complexity of the team's tasks and members' collective lack of experience performing those tasks. Over its first two years, the FCG had four major responsibilities:

- Developing the plant organizational design—including development of the plant philosophy, mission statement, and compensation system.
- Information sharing—including communicating corporate information to plant members, facilitating communication within the plant, and writing corporate reports summarizing plant information.
- Coordinating plant activities—including ensuring that personnel in various functional areas worked together for the

achievement of common objectives, such as successful start-up of the machining lines.

• Setting plant objectives—especially providing direction on the relative importance of various activities in the plant. For example: How much energy should the systems group devote to developing a new accounts receivable program for the finance group, versus debugging the computer that monitored operations on the compressor line?

In a plant oriented toward producing a tangible product—air conditioner components—these tasks almost exclusively involved processing and integrating information. While the other teams in the plant had direct responsibility for getting things done, the value of most of the FCG's activities could only be evaluated indirectly and over a long period. In addition, as the policy-making group for the plant, the FCG was unique in functioning as a quasi-political body, integrating and balancing the competing demands of the different functional areas.

The tasks confronting the FCG were even more difficult because few members of the team had served previously on a plant management committee. Even fewer had been involved in designing a team-based organization from scratch. They, like the other members of the plant, were used to being successful at jobs that allowed for the successful accomplishment of tangible, short-term goals. In fact, one of Barry's criteria for choosing the members of the plant staff had been that they were "accomplishers [who could] cut through all the malarky and get down and put something in place, and not talk about it taking five years, but if it was a three-month job, get it done in three months."

With a relatively inexperienced start-up team confronting a complex and unstructured task, the result—particularly during the first year of the FCG's existence—was often bewilderment and confusion. As one FCG member stated, "I had no sense of what am I going to call an accomplishment. Or where should I be in January versus June. . . . I felt incompetent a lot, [but] I never felt more incompetent than anyone else, which worried me . . . I was beginning to feel like we were in sad shape if I was as competent as anyone else."

Difficulty Managing Intergroup and Interpersonal Conflict. The FCG's work required it to coordinate and allocate resources among different functional areas. Under the best of circumstances, successful completion of this task would have required effective group norms for managing often conflicting functional interests. Yet FCG members typically did not acknowledge or address conflicts within the group. According to one member, "There have been a few times when we have been on the verge of getting into it. But we never got over the hump . . . FCG does not deal with controversial things."

One reason suggested by group members for the difficulties in facing conflict within the FCG was the ongoing split between the members of the operating committee from Joplin and those from Ridgeway and Jacksonville. These two groups had quite different visions of the future direction of the plant. While both groups believed the plant should remain a participative team-based facility, the personnel from Joplin tended to see advanced technology as more essential for the plant's success than did those from Jacksonville and Ridgeway.

Yet an acknowledgment of the difference between the members from Joplin and those from Ridgeway and Jacksonville does not fully account for the FCG's process difficulties. Another team might have used the group's diversity as the spark for creative conflict, leading to improved effectiveness. Because of its unique history, unfortunately, members of the FCG were particularly wary of openly discussing their differences. For example, several members from Joplin saw the replacement of Barry Mackay by Alan Rasky as a betrayal. Although they accepted that Mackay's health had been part of the reason for his replacement, they also wondered whether the members of the FCG from Ridgeway and Jacksonville had undermined him. And they worried that if they were too vocal in the FCG they too might lose their jobs.

Ironically, the members of the group from Ridgeway and

Jacksonville were equally inhibited. They suspected that the Joplin members mistrusted them. Further, because corporate headquarters was in Joplin, those from Joplin had better political contacts than did those who had worked in the outlying plants. Members from the outlying plants feared that if they were openly critical in group meetings, those in the Joplin group might speak negatively about them to their friends at headquarters. The situation was further complicated by Mackay's decision to remain a member of the FCG after he was removed as plant manager. When conflict arose in the group, Mackay often spoke about the importance of "supporting the plant manager." Those from Jacksonville and Ridgeway saw these expressions of loyalty to Alan Rasky as implicit reproaches for their not having supported Mackay sufficiently when he was plant manager.

By the end of the second year of the start-up, group members suggested that the mistrust between members of the FCG from Joplin and those from Ridgeway and Jacksonville had largely dissipated. However, as rumors that the plant might close started to proliferate, individual directors began to worry that they were in danger of losing their jobs. This concern made a number of FCG members even less willing to take the risks they felt they would run by speaking openly in group meetings.

The lack of openness in the FCG clearly led to inefficiency. According to one team member,

> People will challenge each other and back off. You can tell there are differences of opinion [through their] body language. They don't agree. But the relationships are so bad that they run off and do it because you said to do it, even though they don't agree with it. [It] irritates me when someone comes back and tells me afterwards when something is wrong or [says], 'I didn't agree with that. . . .' Part of the reason we don't get consensus is that people have poor relations amongst themselves. . . . There were a couple of times I didn't say anything because I didn't want to catch all the crap. [But] I know that we are walking out of there and don't understand what we are going to do.

Group Size. The FCG's size also may have contributed to its difficulties in managing process problems. The FCG was the only group in the Fairfield Components Plant that members consistently described as too large (everyone else felt their groups were too small). Determining the proper size for the FCG was difficult, according to group members, because the group was used both (1) to coordinate and gain the commitment of the various functional areas in the plant (suggesting the need for a large and representative group) and (2) to develop plant policies and procedures (suggesting the need for smaller and more focused subgroups of experts). As one FCG member explained, "[For functional tasks] there are probably . . . three or four people who have 90 percent of the knowledge and experience in those fields and yet the rest of us who only have 10 percent feel like we want to get our two cents' worth and so . . . it becomes cumbersome to reach a conclusion or understanding. . . . You meet in a group and pick up any small item and beat it to death."

Unclear Group Norms. The FCG described itself as having the least clear norms for member behavior of any group that completed the research questionnaire. Despite the strong emphasis on punctuality in the plant generally, and despite the espoused emphasis on punctuality for the FCG itself, meetings often started late. There was even some confusion about who should attend FCG meetings: one member sometimes was and sometimes was not told about scheduled group discussions. Finally, there was an aimless quality to a number of FCG meetings I observed—a quality well described by one member as follows: "We have a lot of [meetings where] we don't know what the subject is going to be. It's kind of like we have an FCG meeting because we have an FCG meeting. We don't have a set agenda or anything. Everyone walks in with two or three things that they want to get done, that the other people have no idea what that was when they started."

The process problems within the FCG clearly contributed to a lack of clear and consistently respected group norms. One way group members expressed negative feelings that were not explicitly discussable in the FCG was by disregarding group norms. For example, the member who in his interview was most vehement in his frustration with the FCG was also most often late for meetings. Some FCG members felt that one particular individual did not have the requisite experience or position to serve as a member of the group. Rather than confront this issue directly, members often "forgot" to tell him that a group meeting was going to be held.

How Did the FCG Manage to Create a Successful Organization?

Despite all the difficulties described above, the FCG presided over an effective plant start-up. The group surmounted the major hurdles the plant had to overcome—creating an innovative organization design and starting up the manufacturing teams. Virtually everyone who observed the plant or reviewed its performance, from members of our research team to corporate auditors and top managers, had favorable things to say about it. How are we to account for the team's success given its multitude of problems?

First, the employees of the plant, including members of the FCG, often simply managed around the group. Virtually every element of the plant organizational design was developed either by an individual member or by a subgroup of the FCG. Especially in the second year of its operations, the plant manager—not the FCG—set the overall direction for the plant. Instead of coordinating plant activities through the FCG, directors often would meet informally outside of the group. According to one, "It is easier to deal with the people outside of the FCG than with the people in the FCG. If I have a problem with [another director] I go to [him] and we work it out, but if it comes up in FCG we never get it worked out together."

In addition, because the design of the Fairfield Components Plant called for the gradual delegation of responsibilities to lower organizational levels, the plant became progressively less dependent on coordination and direction from the top management team. After the organizational design was completed in the spring of 1982, the shift in plant energies toward preparing the manufacturing teams for production meant that the FCG was more and more often not where the task "action" was. The manufacturing teams, with their team managers, functional specialists, and production associates, were increasingly capable of both directing themselves and coordinating the activities of those in the central functional areas whose expertise was necessary for a successful line start-up. The individual directors on the FCG acted primarily as expert resources to their subordinates and occasionally as mediators of lower-level disputes between the central functional areas and the manufacturing teams. Perhaps the most important task for the FCG during this period was simply to make sure that the various FCG directors did not give conflicting messages to the rest of the plant.

Finally, during certain periods in its history, the FCG did face specific challenges that helped it coalesce temporarily into a more effective team. These tended to be times when the members shared "a common goal that makes us look good as a plant, rather than as individuals," according to one FCG member. For example, the group worked both efficiently and effectively in preparing materials for the corporation to justify allowing the Fairfield plant to remain open. This clear and compelling task provided the group with both a sense of direction and a common external threat that lessened the team's internal conflicts.

Nonetheless, and despite the enormous pride directors had in the organization as a whole, FCG members experienced lingering frustrations with the group. One concluded, "We never got over the hill, and maybe that is too much to ask at this early point. I think we have gained but it has never been what it could have been."

Could things actually have been different for the FCG? We have seen that the team's effectiveness was hindered by unclear direction, high task complexity coupled with member inexperience, large group size, difficulties managing built-in conflict, and unclear group norms. All of these problems are, to some extent, under the control of a group's leader and theoretically could have been solved. For example, Barry Mackay might have selected more experienced team members. He also could have provided the group with clearer direction. Both he and

Alan Rasky might have worked harder to create an atmosphere of trust that made the expression of intergroup and interpersonal differences more acceptable, and they might have fostered the development and consistent enforcement of group norms.

Although such changes indeed would have helped the FCG, they probably would not have helped very much. The FCG was jolted by a series of shocks—ranging from the inevitable frustrations of starting up a plant with an untested organizational design and a new technology, through the trauma of having the group's first leader replaced, to the ultimately fatal economic downturn. Just when the team was beginning to recover from one of these shocks, it invariably was hit by another. The members of the FCG were like a group of sailors in a small, leaky boat in a hurricane. Their captain might have chosen the crew more wisely, he might have got them rowing together better, he even might have done a better job of keeping them pointed toward land; but ultimately the only thing that would have kept the boat from filling with water was for the rain to have stopped.

2

Susan G. Cohen

Corporate Restructuring Team[1]

The meeting to give feedback on our research to members of the structure team at Omega Systems already had been postponed twice because of last-minute changes in senior managers' schedules. This time, we had been assured, all five senior managers on the team would be there to hear what we found in the research and to explore how those findings might help them improve their functioning in the future.[2]

We climbed the stairs to the second floor of the converted warehouse where senior managers at Omega had their offices and found two team members at their desks. They told us that the chair of the committee, Andrea Lehman, was not feeling well and was lying down in the employee lounge. The remaining two members, they said, were out in the production area and should be back soon.

We asked whether a meeting room at the nearby Sheraton had been reserved. We specifically had requested an off-site meeting because, as our research findings documented, meetings at headquarters invariably were interrupted by managers dropping in with quick questions or by urgent telephone calls. No, we were told, nobody had got around to doing that. But surely we could be flexible and find a suitable room somewhere in the headquarters offices.

Andrea was indeed in the lounge, looking pale and pained. When we suggested that perhaps the meeting should be rescheduled a third time, she protested: no, she could manage; we should go ahead and get it done. The team, she said, badly needed to hear our feedback. She would be feeling better very soon, and would join us when we found a place to meet. Space was scarce, but with the help of another structure team member we found an unoccupied meeting room next to the shipping office, and the meeting finally began there forty-five minutes late.

During the meeting, several other managers poked their heads in—hoping they could use the space—and sometimes remained for a minute or two to check something out with one of the senior managers on the team. One team member left in the middle of the meeting to participate in an "urgent conference call that will only take five minutes." He never returned. Members interrupted one another frequently, and sometimes two different discussions were going on simultaneously. Our attempts to point out what was happening, to ask the group to take a look at the meeting dynamics and decide if they wanted to behave differently, were listened to but had little effect.

In all, the anarchy and chaos that characterized the feedback meeting replicated many of the themes that had emerged in our research on the structure team—the findings that we had come to share with the team. And while members agreed both with our findings and with our observations about what was happening in the feedback meeting, their behaviors did not change. Nor did the feedback have any discernible effects on subsequent team dynamics.

Omega Systems was, at the time of the research, a fast-growing and highly successful high-technology firm. Located not far from San Francisco, the firm had been founded two years previously by Tom Justin. A hard-driving, entrepreneurial manager, Justin formerly had been a top manager at a large, traditionally managed technology company. He had come up with an innovative idea for new systems products and services and decided to form his own company to pursue it—taking with him several other senior managers from his former company.

Justin was as committed to developing a new kind of organization as he was to achieving corporate financial objectives. The previous company, he felt, was hierarchical, politicized, and ultimately dehumanizing to the people who worked there. Justin sought to create a relatively flat organization in which people would manage themselves—under his overall direction, to be sure, but with a minimum of day-to-day supervision. This kind of organization, he believed, would be more efficient and profitable than would a traditional bureaucracy. Moreover, it would provide a setting in which people could simultaneously have fun, grow personally and professionally, and potentially make a good deal of money.

Evidence from the company's first year provided striking support for Justin's vision. Despite intense competition and numerous external shocks, the company was both growing faster and making far more money than anyone, with the possible exception of Justin himself, had thought possible. And he had stayed true to his organizational aspirations. When the research began, there were only fifteen senior managers in a company with over six hundred employees, seven directors (including Justin, who was chairman and CEO), and eight division managers.

Although employees generally were doing a good job of managing their own work and coordinating informally with one another, it was becoming increasingly clear to all that senior managers needed some help in leading the company. And the pressure was not about to let up: Justin's stated intention was to continue to grow the firm as fast as possible. As one director, a member of the structure team, saw the situation, "There was a level of frustration in the director and division manager groups as far as being able to get the work done. They didn't have enough arms and legs to accomplish all that needed to be done and sometimes the work was not done well and had to be reaccomplished."

A specific impetus for taking a fresh look at the company's management structure was the upcoming deadline for coordinator rotation. As the organization had grown, some members had been asked to serve as "coordinators" (although without a formal change of title or increase in salary) to help keep production running smoothly. The individuals selected were told explicitly that this was a temporary assignment and that they would rotate back to their regular jobs after six months, at which time others would take their places. As the rotation date approached, both the coordinators (who, by and large, liked the role but felt underappreciated) and senior managers (who had come to depend on the coordinators to make sure things did not fall through the cracks in day-to-day operations) became increasingly uneasy. Should the role of coordinator become a permanent one? What would be the consequences of a whole-sale rotation? What would be the consequences if some individuals were asked to remain in the role but others were rotated back to their former duties?

These questions had no easy answers, and it became clear to Justin that any decision about the coordinator issue would have implications for the future evolution of the leadership structure in the company as a whole. So he decided to convene a group of his most trusted senior colleagues to look into the matter and to make a recommendation to him about whether the management structure of the firm should be changed—and, if so, how. The life and work of that team are the focus of this chapter.

The Team and Its Task

Team Composition

The team consisted of five members—four directors and one division manager. Chair of the group was Andrea Lehman, the director who worked most closely with Justin on organizational design and human resource matters. Andrea also had line responsibility for a significant segment of the production operation. Harry McGrath was the director responsible for operations—

for getting the firm's products and services created and delivered. Karen Miller, who had been Justin's assistant at his previous organization, was responsible for administration. Joe Triandis, the only member of the team who had not worked with Justin at his previous firm, was in charge of technical support. Ivan Williams, the only division manager on the team, handled staff planning and scheduling. The two directors who were not on the team were the chief financial officer and the director of facilities. The team was assisted on occasion by Jeff Steiner, an organizational consultant from a nearby research institute who had been involved with the organization since shortly after it was founded.

Although all members of the structure team shared a deep commitment to Justin and to his vision for the organization, members were diverse in skills and perspectives. As Harry noted, "We have responsibility for very different parts of the company . . . and that is very positive. Everyone has to represent their area, but not to the exclusion of the other areas. We are able to put things in the context of the whole organization." Joe provided this overview of each member's special strengths:

I think Ivan tends to be able to think ahead and look at the implications more than some of the other people in the group. . . . Harry has the writing skills. He can put together volumes of paperwork with a clear thread of the idea running through. But often it tends to be too wordy. . . . Andrea brought her background in personnel compensation and whatnot. Karen is a very balanced and reasonable person as far as someone to bounce ideas off. She is very consistent. I seem to wind up being the devil's advocate a lot. Not that I enjoy that role at all; as a matter of fact I don't enjoy it. It is not always productive. But I do try to look at the business sense of what we are doing on a long-term basis, as opposed to a short-term gratification of any group in the company.

Most members of the team had worked together before, on a task force to reassess the company's compensation arrangements. In general, members felt that the team was well composed. It was small enough for members to work together without encountering the inefficiencies and the coordination problems that invariably develop in a large team. And while members shared a common vision—Justin's vision for the company—they also were diverse enough to have a chance of coming up with a genuinely creative group product.

The Charge and the Constraint

The specific mandate of the structure team was to look into the coordinator problem and come up with a recommendation for solving it. But Justin also was feeling the need for a fresh look at the overall management structure at Omega. As he reflected later, "I provided an initial organizational thrust of a radical organizational style from the foundation of the company, [but eventually] I got tired . . . and I began to feel that I needed some broader perspective. . . . For lots of reasons, I couldn't pay attention to all the things that needed to be paid attention to. . . . It had to stop being a Tom-only deal. . . . [The structure team] was the initial attempt to develop an organizational thrust that was independent of me."

Justin did not make this broader version of the team's charge explicit at the outset. Indeed, when he formed the team, he deliberately kept its charge somewhat ambiguous. Only over time, as members got into their work and had subsequent conversations with him, did the full scope of their mandate become clear. Jeff, the group's consultant, described the process by which the team came to terms with its task: "If I were to paint a picture of it, it would be a picture of a formless shape gradually assuming form, and that form gradually changing in response to a whole lot of things. . . . Throughout its life, the work of the committee was changing and evolving as people learned more about what was needed."

While Justin was comfortable leaving some fuzz around the edges of the team's objectives, he was crystal clear about one constraint on members' work: whatever they did had to be absolutely consistent with his vision for the company. Although

he was willing to entertain radical suggestions about management structure (indeed, he gave the team signals that he would
welcome radical ideas), any tinkering with the overall direction
of the company was completely out of bounds.

"One of the things that I have learned in these two years,"
Justin told me, "is the absolute beauty of direction, the total
power that is in good direction." The direction of Omega Systems was his and his alone to set. He kept a very close watch
over it, and tolerated no deviation from it: "My feeling is that
you cannot tolerate very much sideways movement by anyone
in the top leadership structure. You can tolerate lots and lots
and lots of sloshing around of people who have just joined the
company . . . but you can tolerate very little in the leadership
structure. Therefore, you have to work very hard to make sure
that the leadership structure really understands what you are
trying to do. . . ."

Justin worried, on occasion, whether members of the
structure team had internalized the corporate direction deeply
enough. One member he worried about was Joe, the most technically oriented member of the team:

One thing I learned from the Reuben thing [first president
of the company, who had departed recently], which is why
I am watching Joe very carefully. I knew that Reuben was
a risk all along. . . . He tried to accommodate his views to
the [human resource] strategy but he never made it. I have
to watch Joe very carefully to make sure that he is learning
and not paying lip service and make sure that he is not
being destructive inadvertently because he doesn't understand. Every now and again, I think he does fall off a little
bit, but I think that basically he is learning.

The external consultant to the team also was expected to
keep clear of questions having to do with direction: "Jeff knows
well enough that . . . I have a very defined view of what this
company is, what it is going to do. . . . If he came in here and
started saying maybe Omega Systems ought to do this and this,
it would be intolerable. I wouldn't let him be here for more
than thirty seconds more."

In sum, two features of the structure team's initial charge from Justin were noteworthy. On one hand, the group's specific objective—just what it was that members were supposed to actually accomplish—was a bit ambiguous. As it turned out, the team's objectives did change and expand as time passed. On the other hand, the overall corporate direction articulated by Justin was clear, insistent, and inviolate. It provided a compass that members found helpful as they set sail on what turned out to be a choppy sea with often-changing currents.

Life of the Team

Drawing In

In the early weeks of its work, members of the structure team were not much bothered by the ambiguity of the team's charge, nor were they anxious about the long-term implications of their work. They focused their attention on a more immediate concern: what to do about the coordinators. They jumped into the work immediately with relatively little advance planning or preparation.

The team began by vigorously seeking ideas from everybody and anybody in the company. An open letter went out to all employees seeking their thoughts, and responses were summarized and circulated again to obtain additional comments and refinements. Four task forces were formed from subgroups in the company that had a special interest in the topic (for example, one subgroup consisted of the coordinators themselves). Each subgroup was asked to prepare a report for the structure team giving its views of what ought to be done.

While individuals and subgroups were preparing their responses to the team's requests, members did their own diagnosis of the present strengths and weaknesses of the management structure and they delineated the criteria they subsequently would use to evaluate alternative proposals. Sometimes this work was done at headquarters, but members found it difficult to find and protect the time needed for their deliberations when they met there. Their most productive work was done off site. Members remember one all-day meeting as particularly helpful.

They spent the morning mainly dealing with disagreements among team members, but by the end of the day they had forged a common understanding of the criteria for a good organizational design and they felt they had established a foundation for developing their recommendations.

The ideas and suggestions the group received during this period varied in quality; members were dismayed by some and excited by others. Particularly impressive to them was the report of the coordinators themselves, which showed a commitment to the success of Omega that extended far beyond the coordinators' parochial self-interest. Team members reported that the coordinators' report actually inspired them to try harder to do the best job they could possibly do.

Clearly, the process was working. Team members were working hard and felt productive—despite the fact that meetings were hard to arrange, members were sometimes absent or tardy, and interruptions were the rule rather than the exception. The main problem that members experienced was the sheer volume of input they had received. The team had been flooded with ideas, suggestions, and comments, and it was unclear how they were going to pull them all together.

Pulling Together

An occasion to structure and organize all the ideas soon appeared. Justin decided to hold a retreat of the entire senior management group at a secluded hotel near Newport Beach. After the main work of the retreat was done and most attendees were relaxing on the beach or golf course, members of the structure team holed up and attempted to draft a first cut at their proposals. The work was difficult but engaging. As Harry later reported, "The meeting in Newport Beach was key because Jeff gave us . . . a good framework for discussion, [and] we started putting it down on paper and [writing on] flip charts and talking about the skeletal structure. Some of this came from the [coordinators'] presentation so we had a foundation of information, but we ourselves started really getting into it and testing it."

By the end of the day the team had completed a rough

framing of its proposals, and members invited Justin to review what they had come up with. They were excited because they liked what they had developed and were eager to tell Justin all about it. They also were anxious, however, because Justin had left the team to its own devices up to that point. This would be his first exposure to the team's ideas, and members were worried that he might think they had gone off in an inappropriate direction or that their proposals were worthless.

The team's worries were unnecessary: Justin loved the report. Harry: "I recall Tom's enthusiasm about the effort that had been done so far and his drive for us to continue it. [We recognized] that we were beginning to come together with a recommendation that really would have a meaningful impact for everyone in the organization. [We agreed]: 'We're really getting somewhere on this; let's not slow down now.' "

Soon after returning home, members drafted an outline for a comprehensive final report that would accomplish the following:

1. Review the history of Omega Systems.
2. Review the process used by the structure team to gather ideas and to develop solutions.
3. Set forth the criteria used to design the new managerial roles being proposed.
4. Lay out the new structure in detail, including a new managerial role to be called *team advisor.*
5. Give examples of how the new management structure would work and how team advisors would be selected.
6. Describe a plan and timetable for implementing the new structure.

Team members realized, as they finished their recommendations and moved toward implementation, that they would have to involve other directors and division managers more systematically than they had thus far. Therefore, they established a liaison system in which each member had responsibility for keeping two or three colleagues informed about how the work was going and for relaying back to the team the reactions and suggestions of those individuals. This system, members hoped, would keep everyone in the loop while at the same time maintaining the team's autonomy. They also hoped it would reduce the number of complaints and criticisms the team would encounter when it finally made its report to the rest of the senior managers.

Overall, team members reported, the process seemed to be very much on track as they returned from Newport Beach and began the final push to complete their report.

Coming Apart

Two things happened soon after the retreat that were consequential for the subsequent life and work of the team. One was an expansion of the charge of the group; the second was a marked increase in the team's engagement both with Justin and with the rest of the senior managers. As it turned out, the team's internal processes began to deteriorate rapidly as it took on these new activities.

Expansion of the Team's Charge. Shortly after the Newport Beach meeting, it was agreed that the group would move beyond its original task of laying out a new management structure: it also would make recommendations about who would occupy which slots in that structure. At one level, this meant deciding who would fill the new team advisor positions, but it also involved reflecting on senior management relationships and responsibilities. Should there be changes in who was responsible for which functional area? Which directors and division managers should work together, and which team advisors should report to them? And lurking unstated in the background was the biggest question of all: Should the role of president, held by Justin since Reuben's departure some months before, be filled—and, if so, by whom?

Such questions were new and emotionally charged additions to the original mandate of the team. As one member later reflected, "As you started getting into individuals playing certain roles in the company, having leadership responsibility for different functional areas, [we would say] 'I guess we'd better look into that,' but it created some intense moments."

For the first time, members of the structure team found themselves in competition with each other for choice leadership responsibilities. Alliances were formed and jockeying for position occurred behind the scenes. Members perceived and resented that others seemed to be positioning themselves to become the next president. Moreover, even though Justin insisted that it was the team's job to recommend the best division of responsibilities, he also would tell individual members whom he wanted in specific areas. One member reported, "What would often happen was during the process Tom would have discussions with various people . . . and then inform the group of this discussion so that we could then move in and say, 'Oh, by the way, here is how we are going to structure the equipment area.' Maybe that was necessary. Maybe the role of the structure group wasn't to go into that area of deciding."

Members had secrets based on their conversations with Justin or with colleagues—secrets that influenced their behavior in team meetings and undermined the process of the group. Senior managers who were not on the structure team noticed the change and became increasingly concerned about what was happening. One said, "They were politicized, looking after their own nests." Another said, "Harry was using the structure group to feather his own nest. Maybe some others were, too. There were some backroom negotiations going on."

Greater Engagement with Colleagues. After the Newport Beach retreat, the team emerged from the relative isolation and protection from scrutiny it previously had enjoyed. Most significant for the team was Justin's decision to begin meeting with the team on occasion—a reversal of his previous stance of leaving the team alone.

Members found their meetings with him both helpful and occasionally frustrating. The meetings were helpful in keeping the team on track, and they reduced the risk that members would spend time and energy developing an idea that was inconsistent with what Justin wanted. But they also were frustrating because he sometimes would change his mind about what he wanted from meeting to meeting. As Andrea reported, "It was very frustrating because we would have a meeting and reach some consensus among ourselves. Justin would agree to this and then, at the next meeting, deny that he ever agreed. It wasn't presented as 'I was thinking about this and I am now at a different place.' Instead, it was like 'Why did you ever think of doing this thing?' "

Beyond his own increased involvement with the team, Justin suggested that the team begin a series of meetings with the rest of the senior managers—sometimes with him present and sometimes not—to review and discuss what would be forthcoming in the team's report. These meetings, which occurred even as the team was attempting to complete its report, also brought some new challenges. Andrea continued, "The directors and division managers were doing the same thing as Tom: buying off and then switching positions. This may have been due to people agreeing because they were so tired by the end of meetings. They were all tough issues and maybe people intellectually could agree and then emotionally it wouldn't feel right."

The process looked and felt different to managers who were not on the structure team. One division manager explained why he and his colleagues kept a watchful eye on what the team was doing: "They took care of their own interests. 'It's moving along,' they would say. After they finally started talking to us about what they had decided, we sent them back to start over. While it was going on, we didn't have any influence, and we *cared*."

Some of these problems might have been avoided if the team's liaison system for keeping in touch with their colleagues had worked, but it never really functioned. One division manager reported, "They attempted a little to keep me in touch, but it took a lot of effort on *my* part to make that happen." Another said, "The communications deal didn't work. I never even knew who my person was. So I talked to Andrea, Ivan, and made inferences and interpretations based on questions Harry would ask me. I finally realized that Joe was on the group, and we had some good conversations. But by then the framework was already in place, so I just dropped out."

Deteriorating Internal Processes. Coincident with the change in the team's mandate and its increased involvement with other senior managers was a marked worsening of the team's internal processes. Meetings, always a problem for the team, became more and more chaotic. Members often were absent or late, and frequently nothing was accomplished even when everyone was there. As Joe noted, things seemed to go better when subgroups met than when everyone was present: "[There were some] very productive meetings when we got down to two or three of us. . . . [But] when you got the whole group back together, the work was not accepted by the group. There was a lot of what I would call very substantial progress made when the whole group wasn't there, and it all got unwound again when the group got back together."

The slow progress, disagreements, competitiveness, and distrust exhausted members. When it finally came time to write the report, the group fell apart. There were repeated delays and postponements. One member, asked about missed deadlines, responded, "I think there were six. I'm *sure* there were at least three."

Process difficulties came to a head with the editing and production of the final report. Just about everything that could go wrong in a group did. Some members did not write what they said they would write and withheld that fact from their colleagues. Individuals lobbied Justin directly for their positions on how the report should be presented after they had failed to convince fellow team members. Some members redid work of others in a way that the original author found wholly unsatisfactory. One member went away for the weekend and came back to discover that the team had changed its recommendations at the last minute in a way that removed him from a responsibility he coveted.

Finally, with the first formal presentation of the report scheduled for a Monday, Karen and Andrea stayed up all night Sunday to try to put it together. They did not finish, and they canceled the presentation—to the dismay of some of their teammates. The first presentation finally was made on Wednesday by Ivan and Harry, but the written document still was not available. While they were giving the presentation, Andrea was at home dictating the final revisions to Karen, who was typing them on the office word processor. Ivan and Harry were supposed to get the names of the people who attended their session so the written report could be mailed to them later. But they forgot to do so.

Although the report itself was generally well received in the company, the group had become incapable of further work as a team. As a result, implementation of the group's recommendations stalled. Justin recounts that period:

> The structure group went through a crisis work effort [during that time]; they really worked hard and well. They came up with this pretty long and amazing document—the twenty- to thirty-page communication document. I think that it is a pretty interesting document from lots of points of view; there was a lot of hard work in it. They produced that and once they produced the baby, they all had a case of post partum blues. They all just stopped working and I don't know whether I consciously allowed that to be the case, or if I was busy on other matters, or whether I thought it was natural for them to have a rest, or whether I felt that it was interesting to see what would happen in implementation. But regardless of the reasons they didn't do anything much and the implementation of the whole structure fell flat on its face. . . .
>
> So I got them together and said, you know, you haven't implemented very much. You've done a great job of putting together a conceptual outline . . . but you have not been able to organize yourselves or anyone else to implement this stuff effectively. . . . There has been no transition of leadership from the directors to another leadership group in the company, there has been no real sharing. So you guys have to get back in and really force the process, you have to implement it, teach it, make it clear, follow up on it. So they attempted to get back together again, but they didn't get back together very good.

When members reassembled for the feedback session (recounted at the beginning of this chapter) some two months after the structure report had been distributed, they reported that they had met in the interim only a couple of times and had not accomplished much in those meetings. At the end of our feedback process, we asked the group to complete a brief form summarizing how they, as a team, felt about the session and what, if anything, they had learned from it. The structure team was unable to complete the form. In part, it was because of the press of other business. Yet one member declared that even if the group had had a full hour to complete the form, members at that point would not have been able to agree upon a team response.

Conclusion: The Power of Performance Conditions

Eventually, the new management structure for Omega Systems was implemented. A new level of management was installed, and team advisors were selected and trained to fill the new positions. Work in many functional areas was redesigned and improved. Justin himself took over leadership of the structure team, added two new members, and subsequently relied heavily upon the group as a sounding board for his ideas about the continuing development of the company. But the group never really recovered from what transpired in the months after the Newport Beach meeting.

What actually happened to the structure team? What accounts for the transformation from such an upbeat beginning to such a disastrous end? It seemed that everyone in the Omega management structure had an explanation. Some blamed individuals—notably Andrea (either for being too strong a leader or for not being strong enough) or Harry (either for not working hard enough to help bring the final report together or for working too hard to make sure "his" people were taken care of). Others focused on group process to explain what happened. Behavior in the team simply ran amok, they said, when the pressure got too intense. Still others said that members were just too busy, that the senior management of the company was trying simultaneously to run and to reorganize a young, fast-growing enterprise, and that that was too much for any group of human beings to handle.

All these explanations may have some validity. There is,

surely, no single cause of the problems the structure team encountered. My own analysis, however, suggests that the root of the difficulties was not the motives or talents of individuals, or the hectic pace of work in the firm, or even the relatively uncontrolled group processes. Instead, the key factor may have been the *changes in performance conditions* the team encountered following the Newport Beach retreat. In this analysis, individual and interpersonal behavior are viewed not so much as causes of what happened but as possibly inevitable consequences of it.

Performance conditions changed in two major ways after the retreat. First, the task of the group changed. Previously, the work had been conceptual and integrative, without special regard for the future roles of individual managers. When the group returned from Newport Beach, however, members agreed with Justin that they would "get into personalities," as one member put it. This change reoriented the group: whereas previously, individual, group, and organizational goals were nicely aligned (that is, what was good for one was also good for the others), now there were conflicts between what was best for individual team members and what was best for the collective. What began as an organizational design task became highly politicized when the group's mandate expanded to include recommending changes in senior management roles.

Specific task requirements also shifted as the implementation date approached. The organizing and writing required to produce a comprehensive final report differed significantly from the conceptual work members did in developing their initial framework. In this fast-paced, entrepreneurial organization, senior managers rarely sat down long enough to write anything, let alone a group report. Preparation of a team report is difficult enough when members agree about its content; when they do not, as was the case for the structure team, it can become nearly impossible. And it surely was not accidental that it was the female members of the structure team who finally picked up the pieces—although with considerable resentment that their colleagues' failure to meet their commitments had made that necessary.

The second change in performance conditions was in the relationship between the team and the chairman. Once he had given the team its initial mandate, Justin left the team alone to get on with its work. But then, after the Newport Beach retreat, he increasingly involved himself in the team's day-to-day work. Here, in an interview conducted about three months after the structure team's report was finished, is how he described his pattern of involvement:

> It's been benign neglect throughout much of the history of the task force until very recently, when I decided it needed to be a little less benign. I was distant from the task force in the early days. I got closer to it in Newport Beach, and then I dropped out again from then through the completion of the study work which gave rise to the document. . . . Large amounts of benign neglect were healthy and useful as long as they knew that their direction was in developing stuff—but I had to be careful about when it was appropriate for me to come back in and learn what they learned because I had some new perspectives for them. . . . Now I am feeling the tactics or the strategy needs more hand holding. More time and attention on my part. I am doing that now. I don't know, six months from now I may say, "Boy, they are really in pretty good shape."

Following the retreat, Justin was neither a full member of the group nor an outside authority. Moreover, his degree of involvement waxed and waned in ways that could not be predicted or, sometimes, comprehended by team members. This kept the group off balance and tempted members to lobby him directly about matters they were not able to negotiate successfully within the team. This temptation was impossible for some members to resist, given the enormously high personal and political stakes.

Justin spent some of his time with individual team members discussing their own leadership abilities or exchanging views about the strengths and weaknesses of other senior managers. While he did not fully delegate the task of making recommendations about leadership assignments to the team, neither did he explicitly assume this responsibility himself. Because of the sensitivity of the topic, his sometimes erratic behavior intensified conflicts and political dynamics within the team. Most important, however, the change in Justin's role tended to undermine members' feelings of authority, responsibility, and accountability for their own work. As Joe reflected,

> It wasn't our task to make the decisions, the way I saw it. . . . In practically all cases, there was a lot of dialogue with Tom, and I think that was his intention. The task force was not put together to resolve a problem, [with him getting only] a broad brush overview, and then let it get implemented and evaluate us on how it worked out. Ultimately, he takes responsibility for the whole process because he is the final arbiter of all decisions. I think it was more of a training session for us, he would let us go away for a week at a time to see what we could do on our own, without him being there.

Thus, Justin initially used his authority to specify desired *ends* or objectives, leaving decisions about the *means* that the team would use to achieve those objectives almost entirely up to the members. Early on, Justin provided the team with some leeway to interpret its objectives—as long as the team's recommendations remained aligned with his vision for the company. He used his authority to make sure that team deliberations fit the strategic direction and values of Omega Systems. Late in the life of the team, however, Justin also began to exercise authority about means—the details of what the team was doing and how it was doing it. As he intervened more actively in the day-to-day decision making of the team, members viewed their own inputs as less critical and took their own roles on the team less seriously. As would be expected from the research literature on team empowerment and self-management (for example, Cohen, 1988; Hackman, 1986b), team members' feelings of collective responsibility for the work diminished, and they no longer felt quite so urgently that the ultimate fate of the restructuring activity was in their hands. This, of course, made it possible for other pressing business to take priority over structure team work and for undisciplined behavior to spread in the group at precisely the time in the team's life when discipline was most needed.

The problems the Omega Systems structure team encountered did not have to be as destructive as they were to the team, its work, and its members. If, for example, members had invested in building the team into a cohesive unit with strong, shared norms early in its life, they might have been able to handle the tensions that accompanied the subsequent expansion of the team's mandate. And they might have been able to deal more coherently and competently with Justin's powerful interventions following the management retreat. But they did not make such investments. Members never took time to tend to the development of the team as a performing unit. Such matters did not seem pressing early in the group's life when the team most effectively could have addressed them. Things were, after all, going relatively smoothly back then. Developing the team as a performing unit was always deferred until "later." When "later" finally did arrive, it was too late for the team to recover.

Note

1. The names of the organization and the team members have been changed, as have certain other details, to protect the anonymity of the participants. Richard Hackman participated with me in this research, including the feedback session.

3

Susan G. Cohen

꘏꘏꘏꘏꘏꘏꘏꘏꘏꘏꘏꘏꘏꘏

Hilltop Hospital
Top Management Group[1]

Jean (superintendent):   Wayne asked last week if we could have a special meeting. We will dispense with our usual format. Issues in the hospital seem to be reaching a crescendo. I know that you are feeling a lot of stresses from clinical, nursing, I'm not sure what. Let's talk about what is going on. How are people feeling? I have been feeling some of the pulls and tensions—and I also have been feeling that our meetings have gone very well.

Wayne (clinical director):   I feel a lot of stresses—we ought to look at our role in that—at the top. Also about these particular meetings—the management team meetings—I am not that happy with them.

Andrea (director of residential treatment):   Last week I felt a great deal of tension and stress in the residential care department. . . . I seemed to be a lightning rod for people's anger and people were angry for various sundry reasons.

Bill (assistant superintendent):   I've been clearing up the backlog. What I'm dealing with is not very important to the management team.

Mark (education director):   Last week I worked in isolation on the summer and fall school programs. Summer program got off to a slow and rocky start. Symptomatic of other things.

Andrea: The child care workers are really upset. Throughout the hospital there is a lot of anger.

A long discussion ensues concerning the stresses in the hospital, particularly in clinical and residential care areas. Later, the discussion comes back to the functioning of the management team.

Jean: What has that done to the management team?

Wayne: My feeling is that the meetings have become terribly boring. And I have not wanted to come to them lately. We spend an hour and a half on reports. We have no substantive discussions about anything anymore. . . .

Jean (very softly):   So your response is not to want to have to come?

Wayne: They are not any fun. I used to enjoy coming to them.

Jean: We are back to business. The detail kind of business.

Wayne: We were going to spend ten minutes giving reports around the table. Now we are spending an hour.

Andrea: That was what I was feeling about the management team. I purposefully tried to cut my report short. . . . I did not want to give a report because I wanted to get to the substance. I'd be glad to have dampers put on me. I think that it is important for us to plan, design, and implement. I haven't reached the point that I do not want to come to the meetings.

Jean: I think that it is important for us to talk about it as a group rather than just as individuals. I got back on the old track. Involved not so much in the life of the institution but the details of the institution. The policies that have to be reviewed. The sharing of resources of staff. I sort of skirt the agenda of how the group works. I am willing to get back on track. Get back to the meat and potatoes. The substances that are the life of the hospital.

Sometimes I feel that there is a resistance also for doing that on the part of the members. Certainly I am the leader. I can take responsibility for setting the agenda and how it goes. But there is a responsibility for each member to come in and say something about being bored. . . .

(Transcript from a meeting of the top management team of Hilltop Hospital)

The Hospital and Management Team

Hilltop Hospital is a sixty-bed inpatient facility for seriously disturbed teenagers. It provides emergency psychiatric intervention, psychiatric evaluations, and short- to intermediate-term treatment for those adolescents who cannot be evaluated or treated in a less restrictive environment. The hospital evaluates and treats several hundred teenagers from its catchment area each year.

Hilltop Hospital has three residential units, a school, and a recreation program. Two locked units admit, evaluate, and treat patients. The third unit is unlocked and provides treatment to those patients who have demonstrated sufficient behavioral control to be treated in an unlocked setting. The school is part of a special school district that provides classroom instruction tailored to the special needs of the disturbed teenager.

The hospital employs approximately 140 staff. It is organized by functional departments, and it uses teams as a way of organizing work and providing patient services. The clinical director, Wayne, is in charge of the clinical department, which consists of psychiatrists, psychologists, social workers, medical nurses, and part-time physicians. The director of residential treatment, Andrea, is in charge of the residential care department. The director of education, Mark, serves as the school principal. The assistant superintendent, Bill, is responsible for the administrative service department. The coordinator for quality assurance, George, is a clinical psychologist and is the only member of the team who belongs to the bargaining unit. The management team is led by Jean, superintendent of the hospital.

The Team's Recent Success

The survival of Hilltop Hospital had been at stake in recent years. The management team had assumed power three years earlier with a mandate from the state to restructure the entire hospital program and service delivery system. Problems had reached crisis proportions, resulting in loss of accreditation. If the new management team had not succeeded in turning the hospital around and regaining accreditation, the state would have closed it.

This was the fifth administrative team in Hilltop's ten years of existence. In recent years, administrative and fiduciary responsibilities repeatedly had been shifted from one state agency to another. There had been two moves and several renovations aimed at meeting fire and safety codes. Hilltop Hospital had a poor reputation in the community and had never stabilized its treatment program.

The hospital recently had suffered from searing reports from auditors, large cost overruns, reports of personnel abuse, an inadequate physical plant, fragmentation and duplication of work across units, and general institutional malaise. There was no central leadership and a fundamental distrust of authority. Employee identification was with small subgroups, not with functional departments or with the hospital as a whole.

The department's commissioner recently had replaced Hilltop's administration with an interim management team. The interim team was introduced to Hilltop's staff in a meeting described by the interim superintendent as resembling a "South American army coup." This team developed the beginning framework for restructuring the hospital's program and service delivery system and participated in the selection of the permanent management team. Jean, the superintendent, had been a member of the interim team, providing some badly needed continuity.

The permanent management team succeeded in turning the hospital around in its first year, thereby heading off the state's threat to close it. The team put into place a new organizational structure with clearer lines of departmental accountability and authority and obtained funding to improve the physical facility. In addition, the team developed a strong residential program by transferring unit responsibility from clinicians to child-care workers. The team also tried to foster a new morality in the hospital—one that would reinforce positive interactions with the patients and eliminate patient abuse.

In its first year, the management team directed and mobilized the efforts of the entire hospital toward accreditation. The facility, support services, and treatment programs were brought up to state standards, and the hospital did regain accreditation. State investigators were surprised by the improvements they observed, after having read the earlier reports. Accreditation was a major success for the management team, and Hilltop's superintendent and managers were proud of what they had accomplished.

New Challenges

But now, two years later, the team faces a new challenge. With the hospital functioning acceptably, it is time to move on to the next step in the development of the institution. The management team has the opportunity to develop a hospital-wide service delivery model that integrates hospital departments and focuses them squarely on patients and their needs.

To accomplish this, the management team will have to move the locus of decision making and accountability down from the superintendent and managers to those who are involved in providing direct patient services. Within the parameters of a hospital-wide treatment philosophy, quality of care will be improved by giving more say to the staff members who are most aware of patient needs.

The changes that need to take place—defining an integrated service delivery model and treatment philosophy, increasing the influence of the clinical staff, and decentralizing controls—are in a direction opposite to that taken in the prior restructuring. What the management team did before to ensure Hilltop's survival are the very things that now need to be changed to ensure its continued success.

Can the management team successfully shift gears and

lead Hilltop Hospital in a new direction? The transcript with which we began this chapter suggests that it will not be easy.

One major problem is that managers are not engaged by the team's current work. Some do not want to come to meetings or to work very hard when they do attend. The discussions at management team meetings are not substantive and are dominated by lengthy departmental reports, and many managers feel that the team is not explicitly addressing the most important issues. As one said,

> What we discuss are lots of surface issues. By surface I mean, can we make it through the next month on the dollars we have, should we buy a truck, should we plow the snow, should the teachers work Saturdays, little things. I do not think we delve into issues of extreme importance. I think sometimes we dabble a little, get started, but [avoid] issues like why don't the teachers talk to the childcare workers, why don't the clinicians talk to the kitchen servers? If we could honestly answer those questions, we would have a better handle on managing the hospital.

The superintendent is out of touch with her managers and with life at the hospital. The managers view the superintendent as being somewhat reactive, as not delegating enough responsibility to the team, and as making the major decisions herself. One asserted, "I see the management team as rather passive, frankly. It seems very clear who has the final say and who will make the decision in most discussions. In some cases, and I would say fairly often, Jean will listen to what other people have to say. But there are occasions where she just goes on regardless of how other people may see what happens."

For her part, the superintendent is frustrated with the passivity of the management team. She perceives members as not taking adequate responsibility for running the hospital, as being too passive and lethargic:

> I wish the members of the management team would take responsibility for being in the meeting and getting out of

it what is necessary to do their jobs. Sometimes it seems as if members are willing to sit back and let me be at the helm and flounder and push and then push back rather than take responsibility. Sometimes members look to me to ask permission to talk. I don't know if you noticed that. Something is wrong if the top managers view me as so controlling that they need permission to talk.

Why is the management team having so much trouble getting on with the next steps in developing the hospital? The team already established a foundation of success in earning reaccreditation. It is now more stable than at any time in its history, and yet it seems stuck. How can this be understood?

Understanding the Success

Design of the Team Task

The goal was clear during the first year: to achieve accreditation. The management team knew that the survival of the institution was at stake and that the state central office would no longer fund the hospital if it were not accredited. It was up to them to save Hilltop Hospital—not to mention their own jobs and professional reputations and the jobs of Hilltop's employees.

Members could not have been more committed. The superintendent said it was as though the team were paddling furiously together on a white-water raft through six-foot rapids with rocks and debris all around. She shouted out the orders, and each manager paddled mightily to keep the raft afloat and on course. The collective energy that was unleashed was something that Hilltop Hospital had never seen before.

To achieve the collective goal of accreditation, each team member was given responsibility for completing specific subtasks. For example, the assistant superintendent was responsible for getting the building up to code. The director of residential treatment was responsible for upgrading the residential care program, and she knew the state standards like the back of her hand. Everyone's tasks were clear and important, deadlines were tight, and everybody in the hospital worked to his or her utmost. The turnaround challenge was, in sum, a superbly designed group task.

The External Context

The intervention of the state central office both angered and served Hilltop Hospital employees as they worked to save the institution. Although most team members felt that the previous superintendent was incompetent and needed to be replaced, they felt unfairly blamed for the hospital's problems. This resentment was exacerbated when the deputy commissioner told them that they had not taken adequate responsibility for the hospital's treatment program and patient care. Thus, the state central office became the outside enemy, personified by this deputy commissioner. The entire staff mobilized not only to save the institution, but to prove to the central office that they could do it. Employees were fighting for their self-esteem and professional reputations as well as for their jobs. Having an outside enemy helped.

In a different way, the state served as a friend and supporter of the effort to save the hospital. State officials were willing to do whatever they could to rebuild the hospital, within very broad limits. The person chosen as interim superintendent was the head of another state institution and was highly respected. He adopted the program model from his facility as the basis for Hilltop Hospital's structure. The interim team had access to all previous studies done by the state, which helped members identify and define the tasks they had to complete. And because team members were outsiders, they were not blinded by previous allegiances within the hospital. Their work provided the foundation for the permanent management team. In sum, the state provided the leadership, resources, and conceptual model for turning around Hilltop Hospital—even while serving as the target of much of the anger employees had been building up during the previous difficult years.

Composition of the Team

The composition of the permanent management team was appropriate given the work to be done. It contained some managers hired from outside Hilltop Hospital and some selected from the current staff. In her previous job, Jean, the superintendent, had worked for the state as the director of an outpatient program for children and had served as the administrator for residential care on the interim team. Jean hired Andrea to be the new director of residential care. Andrea had worked previously as the director of a nonprofit residential treatment program for disturbed children and had no experience in a state bureaucracy. Bill, the assistant superintendent, had been chosen just prior to the restructuring; he had worked previously in state hospital administration. Wayne had been a staff psychiatrist at Hilltop Hospital for several years and was promoted to management as clinical director. Mark, the school principal, had worked with the Hilltop program since its inception but was new to the management team.

Team members collectively had the task and interpersonal skills needed to perform successfully. Although the hospital's history and the current turmoil created mistrust, there was so much work to be done that members generally set their worries about one another aside and got on with the work.

Leadership Style

Jean's job history had included moving into crisis situations and turning them around, and her leadership style was directive, decisive, energetic, and action oriented. She structured both the management team's tasks and those to be done by individual members. Before each team meeting, Jean would consult individually with team members and then set the agenda. The meetings themselves were structured, orderly, and very much under her control. Outside of meetings, she sometimes would intervene directly in the activities of her managers—or even take them over herself. Her management style, while controlling, did fit the urgent job to be done at the time.

Jean's management style may have been based, in part, on her initial distrust of the Hilltop staff. Their track record, after all, did not invite confidence. She communicated her distrust through an interrogative communication style and an unwillingness to delegate responsibility fully. Not surprisingly, the staff soon came to distrust her in return. They saw her as an agent of the central office, as powerful, and as someone to be feared and watched carefully. Her petite stature, just over five feet tall and slender, belied both her actions and how she was perceived within the institution.

Jean had accepted the position with the belief that the hospital could be turned around, and as that began to happen, she gradually developed more faith in the staff. While the staff continued to resent her authority, members persisted in working extremely hard to ensure that the hospital would survive. Jean reported that she was thrilled as she saw hospital staff begin to pull together under her leadership. When the hospital did receive its accreditation, she reported being proud not only of her own accomplishment, but also of the collective effort of the entire staff.

Group Norms

The norms of the management team developed directly in response to the urgency and clarity of the task, coupled with Jean's leadership style. The team knew that it had just a few months to bring the hospital up to state requirements. This urgency created an emotional intensity and a norm of incredibly hard work. The interim management team already had developed plans that specified the tasks to be done. Each manager was responsible for completing these specific tasks within narrow time frames. Meetings consisted of sharing information, reviewing individual progress, and discussing ways of getting around obstacles to change. The team developed the norm that individual managers would do the work and meetings would be used mainly for sharing information and coordinating activities.

Because Jean kept most of the major decisions to herself, the team also developed a norm of passivity. While members would work very hard on their own assigned tasks, they would wait for her to make decisions or to change the definition of their assignments. Because there was so much work to be done to pass accreditation, and because Jean's decisions generally were prompt and appropriate, the team's passivity was not a problem. Indeed, that norm may have freed members from the need to spend precious time and energy on decision making, allowing them instead to apply their full talents and efforts to the actual work toward accreditation.

Summary

The conditions were right for the management team's success during the reaccreditation period. The task could not have been better designed. The state bureaucracy provided the resources necessary for success and simultaneously served as the outside enemy, thereby mobilizing staff effort. The composition of the management team was appropriate given the work to be done. Jean's directive leadership style—her willingness to take charge—fit the task at hand. The norms of the management team were well crystallized and focused on getting the actual work done. The cards were stacked for success—and success the team had.

The Present Challenge

Now that survival is no longer at stake, the top management team is wallowing and lethargic. Much work remains to be done—albeit from a new and stronger position. The challenge is significant because now the team needs to manage the hospital in a different way. Indeed, the very things that the management team did to ensure Hilltop's survival are now the things that need to be changed to run an effective hospital. Are the conditions favorable for the team to move ahead, or will the team be unable to succeed in its new challenge—as the excerpts from interviews and meeting transcripts presented at the beginning of the chapter seem to suggest? Let us look again, in this new context, at the conditions that helped the team regain accreditation.

Design of the Team Task

The task of the management team is not clear. Although managers talk about doing long-term planning, about the need to integrate services, and about the need to push decision-making authority down, they have not concretely defined their tasks. Their reluctance to do this stems in part from fundamental disagreements about how the hospital should be managed. Members find it easier to hide their disagreements behind a veneer of ideological agreement and to do busy work than to confront their real differences.

All members do assert that the management team should integrate hospital services in response to the needs of the children. However, they have different pictures of what that actually means. Some view integration as cross-departmental cooperation. Others view it as the establishment of stable interdisciplinary treatment teams located in each residential unit. Still others view it as an approach to therapy—integrating the fragmented personalities of the patients. Managers never talk through these differences. Instead, they affirm their general agreement, and thereby avoid setting a specific direction for Hilltop Hospital.

The managers also agree ideologically that decision-making authority and accountability should be pushed downward in the organization. They seek to build collaboration and trust between themselves and hospital employees. At the same time, however, the superintendent and some team members are concerned about employee abuses—inappropriate absences, overtime, use of workmen's compensation, and so on. This concern often prompts them to monitor employee behavior closely and to tighten up centralized controls—an approach that has worked in the past. But the team is unwilling or unable to put into practice the philosophy of management that it espouses.

The team keeps busy with reports and specific operational tasks. Focusing on details reduces the anxiety generated by the ambiguity of the larger concerns. Team members do not feel challenged by these smaller issues, nor do they perceive operational activities as setting the direction for the hospital. Team members recognize that they are not steering the ship, and that makes them uneasy.

The superintendent used the metaphor of a tired crew team to describe how the management team currently functions. She said it feels as though she were at the helm with a mega-phone and the team members were at the oars. But the crew members are tired and not coordinating their strokes. They are having a hard time putting the boat in competition because everybody is not at the same place at the same time—and they are not sure where they need to go. A tired crew is an image that dramatically contrasts with the previous metaphor of white-water rafters paddling like hell to save the ship.

In fact, the hospital is no longer in crisis, and what actually needs to be done next is indeed ambiguous. The direction and tasks have not been predefined by external authorities; the team itself must now do that. And while the team has taken some preliminary steps toward task definition (for example, by emphasizing integration of services and by seeking to push deci-sion-making authority downward), little has been done to im-plement these new directions.

The challenge, then, is to make future plans more con-crete and to determine the specific action steps that need to be taken. How will team members actually achieve integration of services? What does this mean for how the hospital will be orga-nized and how it will operate? How will the hospital need to change patient services? What mechanisms will the team put in place to support decentralized decision making? How will em-ployee abuses be handled? Grappling with such specifics is diffi-cult for the team because it requires members to confront their real differences in values and perspectives. Yet confronting those differences may be the only realistic way for the team to pro-vide the leadership that is its ultimate responsibility.

External Context

The external context of the hospital has been relatively static and neutral in the last year. Managers have not had to respond to externally generated requirements for change. Although the hospital did have to go through a regularly scheduled reaccreditation, the structure for accomplishing that was in place and the process was routine. Reaccreditation pleased the hospital staff, but nobody viewed it as a major achievement.

The superintendent buffers the hospital from the state central office. She is the one who brings legislative rulings, departmental mandates, and accreditation information to the attention of her managers. The state bureaucracy is always the focus of complaints, but managing external relations overall has been business as usual. There are no significant external factors to impede the management team from asserting control of the hospital's direction and destiny.

Team Composition and Norms

The management team is structured along departmental lines, and it is composed of the same people who guided the hospital through its accreditation crisis. Members of the team represent functional departments and advocate departmental interests when resources are discussed. The superintendent makes decisions after listening to managers' competing claims—sometimes in a team meeting and sometimes in private one-on-one conversations with individual managers. The management team generally rubber-stamps Jean's recommendations. The team, then, is a site where managers individually represent their departments to the superintendent, rather than a body that collectively sets direction for the hospital.

There is a strong group norm inhibiting the overt discussion of differences in members' needs and priorities. This norm makes it virtually impossible for the team to make tough resource allocation decisions and is one reason why members rely so heavily on the superintendent for such decisions. While information is shared in the management team meetings, much of the real work is done outside or in private discussions with the superintendent.

Team norms also inhibit the expression of conflict, even though it is present under the surface. In the words of one manager, "People are exceedingly polite in the management team. I see people becoming more open now than before, but I still sense members are holding back. I don't believe managers go to different constituencies and say 'You won't believe the decision we made today!' but I do think subtle messages of disapproval and disagreement are communicated."

The team's failure to make real progress toward its espoused goal of developing a hospital-wide service delivery model and treatment philosophy provides an illustration of how the design and norms of the team impede its progress. Wayne, the clinical director, must be a key figure in any attempt to revise patient services because the clinical director is responsible for shaping treatment philosophy in a psychiatric hospital. It is unlikely that the management team could ever develop a comprehensive and viable treatment philosophy without Wayne's leadership.

Yet Wayne's part-time status, his history in the hospital, and the team norms that inhibit dealing openly with disagreement and conflict make it exceedingly difficult for him to lead. Wayne was a staff psychiatrist when the clinical group was disenfranchised by the interim management team during the initial accreditation crisis, and his clinical colleagues are still smarting from the events of those days. Although he shares the frustrations currently experienced by the clinical staff and represents clinicians' concerns at team meetings, Wayne has not been able to provide a viable model for clinical leadership at the hospital. Nor have his fellow team members provided him with the support and encouragement he would need to be able to do so.

If an integrated service delivery model is to be created, the management team will have to move beyond the norms that currently guide member behavior. It will be necessary for members to openly represent the needs of their departments, to acknowledge and deal with disagreements and conflicts that exist within the team, and to draw on the different information and expertise held by individual team members.

Such a change is unlikely to occur spontaneously. The team, at the moment, may be so deeply stuck by its present norms that it will be unable to get back into motion without active intervention from Jean, the team leader. She might, for example, insist that the team as a whole take greater responsibility for making decisions on behalf of the entire organization, or she might help members address substantive issues having to do with patient services that are now glossed over, or she might aid Wayne in developing and building support for a treatment model that could reempower the hospital's clinicians.

Leadership Style

The superintendent's style has not changed much since the days of the accreditation crisis, and there are few signs that she is likely to take the kinds of initiatives mentioned above. Jean continues to be very directive in dealing with team members, and no one harbors any doubts about who is in charge. She structures all meetings, introduces the agenda, and forcefully argues her position. She has little difficulty making decisions and sometimes does so prior to receiving input from her managers. She does listen to opposing points of view and occasionally reverses her stand based on cogent arguments from the team. However, this occurs only when managers feel strongly enough about a particular issue to challenge her. Most of the time, Jean makes the major decisions herself and thereby continues to keep the team as a whole from becoming fully empowered.

The team relies upon Jean's decisiveness to resolve conflicts among members. In meetings, managers more frequently respond to Jean than to each other. While this hub-and-spoke style of meeting leadership does keep overt conflict low, it also further contributes to member passivity. And although both Jean and the team members report frustration with such passivity in meetings, no one has done anything to change it.

Jean's leadership style was appropriate at the beginning of her tenure. With no direction, few controls, and little accountability, her strong leadership was the glue that brought and held the organization together. However, three years later, the situation is different. The present challenge is for Jean to develop a style of leadership whereby she would share responsibility for running Hilltop Hospital with her management team. The top managers do want to participate more in setting the overall direction for the hospital, and they genuinely would like to push the authority for operational decision making down to Hilltop's middle managers. The difficulty continues to be how to put these ideas into practice.

Postscript

Two years have passed since the management team had the meeting excerpted at the beginning of the chapter. What changes has the management team made? Has the team made progress in developing an integrated service delivery model and treatment philosophy? Has the superintendent delegated more decision-making responsibility to her managers? Has the team pushed some of its authority down in the organization? Have the managers become more willing to confront their disagreements openly? Is the management team now steering the ship?

The team indeed has made some progress, but change has been slow. The team requested and received input from all hospital groups to formulate a treatment philosophy and service delivery model. It developed and implemented a new unit and treatment team model and is working on a new organizational structure. It also made progress in developing and implementing a new service delivery model, and its approach in doing so was participative.

Hilltop Hospital hired a new clinical director after Wayne left to pursue a private practice. The new clinical director has been very influential in both the management team and the hospital. He led the effort to refine the hospital's service delivery, treatment philosophy, and unit structure. He is reformulating and expanding the role of clinicians, particularly psychiatrists, in the residential units. Moreover, for the first time in Hilltop's history each unit has its own staff psychiatrist.

The superintendent reports that the management team once again is energetic and enthusiastic. The superintendent and managers have responded favorably to the leadership asserted by the new clinical director. His presence has energized the team.

The state has formulated new accreditation requirements that expand the role of psychiatry and nursing in psychiatric hospitals. Hilltop Hospital has three years to conform to these new specifications, and the plan is to gradually shift hospital staffing patterns in response to them. This change in direction will reinforce the changes made by the new clinical director.

Although the team has involved all hospital staff in the development of its new service delivery model, movement toward a more participative style has been gradual. Managers still are reticent to disagree with one another and with the superintendent, and the superintendent's leadership style remains quite directive.

Conclusions

Implications for Organizational Change

The team and leadership challenges that confronted Hilltop's top management team changed as circumstances changed. Conditions that enabled the team to be successful in a crisis situation became dysfunctional during a time of relative stability. Success did not automatically breed more success but instead created conditions that required the team to change its leadership, group design, and group norms. Ironically, it was the team's previous good work that created the need for it to change its approach and operating style.

The challenges that Hilltop's management team faced are likely to be experienced by other top management teams that succeed in turnaround situations. The following four challenges are representative.

A Leadership Challenge. Strong directive leadership frequently is required in a crisis situation. Once stability is achieved, however, a more participative style may be required to build employee commitment and to improve services. Changing to a more participative style can be difficult. Someone who is good at managing a turnaround situation may not be as effective at managing a stable organization—and may have difficulty modifying his or her style to fit the new situation. Team members also may not be eager to take on the new, additional responsibilities that appear after a crisis has passed. They may have become accustomed to depending upon the leader to make the tough organizational decisions and, therefore, may hold back from accepting their own new leadership challenges.

Redefinition of the Team Task. A crisis situation demands action and provides clear direction for that action. In the case of Hilltop Hospital, accreditation requirements sharply defined the tasks of the top management team. If, on the other hand, an organization is relatively stable and well functioning, the tasks of a top management team often are ambiguous. To overcome this ambiguity, the team must be proactive in defining a direction for the organization. That is much harder to do than it is to respond energetically to a consequential, externally imposed challenge.

Changes in Team Composition. New circumstances require new behaviors and new skills. There is no guarantee that any individual will be able to gain these skills and make the behavioral changes needed for success in the new circumstances. Thus, a change in membership sometimes may be required to unfreeze the group—particularly if the patterns of member interactions have become so firmly entrenched that the group does not permit current members to veer from established behaviors.

Hilltop Hospital's management team remained stuck until there was a change in clinical directors. This change was accidental, due simply to Wayne's desire to devote more time to a private practice. His replacement, untainted by the hospital's history, was fresh, energetic, and highly competent. He quickly gained the respect of the superintendent and fellow team members. He turned out to be the right person to lead the effort to move decision-making authority downward and to reempower hospital clinicians. Moreover, his strong influence on management team decisions helped break the norm of member passivity. In Hilltop's case, the change in team composition broke up the team's logjam—a logjam that the team and its leader had been unable to do anything about while Wayne was still clinical director. It is noteworthy that this change, which was probably the most powerful one that could have been made, happened accidentally.

Changes in Group Norms. Group norms that develop during a crisis situation are likely to be dysfunctional during periods of stability. During the crisis, Hilltop's management team developed the norm that individual managers do the work and report their progress in team meetings. It also had norms that minimized overt conflict among members and that deferred all resource allocation decisions to the superintendent. These norms made sense when survival was at stake and deadlines were tight. They were no longer functional, however, when the management team needed to set a strategic direction for the hospital and revise how resources were allocated.

Implications for Human Service Organizations

Because Hilltop State Psychiatric Hospital is a public human service institution, the management team confronted some special management challenges. Its funding came from the state and was contingent on conforming to hospital accreditation standards. The superintendent and management team rightfully paid careful attention to any changes in accreditation standards and pinpointed those standards as its critical environmental benchmark. Other management teams in public organizations also may need to focus upon external benchmarks, such as statutes, administrative regulations, and so on.

However, an external focus also can divert a management team's attention from its primary task—in Hilltop's case, providing psychiatric treatment to disturbed teenagers. The professionals within the organization, with some justification, viewed the management team as more concerned with rules than with the quality of patient treatment. The clinical director, who sat on the management team, was the person most likely to voice the professional perspective and to experience the tension between representing clinicians and being a member of management. This schism between administrators and professional staff is typical of human service organizations and is reflected in the dynamics of many top management teams in such organizations.

Top management teams in human service organizations often espouse clinical ideologies and values but frequently experience difficulty putting them into practice. "Integration of services" was a salient ideology at Hilltop because psychiatric treatment was seen as a method of integrating a disturbed and fragmented personality into a coherent and functioning whole. However, the management team's functional structure forced managers to advocate departmental interests at management team meetings at the expense of hospital integration.

Therapeutic ideology also advocates taking responsibility for oneself and self-management. Although Hilltop's top management team espoused a management philosophy of participation and collaboration, members behaved autocratically to control employee abuses. Finally, therapeutic values foster the expression of feelings and open reflections on group process. Hilltop's management team did permit members to express feelings and to make "process comments" during meetings, yet such talk did not result in the resolution of process problems. Although Hilltop's managers commented at meetings about the team's avoidance of conflict and its passivity vis-a-vis the superintendent, such discussions did not enable the team to forge new patterns of behavior until after its composition had changed.

Discussions that were appropriate among members of the management team at Hilltop Hospital would be unacceptable in many corporate settings. Yet the behaviors of the Hilltop managers were strikingly similar to those observed in meetings of corporate top management teams. While clinical ideology and values do influence the conversations of senior managers in human service organizations, actual behavior may be more strongly affected by the imperatives of a team's organizational tasks—such as setting organizational direction, coordinating among different functional units, allocating resources, and ensuring satisfactory organizational performance.

Team Leadership

Leading a top management team offers some special challenges. The leader must help his or her team set overall direction for the organization and then make sure that the team implements those directions. This requires that a number of tensions be managed on a continuous basis—for example, exercising authority regarding ends versus means and the allocation of team attention between internal and external challenges.

Jean focused almost entirely on means, never exercising authority directly around questions of direction. She was strong (probably too strong) and directive (probably too directive) in setting agendas, allocating resources, and assigning tasks to managers. And she was far too hesitant in using her legitimate authority to establish clear and engaging directions for the team and the hospital. It is not surprising, given Jean's tilt on the means-ends tension, that the group had problems with questions of direction, that a norm emerged to suppress disagreements and conflicts among members, and that the top management team was unable to push authority downwards in the organization.

Jean's greatest strength was in mobilizing the troops to meet external challenges. In the absence of such challenges, she did not seem to know what to do or how to lead. Because she was unable to define a direction for the hospital, she needed help in responding adequately to the endless flow of internal challenges. The new clinical director provided this help by suggesting a concrete, operational direction for the hospital's services. Once he had done that, Jean was able to specify the next steps to be taken. Together, they are now gradually moving the management team and Hilltop Hospital to the next stage in its development.

Note

1. Hilltop State Psychiatric Hospital is a pseudonym created to protect the anonymity of the institution.

Russell A. Eisenstat
Susan G. Cohen

Summary: Top Management Groups

Leadership. Images of George Washington taking his band of patriots across the Delaware, precariously but fearlessly perched at the bow of his boat. Winston Churchill in a bomb shelter leading Britain through World War II. Lee Iacocca leading Chrysler out of its financial abyss. When we think of leadership, we usually conjure up images such as these—charismatic figures unifying the disparate elements of an organization or nation into a smoothly functioning whole that overcomes external adversity.

The leadership exhibited by the teams in this section is at variance with this view because it is, to a considerable extent, collective. Each team studied was at or very near the top of its organization, and in each case members were working together to develop strategic directions or to make highly consequential organizational decisions. What might justify such a departure from the traditional model? Why might an organization turn to a team rather than to a single individual for leadership at the top? Several reasons can be suggested:

- A team's decisions are more apt to represent the wide range of interests present in any organization than would those of an individual leader acting alone.
- There is a possibility for more creative organizational solutions from a group of individuals with different skills, per-

spectives, and information than there would be from any individual leader.

- Team members, as well as the organizational constituencies
  they represent, should better understand and be more apt to
  support organizational decisions that they have played a role
  in shaping.
- Communication among top managers should be more efficient because they meet together regularly.
- The job of managing the organization is simply too vast to
  be accomplished by any one individual leader; a team can
  spread the burden and ensure that important tasks receive
  adequate attention.
- Serving in a top management group can provide valuable developmental experiences for members.

Opportunities and Obstacles

There are, then, some plausible reasons for believing that at
least some of the work that traditionally has been the responsibility of individual senior managers can be more effectively accomplished collaboratively. However, the ultimate responsibility
and accountability for management actions rarely rest with a
team; there invariably is one person with whom the buck really
does stop.

This clearly was the case for the three teams discussed in
this section. At Omega Systems, for example, there was no
question that Tom Justin ultimately called the shots, that the
structure team served at his pleasure and for his purposes. In
each of the other two teams, one individual took almost all the
blame when things went badly wrong: when the Fairfield plant
fell behind schedule and when the psychiatric hospital lost its
accreditation, the plant manager and the hospital superintendent
were the first to be replaced. Because of the irreducible fact of
the top executive's accountability, all three groups existed at
the sufferance of those executives; they served the functions he
or she set out for them, and they had only as much power as he
or she gave them.

The power delegated to the three groups we studied varied

enormously. At one extreme, the first plant manager at Fairfield was perceived by group members to have almost abdicated his authority in his attempt to encourage group participation. At the other, Tom Justin at Omega sometimes would intervene directly in the work of the structure team, telling members specifically how he wanted them to operate or what decisions they should make.

These groups did, nonetheless, perceive themselves as quite powerful—and were seen by others in their organizations as even more so. All three teams were involved in setting the basic strategic directions for their organizations, and their decisions had major consequences for the distribution of organizational resources. The results of their deliberations also had profound effects on the careers of both team members and others in their organizations. When the decision was made to cut back on the scope of operations at Fairfield, for example, the FCG was called on to decide who would continue to work at the plant and who would be transferred. The chairman of Omega Systems asked the structure group to recommend the managers who would lead the functional areas delineated in the group's new organizational design. And the hospital team decided about promotions and lateral moves for other hospital staff.

Although each of the groups was, at one time or another, frustrated by unilateral decisions made by the senior manager, they generally enjoyed considerable autonomy in how they carried out their work. Both the FCG and the structure team were responsible for the design of organizations that were committed to experimentation—and there were few constraints on what constituted an "appropriate" design as long as it worked. Moreover, these two teams operated early in the lives of their organizations when the range of possibilities for the future was great. The hospital team, functioning within the constraints of a mature government bureaucracy, had substantially less discretion. Although the accreditation crisis did bring this team more freedom of action than it otherwise would have enjoyed, the team's discretion became more circumscribed once the crisis was over and the hospital's organizational structure had been refined.

Because of the importance and scope of top management

teams' work, other organization members closely scrutinized their actions. Before meetings of the FCG, group members often were questioned closely about what the group was going to be discussing. Speculation about what really was going on in the team was a popular discussion topic at the plant. Moreover, organization members often attributed responsibility to the teams for actions that were, in fact, beyond their control. For example, as questions started to surface in corporate headquarters as to whether the Fairfield plant was economically viable, the FCG had to spend increasing amounts of time preparing financial reports for review by corporation officers. Soon, managers in the plant began to accuse the team of failing to provide them with adequate direction. Team members reasonably protested that the absence of direction was not the result of their actions, that it reflected real corporate uncertainty about the future of the plant. A similar phenomenon occurred at the hospital: employees often blamed members of the management team for inequities in policies that were, in fact, the result of state regulations.

Because the teams were highly visible, because they wielded considerable organizational power, and because they were in ongoing contact with the top executive, members viewed team membership as providing significant personal and professional opportunities. Membership also created some problems for members and brought some measure of risk. Some managers who had not been chosen for team membership, for example, made no secret of their resentment and their feelings that they could have done a better job on the team. Moreover, the top executive, who now had a close view of each member, was the person with the greatest influence on individuals' opportunities for career advancement. It was not uncommon for team members to become preoccupied with speculations about which of them were currently in and out of the top manager's favor. These concerns prompted some team members to play it safe by telling the top executive what they thought he or she wanted to hear. For example, when the future of the Fairfield plant began to seem in doubt, team members became noticeably more cautious in their behavior in team meetings. A number of team members stated privately that they were not going to stick their necks out in team meetings because decisions were going to be made shortly about who would remain in Fairfield and who would be transferred. We observed similar dynamics at Hilltop Hospital and Omega Systems, particularly when managerial reassignments were in the offing.

The high levels of discretion the top management teams enjoyed, coupled with the diversity of members' skills and interests, provided each team with opportunities to develop innovative solutions to organization problems. The teams also had ample room to fall on their collective faces. It is not surprising, therefore, that they exhibited wide variation in their levels of performance. The FCG created an organizational design that was a model for its corporation, but it also spent countless hours in frustrating and unproductive meetings. The Omega structure team developed a comprehensive new management structure for the firm but suffered extended periods during which nothing at all got accomplished—and the team fell apart completely when it came time to implement the new design. The hospital team performed very well during times of crisis but became lethargic and unproductive once the crisis had passed—even though there was still important management work to be done.

Fragmentation and Avoidance

When the top management teams we studied did not function effectively, it was typically for two interrelated reasons. The first involved the internal processes of the team and was seen in both the FCG and the Omega structure team. When things started to go wrong in these teams, they tended to come apart. Members showed up late for meetings or did not come at all. Decisions were made in one meeting only to be undone in the next. Major conflicts developed among members, but either they were not discussed in team meetings (in the FCG), or they exploded in a way that made it impossible for the group to move forward with its work (in the structure team).

The second troublesome dynamic, avoidance, followed from the first and had to do with the relationship between the team and the top executive. When the executive perceived that the team was fragmenting, he or she began to avoid using the team for organizational decision making. In some cases, the executive would unilaterally make decisions that the team felt were within its mandate. In others, he or she would consult with some group members and not with others before coming to a decision. These actions tended to intensify competition among team members for the executive's attention, to encourage dissension among them, and to further increase group fragmentation.

Once a cycle of fragmentation and avoidance gets established, it can be very hard to stop. Yet these dynamics do not occur in all top management teams. The hospital team, for example, rarely encountered them; and at some times in their lives the FCG and the structure team were free of them as well. What are the conditions that reduce the chances that a top management team will fall into the fragmentation-avoidance cycle?

Favorable Conditions for Management by Teams

Considering the history of all three teams studied, we can identify a number of factors that distinguish those times when top management teams are likely to perform effectively from the times when they are prone to problems. The first factor is simply the amount of members' task-relevant experience. Few members of either the FCG or the structure team had much experience with the full range of top management tasks. For those tasks that did allow members to draw on their previous experiences, the teams generally performed well. Problems emerged when the team had to do work that was obviously of great consequence, but for which members were novices. One reason the hospital team may have functioned more smoothly than the others is that it rarely had to perform tasks that required members to stretch beyond skills they already had mastered.

A second factor that contributes to top management team effectiveness is organizational stability. The hospital team operated within a relatively mature organization, the structure team was in a relatively young and still unsettled firm, and the FCG was right in the midst of a plant start-up. As might be expected, the greater stability and maturity of the hospital resulted in more clearly defined team tasks, more time for the team to clarify its norms without the context changing radically, and more opportunity for members to do the kind of trial-and-error learning that is necessary to develop new management skills. In the other two teams, members had to develop their organizations, their teams, and themselves simultaneously—an extraordinarily challenging undertaking. It is difficult to learn, to create new organizational forms, and to develop a team if virtually everything is unsettled, if nothing can be counted upon to stay put.

Each team also performed better during those periods when members were actively learning from their experiences. When in a learning mode, members were able to bootstrap themselves to greater skill and performance even when they encountered failures. For the teams we studied, the capacity for learning was directly related to the amount of trust that existed among members—and that varied substantially across time. The experience of the Omega structure team is illustrative. Once the team task was expanded to include making recommendations about which members would occupy which roles, trust among members decreased, learning deteriorated, and performance suffered. The same kind of thing happened at Fairfield. After the first plant manager was replaced, the level of openness among group members dropped substantially. After about six months, trust levels had returned to near their former levels; but when the survival of the plant was threatened, trust and openness decreased once again. The capacity of the FCG to learn, and its level of performance, paralleled these swings in members' willingness to tell one another the truth and to take individual and collective risks.

The behavior of the top executive critically affected the level of trust within the top management teams at any given time. Most salient was the degree to which the executive, whether implicitly or explicitly, encouraged team members to compete for his or her attention and favor. When the executive conducted team-relevant business with certain members outside the group, for example, trust and learning within the team inevitably deteriorated. On the other hand, by insisting that the team deal explicitly with difficult topics as a group, and by recognizing and rewarding the team when it did so, the executive could noticeably boost the ability of the team to learn from its own experiences. In the three teams we studied, there was variation across time in the degree to which the senior executives did this—reflecting, perhaps, the stress they were under at the time.

Finally, the senior executive also was critical in establishing the boundaries of the team and its work. When boundaries were clear, team performance generally was good; when there was chronic uncertainty about which issues were in the team's domain and which would remain the prerogative of the executive, difficulties emerged. Team members could accept whatever boundaries the executive established as long as they were clear. One of the major problems encountered by the structure team at Omega was that Tom Justin was constantly adjusting the team's boundaries. After any given change, members who did not like the current directive could simply sit back and wait because it was likely that yet another change would soon be made. This, of course, seriously impeded the team's ability to move forward. Similar dynamics occurred at both Fairfield and Hilltop: on more than one occasion, each of these teams felt their authority was undermined when the senior manager took unilateral action on an issue that members had felt was their prerogative. The team's momentum dipped noticeably each time this happened.

Conclusion

We began this chapter by suggesting that the presence and behavior of a charismatic leader are just one part of the story in understanding organizational leadership, that top management teams also can and do play significant and constructive roles in setting strategic directions and in making organization-wide decisions. It is true, however, that top management teams can be only as effective as the senior executive chooses to let them be. It is the executive who plays the critical role in selecting members with the skills and experience that are needed, in defining the boundaries of the team and its mandate, and in helping members establish and sustain the group norms they need to manage their work. If executives do not perform these roles, or if they perform them poorly, they subsequently may have to face a far more difficult choice—between tolerating the anarchy of a fragmented team and accepting the sterility of autocratic decision making.

Part Two

TASK FORCES: ACCOMPLISHING ONE-SHOT PROJECTS

At one time or another, almost everyone is in an ad hoc task group—a team brought together specifically to do a special project in a limited time. The value of these groups, and the reason they are so frequently used, is that they offer a ready and seemingly straightforward way to depart from routine ways of doing things to accomplish nonroutine tasks.

Task forces, sometimes called project teams, are distinctive in several ways. First, team members typically do not work closely together in their regular organizational roles; instead, they come together from different jobs (or even different organizational units) specifically to perform the team task. Second, the work of the team is nonroutine: the team task is a special one that requires the creation of a unique, often one-of-a-kind or one-time-only group product. Third, task forces have an unusual mix of autonomy and dependence. On the one hand, they typically are free, within broad limits, to proceed with the work in whatever way members find appropriate; on the other, their work is done at the behest of some other person or group, and therefore members are considerably dependent on the client's preferences. Finally, task forces are temporary groups. Typically, they are given a specific deadline for accomplishing the work. Even when there is no firm deadline or the deadline is fuzzy, everyone knows that the group is temporary and will disband when it completes the task or project.

A task force has both special opportunities and significant challenges. To succeed, members must find acceptable ways of working with each other, figure out how to structure and execute work for which there are no existing performance programs, to assess and deal with the expectations of outsiders (such as higher management, clients, and other stakeholders), and to keep track of time—all within a finite group life span. As is evident from the task forces discussed in this section, these challenges can be daunting.

The first two teams examined, in Chapter Five, are groups of management students contending with problems posed by their instructor. Members of one group, the Novices, were essentially strangers to one another and had to work on a task with which they had no previous experience. Members of the other group, the Strategic Planners, did know one another and had some already formed ideas about their problem and what its solution would entail. As will be seen, the dynamics of these two groups were markedly different in some ways but similar in others—particularly around the role that time played in the teams' dynamics.

Chapter Six examines a team of relatively high-level bank executives charged with designing a new financial product by a certain date. In Chapter Seven the team consists of civil servants in the executive branch of the federal government. This team's task was to prepare a series of reports for consideration by top policy-making officials—again, by a given deadline. It turned out that the bankers completed their work successfully and met their deadline, but the civil servants did not.

Together, the groups in this part point to a number of commonalities in how task forces function and they illustrate as well the varied strategies such groups use in dealing with the special hurdles encountered in project work. By comparing the design, leadership, and internal dynamics of successful and unsuccessful task forces, some lessons can be learned about the factors that are critical to the effectiveness of such teams.

5

Connie J. G. Gersick

The Students

A multitude of doors opened, and students streamed into the sunny hallways of the management school. Alexandra, Louanne, and Will[1] emerged from their section of Introduction to Organizational Systems (IOS). They had just been briefed about an upcoming "live" case—a real organizational problem to be brought to the class by a senior manager from a well-known local company. Now they were looking for Ken and Grace, students from another section of the course, with whom they would analyze the case and write their report for the client. The first task of the group, according to the instructor, was to plan the questions they would ask the client when he visited the school the following week. The team did not yet know which of three potential issues the client would ask them to work on.

#1:   On the way to the dining room where the group would have its first meeting.

[1]*Grace (to Ken):*   Did the teaching fellow tell you the six questions to ask a client?[2]

[2]*Ken:*   No. But we did get some information on how to question clients.

[3]*Alexandra:*   Didn't you say that Professor Sokon's project on race relations took place at Ibacorp last year?

[4]*Grace:*   Shh! It's supposed to be secret!

[5]*Ken:*   What! Secret that Ibacorp is racist?!

After the students are seated for lunch in the dining room:

[6]*Alexandra:*   I know the client. He's well respected. . . . I wonder which issue we'll be given to deal with?

[7]*Ken:*   The race issue. I hope we do. I worked on that stuff at the state capital.

[8]*Grace:*   I'd like to know how Ibacorp got into difficulty about their affirmative action plan in the first place.

[9]*Alexandra:*   Should we talk about who we are so we know what resources we have to pull from? (looking at Will) Want to start?

(Everyone in the group introduces himself or herself. Once the last person finishes, there is a silence.)

[10]*Alexandra:*   I talked to someone who said these projects take at least twenty hours per person. . . . Twenty hours per person!

[11]*Ken:*   Somehow I don't see it that way, but if that's what's required . . .

[12]*Grace:*   Once we find out what issue the client's going with, I'd be interested to know how much information we'll need that he's not giving us.

[13]*Ken:*   Black people from Ibacorp go to the Rose Cafe after work.

[14]*Alexandra:*   You have connections?

[15]*Ken:*   Yes!

[16]*Alexandra:*   You can be the industrial spy! (Pause) We don't really need anything formalized for Monday.

[17]*Will:*   We don't have enough information to do that. In class

on Monday we'll just be five of the class of people. We'll see how the thing unfolds—and we can call him later. I just think getting together once—that's the real purpose of this anyway.

(The group sets a time for its next meeting, and breaks up.)

A Team of Novices

Ken, Grace, Alexandra, Will, and Louanne were a collection of novices: new to each other, unfamiliar with the task, and barely acquainted with their professor when the group started up. They were all students in their first year of a graduate management program, placed in a group by the professor, and given two weeks to prepare the opening case of the fall term. The group's shared grade for the paper would determine 25 percent of each student's final evaluation; it was a major assignment. The case dealt with an affirmative action issue brought into the class by the personnel manager of a local business. Because of the nature of the case, it was important that the group included three white members (Will, Grace, and Alexandra) and two black members (Louanne and Ken), and that Ken had done affirmative action work in a previous job.

Getting Started. The dialogue above, a telescoped transcript of their first meeting, shows the full range of topics that members discussed as they started out, and it reveals a great deal about the issues that dominated this team for some time to come. The group ran the meeting as if the work had not begun. Members spent most of their forty-five minutes together introducing themselves, speculating about exactly what the case problem would be, how much effort it would require, and what the client was like. The topic of questioning the client was not forgotten—it came up four times in their discussion—but members explicitly rejected the idea of doing any planning for it: "We don't have enough information to do that." Further, they were not yet prepared to act as a coordinated team: "In class on Monday, we'll just be five of the class of people."

There are hints in the dialogue that a lack of information may not have been the only obstacle to the team's starting in to work together. Members were already approaching the task from different directions. A few minutes after Ken exclaimed that it was "[no] secret that Ibacorp is racist," Alexandra mentioned that "[she knows] the client. He's well respected." While a couple of members wondered which of a few potential topics the client would give the class to deal with, Ken had a definite opinion: "The race issue. I hope we do." When Alexandra worried that the project might consume "twenty hours per person," Ken replied that he didn't "see it that way, but if that's what's required. . . ." At the end of the meeting, when Grace wondered how much information the client would withhold from the class, Ken said that he knew a cafe frequented by black employees of the organization. Alexandra treated this as a joke, saying he could be "the industrial spy."

These questions and issues defined important dividing lines for the group. Through the first half of the team's life, the three white members continued to express hesitancy about the work. They thought that they did not have "enough information" to do the instructor's assignment; they were worried about taking on too much and overstepping what they were "supposed" to do. In contrast, the black group member who had job experience with affirmative action seemed highly invested in the task, sure about what the problem was, and ready to decide for himself what to do. Most significant, the team was conflicted about how to relate to the client and what its task was to be—working for a client whom they respected or working around a racist client.

The Novices met again immediately after the client's presentation. They now had much more information, but they echoed the uncertainty of their first discussion: "I've got to admit I'm unclear about what to do. . . . It's going to take some time to . . . put this together and really decide what [to look] for." Will and Alexandra proposed that "since we can't do much today, we should just work on process . . . maybe something concerning—what's a good way [to operate], given this task." Ken was eager to plunge in, though, and he began talking about the client. The group dropped the idea of planning the work and soon returned to its initial question of how to define the task. Excerpts from two different meetings indicate the tenacity of that issue:

#2: Early in the Novices' second meeting (immediately after the client's presentation).

[1]*Ken (referring to the client's definition of the problem):* You don't meet affirmative action by just hiring black people!

[2]*Alexandra:* Yeah, but I think—they just took one problem—

[3]*Will:* Yeah . . . for us to be able to do in two weeks—

[4]*Ken:* Yes, but you don't meet an affirmative action goal . . . by just hiring black people.

(Later in the meeting):

[5]*Ken:* Basically they [the client] all do nothin'—that's the thing they share in common.

[6]*Alexandra:* I don't know how you can say that! You don't know that!

[7]*Ken:* Yes I do! That's part of the whole problem . . .

[8]*Will:* I guess I'm thinking that . . . he just picked up this as one manageable project for us in two weeks. If we had to look at [other ethnic groups] and everybody—I mean, in two weeks, it would just have been—

#3: Fifteen minutes into the third meeting.

[9]*Alexandra:* Ken—do you think that what you're focusing on is . . . an addendum to the problem of this paper? Because we're being limited in scope.

[10]*Ken:* I think we're limiting ourselves, if that's what we interpret it as.

[11]*Alexandra:* If we were real consultants we'd have to look at the whole problem . . . but . . . for the purposes of this exercise we should focus on issues *they* raised.

The Novices had great difficulty making progress during this period. Group members, separated simultaneously by race and experience level, were far apart in their estimates of how much they could "do in two weeks," in whether they should treat the task as real or as just an exercise, and in their inclinations to go along with the client ("focus on issues *they* raised") or to overrule him. Alexandra said later that she felt inadequate, being white, to argue with Ken; he seems to have been too intimidating to the group for the team to benefit from his knowledge. The transcript of dialogues 2 and 3 illustrates (statements 2, 4, 8, 11) the extent to which opinions and ideas were dismissed as inappropriate to the problem, rather than discussed. Unable to agree on what their task ought to be, the Novices were not producing anything on paper.

Some time into the team's third meeting, the deadlocked argument came to a halt. Louanne, the other black member of the group, suggested that Ken's position be included in the group's paper; but she said that, since she was not the expert that Ken was, she felt "more confident" just focusing on the task the client had defined. Ken leaned his chair away from the table and became silent as the other group members turned from the content of the task. They finished the meeting by discussing how to divide the labor for the paper.

Halftime. The class papers were due two weeks after the client presentation, and the Novices' next meeting took place on the last night of the first week. This meeting marked a major change in the way the group had been operating—and a dramatic leap forward in progress. The meeting was set apart from the others in several ways. It was their first evening gathering and the first one to start on time. People had done some homework and seemed to have a much better sense of what they were doing. Significantly, the course instructors had just transferred Ken to another group. (The Novices' explanation was that the other group needed his expertise more since it was doing an oral presentation for the client.) As excerpts show, this meeting felt very different for group members.

#4:   Opening comments of Sunday evening meeting.

[1]*Alexandra:*   This is due next Monday, right?

[2]*Grace:*   Right. Time to roll.

[3]*Alexandra:*   Want to set a time limit?

The members agreed on a time limit, and they structured their discussion around a list of issues to cover in the paper. After two hours their spirits were high.

#5:   Later Sunday evening.

[1]*Grace:*   So we're ready on section two, number one, *recruiting.*

[2]*Will:*   Not bad! We spend one hour on one topic, and an hour on another!

[3]*Will and Grace:*   Yay!

[4]*Will:*   We're moving along here—I feel a lot better about this at this meeting than I have . . . and I think we are getting a lot done.

[5]*Alexandra:*   (agrees)

[6]*Grace:*   Well, I think we're also making—decisions to be task oriented and—take the problem at its face value . . .

[7]*Alexandra:*   Instead of—

[8]*Grace:*   Part of our trade-off with losing Ken is—the social consciousness—

[9]*Alexandra:*   Um hum—

[10]*Louanne:*   He comes in with a lot of experience, though, I mean, he—

[11]*Alexandra:*   *Too* much, I think, for us—

(Louanne defends some of the points that Ken had made.)

[12] *Grace:*   That's—I think, his good point that he left us with
. . . and that should be a very strong point.

[13] *Will:*   I think it should be, too.

This segment of the meeting reveals that the members felt
they were finally getting someplace—and that they were quite
relieved to have taken a turn for the better. Ken's departure
made a big difference to the group, and they tied much of their
new-found efficiency directly to his absence. Nonetheless, Alexandra and Louanne (now the only black member) showed signs
of continuing the debate that had centered around Ken (statements 8–13). When this happened, the other two group members quickly moved to confirm Ken's value; the conflict was
stopped.

It is impossible to know what would have happened if
Ken had remained; however, his absence was far from the sole
change in the group. The longer the members had worked together, the more impatient they had got, and the more salient the deadline became. Grace and Alexandra opened the
meeting by noting the due date and announcing that it was
"time to roll." Meanwhile, their understanding of the task had
grown. They were able, for the first time, to create a structure
to organize their ideas. There was a strong contrast between this
meeting and earlier ones when the group did not even know
"what to look for."

The Second Half. The Novices had decided that the three wom-
en in the group would develop idea outlines based on the material they had generated at their halftime meeting. Each woman
would handle about one-third of the paper. William was to draft
the paper based on these outlines. Their next two meetings
went smoothly as the group discussed the outlines. At the close
of their penultimate meeting, Will collected his teammates' contributions. Everyone expected him to write them into a draft
without too much difficulty.

Finishing Up. The group's next and final meeting was the day before the paper was due. The plan was to go over Will's draft. A

few lines from the beginning of the meeting indicate something of the group's position at that time.

#6: Beginning of the final meeting.

[1]*Alexandra:* I don't remember—did he call for an analysis of the problem?

[2]*Will:* Yes it does—our assignment—that's what made things a little rough, for when I read what we're expected to have in the memo as a course requirement, we really have to have about four things (he lists them). . . . I sort of had to come up with all of that.

[3]*Alexandra:* . . . God, I never thought to look at it. I just thought it was recommendations.

[4]*Grace:* I looked at it after we finished.

None of the Novices had looked at the paper requirements during the time the group had worked on the case. As a consequence, members' outlines did not match the assignment well, and Will had to "come up with" much of the *group's* paper himself.

One result of this situation was a problem of perceived inequity. As the other members made their suggestions for how "you" (Will) should revise the paper, it became clear that they were still invested in the ideas they had outlined but assumed the writing was Will's responsibility. Will, placed on the defensive, had to do much more than he had expected. He finally refused, in an increasingly uncomfortable exchange, to accept the job of producing the final product.

A second consequence was that the team reached its last meeting with major flaws in the work. As the group compared the draft to the requirements, it became painfully clear that large chunks of the assignment were simply not done.

#7: The final meeting.

[1]*Will:* One of the things we're probably weak on . . . because we just never thought to talk about it, is implementation. . . .

We'll be judged poorly if we just toss out a simple thing like "verify" and don't tell how to do it.

[2]*Alexandra:*   So we need something else to cover "verify." (Long pause) How *do* you normally implement that?

(Alexandra and Will discuss a possible solution.)

[3]*Grace:*   Or we could just do—it's not good implementation. . . . (Pause) All right—let's come back to it.

(Pause)

[4]*Alexandra:*   So number four's OK, though? (Getting no reply, she goes on to the next point.)

[5]*Grace:*   On number four and number five—we could . . . reorganize them so the recommendation is. . . .

(Pause)

[6]*Alexandra:*   We're reaching though—in all of this we're really reaching. We don't have much time to substantiate . . .

[7]*Grace:*   I think our content is good but I think we weren't clear when we were talking about it on—what's a recommendation, and what are the steps, and it's just a matter of reorganizing it in that light.

The numerous pauses in the dialogue are testimony to the difficulty of recognizing large gaps so late in the process. Statements 5 and 7 show one way the group tried to pull itself out of this hole—by construing flaws as a simple problem of reorganization. The paper was due the next day, and they had to repair the structure they had, not build a new one. The group finally finished the paper, but only after a very long and difficult day.

Generalizing: From the Novices' Life to a Model of Group Life Cycles. Looking back, we can summarize the life history of this team in terms of a few distinct periods, starting with the first meeting. As the dialogues show, the group's initial discussion established its position on several fronts. Regarding team interaction, members immediately fell into opposing camps whose members were not ready to work together; their interaction pattern was to argue without doing any active problem solving. Regarding the task, members disagreed on how it should be defined. They split into an inexperienced majority, uncertain how to begin, and a confident minority, eager to start. Regarding the team's relationship to its context, the group disagreed again. Though members unanimously dismissed the professor's instructions, they diverged about the client: whether to trust him and wait for him to define their task or to mistrust him and define the task for themselves. All these positions were inextricably tied to one another. The team's arguing was about the task and the client, and members' attitudes toward the task, the client, and each other were mutually reinforcing. For several meetings, the team stayed on this track—recycling the same debates about the same issues with very little movement, either on the task or on its own interaction patterns.

Just before the halfway mark between the time the group started work and the project deadline, movement suddenly occurred. The professor changed the group's composition, the debate ended, and the team shifted into high gear. In one meeting, it accomplished a leap forward that made members feel "much better" and established an overall outline for their product. The next several meetings constituted another distinct era—a period of relatively smooth production work, guided by the decisions made at the midpoint. The final period in the group's life was its last meeting. As members shifted from generating ideas to repairing and finishing off the material they already had, the group felt the consequences of its own past choices about how members would work together, about the amount of effort they had invested, and about how well they had attended to external requirements.

The underlying pattern that this team followed was identical to the pattern found in seven other naturally occurring groups (whose tasks ranged from designing a new bank product to founding an academic institute), all studied over their complete life spans (Gersick, 1984; 1988). And the pattern discovered in these groups was not one that would have been predicted by existing group development theories.

Traditionally, group development has been portrayed as a universal sequence of stages or activities through which groups gradually and explicitly prepare to perform and then perform their work (Hare, 1976; McGrath, 1984). Two characteristic models are: *orientation, evaluation, control* (Bales & Strodtbeck, 1951) and *forming, storming, norming, performing* (Tuckman, 1965). These models are grounded in the paradigm of development as an inevitable, hierarchical progression: a group cannot get to stage four without first going through stages one, two, and three. Development is construed as movement in a forward direction, and every group is expected to follow the same basic path.

This research found no universal sequence of activities in the groups studied—nor was group progress steady and gradual. They varied widely in the way they began and in the sequence of issues that preoccupied them. However, there was remarkable convergence in the *times* that groups formed, maintained, and changed their interaction patterns. Every group's life progressed as a *punctuated equilibrium* (Eldrege & Gould, 1972), a pattern in which unique forms appear suddenly, persist for considerable periods of time, and change in compact, revolutionary bursts. In this paradigm of change, systems' histories are expected to *vary*, because the paths a system takes at its inception and during periods of revolutionary change are expected to be significantly influenced by unique characteristics of the system and its environment.

Instead of orienting themselves to their tasks and members before arriving at views about their projects, as traditional theories suggest, each group immediately formed a framework of "givens" about its situation and how it would behave. This framework, in effect, constituted a stable platform from which the group operated throughout the first half of its existence. The framework included behavior patterns (ways the group did things) and premises (ways the group construed things) about its task, its environment, and its internal interaction.

Occasionally, members clearly indicated their approach to something, stating their premises and how they planned to behave ("The key issue here is X; let's work on it by doing Y");

however, teams seldom formulated their frameworks through explicit deliberation. Frameworks were established implicitly, by what was said and done repeatedly in the group, right from the start. Teams' initial frameworks, in place by the end of their first meetings, persisted until almost halfway through the calendar time they had for their projects. I refer to this period as *Phase I.* Then, precisely halfway between its first meeting and its official deadline, each group underwent a *Transition.* Central approaches and behavior patterns that appeared during first meetings and persisted during Phase I disappeared at the halfway point, as groups explicitly dropped old approaches and searched for new ones. The clearest sign of Transition was the major jump in progress that each group made on its project at the temporal midpoint of its calendar. The revised frameworks that groups formed at Transition carried them through a second period of momentum, *Phase II,* to a final burst of *Completion* activities at their last meetings.[3]

The portrait of one team, the Novices, helps illustrate these phases. We can now look briefly at a second group to see how a team can differ radically in the style, pace, and content of its interaction, yet duplicate the same pattern of alternation between long periods of continuity and compact periods of change.

The Second Group: The Strategic Planners

For the Novices, the first assignment of the term was slow and often frustrating work. The team did not begin developing a plan for the case until halfway through its time—and no one even looked at the requirements for the paper until close to the deadline, after the group's planning was done. The second group had a very different experience.

First Meeting. The Strategic Planners were part of the same management course as the Novices. They were three white men: Bert and Rajeev, first-year students, and Jack, a second-year student. Jack and Bert had worked together on a previous assignment; Rajeev and Jack had known each other outside school.

The team began much later in the term, after the class had completed three cases. The client was an entrepreneur who had invented a new technology for which demand was rapidly increasing. He wanted advice on how to expand his business. The case was set within the course instructor's unit on organizational design.

The excerpt below, a clip of less than one minute from the very start of the team's interaction, shows a beginning that was not at all like that of the Novices. In contrast to the Novices' initial paralysis, the Strategic Planners started immediately on the task. Not only did they begin under different circumstances (they had already heard the case, they had a definite assignment, and they were familiar with the work and each other), they seemed to think they knew exactly what the case was about. Moreover, the three members immediately agreed on what to do.

Nevertheless, their opening discussion was the same as the Novices' in the way it positioned the team for the first half of its life. The dialogue illustrates the group's opening framework with its four interrelated facets: the team's stance vis-a-vis its outside context, its approach to the task, its pattern of internal interaction, and its performance strategy.

#8:   The team, talking right after class to plan its first meeting to work on the case, has just heard the client present his problem.

[1] *Jack:*   We should try to read the [assigned] material.

[2] *Rajeev:*   But this isn't an organizational design problem, it's a strategic planning problem.

[3] (Jack and Bert agree.)

[4] *Rajeev:*   I think what we have to do is prepare a way of growth.

[5] (Nods of "yes" from Jack and Bert.)

In just three statements (1–3), the members express a clear set of assumptions about their relationship to the organizational context (the professor and his requirements). They are not going to read the material, they disagree with the professor's definition of the task, and they will define their project to suit themselves, not external expectations: "This isn't an organizational design problem, it's a strategic planning problem."

The members' approach to working together is just as visible. When three consequential proposals are made—about the definition of the task, the team's (non)obligations to the professor, and the goal they should aim for—everyone concurs. There is no initial "storming" and dramatically swift "norming" (Tuckman, 1965) in this group. The members establish basic norms instantly and begin working together in synchrony.

Finally, the clip shows the team's starting approach to its task and its performance strategy: members are confident about what the problem is, what the goal ought to be, and how to get to work on it. The team will use strategic planning techniques to "prepare a way of growth." As did the Novices, they make all these assumptions virtually simultaneously.

Phase I. The first meeting was, for each group, a good preview of the entire first half of its life. Just as the Novices' initial uncertainty and differences of opinion persisted to their midpoint, the Strategic Planners maintained the agreements and the pace they established in the first minute of their group's life. At their subsequent work session, two days later, they picked up right where they had left off. The following excerpt gives some indication of how well their initial dialogue predicted lasting patterns.

#9:

[1]*Jack:*   I have not looked at any of the readings—did you look at all?

[2](Bert and Rajeev laugh.)

[3]*Jack:*   . . . I was thinking . . . we could do alternatives—different ways to grow . . . like a prospectus for a consulting study.

[4]*Bert:*   That's exactly the way I'd go.

[5] *Rajeev:*   (agrees)

(After five minutes of discussion about the client and his situation, Rajeev suggests they start work.)

[6] *Jack:*   We've got some more time. . . . I think it would be premature to describe alternative goals yet . . .

[7] *Rajeev:*   If we can generate some of the assumptions now and talk about the alternatives later—it's a two-step thing.

[8] *Jack:*   OK, that's fine. Let's start that.

[9] *Rajeev (going to the blackboard):*   What are the things on which the business depends?

[10] *Bert:*   Supply—operations.

[11] *Jack:*   The technology is the key.

The dialogue shows that the team is still disregarding the professor (statements 1 and 2), still working in easy agreement (4, 5, and 7), and still taking the same approach to the task (3). It also shows the group acting on the intentions expressed earlier and employing a logical, orderly technique to construct its product (6–11). The team followed the interaction pattern shown in statements 6–11 for two full meetings—Rajeev led the group through a structured set of strategic planning questions. At that point, the team had a complete first draft outline of a growth plan for its client.

It is interesting that, although the Strategic Planners had a much faster, more confident start on the case and some experience with the course instructor, they mirrored the Novices' pattern of ignoring the paper requirements until after they had a draft planned out. Their first expression of concern about requirements occurred in the last ten minutes of their third meeting.

#10:

[1] *Rajeev:*   I still don't understand what the professor wants.

[2] *Jack:*   I know—I'm just saying hopefully by the time we've

decided what he wants, we can then give him something. We're still at the earlier phase and I'm not sure how long that's gonna take.

As it happened, the "earlier phase" was about to end.

Transition. Both the Strategic Planners and the Novices experienced major changes at the halfway point in their calendars—even though they were far apart in the amount of work they had accomplished by that time. The Strategic Planners' next meeting bisected the time span from their first work session to the day the paper was due, occurring on the sixth of eleven days. They were supposed to meet right after a class lecture, but they started late, in a state of uncharacteristic disarray. The members took about twenty minutes to find each other and, by the time they finally converged, no meeting room was available. Instead of their customary quiet setting, they ended up talking in a busy hallway lounge. Jack commented, "It's like a three-ring circus." The group's tight, orderly routine was disrupted.

Another change occurred in their approach toward the instructor. The group had started out very confident that his definition of the case was incorrect, but they now thought differently. The major portion of their hallway meeting was spent reevaluating the work they had done and planning revisions based directly on the lecture they had just heard.

#11:

[1] *Rajeev:* I think what he said today in class—I have already lots of criticism on our outline. . . . What we've done now is OK, but we need a lot more emphasis on organization design than what we—I've been doing up to now.

[2] *Jack:* I think you're right. We've already been talking about [X]. We should be talking more about [Y].

[3] *Rajeev:* We've done it, and it's super—but we need to do other things, too.

[4] (Bert agrees.)

(The group goes quickly through the outline that they had prepared, noting changes and additions they want to make "after
hearing today's discussion.")

[5] *Rajeev:*   The problem is, we're very short on time.

   With this meeting, the Strategic Planners stopped barrel-
ing along on their first agenda. They paused to take stock of
what they had already accomplished and to decide what they
wanted to do with the rest of their time. For the first time, they
allowed the instructor to influence their ideas: they decided
they should do the organization design after all. They also were
more sensitive to the approaching deadline, having shifted from
their earlier sense that "we've got some time" to a feeling of
being "very short on time." Along many dimensions, then, this
meeting represented a major transition for the group.
   A close comparison between the two groups' transitions
demonstrates, in more detail, how the structure of groups' development can be consistent, even though the substantive activities they engage in are very different. The similarities highlighted
below were characteristic of the midpoint transitions for all
eight groups studied in my research.
   First, the Transition was preceded by a break in the
groups' momentum. Groups completed (or dropped) major aspects of their starting frameworks. The Novices closed the debate that had occupied the first half of their time. The Strategic
Planners finished roughing out the "growth options" they had
agreed to construct the first time they met. These breaks occurred just before each team's midpoint.
   Second, groups showed fresh awareness of their deadlines
at transitional meetings. The Novices began by noting the due
date and saying it was "time to roll." The Strategic Planners
talked about running "short on time." This explicit discussion
of time, always occurring at the same calendar point, suggests
that the midpoint milestone functions like an alarm clock—a re-
minder of the deadline that catalyzes teams' feelings of urgency
to make progress.
   Third, transitional meetings broke routines of meeting
times, places, styles, and sometimes attendance. For the Novices,

meeting in the evening, starting promptly, setting a definite agenda, and following it were all departures from routine. The Strategic Planners changed from quiet, enclosed meeting rooms and a punctual, orderly style to a late, disorderly meeting in a bustling lounge.

Fourth, teams' supervisors played important roles in their transitions. The instructor made a significant difference to the Novices by removing a member from the group halfway through the project. The Strategic Planners suddenly shifted from ignoring the instructor, or being unable to understand him (excerpt #10), to making enthusiastic use of his views after a midpoint class lecture. (Although outside stakeholders played important roles in all eight teams' transitions, there was variation in whether the supervisor, the team, or both initiated actions.)

Fifth, transitions yielded specific new agreements on the ultimate directions teams' work should take, and teams made a burst of progress on their projects. The advances the two student teams made were qualitatively different, but equally radical. The Novices spent the first half of their time in unstructured exploration and argument. For them, the Transition was an occasion for choice making, structuring, and pulling together. The Strategic Planners, in contrast, had begun with quick decisions and unhesitating construction of a chosen plan. For them, the Transition took the form of evaluating the adequacy of what had been created and making major revisions: "We've done it, and it's super, but we need to do other things." The Transition, then, is not a uniform script enacted in every team, but a predictably timed opportunity for each team to take its own next step.

Phase II. Like the Novices, the Strategic Planners used the second half of their calendars for construction work on their projects. For both teams, the content of Phase II meetings was different from Phase I because the groups were carrying out agendas newly made at their transitions. The Strategic Planners' Phase I meetings were used to outline possible growth options; the group now fleshed out the organization design to realize those options. Members returned to their closed meeting rooms and orderly question-and-answer format but with a shift in leadership: Jack took over from Rajeev as lead questioner and keeper of the chalk.

Completion. For the Novices, life changed one last time just before the deadline. The team mounted a final burst of energy and changed the type of work it was doing from activity designed to generate output to activity designed to repair and finish off the output it already had. The team's discussion of external expectations became more prominent as it prepared to release its work for outside review. The same changes in activity occurred for the Strategic Planners but, again, with substantial differences in character. Having managed their task, their team interaction, and their attention to external requirements differently, the Strategic Planners arrived at their completion meeting with a legacy different from that of the Novices.

   The day before the paper was due, Rajeev, Jack, and Bert, each with a draft of one section in hand, met to put the pieces together into a paper. About ten minutes into the meeting, having made one quick pass through all their materials, Rajeev remarked, "I think we have all the ideas. We have a good handle on the thing. The main task is how to arrange them." This brought the group to a conclusion similar to that of the Novices; both framed their completion work as "arranging" what they already had (see excerpt 7, statement 8), but the sense of the material's adequacy was very different for the two groups. Compare the Novices' painful realization of the gaps in their work with the following discussion:

#12:

[1]*Jack:*   Let's take it through orderly. What goes in the memo versus what goes in the technical backup? (He goes to the blackboard.) I'm just going through the list we made up—

[2]*Rajeev:*   Well, we have the list—

[3]*Jack:*   OK—How would we refer to [X] in the body of the memo?

(He writes a suggestion on the board.)

[4]*Bert:*   That could be the strategy for the cash flow.

[5]*Jack:*   Yeah, OK!

[6]*Bert:*   We have to make sure that's stated in the technical backup.

[7]*Jack:*   OK. Then we had implementation. I think we want bullets.

[8]*Rajeev:*   Yeah.

(Jack and Rajeev list the points they want for the bullets.)

[10]*Jack:*   That's good!

This team's completion meeting was significantly shorter and easier than that of the Novices. First, the teams ended differently on the dimension of intermember relations. The Novices had planned their division of labor based on a seriously incomplete map of the task. This led to resentment about equity and contributed to an uncomfortable last meeting. The Strategic Planners, who had a much clearer sense of the type and amount of work involved, negotiated a more accurate division of labor all along. When members finished, they were pleased with each other's work, and they said so: "Mr. Rajeev is gonna be our star!" "He's good. He'll talk 'engineering speak.' "

The teams also ended differently on the problems of creating a product and meeting external requirements. In statements 7–10 of the above excerpt, for example, the group is not wondering what "implementation" means, nor are they trying to think of an implementation plan; it is putting completed ideas into place. The Strategic Planners entered their completion meeting with a product that was much more nearly ready to go. This difference is not simply attributable to the experience gap between the two groups. A more complex explanation—one that takes into account the way the two teams used their transitions—is required.

Neither team attended to external requirements until after it had a first draft. But the Strategic Planners took only half as long as the Novices to get that draft. When they rethought their approach to the work at the Transition, they revised it in line with requirements. The Novices, who used the Transition to define their task and to get started, may have had too little done at that time to understand the requirements—even if they had thought to look at them. And, once their Transition was past, they did not stop to question the adequacy of their plan. The Novices were the slowest team in the study and the only one whose transitional meeting did not include some comparison of outside requirements or resources to the team's developing plans. It appears that it may be more difficult than we think to educate a team about requirements at the beginning of a project—and more important than we realize to clarify requirements at the project's midpoint.

Conclusion

Special project teams face four intertwined challenges: (1) to develop a creative product that (2) commands the shared support of the group and (3) matches external resources and requirements, and (4) to do all this by a deadline. Groups approach the first three of these challenges simultaneously and with great individual variation. They begin at different places and work with different speeds and styles.

Within the variation in content, however, there is surprising regularity in the rhythms of continuity and change in group life cycles. Each group begins on its own distinctive track and stays on it until halfway through the calendar time, then makes a concentrated leap ahead. This leap, the midpoint transition, appears to be catalyzed by a pacing mechanism—members' awareness of time and deadlines. This mechanism may be one important way groups handle their fourth challenge—fitting an indeterminate amount of work into a fixed amount of time. Halfway into a project, members can readily estimate what they have accomplished in a specific amount of time and how much they have yet to do with the same amount of time remaining.

Two periods of the life cycle emerged as especially significant: groups' beginnings, as potent predictors of the first half of their life cycles, and groups' calendar midpoints, as key opportunities to revise their directions. The quality of groups' endings appears to depend significantly on the stances that groups take at those first and midpoint meetings. The implication is that the initial design and the midpoint are especially good times to influence the outcomes of special project groups.

Notes

1. All names of people and organizations are fictitious.
2. Parts of some sentences in the dialogues are paraphrased for clarity. Readers may find more complete dialogues for all eight groups, without paraphrasing, in Gersick (1983, 1984).
3. A more extensive discussion of the group development model that grew out of this study is presented in Gersick (1988).

6

Connie J. G. Gersick

The Bankers

> This is a big deal, this new account. Huge deal! And very significant in the banking industry, and—it's kinda fun to be right in the middle of it!
>
> —Don, Vice President and
> Compliance Officer[1]

> It was . . . the first time in a long, long time where you could become creative . . . innovative. In the past, we were so regulated—everyone offered exactly the same instrument. Just a whole lot of sameness.
>
> —Gil, Vice President for
> Operations

Gil and Don were members of a team of four senior executives who designed the first money market account for a large East Coast bank. Their work began a few days after Congress approved a new product—an account that, for the first time since the early 1930s, allowed banks themselves to determine the interest rates they would pay. The change would enable the banks to compete with the money market funds that had attracted away a substantial fraction of their deposit base; it would also place banks in much greater competition with each other. Any bank could offer the product exactly sixty days after the bill was signed.

The bill clearly promised a watershed opportunity for banks, but there was considerable uncertainty about exactly how the new account might look. The legislation had laid out some broad outlines, but the Depository Institution Deregulation Committee (DIDC) was to establish more specific regulations in the coming weeks. Because the DIDC had not yet met, the team started its deliberations in the dark. For instance, banks did not know whether a minimum deposit would be required, and if so, what the amount would be. There were limits on the number of checks that could be written, but no one knew how those limits would be enforced, and so forth.

In addition to the uncertainty, several other challenges were built into the project. The new account had to fit the bank's operating systems ("Computers are very inflexible," one member explained). It also had to be "easy for the branches to use. In the back of my mind the whole time was how we were going to explain it." And the account had to be highly competitive without "giving away the store." All these considerations were colored by the challenge to be ready by the deadline: ". . . if we didn't [offer it on the legal opening date] we would lose a lot of points, so . . . my only concern was, can we do this, and do it well in the time that we have."

The four team members were all part of a larger management committee (ranked just below the top policy group) that met regularly to discuss bank operating tactics. The four men initiated the group themselves as soon as the legislation passed: "We immediately got in touch with each other as the seniors on the committee [and collected] a nucleus of the bigger group." Each one talked, in interviews, about thinking through which departments would have to be represented and planning the composition of the team. Members wanted the team to be as small as possible with the right mix of experts so the work could be done quickly. The resulting group was high powered, enthusiastic about the task, and well connected to the top as well as to critical functional areas of the organization. Its members were Don, Porter, Rick, and Gil. Don, a vice president, said he was the junior member of the group. But since he was the bank's compliance officer, and because it was essential that the account conform to regulations, he was the chairman. Porter, a senior vice president and treasurer of the bank, provided a direct link to the small top management group that set the bank's rates and overall business policy. Though he was the team's ranking member, none of the others reported directly to him, and he said his style was to work for consensus rather than "use my clout." Rick, as marketing vice president, was responsible for making sure the bank's design and presentation of the account would make it a competitive success. Gil was vice president of operations—the side of the bank that processed all transactions. His contribution was necessary to make sure the bank's information and computer systems could actually handle the new design.

The men's offices were in three different cities: Don and Rick were in the same building; Porter was at corporate headquarters, about an hour's drive from them; and Gil was at the operations center, located between the other two offices.

Chronology

The team met four times, irregularly scheduled over a thirty-four-day period starting a few days after the law was signed. The team's deadline for finishing the design of the account was a few weeks before the opening day, to allow time for the bank to get ready. Members determined the main characteristics of the account in these meetings. But as the project unfolded, they increased their communication with each other outside meetings—and they increasingly talked with other people in the bank to get the concrete details ready to go.

First Meeting. The group's initial conversation showed much about its character.

#1:

[1]*Don (referring to a written list of topics):*   What do you think we ought to do to start this, Rick? Just go through each of these?

[2]*Rick:*   Well, I want to explain to Gil and Porter—we had a little rump session the other day just to say "What the hell *is* this

thing? What does it say, and what are the things that we have to decide?" And what we did was go through a group of 'em. . . . These are not necessarily in order of importance—they're in order of the way we thought of 'em, really.

This excerpt shows the first twenty-five seconds in the life of the task force, and it is an elegant summary of the group's enduring work style. It shows that Don prepared for the meeting beforehand, that he did this by consulting with one other member, that the preparation consisted of generating an unadorned list of topics to be covered, and that this list was not arranged in any hierarchy other than "in order of the way we thought of 'em." The team followed this strategy in every one of its meetings. Before each one, a pair of members prepared skeletal documents for the group to work from. The documents anchored the discussion, and the group checked off items as they covered them. But discussions were much less like logical progressions than like pinball games: each question ricocheted the conversational ball onto several new questions, and occasionally bells and lights went off as the team made a decision about a specific point.

Second, excerpt #1 gives a concise statement of where the group members felt themselves to be as they started out on the task. The team's main question at that point was, "What the hell *is* this thing? What does [the bill] say?" Members' approach to the task, as they began, was to absorb the new legislation and develop a comprehensive map of "the things we have to decide." For the account to work, every part of a complex set of organizational systems had to mesh. This requirement helps explain the link between the team's pinball style of work and its definition of the task as *mapping.* As one member put it, ". . . it's all intertwined because . . . we're trying to talk about what system we're going to have to use—and the whole structure of the account." Their loose style allowed the team to use free association to catch problems and ideas that might have been neglected in a more orderly approach.

Partly because of the lack of regulatory information, members raised more questions than they answered; however, the few decisions that did come out of the first meeting established important foundations for broad policy. The group did set the central character of the account at this meeting. Appropriately enough, this key point fell spontaneously out of a discussion that started on an entirely different topic.

#2:

[1] *Gil:*   Is it gonna be tied to a cash reserve?

[2] *Porter:*   Well, we can't figure out how to do it . . . we couldn't with a couple of hours yesterday—

[3] *Gil:*   You could say, you have a checking account, too . . . [suggests tying in the cash reserve feature from a checking account].

[4] *Porter:*   I think, really, the point that we have to get to is, are you going to link a checking account to this. . . . That's the only way a [cash reserve] *works.* . . . If I were the typical customer, which I'm probably not—what I would do is set up my [money market] account, then set up my cash reserve—

[5] *Don:*   And once a month, transfer money to the checking account.

[6] *Porter:*   That's right. I know I pay my bills on the fifteenth of every month—

[7] *Don:*   Yep!

[8] *Gil:*   And write checks—

[9] *Porter:*   And write checks out of that!

(two or three excited comments at once)

[10] *Gil:*   You'd get a lotta mileage out of that!

This idea, to define the product as an investment account with a link to a checking account, was the point of departure for many of the details that came later.

The meeting ended with a three-minute discussion about what the members wanted to do as a closed team and whom they wanted to include. On one hand, they recognized the need "to bring in the whole group at some point." They did not want "to miss anything that somebody else would catch." At the same time, however, they did not want to be slowed down. "We didn't have time to get into the ego-political situation that larger groups might create," one reported afterward. Members decided to stick with the group of four until they had the general design laid out and then to bring in other people to help plan how to execute it: "What'll happen is, once we know how we want to handle this, Gil can come in with his staff and say, 'Look, work on the details here.' "

Second Meeting. Progress on the task at the second meeting was quite similar to the first in that there was still very little information about regulations, so the team still had many questions: "We still don't know what's coming." A change at this meeting was a shift in sentiment. The first meeting was very much a case of the four team members pulling in outside information to explore and define the task among themselves. By the second meeting, the feelings of uncertainty were mixed with a stronger expression of the team's wish to guard its independence in designing the account—independence from other managers inside the bank and from the government.

The discussion at the second meeting concerned three issues. First, other officers in the top management group had become aware of the new opportunity. The team spent a few minutes at the beginning of the meeting trading stories and concerns about the pressures they were getting from colleagues who wanted to know exactly what was going on or who wanted to influence the design to fit with their own programs. During this conversation, much to the team's amusement, the bank president called Porter on the telephone.

#3:   Secretary calls Porter to the telephone—team members all laugh.

[1] *Rick (gleefully):*   You're on the list! Last week, week before that, I was on the list! He kept calling me every day!

(Later, when Porter returns to the room.)

[2] *Don:*   Back from the lion's den?

[3] *Gil:*   "By twelve-thirty, have all the answers!" Right?

[4] *Porter:*   You better believe! He just wanted to transmit to me that he had a long conversation with [the chairman] on Friday, and there is no question that this is . . . priority number *one*, and that—it better be good!

(They laugh.)

Members devoted the bulk of the meeting to going over a letter Don and Porter had drafted in response to the DIDC's request for comments about potential regulations. The consistent message of the team's comments was to minimize regulations and maximize bank control: "Whether or not the bank wants to do that . . . that's their own decision, and that's what you're saying." After reviewing the letter, the team debated a few policy issues thoroughly and came up with two new ideas about what the account package would include.

Toward the end of the meeting, members again picked up the matter of communication with the rest of the management group. They first decided to test the top management waters before working any further on one of their policy ideas.

#4:

[1] *Rick:*   Just play [the chairman] for a minute. Isn't he likely to say "Why should we tier our accounts when the money funds didn't?"

(Porter raises the possibility of discussing the tiering idea with others, but has some doubts about it.)

[2] *Porter:*   Do you want to *play* with that kind of question?

[3] *Rick:*   Sure! . . . I think the way to present this is, "the task force has come up with an idea. . . . One of the things we have been considering is a tiered balance. . . . Before we go ahead with that, we need to have some thinking about it. *We* know the

money funds didn't have a tiered balance thing; on the other hand, this is an opportunity for us to stick out some, maybe, from the pack."

Second, they decided that their letter to the DIDC would provide a way for them to answer people's questions and let them in on the story—without jeopardizing the team's discretion to plan policy. Porter offered "to read this to the management committee tomorrow. The disclaimer is that all we're doing is making comments to the DIDC. It's not what we're planning to offer. We're still thinking."

The Third Meeting: Designing the Account. The third meeting occurred four days later, precisely in the middle (the seventeenth day) of the thirty-four-day span of team meetings. There were changes on several dimensions—who came, where and when the meeting took place, and the kind of work the team did on the task. The first two meetings, and the last, took place in the morning at the centrally located operations center; but this time, the group met in the afternoon at corporate headquarters. The attendance of the meeting also changed; two members of Gil's operations department joined the group.

During the short period of time between the second and third meetings, each team member had initiated some important work in his own department. At the previous meeting, Rick had mentioned that he wanted to start on advertising soon, and he now announced that the copy for the first "statement stuffer" about the new offering would be ready that afternoon. Also starting after the last meeting, Gil had worked with his staff to begin getting ready for the software changes. Don had talked with some of the service departments in his division about upcoming plans, and Porter said that he and his colleagues had just finished drafting the source budget—a projection with critical implications for the kind of performance that would be needed on the new account.

As the meeting began, the team members were neither as uncertain about the account as they had been at the first meeting nor as sanguine about their control over it as they had been

at the second meeting. They were more concerned about succeeding with it. The members were worried. In the first remark
of the discussion, Don expressed some concern that Porter's
group was not moving fast enough.

#5:

[1]*Don:*   . . . Porter, you guys on the eighth floor are gonna hafta
make some decisions . . . about how we're gonna price 'em,
whether we're gonna have tiers—

[2]*Porter:*   Tiers and that kind of thing is something different
than "how."

[3]*Don:*   Um hum. (Pause) We've been working on "how." Fine.
We can explore all the ramifications, but I just hope we don't
get *stuck,* toward the end, without—

(A few sentences later, Rick talked about his marketing worries.)

[4]*Rick:*   I don't worry about the money market funds. . . . It's
the other people like *us* that I worry about—the crazies that are
gonna come out with fourteen percent. (Others agree.)

[5]*Don:*   It's the marketing that scares *me* most. 'Cause everybody's gonna hit with roughly the same thing all at once, and
how do we stand out in that crowd?

Because customers were expected to transfer money from
low-paying savings deposits to the new, high-paying account, the
team anticipated serious costs as well as opportunities for banks.
Team members knew this, but they had not said much about it
in the first two meetings. Porter's source budget figures brought
home the magnitude of the risk as well as the need to put bank
resources on the line to bring in the customers.

#6:

[1]*Porter (concluding his explanation):*   . . . so you gotta bring in
another [x] hundred million dollars, on which you earn over
[x] basis points, to make your profit goal.

[2]*Gil:*   Lots of luck!

[3]*Porter:*   That's one big job!

[4]*Rick:*   It's scary!

[5]*Don:*   What have you been told, Rick, about the resources allocated to marketing?

[6]*Porter:*   Well, that's why we're doing this right now, because this has got to get to Ted [the chairman]. We're going to run it this afternoon, . . . and we're gonna say, "Ted, produce your profits, but this is what you gotta do!" And convince him that you *gotta* put the marketing money behind it or you're not gonna—

Despite the importance of this topic, it was not the agenda of the meeting, and the team did not spend more than ten minutes on it. When Rick asked whether the team was "just going to answer a lot of questions today, or . . . ?" all four original members concurred that "We want to design the skeleton the way we think it's gonna be." "Basically, we're gonna lay out the characteristics of the account." The team spent the next two hours on detailed problem solving with the two additional operations experts and dealing with the nuts and bolts of the account— such as what the related transactions and calculations would be and how they would flow through the bank's machinery. After an hour and forty minutes, when Rick asked how much longer they were going to meet, Gil replied, "Until the bitter end, Rick! We gotta get this thing done!"

By the end of the meeting, the anxiety about succeeding in the marketplace had given way to excitement with the design they had hammered out: "Oh, I think that's super!" "It's creative!" "I think we got a good product!" "Well, I'm pleased to announce that . . . so far it sounds legal."

The bankers did not convene as a group for another seventeen days. They spent that time working individually or in pairs with various departments throughout the bank to prepare the marketing package, the operational machinery, and the documents needed for the account they had outlined at the third, midpoint meeting.

The Final Meeting. The main work of the team's last meeting was to nail down the final features of the account with precision and to get ready to export it from the team to the rest of the bank and to the general public. To help with this, the team again called in a couple of nonmembers—an operations vice president who dealt with setting up new accounts and an assistant vice president responsible for personnel in the branch offices. A comment that Rick made early in the meeting sums up the progress the team had made so far and the work that remained: "It's one thing to stand up there and say we're gonna offer the thing. [But now] we've gotta get something out there that says 'These are the characteristics of the account.' Then we've gotta get something out [to the staff] on how to *handle* it."

The meeting started off with team members' reactions to some of the points that had not been decided as they had hoped by the DIDC ("What kind of dummies *are* they?!") or by other executives in the bank. As in the second meeting, members expressed their reactions succinctly and then turned to other matters. The team quickly roughed out an idea for training sessions.

#7:

[1]*Porter:*   We gotta be prepared to train our people to discuss this with customers. . . . I think we're *all* gonna go out. . . . Sell our people on the fact that this is our life!

[2]*Don:*   Your point is well taken, because . . . if you really want the field to understand how important it is—the heavyweights can take 'em on home.

Rick suggested that the team, along with selected members of the top management committee, meet with all the branch managers in a series of regional meetings, and the rest of the task force agreed.

The group spent the rest of the meeting finishing the description of the account and working out exactly what kind of supplies would be needed for the first day's customers to open accounts. Rick asked Porter to "see if you can get this thing written in blood, so that when I go to the [advertising] agency this afternoon, I know what I can and cannot give 'em." By the end of the meeting, the team's design work was complete; everyone dashed off with his own new assignment.

Postscript: The Outcome. The two weeks between the team's last meeting and the opening day were hectic but exciting. The "inspirational" meetings the team had recommended were especially successful; to members' delight, the bank's chairman ("who has been characterized in the press—and he won't deny it—as being 'crusty' . . . ") came to every meeting. It was "a first for this institution, to take all the senior management out and troop 'em through the whole damn system—to hype these people to do what we wanted 'em to do. . . . Oh, it was exciting. It almost brought tears—because it worked!" The project closed with a final rush, with team members and their staffs working on the openings kits and driving them out to the branches. Thanks to a coordinated push throughout the company, everything was ready for opening day.

Conclusion

The bankers provide an informative example of a team that must communicate extensively and well with its surrounding organization. Members needed complex information from every bailiwick in the bank. They needed to generate quickly an approvable design—neither wasting their own time on ideas that would be unacceptable to key executives nor taking the time for widespread negotiation in the design process. They had to install their product into all the bank's systems, and they had to teach and motivate the work force to handle it effectively.

The team met that challenge through skillful, deliberate planning. Success began with the *composition* of the group. The team stayed small, to safeguard its discretion and agility—but it brought together a mix of people with the expertise and clout needed to conceive the account and coordinate its implementation. Second, the team planned the *timing* of contacts carefully. They purposely settled on their general policy first, and then brought in subordinate experts halfway through to help work out the details of execution. Finally, the team carefully *planned its interaction* with peers and decision makers. As shown in the discussion about how to test people's reactions to tiering (#4), members thought carefully about how to communicate so as to influence people *and* to learn from them, without jeopardizing the team's independence.

The team had several advantages in its work. Members were high-status people with wide access to information above and below them, and they were working on a high-status project. This was evidenced by top executives' willingness to go along with their training plan for "the troops." Further, the team had expert power. The chairman telephoned during a meeting to say "It had better be good," but he did not tell the group what to do. The team clearly was the body with the expertise needed to design an intricate product. Finally, the team had both the norms and the skills appropriate to the challenge. Members were willing to devote time to planning how to interact with their surroundings—and the marketing vice president was especially good at suggesting how to include others while preserving the team's primacy on the project.

And, as Porter said, "It worked." In terms of the criteria of team effectiveness discussed in the introduction to this book, this group was a clear success. The members learned individually *and* became more competent as a team as each one explained the special constraints of his own department and the group collaborated to fit the pieces together. Porter, who commented on the outcome of all the work several weeks after opening day, best summarized the satisfaction that team members (and the wider organization) derived from the product:

We did *exactly* what we wanted to do. We have opened close to [X thousand] accounts! . . . And can you imagine the herculean effort that our employees put in? . . . [The chairman] went so far as to send out a general bulletin, to the whole—every employee in this bank, the first time I've ever seen it done—thanking them for their cooperation in getting this product out.

Note

1. The names of the team members and the bank are fictitious.

7

Mary Lou Davis-Sacks

Credit Analysis Team[1]

The setting is Washington, D.C. It is late fall and the federal budget cycle is about to begin. The work of the Credit Team is just about done.

The Credit Team, which consists of ten or so members, was created in May to develop a series of reports describing credit programs in the federal budget and their impact on the national debt. Although no one is sure of the exact composition of the team, most of the members (and Cynthia, the team leader) work in the same branch of a major federal agency. Other members have been recruited from other agencies for temporary duty on the project. Most team members are senior to Cynthia, and all are regarded as highly competent professionals.

Both senior civil service and political leaders view the credit project as an important one. The hope is that the team's reports will structure and guide the decision making of the Credit Policy Working Group, a group of top-ranking political appointees from various federal agencies formed to make recommendations to the administration on credit programs in the federal budget.

It is now 9:30 A.M., an hour before the working group is scheduled to meet to discuss the penultimate report. Cyn-

126

thia is getting nervous. Earlier this morning, Loman, the chair of the working group, called to tell her that the report looked good—and to ask her to prepare an opening statement summarizing it. Cynthia is on the telephone trying to get back in touch with him to find out more about what he wants, but he is out of the office. Tersely, she leaves a message and gathers her materials to leave for the meeting.

Outside Cynthia's office, Credit Team members who contributed to the report are picking up copies of the report and checking on the time and place of the meeting. Cynthia says little to them as she rushes by on her way to the conference room where the meeting will be held. She and Kitty, an undergraduate student intern borrowed for several weeks from Loman's office, hastily arrange chairs for the sixty or so people who have been granted clearance to attend.

Members of the working group will sit at the long conference table, with members of their staffs sitting immediately behind them. Cynthia, members of her team, and the chief of her branch will sit in chairs placed against the walls of the conference room. From this vantage point, Credit Team members will be able to follow the actions of the working group and to determine for themselves the impact of their work on decision making about national economic policy. It is a relatively rare opportunity for civil servants, and other team members share Cynthia's excitement about what is about to transpire.

An Effective Team?

The Credit Team's report was well received by the working group, and members returned from the meeting ready to dig into work on their sixth and final report. This report was the most critical of all because it was to include a set of policy recommendations which, if accepted by the working group, would be used in preparing the president's budget for the next fiscal year.

Because the budget preparation process runs on a tight, predetermined schedule, it was important that the report be ready by early November—a fact that Cynthia's branch chief made certain she understood. Team members also accepted the deadline. As one commented, deadlines were sacred at the agency, and the rule was that when a delivery date arrives, "You turn in what you have and hope it's in good enough shape."

The credit team did not meet its deadline for the final report. Submitted a full month after the deadline (which had been changed several times by the team's clients), the report merely summarized decisions which, by that time, the administration already had made. It had no influence on the president's budget.

Was the credit team therefore ineffective? The answer is not simple. In fact, almost everyone we asked—team members, the branch chief, Loman—said that the team had done a good job. The team had tackled a tough, new assignment, they said, and had generated reports that met the branch's high quality standards. The branch's good reputation had been maintained. Few noted that the final report was submitted too late to serve its intended purpose.

Some, including the branch chief, acknowledged that the work of the team did not have as much impact as they had originally hoped. But that, one senior staff member (who had worked on the project) reported, was because too few personnel had been assigned to the project. The branch chief agreed and expressed regret that Cynthia had not taken to heart his recommendation that she draw on the outside resources he had secured to help in preparing the reports.

In general, however, the work of the Credit Team was evaluated on the basis of the acceptability of the reports themselves rather than on what the team potentially could have achieved—the impact on national policy it could have had. The reports themselves were almost universally viewed as high-quality documents.

The acceptability of a team's output, however, is but one

criterion of a team's effectiveness. Also relevant is what happens within the team. Some get better and better the longer members work together, and by the time they submit the final product, the team is a beautifully functioning unit with members far more knowledgeable, motivated, and satisfied than they were when the work began. Other teams show the opposite pattern, with escalating cycles of internal "process problems" eventually incapacitating the team and alienating its members. Things can get so bad in such groups that they become unable even to finish the work, and members, in such cases, often lose whatever interest or ability they originally had in working together. A group can, over time, lose its viability as a performing unit.

The credit team showed signs of this pattern as members' ability to function as a team deteriorated over the course of its life. This was most evident while members were preparing their final report. One team member, a senior member of the branch, reported during this time that he had never before felt he had so little influence on a project of which he had been a part. Moreover, he and Cynthia had become embroiled in a heated conflict during preparation of the final report. The conflict arose because he contacted Loman directly about changes that Loman had requested in a section of the report the team member had prepared. Cynthia saw his direct contact with Loman as a threat to her position. She complained to the branch chief that the incident indicated that "clear signals were sent to other staff that my level of responsibility had decreased and that it was no longer necessary to coordinate through me."

Another team member, who had been recruited from another branch within the agency, also was bitter about his role on the Credit Team. He reported that a section of the final report he had written was sent back to him with many requests for revisions. He claimed that when he refused to make the changes, he was "fired" from the team. No other team members were aware of this particular incident, but many expressed similar dissatisfactions. Several, for example, reported feeling "jerked around." And the student intern who had worked closely with Cynthia during the preparation of the fifth report described Cynthia as becoming more and more flighty as the final report was being prepared. Eventually, the intern returned to Loman's office earlier than planned.

Cynthia also experienced major frustrations as her team wrapped up its work. Indeed, she submitted an angry letter of resignation just days before the final report was submitted. In the letter she indicated that her morale had "reached an all-time low." She noted four major reasons for her dissatisfaction: (1) erosion of her ability to maintain control over major assignments, (2) contradictory instructions from Loman and a senior member on the Credit Team, (3) overtime for which she received no financial remuneration because of an unexpected policy change, and (4) the lack of office space for two people she had recruited to work on the team.

Not surprisingly, when the final report eventually was finished, the team simply faded out of existence. Contrasting the eagerness with which team members sought personal copies of the fifth report, copies of the final report sat outside Cynthia's office gathering more dust than interest.

What Happened?

The Credit Team had been assigned an exciting, challenging task that could have had considerable impact on national policy. Its members were knowledgeable, skilled, and initially highly motivated. Senior managers were fully behind the team and its work and offered to provide whatever additional resources and support the team required. Yet the team ended its life having turned in its final, and most important, report too late for it to be of much use—and having frustrated and alienated most of its members, including the team leader. How are we to understand what happened to this team?

To construct an answer to this question, we will examine first the task of the group, then the group itself (including both its composition and its internal structure), and then the organizational context within which the Credit Team operated. We will find that performance conditions for the team were less than optimum. Was the team doomed from the outset, or could something have been done, perhaps by Cynthia or perhaps by her branch chief, to have overcome the built-in difficulties the team faced? The chapter will conclude with some reflections on that question.

The Task: Challenging and Important

Alan, the branch chief, had planted the seed for the Credit Team long before the group itself was formed. Alan strongly supported the formation of a special working group composed of top-level political appointees from across various federal agencies to address credit programs in the federal budget and to make recommendations about these programs to the administration. He believed that rising costs of credit programs in the federal budget warranted a more comprehensive and thoughtful treatment than they had received so far.

More important, Alan saw the Credit Policy Working Group as providing justification for his branch to prepare an integrated, comprehensive set of reports on credit issues in the federal budget. He believed the working group could serve as an excellent vehicle for sending recommendations based on careful empirical analysis to the administration. In the past, his branch had been asked on an ad hoc basis to prepare informal reports for the administration on credit issues. What Alan now sought was the authority to prepare a comprehensive and integrated set of reports that could, if taken seriously, educate federal policy makers and constructively inform their actions. After considerable negotiation with administration representatives, Alan secured the mandate he sought.

The major project of the Credit Team was to be a series of six integrated reports. The first was to provide an overview of credit issues in the federal budget. The next four would address specific sets of federal credit programs, and the last report would summarize the recommendations of the working group and provide unbiased forecasts of their likely impact. The hope was that the nonpoliticized projections drawn in the final report would guide the administration in making rational decisions about federal spending.

Members of the Credit Team (and others in the branch)

found the team task exciting and challenging, both professionally and personally. The task was meaningful for them as professional economists because the issues they were to describe and analyze were complicated, and the task would stretch their skills. The task was important for them as members of the branch because the reports would be highly visible throughout the government, and therefore would affect the branch's reputation. Finally, the task was important for Credit Team members personally because the growing impact of federal credit programs on the national debt had become an issue of national concern—and team members now had the opportunity personally to do something constructive about this problem.

When Alan designed the team task and when the working group confirmed it, few specific guidelines were provided about how the reports should be prepared or what their format should be. They were, of course, expected to meet the branch's usual high standards of clarity, succinctness, accuracy, and objectivity. The reputation of the branch for producing high-quality reports was something that Alan and other senior staff members valued enormously and protected carefully. Everyone involved with the work of the Credit Team understood that this project, especially, demanded the finest work that branch members could produce.

The reports also had to meet Loman's standards and be responsive to his suggestions and demands. As a senior political appointee, Loman had different criteria than did the civil servants in the branch. Branch members assumed, however, that their standards would be higher than his and, therefore, that meeting branch standards would ensure that they would exceed Loman's. They gave little thought to managing potential conflicts between the two sets of standards. In the past, whenever such conflicts had arisen, the branch had always maintained adherence to its own standards and had never got into serious trouble for doing so. It would turn out that conflicts about criteria and standards for the credit reports would be far more difficult to resolve than they had typically been in the past. Unfortunately, no one realized this at the outset, and therefore no special attention was given to the matter when the task initially was presented to Cynthia and her team.

In sum, the task of the credit team was motivationally engaging to team members, the team had enormous autonomy in deciding how to accomplish it, and the reports they were to produce could have considerable constructive impact on national economic policy.

The Team: Competent Members but Barely a Group

The people on the Credit Team, or otherwise involved with its work, were uniformly competent and well regarded by their colleagues. Cynthia herself was an up-and-coming star in the branch who had received one of the agency's most prestigious achievement awards the previous year.

Most of the team members were senior to Cynthia and had worked in the branch for at least five years. One member had left the branch several years before to accept a high-ranking position in another federal agency but then returned to the branch because of the professional satisfaction she derived from her work there.

The three people Cynthia recruited from outside the branch to contribute to the Credit Team were young, but they carried impressive credentials. One was a student intern from Loman's office who was on an extended leave from a prestigious private college. Another was a young woman who had already published an impressive piece on federal budget credit issues in a well-respected national journal. This woman and a man recruited from a different branch within the agency because of his expertise with the agency's computer system were at the same grade level as Cynthia.

In sum, Cynthia had a set of highly qualified people available for work on the Credit Team. Moreover, Alan, Cynthia's boss, assured her that she could recruit additional people from outside the branch if the expertise of those within the branch did not meet the team's needs. Availability of talent simply was not a problem for the Credit Team.

The problem, instead, was in the very definition of the team. Alan's agency, in the year or two before the credit project began, had developed a way of operating that was unique within the larger agency. Alan believed strongly in the use of groups as a way to distribute heavy work loads among staff members and to help junior staff members learn from their more experienced colleagues. A given group might last for a single day (for example, to prepare an analysis needed immediately by a client) or for many months, as was the case for the Credit Team. Each team had a formal leader appointed by the branch chief, but the teams were essentially self-managing with broad latitude; how any given team operated was up to the team and its leader. Individual members of the branch usually were on several teams concurrently. Therefore, they needed to allocate their time carefully among various teams and tasks and to balance among diverse demands that sometimes conflicted with one another.

Alan, the branch chief, assumed that the task of preparing the credit reports would be a group effort. That was the way things were done in the branch. The teams typically worked very well, and there was no a priori reason to expect that it would be different this time. Indeed, it appeared to Alan that a self-managing team was just what the credit project needed. It was clear that preparation of the reports required specialized knowledge about the many credit programs the federal government funded. It was equally clear that no one person possessed the necessary expertise to complete the task alone. The task demanded a pooled effort and coordination—just what a team could provide.

Yet the Credit Team never really coalesced. I saw the first sign of this problem when I attempted to obtain a list of team members so I would know whom to speak with to learn about the life and work of the Credit Team. No such list existed—quite unusual for teams in the branch. Precisely because there were so many teams, everyone took pains to make sure all parties knew exactly who was on which one. But that was not the case for the Credit Team.

Cynthia was the only person in the branch assigned to work on the Credit Team full-time, and everyone confidently identified her as the team leader. Beyond that, confusion reigned. One person who had been identified as a team member by at least three other people denied it. Because he reviewed draft reports of all teams in the branch, he said, he should be viewed as a resource to the Credit Team rather than a member of it. Besides, he asserted, the credit project was not a real team task like others in the branch.

Despite this confusion about membership, most (but not all) members of the team, and most other members of the branch, did refer to the Credit Team as a team. And eight to ten individuals in the branch were closely identified with each of the team's reports. The problem was that exactly who those people were changed from report to report. Moreover, since preparation of the reports overlapped in time, the membership of the team on any given day was unclear throughout the life of the project.

Team Structure: Hub and Spokes

Despite Alan's assumption that those working on the credit project would operate as a self-managing team, much as others in the branch operated, this never happened. Cynthia decided not to use the group as a *group* to develop strategies for accomplishing the work, to coordinate members' activities, or to manage relations between the team and Loman. Instead, she personally developed the grand design for the reports and then met individually with team members to assign them portions of the reports to write. She also personally coordinated the efforts of those who wrote the reports, those who reviewed them, those who physically produced them, and those who received them. Occasionally, some subset of the team worked together for a period of time, but generally individual team members worked independently under Cynthia's direct supervision.

Indeed, Cynthia tended to become upset when team members took initiative to coordinate the work or, especially, to deal with the team's client. When explaining why she submitted a letter of resignation shortly before the final report was finished, she cited, as one reason, a team member's initiating contact with Loman during the preparation of the final report. On another occasion, she asserted that she intended to design the team's reports even if Loman objected to her proposed report format. Without question, Cynthia was in charge and was strongly motivated to stay precisely at the center of the team's work. The team's structure was as clear an example of a hub-and-spokes model as one is likely to find.

Alan was surprised by Cynthia's decision to go it alone and deal with other team members almost exclusively as individual contributors to the project. When he returned from vacation in late August, near the midpoint of the team's projected life, he was dismayed to find Cynthia trying almost single-handedly to prepare all of the team's reports. He immediately met with her and suggested that she call upon others in the branch—or outside the branch, if need be—to help complete the reports. Cynthia's reaction, as related by Alan, was to become insulted and to interpret his suggestion as reflecting a lack of confidence in her ability. It took her a full day to cool off, Alan later recalled. After a day had passed, she called to tell him how much his suggestion had angered and hurt her but that, upon further reflection, she realized that perhaps she could indeed use some help from other staff members.

Cynthia did ask others to contribute to the fifth and final report but, still, she never asked them to contribute as a group. Nor did she ever convene a meeting of those working on the reports. As a result, most credit team members wound up contributing to the reports only in narrow, specific ways. Only a small part of their expertise was used—that part of specific relevance to a particular section of one of the reports. Senior members of the branch did have knowledge, skills, and access to information that could have been useful in developing strategies for proceeding with the work and for managing the relationship with Loman. But Cynthia did not tap those resources. Indeed, the people with whom Cynthia worked most closely throughout the project were the three individuals recruited from outside the branch.

The Organizational Context: Changing and Turbulent

Ideally, a team would operate in an organizational context that is rich with resources, that has competent technical assistance available, that provides the team with all the task-relevant information needed, and that supplies ample feedback and performance-contingent recognition. Moreover, it would be good if the environment would hold still while the team accomplished its work.

Teamwork would be easier if all this were true, but organizational contexts inevitably are less than ideal in some ways. For the Credit Team, two features of the environment were fine: sufficient resources and technical assistance were available. It is true that the team did not draw on them as much as it could have, or perhaps should have, but they were available. Feedback and recognition were mixed for the team, as will be seen. Obtaining reliable, complete information was a major problem. And the environment decidedly did not hold still for the Credit Team.

Feedback and Recognition. Obtaining feedback on work in progress was not a major difficulty for the Credit Team. When the project was initiated, a feedback process was put into place that provided individual team members with detailed feedback about the quality of the sections they prepared. The process worked. Moreover, Loman sometimes called to comment on a report. Ultimately, there was the possibility that the group would see the effects of their reports on the deliberations of the working group and perhaps even on national economic policy. None of the team members complained about an insufficiency of feedback.

Recognition was a somewhat more touchy subject. Some team members did not seek recognition and, indeed, felt it would be superfluous. One said, "Professionals in the branch are *expected* to do top-quality work. Unless work falls below this standard, no further comment is necessary." When Loman sent a letter to team members congratulating them on their work, a number of them regarded the letter as unnecessary and almost condescending. Did he really expect that they would have submitted anything that was *not* top quality?

Others on the team, including Cynthia, appreciated the recognition—such as a telephone call from Loman complimenting her on the quality of the team's fifth report. Indeed, Cynthia felt that she and the team deserved more recognition than they received. She was unhappy, for example, that Loman did not publicly acknowledge the work of the Credit Team in his opening remarks at the meeting of the working group. Overall, however, there was no evidence that either the work or the morale of the team suffered because of insufficient feedback about the team's efforts or insufficient recognition of its accomplishments.

Information. Team members did express considerable frustration that they could not always obtain the information needed to complete their tasks. Sometimes the problem was within the agency itself, as when the Credit Team asked another branch for data the team needed for the final report. Frustrated, Cynthia wrote in a memo to Alan that the other branch was "not in a position to provide the rudiments of assistance." Cynthia went to Alan with the problem. Alan responded by instructing Cynthia and another member of the Credit Team to assist the other branch in pulling together the data needed by the Credit Team. They did this, but, according to Cynthia, it took a considerable personal toll on her and the other two Credit Team members who pulled the data together. She described it as a "grueling exercise," and she cited the experience as among the reasons for her letter of resignation.

More problematic for the team was the lack of clarity about what standards would be used to assess its work. It was clear to all members that the branch had different standards than did Loman and his political colleagues. The former stressed objectivity and analytical thoroughness, while the latter emphasized political utility and persuasiveness. Members were unsure which standards were to apply to their work. The work was being *done* by the branch, which would suggest that the usual standards should apply, but it was being done *for* a very high level political group, which perhaps meant that the clients' standards should be used.

The question was never resolved. One team member, for example, expressed great frustration over having to revise a section of the report he had written. He was frustrated because, while the report did conform to branch standards, it did not meet Loman's expectations. He felt he should have been told before he started to write just what standards would be applied in judging his work. Alan, the branch chief, maintained that such information was readily available to the team if they would only ask for it—yet no one did. The team struggled with incomplete or ambiguous information about standards throughout its life.

Most difficult of all for the Credit Team was getting clear, reliable information from Loman. Part of the delay in the final report was the result of Loman's unwillingness or inability to schedule a meeting at which the working group would make its final recommendations to the administration. This, in turn, caused deadlines for the final report to be postponed. Cynthia tried repeatedly, but without success, to obtain a date from Loman for this meeting. And she faced similar frustrations with the other meetings of the working group. They would be either canceled at the last minute or scheduled so quickly that the team had to rush to complete its reports in time.

One Credit Team member described Loman as someone who "shoots from the hip." His actions seemed unpredictable and his demands unreliable. It appeared to team members that what he wanted shifted constantly as the political environment fluctuated. Team members were constantly scrambling to respond to changes in his expectations. As a result, "managing Loman" became one of the team's major challenges. How well that was done was viewed by all as highly consequential—not just for the life and work of team members, but for the eventual impact of the credit project overall.

Managing the Client. Cynthia, consistent with other aspects of her leadership style on this project, took personal responsibility for managing relations with Loman, and she positioned herself as the team's only link with him. She explained that she wanted to be the sole link with Loman so she could limit his personal involvement with other team members and thereby protect them from being usurped by him. In describing her plans for preparation of the final report, for example, Cynthia reported that she was going to try "to keep Loman out of it." She believed the format she would design would be preferable to his. She did not see any advantage to expanding the relationship with Loman or to negotiating standards for the team's work with him prior to drafting the reports.

Cynthia's attempt to restrict communication with Loman may have been a reaction, in part, to an earlier mistake she had made. A generally accepted norm in the branch limited contact between civil servants and political appointees. The norm was important because it helped protect the branch's image as a staff of objective professionals. Cynthia had violated this norm some months earlier by accepting an invitation from Loman to breakfast with him at the White House. Her colleagues gently reprimanded her for this small transgression, and she subsequently seemed eager to prove that she was not "in Loman's pocket."

Whatever her motivation, Cynthia's decision to limit Loman's involvement and contact with the team did have some costs because it also limited the amount of information the team obtained from him—information it could have used to refine team strategies for accomplishing its work. Her decision also effectively eliminated opportunities that team members might have had to influence Loman—for example, to convince him to hold fast to established meeting schedules or to shape his views of what the reports to the working group should include and what their format should be.

In the end, Loman remained something of a moving target, which required team members to do considerable reworking of their drafts—and, frequently, to move quickly to adjust to his frequent changes in schedules and priorities.

What Kept the Credit Team from Being Great?

The Credit Team had enormous potential. The task of preparing a set of integrated papers addressing the impact of federal credit programs on the growing national debt was an exciting and challenging task for the professional economists on the team. It was an assignment that had been carefully developed, and many branch members viewed it as one of the most significant professional challenges they had faced in their work for the agency.

Team members did invest heavily in the task, working long hours to perfect the team's reports. Several members worked fourteen to sixteen hours a day for five consecutive days to compile the data needed for the final report. One member even scheduled elective surgery so that it would not disrupt the Credit Team's work schedule.

Collectively, members of the team also had ample knowledge and skills to accomplish the task. Team members were among the nation's experts on credit issues in the federal budget. Furthermore, the branch chief was willing to recruit people from other agencies in the government if their special expertise was needed. The team did not use all the talent of its members as well as it might have, but the talent was abundantly present.

What kept this team from being a smashing success? Why did the reports it prepared merely meet organizational standards for acceptability rather than fulfill the dreams that many had of great impact on national economic policy? Why were so many team members angry, frustrated, and ready to quit when the final report was submitted?

Is it that the work was just too much or the task too challenging for any team to do? Or did the team fall victim to the conflict in standards between the branch and its client? Neither explanation is plausible. Although the task was indeed difficult, the team had ample resources—and groups commonly must thread their way among multiple and conflicting client standards.

A more likely explanation has to do with a different kind of conflict—one that was never addressed explicitly—namely, that between Alan and Cynthia over how the team should accomplish its work. Alan took it as given that the Credit Team would operate pretty much like the other self-managing teams in the branch. The resources and advice he offered were all predicated on this model. Cynthia, on the other hand, preferred and insistently implemented a hub-and-spokes management model. Her actions and requests were all predicated on *that* model.

The team members surely must have been confused. Were they to act in accord with branch tradition and with the obvious if implicit wishes of Alan, the real boss of the branch? To do that would violate the wishes and, in many cases, the explicit instructions of Cynthia, their immediate team leader. To go along with Cynthia, on the other hand, demeaned their roles and limited the contributions they could make to what was clearly a very important project.

It was a disturbing dilemma, and it is not surprising that team members behaved in quite different ways at different times. This, too, added to the confusion and uncertainty. For example, what should one *do* when Loman calls? In the past, it had been more than acceptable to take the call and deal with whatever he wanted. But now? Should one decline to talk to the client and insist that he speak only to Cynthia? Or should one take the risk of answering? There were no clear rules for dealing with questions such as these, and they came up all the time.

One could fruitfully debate whether the self-managing team model or the hub-and-spokes model was objectively more appropriate for the work the Credit Team had to do; reasonable arguments can be made on both sides. For example, the hub-and-spokes model is not much at variance with what was done in the branch before Alan became chief, and back then the work generally got done just fine. Moreover, other branches in the agency continued to use that model, and they also got their work done. On the other hand, everyone in the branch had become accustomed to the additional responsibilities and they welcomed the flexibility offered by the self-managing team model. That was how the branch now did its business, and many staff members found it both more suitable for dealing with a fast-paced, uncertain environment and more agreeable personally and professionally.

In my view, either model could have worked quite acceptably in the circumstances the Credit Team faced. What if the self-managing team model had been used? How would Cynthia's behavior have been different? She would, first, have clarified the boundaries of the team so that everyone—team members, managers, and clients—would know who was on the team and that the team was the unit responsible for getting the work done. She would have held a kick-off team meeting at which the team would have reviewed the tasks to be done, assessed the resources needed for the work (and compared them to those available), and established the team's basic time lines and norms of conduct. As the work progressed, she would have helped members clarify their roles and assisted them in finding ways to deal with whatever problems the team encountered—an insufficiency of resources, an obstreperous client, an uncooperative data source, and so on. If some extra clout were needed to solve an external problem, she would have supplied it—either by taking action herself or by enlisting the assistance of Alan. Around the midpoint of the group's life, she probably would have held a fairly formal stock-taking meeting and involved both the branch chief and the client in discussions about how the work should proceed as the team began to pick up the pace and head for the finish line. Throughout, she would have been around—coaching, helping, running interference, and generally doing whatever she could to facilitate the work of the team. And, after all the reports were turned in, she would have held a debriefing meeting at which team members could celebrate their successes, commiserate over their failures, and see what they could learn from their experiences that would help them be better team members and leaders in the future.

The hub-and-spokes model also could have worked considerably better than it did. But because it deviated from the way business typically was done at the branch, it would have been necessary for Cynthia, at the outset, to have made sure that both Alan and her team members understood and accepted that this project was going to unfold in a nontypical fashion. Those discussions surely would have prompted some debate about the rationale for Cynthia's preference about how the team should operate. That debate, in turn, might have altered some of her management decisions. However, once all relevant parties did come to understand and accept how things were going to operate, the work would have unfolded without as many miscues, misunderstandings, and inefficiencies as actually did occur during the credit project.

So, once again, why was the Credit Team not more successful? In my view, three parties share the blame. First, Cynthia, for putting her head down too soon and too insistently, and for failing to read the imperatives of branch history and the constant stream of cues sent to her by both Alan and her team members. Cynthia had in her mind a single model for how to run a project—a model that may have fit her personal style and one to which she may have been especially attracted because of her relatively junior status in the organization. Her failing was not that she had that model in her mind or that she preferred it (for whatever personal or historical reasons)—her failing was that she did not systematically assess the model's appropriateness for the situation in which she was applying it.

Second, Alan, for failing to detect the poor fit between the way the credit project was being structured and managed on the one hand and the generally accepted mode of operating in the branch on the other. Throughout the project, Alan continued to behave as if he were the second-level manager of a self-managing team. He was not, because there was no self-managing team. For this reason, Cynthia understandably found his proffered advice and help either irrelevant or actually detrimental (it was, after all, aimed in the wrong direction). Alan reported that he often found Cynthia's behavior hard to understand—but, invariably, he attributed that to stress, to her being a highly talented, high-strung, relatively junior staff member who, for the first time, was leading a team of seasoned professionals on a task of the highest importance. Alan may or may not have realized that Cynthia was using a model of team leadership quite different from the one he personally espoused. Whether or not he had this realization, he did not *do* much about it—either by trying to change her behavior or by changing his own.

Finally, the Credit Team members themselves. They actually experienced the competing pulls—from Cynthia, from Alan, from the client, and from their own histories in the organization. Yet none of them sought a pause in the process so that all parties could take a look at the crosscurrents that pervaded the life and work of their team.

How about the client, Loman? Did he also contribute to the team's being less than it could have been? Were not his constantly changing demands and priorities a significant impediment to the team's effectiveness? My answer is a qualified no.

Loman was indeed a difficult client who created far more turbulence than was really necessary. But the client gets to be the client, and if his preferences or priorities change, then they change. It was the team's job either to adapt to those changes or to convince Loman that it was in his best interest not to change. In my analysis, Loman—who was viewed by many on the Credit Team as a direct impediment to their performance—may have been the only real innocent in the entire drama.

Note

1. The names of individuals and of the team, as well as certain other details, have been changed to protect the anonymity of the participants.

8

Connie J. G. Gersick
Mary Lou Davis-Sacks

Summary: Task Forces

All task-performing teams must make choices about how they will approach and execute their work, how members will work together, how they will manage relations with significant external persons and groups, and how they will pace themselves. As will be seen below, these choices can be especially salient for task forces because of the novelty of the work (and, often, of fellow group members) and because of the special salience of time and deadlines for such teams.

The Work of Task Forces Requires the Creation of Nonroutine Products. Such teams, by definition, start out not knowing exactly what they eventually will come up with. Uncertainty, learning, invention, and change therefore are integral to the work because members are creating something that did not exist before.

Is there a natural sequence task forces go through to create their products? Our evidence suggests not: the teams we studied used a variety of sequences to accomplish their work. Gersick's teams in Chapters Five and Six, for example, started at different points (contrast the student Strategic Planners' immediate confidence about what to do with the student Novices' slow start) and worked with different styles. Further, there appears to be no one best way to work. Highly divergent styles

146

can be equally effective in getting the job done (contrast the orderly style of the Strategic Planners with the loose "pinball" style of the Bankers).

Despite this variation, we did find one pattern in how task forces moved from start to finish on their tasks. Three of the groups we studied evidenced a clear pattern of "punctuated equilibrium"—alternating between relatively long periods of inertia and dramatic bursts of change. They did not change or progress in gradual increments throughout their lives; rather, members established unique behavior patterns very quickly (and without much conscious deliberation) as teams started out, and they worked within these patterns for a considerable time. New ideas and information coming into the groups did not continually turn them in new directions. Then, as they neared the point halfway between the time they started work and their expected deadline, the groups made considerable progress in a compact transition period, incorporating previous learning with new insights and changing their approaches to their work.

We are less certain whether this pattern of inertia and revolutionary change, clearly present in the teams Gersick studied, also occurred in the federal agency Credit Team observed by Davis-Sacks in Chapter Seven. Because that team faced multiple and constantly changing deadlines, it was impossible for members (or for us) to know precisely when the midpoint of their work time had arrived. Nonetheless, that team, like the others, did undergo a period of intense effort followed by heightened interpersonal conflict at the approximate midpoint of the work on its last and most significant report.

The Team That Does the Work Is Itself Nonroutine. Given responsibility to design and produce a nonroutine product, the need for decisions and choices is inescapable. With individuals, the trick is to decide what to do and then to do it, but that is not sufficient for interdependent group work: some level of *agreement* among members also is required. If members do agree, the group can act as one; if not, the group may experience either the special benefits or the special problems of having a mix of minds at work on a task. The challenges to the team are to figure out how the relevant expertise is distributed among members and to negotiate agreement about who is to do what. This can be daunting for a group of people who are unaccustomed to working together.

The Novices provide an example of how incapacitating such negotiations can be: fully half of the group's time was used up in deadlocked argument. Two factors that may have contributed to their difficulty were the uncertainty of their task (there was no clear way to proceed) and the heterogeneity of the group (members were so different from one another that they simply could not work together). The Bankers, on the other hand, illustrate one of the benefits of heterogeneity in a group: productive argument. This team had to weigh many trade-offs in designing its new product, but members (who represented competing points of view) were able to work through these trade-offs by debating each other in group meetings. This team did have an advantage over the students from the beginning: members had a relatively good idea about who had what expertise, and they knew they were highly interdependent in their effort to reach a shared and consequential objective.

Members of the third team studied, the Credit Team, rarely met as a group. The team leader conceived of the group project as a set of loosely connected subreports. She achieved coordination through her own efforts rather than through the team members, so there was little for members to negotiate with one another. Less an integrated group than members originally had expected, the team enjoyed few of the benefits of group work—except that there were more hands to help and a broader base of expertise from which the leader could draw.

Because task forces typically have both a nonroutine task *and* a new mix of people, such groups are unlikely to have already prepared routines for coordinating members' efforts or for determining how work and influence will be distributed among them. These matters, too, must be invented or learned from experience as the group proceeds.

Two factors make this learning especially challenging for task forces. First, the optimum distribution of influence may change as the work progresses and members discover what the task actually requires. The Strategic Planners, for example, started out by developing a strategic plan for their client. One team member was most experienced with this technique, and he emerged as the group's informal leader early in its life. At the group's transition, however, members decided to change focus and generate an organizational design for their client. A different team member was the expert in that area, and he then took the lead. The success of this team surely would have been compromised had members not been flexible enough to shift the balance of influence as the work changed or had they not taken the trouble to determine how members' expertise was distributed.

The Credit Team did not do this, and both interpersonal and task problems resulted. The team never explicitly explored differences in members' expertise for various parts of the work. Instead, the team leader kept for herself virtually all the say about the team's reports. As a result, the team did not use all the available expertise. Moreover, the leader's domination contributed to members' frustration and alienation—and, eventually, to significant delays in the production of the final report.

The second factor that makes learning a challenge in task forces is members' inability to know in advance exactly how much work the project will require. As a result, they may bungle the division of labor even when they want to parcel out the work fairly, thereby spawning feelings of inequity among members. If some members do succumb to the temptation to become free riders (perhaps because they anticipate little future involvement with the present teammates or because they have competing demands from their regular duties), feelings about equity can become intense. This kind of feeling was present in both the Credit Team and the Novices, and it resulted in resentment and suboptimal work processes in both teams, especially in the final stages of their projects.

Task Forces Are Simultaneously Autonomous and Dependent. Because task forces do work that is both nonroutine and delegated, members must simultaneously make independent decisions and conform to external requirements. Because the group is created by someone else for his or her own purposes, members must be open to influence by the person who created it or by others that person designates. Because the work is nonroutine, the product cannot be fully described in advance: the group must make choices based on members' own judgments as the work progresses. So, on one hand, the group is being "paid to think" and must make decisions, while on the other, unless members make sure relevant outsiders have the chance to influence their work, the product may be inappropriate or unacceptable. The challenge for the group is to find the right balance of independence from and sensitivity to outsiders. The corresponding challenge for the external manager of the group is to influence and guide the group while remaining open to learning from it. The team, after all, should be discovering things that no one knew when the assignment was made.

The student groups used a simple, sequential strategy for dealing with the independence-responsiveness tension. Both of them gained independence by initially ignoring their nonintrusive instructor. Subsequently, both took initiatives to learn what the instructor's requirements actually were and then modified their work based on what they learned. The key was to know *when* to attend to the views of the instructor and when to keep the group's collective head down and plug along with the work. At the start, each student team's grasp of its requirements and of the instructor's expectations was limited because members did not yet know enough about what they were doing. By the end of their projects, they knew well what they were doing, but the cost of waiting until the end to learn what the instructor really wanted was quite high—as the Novices discovered to their dismay. The midpoint, when the Strategic Planners took their look outside, was just the right time.

Whereas the direction of the learning process for the students was skewed, in that information flowed from the instructor to them but not vice versa, the situation at the bank was different. There it was critical for the team to establish two-way communication with others about how the product was developing and what resources the organization would devote to it. The Bankers were active, skillful, and deliberate in balancing between open communication with the organization and protection of their own discretion.

The Credit Team provides a final, contrasting example. Here, the team leader was the sole link between the team and its stakeholders. As a junior staff member without much clout, she had less power than did the stakeholders, so she needed to be responsive to them. Rather than negotiating and clarifying the stakeholder expectations at the outset of the project and then using this information to guide team efforts, the team leader avoided such discussions and left team members to prepare their reports based on their own beliefs about what would be acceptable. This "do what you think is best and wait to see" strategy provided members considerable discretion but little recourse when reports were subsequently rejected.

Balancing the relationship between the team as a whole and its outside context as a whole becomes more complex when outside stakeholders have heterogeneous demands. A team, whether planned or by default, must necessarily make some concrete response to competing stakeholder interests in its product, and hammering out a solution to a complex gestalt of external demands can be challenging indeed. The group's composition affects its ability to respond, partly because the people in the group represent (through members' identifications with various outsiders) a particular collection of attitudes toward, and information about, those stakeholders. The Bankers illustrate how members' stakeholder identifications can be put to work in a fruitful way; the Novices' deadlocked disagreement, which arose partly out of members' differing views about how to relate to outsiders, shows how problems can arise.

Task Forces Must Accomplish Nonroutine Work in a Fixed Time. A task force must somehow pace itself so that a project whose requirements are unclear at the outset is completed on time. This is hard enough when the deadline is clear and fixed. It can be nearly impossible when the deadline is fuzzy or changes frequently because then there is uncertainty about *both* the work demands and the time constraints. The four teams we studied varied considerably with regard to their difficulties in developing and sustaining an appropriate work pace. The students had it easiest. Their deadlines were completely clear and were not going to flex either way. Moreover, these teams were not dependent on anyone other than their instructor for resources or information.

The Bankers' deadline also was completely clear: the new account would be legal to offer on a certain date, and it had to be ready on that date if the bank was to be competitive. Unlike the students, however, this team had more than itself to worry about. Members had to secure approval for their plans from senior management, coordinate with outside vendors for supplies, and get a whole organization ready to offer the product. Nevertheless, the team was largely calling the shots, and the rest of the organization was generally ready and eager to cooperate. Although managing the pace of the work was more complex for the Bankers than it was for the students, members were just as much in control of the process.

In these three cases, time was a great organizing force. The midpoint transition was a concentrated, powerhouse time to touch base with outsiders, revise the work in accord with what was learned about external requirements and stakeholder expectations, and reset plans for the second half of production. The deadline itself was another powerful motivator and organizer, which resulted in a period of flat-out work to finish up. And all three of these teams did complete their work by the deadline.

The Credit Team had to contend with a far more difficult performance situation, and it wound up missing its final deadline. Because there were so many changes in the team's deadlines, it was virtually impossible to know which one was the true "drop-dead" due date. Members also shifted internal deadlines because of events occurring outside the group and because of delays in getting information from outsiders, who often were not responsive to the team's need for information about schedules. Whether the ambiguous and uncertain deadlines caused the final report to be late, or whether problems within the group caused members to shift deadlines and created a cloud of confusion around them, the lack of a consistent time line frustrated team members and resulted in some significant personal and collective costs.

It is, of course, obvious that a team dependent on outside

groups for resources will have problems if those groups cannot be counted upon to deliver the goods. What is less obvious is the role of timing and clear deadlines in synchronizing and ordering the multiple adjustments that teams have to make throughout an ad hoc project. Confusion and shifting ground with regard to deadlines may not just make the team late; they may have an effect similar to that of fibrillation during a heart attack. In heart fibrillation, the problem is not that the heart stops but that synchronization is lost, and therefore heartbeats are ineffectual. Instability of a team's deadlines can undermine members' ability to synchronize their efforts in managing the multiple demands that task forces invariably face.

Summary. Uncertainty and heterogeneity have been prominent concepts in the chapters of this part—uncertainty in the task, in how team members will work on it, and in how much time it will consume; and heterogeneity among both team members and stakeholders. The more that uncertainty and heterogeneity pervade a project, the more a task force must be prepared to learn, invent, change, and negotiate. Uncertainty and heterogeneity do offer higher potential creativity, but they also bring higher risk and harder work.

Task uncertainty is built into a task force's work; it is part of what being a task force or project team is all about. And heterogeneity, both internal and external, is more the rule than the exception for such groups. Our findings suggest that the skills of team members—and of those who establish and manage the teams—in dealing with uncertainty and heterogeneity strongly influence the ultimate effectiveness of task forces.

Part Three

PROFESSIONAL SUPPORT
TEAMS: PROVIDING
EXPERT ASSISTANCE

Professional support teams serve their organizations indirectly by providing expert assistance to those who directly generate the organizations' products or services. Perhaps the most distinctive feature of such groups is that they typically are in a reactive mode vis-a-vis the rest of the organization. Those who are served define the work and specify the objectives. Typically they are individuals or teams with "line" responsibilities rather than the team's own managers. Moreover, because professional support teams operate at the pleasure of their internal organizational clients, members may occasionally find themselves all prepared for work but, in the absence of a specific request for assistance, with no work to do. It is a continuing challenge for these teams to help clients (and potential clients) understand and value the special expertise they offer.

The three teams examined in Part Three are quite diverse. Chapter Nine describes a team of analysts in an agency of the federal government whose job was to track a certain piece of legislation as it wended its way through congressional deliberations and to report its findings daily to senior political officials in the executive branch. The work was high pressured and fast paced, but entirely dependent on others—dependent on congressional committees, which sometimes changed the schedule of

155

hearings with no advance notice, and dependent on the team's clients, who occasionally made special requests of the team, also with little notice. The tracking team's attempt to prepare for its work and the ultimate futility of those preparations provide a good illustration of both the challenges and the frustrations of professional support work.

The second team, described in Chapter Ten, is the systems group at a new plant where air conditioner components were to be produced. This team was charged with creating and maintaining the computer systems necessary to support the office, factory, business, and engineering needs of the plant. Its history highlights the kinds of conflicts that can occur between a professional support team and its clients. Team members, dedicated to developing a state-of-the-art information system for the fledgling plant, had to deal with line managers who were not terribly excited by the team's vision. Moreover, the corporate systems group, back at headquarters, saw no reason why existing systems could not be adapted and used at the new plant. It was a continuing challenge for the Fairfield Systems Group to find ways that the team could actually *use* its considerable professional expertise to help the new plant succeed.

Chapter Eleven describes a team of airline maintenance managers. This team had to manage two very different tasks simultaneously: dealing with immediate maintenance problems as they occurred and conducting longer-term engineering and organizational projects. Life at work was unpredictable for members of the maintenance control team, and the team had difficulty balancing the reactive and proactive parts of its work. This difficulty was compounded by the fact that members could almost never meet as a group—because they had to provide around-the-clock coverage of airline operations in case a maintenance problem occurred and because project work sometimes kept one or more members away from headquarters for days at a time. The way the maintenance control team and its managers designed the work and the team to deal with these difficulties offers some interesting ideas about how professional support work in other kinds of organizations might be structured and managed.

9

Mary Lou Davis-Sacks

The Tracking Team[1]

Elaine used every minute of the sixteen-block cab ride to the Capitol to review with Jim, one more time, details of the congressional committee meetings they were about to observe. She had prepared the team better this year than in past years, and she hoped her efforts would pay off. But she was worried. She had a gut feeling that something wasn't quite right.

The team was ready—all four of them. They had been preparing for nearly two months and were anxious for the committees to turn their attention to the piece of legislation the team was expected to track for the executive branch. Once committee action began, the team members would drop all their other assignments and devote themselves full-time, and more, to the tracking task.

Based on experience in past years, the team anticipated long hours, hurriedly prepared reports, and rushed cab rides to and from the Capitol. Although the upcoming activities would be grueling, team members admitted to excitement about them. This was the race for which the team had been preparing for months. Now it was time to test the team's strength—to show what it could do.

Every year, the administration submits a certain piece of legislation to Congress, and both a House and a Senate committee review it. During the review period, each committee meets for days on end—hearing testimony, asking questions, and preparing recommendations for consideration by members' congressional colleagues.

The hearings take place in a large chamber, with members seated on a dais at long tables. The tables are arranged in a semicircle facing an audience of approximately 200 people. Television cameras and lights fill the side aisles. The first few rows of audience seating are reserved for congressional staff and official visitors. Outsiders, those without passes, wait to be seated in long lines at the back of the chamber. Many stand throughout the proceedings.

Team members sit in audience seats the committee staffs reserve for them. Even there it is crowded. It is difficult to take notes or to open a briefcase without bumping the person in the next seat. Moreover, team members cannot always see who is speaking and sometimes have to refer to seating charts they prepare ahead of time to figure out who is saying what.

Two members of the tracking team attend each session so they can cross-check notes, fill in gaps for each other, and generally provide better coverage of the committee proceedings. This arrangement also allows each member to take a break now and then, to have a mind-clearing stroll down the corridors. Sitting for hours at a time in these crowded conditions is exhausting.

Typically, team members prepare their reports at the end of the day, after returning from committee meetings. If critical events occur in a morning session, however, they may return to the branch and prepare a report over lunch for submission to administration officials in the afternoon.

Ideally, one or more team members remain back at the branch to provide back-up support for those members at the hearings on the Hill. During breaks in the meetings, those attending often call their colleagues at the branch to update them on committee activity, to ask them to ferret out some background information, or to begin planning the report that they will submit at the end of the day.

The Team and Its Work

The Work. The team's primary task is to track committee action—to monitor the activities of two congressional committees as each considers the annual piece of legislation, to be the eyes and ears of the administration in following what Congress is doing. The team submits its reports to high administration officials, who expect them to be reliable, timely, and detailed enough to serve as a sound basis for the development of political strategy. Occasionally, executive branch officials also ask the team to prepare background reports for use in interpreting committee actions. For these reports, a team can take longer than is possible for reports that track congressional activity in real time.

Most, but not all, of the team's activity occurs during the relatively brief period each year (four to ten days) when the committees consider this particular piece of legislation. Those who have been a part of the team previously, and those who simply have watched the team in previous years, know that once the committees turn their attention to this legislation those on the team will have to drop everything else and "crash." There is much folklore in the branch about the strategies team members have invented in past years to survive during the "crash" season.

In general, the team's reports are expected to be relatively straightforward accounts of what happens at the committee meetings. When, however, a committee comes up with a proposed change in what the administration has submitted—a change that involves specific dollar figures—team members have to translate those dollars into the metric the administration uses. This is technical work involving use of the executive branch's forecasting procedures and economic assumptions. Administration officials expect the team to tell them whether their figures and those proposed in committee reflect differences in technical forecasting procedures, in underlying economic assumptions, or in political views about how government funds should be allocated.

This subtask requires that team members be knowledgeable about the forecasting procedures and about economic assumptions used by both the executive branch and the two committees. Obtaining this information can be difficult and time consuming. Some facts and figures are hard to locate or retrieve in the federal bureaucracy. Others are politically sensitive and cannot be easily extracted from the committee staffs who have them.

While team members do sign their names to the reports they prepare, administration officials hold the team's leader and the branch chief responsible for the accuracy and timeliness of the reports. Team members' colleagues in the branch, however, do give them credit for the reports and recognize the contributions of individual members. They know that the reports are the result of intense, collaborative effort by team members and that they require a great deal of preparatory work that usually is not obvious in the final reports themselves.

This year, the team was working without any specific guidelines or deadlines for its reports. Previous administrations had provided quite clear expectations—for example, by establishing specific time schedules for submissions. But this year, the request was simply that reports be filed as soon as possible, and team members had the distinct impression that "as soon as possible" would never be quite soon enough. Members felt rushed even before committee hearings began. This year, the work would be harder than before. That was a problem, because this year the team also was less experienced than usual.

The Team. The tracking team consisted of four professional civil servants employed in one branch of a large federal agency. All four had other responsibilities in the branch besides this team—responsibilities they would temporarily set aside once committee hearings began. Elaine was the team's leader, as she had been for the past five years. Two of the other team members had served the previous year, and one person was completely new to the team.

Elaine was a middle-aged woman who spoke rapidly in a quiet, low voice. She gave short, concise explanations and she organized her thoughts carefully before speaking. She never rushed conversations but did routinely interrupt them to take phone calls. Elaine was well regarded by her professional colleagues in the agency and on Capitol Hill. She had built strong connections with her professional counterparts on the Hill, and they viewed her as both competent and trustworthy.

Karla was ten years younger than Elaine. She spoke her mind freely and did not hesitate to voice criticism. Karla had been a member of the team the previous year and only reluctantly agreed to serve again this year. She did not feel the team made good use of her professional expertise. Karla did not want to make a career of merely watching the political process. Instead, she said, she sought work that would allow her to stretch and develop her technical and analytical skills.

Mike was about the same age as Karla. While Mike and Karla had exchanged sharp words in the past, tensions between them began to ease as the committee season approached. Both assured me they were once again ready to work together, although Karla still harbored some residual anger. Mike liked politics, and he was looking forward to going to the Hill and watching what transpired. Having a front-row seat to observe national decision making excited him, although he kept that private: it was not good for one's reputation to appear to have caught "Potomac fever"—to seem to actually care about the power and political currents that pervade the Capitol.

Like Elaine and Karla, Mike had been a member of the team the previous year. Under the pressures of last year, four students had been hired temporarily to assist the team and Mike had supervised them, working in what came to be known as the "emergency room." Mike perceived this as a signal of his status on the team and considered himself to be second in command to Elaine (although none of the other team members viewed him this way). Mike privately hoped that he might be asked to fill Elaine's position as team leader should she ever relinquish it.

Jim was the novice on the team—new both to the branch and to Washington. Having just arrived from the Midwest, Jim was wide-eyed about everything that happened inside the Capitol Beltway. He was excited about being so close to the center of political power, and he had not yet learned to conceal that. He was still learning—both about the technical parts of the work and about how a branch staffer is supposed to act.

The Context

The Network. Elaine's years of experience were valuable to the team, not only because she could see the patterns in small pieces of information—patterns that eluded others—but also because she was able to obtain such information through connections she had cultivated over the years with staff members around the Capitol. In her view, having informal relationships with staff members in various other agencies and in Congress was critical to getting the work done, and she strongly encouraged her team members to develop their own contacts.

Mike and Karla had begun to develop contacts the previous year and expected to strengthen these relationships this year. Elaine explicitly instructed Jim to stop by the offices of the committee staff before the committee's preliminary meeting to establish contact with people there. Some members of the team were worried about Jim's ability to do this successfully. Karla, in particular, was afraid that Jim would innocently and inadvertently jeopardize relationships that she had worked hard to develop by asking "stupid" questions of committee staffers.

The contacts the team developed were not only important sources of information about such mundane (but important) matters as the schedule of committee activities, but they also were critical in obtaining information about the forecasting procedures and economic assumptions the committees used. Since some of this information was difficult to locate and some was politically sensitive, the team needed to cultivate sources that would trust the team to be discreet with the information and to use it judiciously.

These contacts were the team's professional network. It is not unusual for people in the federal government to move from staff to staff every few years, so a contact developed for one purpose this year might turn out to be useful for another purpose in a subsequent year. Furthermore, members of the team's network were among the very few who fully understood the technical aspects of the team's task. It was important to the team members, and to Elaine in particular, that the team develop and maintain the respect of these people.

The Branch. The immediate organizational context of the tracking team was a branch of an agency in the executive branch of the federal government. Alan, the branch chief, liked to use self-managing teams whenever he could to accomplish the branch's work. He felt that such teams were able to be more flexible and responsive to the constantly changing political environment than were more traditional organizational forms and that they were a good device to help new staff members learn from old hands.

When Alan created a team, he composed it carefully by building in a mix of new and experienced members and making sure that collectively the team had enough knowledge and skill to accomplish its work. And he appointed a trusted senior staff member to be team leader. He tried to be as clear as possible about the team's task, the standards that would be used to assess its work, and the limits on its authority. Beyond that, he gave the team wide latitude to decide how members would manage themselves and their work. Once a team was under way, Alan stayed in the background as much as possible—providing support where he could and running political interference if asked, but not intervening in the team's day-to-day activities. This organizational design was decidedly nonbureaucratic and was viewed in the agency as something of an innovation. But Alan liked the design, it seemed to work, and it was the way he dealt with the tracking team.

One implication of Alan's organizational design was the team's need to manage its own relations with clients and information sources. Normal practice in the agency was for information requests, and responses to those requests, to be passed up and down hierarchical chains within each organizational unit before being passed across organizational boundaries. Alan thought that was cumbersome and inefficient, so he encouraged clients to deal directly with those staff members who had (or could get) the information they needed. And he, like Elaine, encouraged staff members to develop their own informal networks of contacts. Alan had found such networks essential to his own work before he became branch chief, and he felt so strongly about their importance that he regarded the relationships a team built with people on the Hill and in other agencies as one sign of a team's overall effectiveness.

Still, the most important indicator of a team's performance, in Alan's view, was the quality of the reports it prepared. Alan insisted that every report his branch issued be as near to perfect as staff members could make it—in technical accuracy, certainly, but also in the clarity of data tables and in the quality of the written presentation. Indeed, one of the limits Alan placed on the authority of the tracking team was a review process that made sure each report was checked and double-checked. Alan personally reviewed most of the reports that were prepared by the team before they were sent to the executive branch—and when rewrites were required, it was usually Alan who insisted on them.

The Clients. Senior administrators in the executive branch were the sole clients of the tracking team's reports. The team received little feedback from those individuals, nor did it expect much. Team members knew their clients were always very busy and assumed they would not take time to comment on a report unless they found a problem with it or unless they needed additional information.

It was, nonetheless, very important to the team that its clients in the administration think well of its work. These people did, after all, wield enormous power. They could, if they wished, ask the team to rewrite any report they did not like. They could demand that the staffing of the team be changed, and agency management would almost certainly accede to such a request. Or they could disband the team entirely and find another means of getting the information they needed. Even though there was very little direct contact between the team and its clients, the team took them very seriously indeed.

Elaine was wary of executive branch officials. Although it was not necessary for her to do so, she tried to channel most communications between the team and administration officials through Alan. In contrast to her unceasing efforts to build informal relationships with staff members on the Hill and in other agencies, she saw no particular advantage to trying to build such relationships with administration officials. The power differential was just too great. Besides, while civil service staffers tend to stay around Washington for a long time, administration officials generally are here today and gone, if not tomorrow, then certainly in less than four years.

The power differential between the team and its clients, combined with the uncertainty of the committee process, kept the tracking team in a reactive posture. Members could not prepare very far in advance because they had neither the power to control future conditions nor the relationships with clients to enable them to shape the demands made of them. They frequently had to scramble, using whatever methods they could devise quickly to get the work accomplished. Elaine did not like to scramble because she feared it might jeopardize the quality of the work. Therefore, she decided to invest heavily in training and strategy planning this year, to see if the team for once could get ahead of the game and stay there. If she succeeded, it would be a significant change in the traditional work style of a tracking team.

Running the Race

Get Ready . . . In previous years, Elaine had tried to develop written materials to train new team members. She had given up on that project, however, and she now believed that new members required direct, hands-on coaching. The key target this year was Jim. Elaine invested a great deal of time working with him before the start of committee hearings and insisted that Karla and Mike do the same. With such a small team, she said, it was absolutely essential that all members be as prepared as possible when committee action started.

Part of Jim's training took place in hour-long, intensive question-and-answer sessions. Another part involved short, periodic checks to make sure he was progressing adequately on tasks and to see how ready he was for committee action to start. Elaine's instructions included everything from explanations of the complex decisions the committees might make to the materials Jim should take with him to committee meetings.

Elaine rarely complained about the time she spent training Jim, although she did worry some about how much success she was having. Karla and Mike, on the other hand, expressed frustration with the time they had to spend with him. Karla, in particular, became irritated by Jim's questions and lack of knowledge. She became especially incensed when he once asked an inappropriate question in the presence of a House staff member with whom Karla had worked hard to develop a relationship of mutual respect. Jim also contributed to Karla's frustration at least once by questioning her authority to ask him to redo a task that he thought he had accomplished adequately.

While Karla and Mike were more experienced than Jim, they did have only one year more than he did. They, too, lacked the depth that would be required to report on and interpret the diversity of things that would occur once committee action started. Moreover, their knowledge about committee operations was limited to relatively specific content areas. Elaine tried to expand their knowledge by assigning them preparatory work on topics outside their areas of expertise. Both objected to this, and neither actually completed the assigned work.

Get Set . . . Elaine had more success in training her team by doing it implicitly in a series of meetings she held starting two months in advance of the first scheduled committee hearings. The manifest purpose of these meetings was to compile intelligence about what was likely to come up in this year's hearings, to gather in advance information that might later be needed on short notice, and generally to plan the strategy that the team would use when the "action" began. The less obvious purpose of the meetings was to continue training her team—including Jim, who so far appeared not to be "getting it," and Mike and Karla, who had clearly signaled that they did not think they needed it.

One information-gathering task the team accomplished in these meetings was to obtain the data needed to translate committee dollar figures into the format used by the executive branch. This information was stored in the agency computer in the form of algorithms that could be used to quickly perform the necessary translations.

The team also developed a set of norms to guide its reporting practices. The previous year, administration officials had pushed the team so hard that members resorted to phoning in reports rather than writing them, which created two major problems. First, telephone reports bypassed the standard review procedures the team leader and branch chief had established for ensuring the quality and accuracy of reports. Second, telephone reports provided no written documentation of committee action that could be circulated among team members. The team had encountered some difficulties the previous year because of the telephone reports, and the guidelines members developed in the strategy-planning meetings were expected to head off any such problems this year.

The team established other time-saving devices and guidelines for member behavior in these meetings. Elaine pushed hard on this, partly to see if the team could come up with better ways of doing an inherently difficult and frustrating job, and partly because she was worried about the fact that the team was so small and inexperienced. Although Alan had promised that she could call upon others in the branch for help if she needed it after committee hearings began, Elaine took it as a leadership challenge to see if she could develop her small, inexperienced team to the point that she would not need additional staff.

As the projected date of the first committee meetings approached, Elaine became increasingly confident of the tracking team's readiness. Yet uncertainty nagged at her. Information she was picking up between the lines of stories in the *New York Times* and *Washington Post* and from her contacts on the Hill suggested that something unusual was afoot. She could not figure out exactly what it was, but she had a strong intuition that somehow, in some way, the legislative process was floundering.

. . . and Stop. The tracking team never got a chance to test its strength. The committees met only briefly in preliminary meet-

ings and then, for the first time in history, decided not to take action on this particular piece of annual legislation. The effect on the team was devastating. They were all dressed up but had nowhere to go.

Elaine's efforts to introduce more planning and preparation into the team were not rewarded. There would be no harvest from the energy and effort the team had invested in getting itself ready. Nor would the team pass on to its successors a proven new way of accomplishing tracking work.

There would be no real test of the team's success in training Jim. He would not have a chance to prove himself, and questions about his competence would remain unanswered. Worse, without an opportunity to apply what he had learned, it seemed unlikely that he would retain his newly gained knowledge for use the following year.

Mike, who had not completed the preparatory work Elaine had assigned him, would not be able to redeem himself by investing long hours and much effort during the committee proceedings. Nor would he have the opportunity to earn "credit points" that might move him toward a team leadership position in a future year.

The team would not have a chance to live through the committee season together, face adversity together, and enjoy the special spirit that so often develops in a team when adversity has been overcome. There would be no stories circulating in the branch in subsequent years about this team's herculean efforts. Members would not have a chance to develop new contacts on congressional staffs or to strengthen old network ties. Nor would they have the opportunity to further strengthen the branch's reputation with its clients in the administration.

Shortly after committee action had been canceled, Elaine called a meeting to review the work the team had accomplished and to thank members for their efforts. It was difficult for members to feel much pride in what they had done or to talk with any enthusiasm about how helpful that work would be to next year's team. There was just too much frustration and disappointment in the room.

By the following year, Karla, Mike, and Jim had all left the branch.

Conclusion

There are some real costs to a team when it has prepared intensively for a piece of important work—and then that work vanishes. Individual members are disappointed and frustrated, of course, because their efforts to prepare have been wasted. And they do not have the chance to make the contributions or gain the learning that the work itself would have brought.

There also are costs to the team as a whole, including diminution of its capabilities as a performing unit. For the tracking team, the hectic but challenging conditions that members would have encountered during the congressional hearings almost certainly would have strengthened team spirit and heightened member commitment to the team and its work. Moreover, members would have had the chance to work through some of the tensions that had built up during the preparation period. Members' energy and attention would have turned from internal matters (such as questions about Jim's competence or Mike's commitment) to real and pressing work demands. As it turned out for the tracking team, the questions remained unanswered and the tensions were not resolved.

It is ironic that Elaine's extra efforts to train individual members of the team and to help the team develop task-appropriate norms and performance strategies probably exacerbated these problems. The team suffered more over its missed opportunities and its wasted effort than it would have if competent preparatory work had not been done.

At the end of the team's life, Elaine tried to relieve members' frustration and unhappiness by pointing out the good work that the team had, in fact, done. But the reassuring talk at her debriefing meeting about what had been accomplished was small consolation for members' disappointment at having been prevented from performing their major task.

The problem the tracking team faced may be a common one for support teams that provide services on an as-needed basis. Teams that must wait for a request or a signal from the environment before they can perform are inherently vulnerable to the kinds of problems and frustrations the tracking team experienced.

A support team can, of course, try to head off this kind of problem. It might, for example, try to stimulate client needs or actively seek out tasks it is ready and willing to perform. The tracking team, for example, could have "planted some seeds" with its clients in the administration and perhaps could have generated some work in addition to its basic tracking responsibilities. But that is unlikely for a team whose main business is support. Such teams prepare themselves for reactive work and define themselves that way. Once that definition is in place, the chances of members taking proactive initiatives diminish.

For the tracking team, the major concern was that its resources were barely sufficient for the upcoming reactive work. How wise would it have been, in those circumstances, for members to have generated additional tasks just to have interesting work to do if the major task should fall through? How legitimate would it have been for them to have taken such an initiative in any case? How high is the risk that such initiatives from support teams will turn out to be make-work—things that do not really warrant the organizational resources they would require? A support team, because of its interest in providing services to its organization, may run a real risk of overestimating needs for its services and wind up wasting organizational resources.

It is *hard* to be a support team, to have to wait for others to give the signal to begin work. It is hard to find the right balance between a reactive and a proactive stance. Also, as the tracking team vividly illustrates, it is hard to find the right balance between getting all prepared ahead of time for the anticipated work (and risking the kind of disappointment and frustration the tracking team experienced), on the one hand, and waiting until the call actually comes (and risking being unprepared), on the other. Finding ways to balance tensions such as these is, perhaps most of all, what good leadership of support teams is all about.

Note

1. The names of individuals and of the team, as well as certain other details, have been changed to protect the anonymity of the participants.

10

Russell A. Eisenstat

ᶻᶟᒪᓓᴿᶟᶻᒪᓓᴿᶟᶻᒪᓓᴿᶟᶻᒪᓓᴿᶟᶻᒪᓓᴿᶟᶻᒪᓓᴿᶟᶻᒪᓓᴿᶟᶻᒪᓓᴿᶟᶻᒪ

Fairfield Systems Group

The members of the systems support team were furious. Alan Rasky, plant manager of the Ashland Corporation's Fairfield Components Plant (FCP), had walked through the group's offices the preceding evening and berated team members for having messy desks. Rasky felt that good housekeeping was critically important in a sophisticated manufacturing facility such as the FCP because sloppiness anywhere in the plant could lead to safety and product quality problems. "Even though you aren't producing parts," he insisted, "if you don't keep your desks clean it sets a bad example for everyone else."

Systems team members felt differently. One explained: "You are working eighty hours a week and the last thing you need to tell people is that your desk isn't clean. . . . Alan has said that is just a piece of what you are supposed to do. But it comes across as it is ninety percent of the job to keep the desk clean, and the fact that I wrote twenty-eight programs and they all work perfectly and our productivity has increased by one thousand percent doesn't mean [anything] because I don't have a clean desk. In Joplin [Missouri, corporate headquarters] some of the most unproductive people in the world had the cleanest desks. So it was coming across to me as this is how I am judging whether you are a good person or not, is whether your desk is clean."

171

Working on a professional support team at a team-based manufacturing facility can be frustrating. Production teams in such plants get most of the attention and praise. Worse, mature production teams often take over many of the tasks that functional specialists handle in traditional plants. However, even in advanced manufacturing facilities, functional professionals do have a significant role to play in, for example, creating and maintaining plant-wide computer systems, in training manufacturing personnel to perform functional tasks, and in continuing to handle those technical tasks for which manufacturing team members lack the requisite time or skill.

Relative to knowledge about the design and leadership of production teams, knowledge about the best strategies for managing teams of functional support personnel in high-commitment manufacturing facilities is scarce. Senior line managers in such organizations typically have taken one of three stances toward professional support groups: ignore them, view them as sources of resistance, or manage them in the same way as manufacturing teams. This chapter, by focusing on the history of one technical support team, seeks to illuminate some of the problematic consequences of taking each of these three stances toward such teams.

The team we studied is the systems support team at the Fairfield Components Plant (FCP).[1] An air conditioner components plant, the FCP was a high-commitment organization that used teams as the basic performing unit for both line manufacturing and staff support activities. The systems team at Fairfield was responsible for creating and maintaining the computer systems necessary to support the office, factory, business, and engineering needs of the plant.

The challenges that confronted the systems team at Fairfield derived from a fundamental tension about the purpose of the team. Was it to be an experimental laboratory for developing state-of-the-art computer systems for the FCP, or should it serve a more modest support function by drawing on already proven technologies to provide technical assistance to plant personnel? In examining the roots and consequences of this tension, we will discover a number of issues that directly affected the productivity of the systems team and that are germane to the design and management of functional teams more generally.

Innovation Versus Support

The Roots of the Tension. In December 1981, the FCP's first plant manager, Barry Mackay, convinced Bob Jones to join the plant as the first manager of the systems team. The team was not yet formed, and Jones was excited about his potential contribution to the new plant. Jones's enthusiasm was reinforced by Mackay, who had a background in industrial engineering in Ashland's traditional manufacturing plants. Jones, at the time a corporate systems manager, had experience in two of Ashland's innovative plants. He had been involved in developing the inventory system for the Ridgeway, Pennsylvania, plant and subsequently had studied the manufacturing resource planning system being developed at the Jacksonville, Florida, plant.

Jones shared with Mackay a belief in the importance of developing a state-of-the-art information system to support the organizational innovations planned for the Fairfield plant. Traditionally Ashland used computer systems primarily to process financial information—most of which was done centrally by the corporate systems group in batch jobs on large mainframe computers. Mackay and Jones wanted to break out of traditional patterns. They sought to create an integrated computer system that would allow for the immediate transfer of information not only from one plant system to another (for example, from the computers monitoring manufacturing to those processing financial information) but also from the plant to the mainframes at headquarters in Joplin. The system would also decentralize data processing to the greatest possible extent. Whenever possible, end users, rather than systems staff, would perform data entry, data access, and data manipulation.

The opportunity to play a part in creating this innovative system was a major incentive for the people Jones hired to work on the systems team at Fairfield. They were excited about creating a new, integrated system, not only because of the impact they felt it would have on organizational effectiveness, but also because developing the system would provide an unprecedented opportunity for them to exercise and refine their design and programming skills.

However, the systems team did not have an easy time implementing its vision. At about the same time Bob Jones hired the final member of his team in June 1981, Barry Mackay was replaced by Alan Rasky as plant manager (see Chapter One for details). Whereas Mackay's technical background had spurred his interest in advanced computer technologies, Rasky's experience was exclusively in manufacturing; he had previously served as a business manager in the Ridgeway plant and been director of manufacturing in the Jacksonville plant. Although he did not oppose the use of advanced technology, he placed far greater emphasis on developing innovative administrative systems. According to one systems team member,

> We [in systems] stress technology, moving forward. But there are some people who stress getting done what we have to do today, [with] very little emphasis on where are we going to be ten years from now. We do that much more on organization than we do on technology or information systems. Organizational systems, pay, and those sorts of things, we give a lot of attention, but settle with what we have on information systems. You get into details that people don't understand. . . . Alan [Rasky] is learning more every day. But there are a lot of things that he says that tell you he is not on board.

The systems team also faced substantial resistance from the corporate systems group. The Fairfield systems team wanted the FCP to have its own computer system, but the corporate group felt the plant should use corporate mainframes. While the FCP team wanted to develop a new set of programs to meet the plant's unique requirements, the corporate group thought FCP should merely modify preexisting Ashland programs. One team member complained,

> I've had some extremely stressful times working with central systems. . . . They want you to march to a complete

corporate plan, their plan, not one that they get any input into. . . . Their intentions are good. They say, "It's cheaper to do everything centrally." But it isn't cheaper because they don't get the buy-in. It's their idea and you implement it, rather than it is my idea and I am implementing it.

I don't agree with their approach to doing new plants. Their approach is to put in some old start-up systems to help them get started up. But then you never get rid of them. The history has been that way. "Interim systems" is what they call it. They put a pressure on you so great that it is cheaper to do it that way. But no one ever had to justify how much time was spent taking those old systems and bringing them up to standard, and they still aren't any good. . . .

Members of the systems team perceived that they were caught between a technically unsophisticated plant management team and an unsympathetic corporate systems group. This left them feeling both unappreciated and unsupported.[2] One team member explained, "We have a knowledgeable set of people that are not recognized enough for their ideas. For what we have done over the last year and some of the ideas we have come up with, we have gotten very little direct recognition. There might have been a pat on the back from one of the users that we are doing it for. But from management, no."

While the systems group was supposed to provide expertise for the rest of the plant, few people in the immediate environment could provide *it* with technical assistance. Although group members did recognize that technical assistance generally was available somewhere within the larger Ashland organization, it often was logistically difficult for them to draw on such resources. According to one member, "I think we have the expertise in Ashland. But whether we can get it when we need it is not necessarily true. There are a lot of things going on. They have training classes over there [at corporate headquarters] that would help us out, but we are not necessarily able to get there, because we have things to do, or financially we can't do it."

Managing the Tension. Systems team members were faced with resistance from the corporate systems group, a plant manager unsympathetic to their vision and system development strategy, and a relatively immediate need to get some kind of computer system up and running. It was too much to overcome, and the systems team finally agreed to "implement various business systems already existing in the corporation." At the same time, however, they got Rasky to agree that, in addition to setting up these interim systems, they could begin working on a plan for a state-of-the-art computer system that, as described in a systems planning document, ultimately would "more adequately support [the plant's] information needs."

In some areas, such as office automation, this two-track strategy worked well. The systems group itself was not sure exactly how office automation should be handled in the plant. Consequently, the team simultaneously began work on a long-range office automation strategy and leased stand-alone word processors so employees could become accustomed to handling paperwork electronically. According to one team member, "It looked like it would give us the experience that we needed to check some things out about how people felt about things. It probably wouldn't have made a difference what system it was." This strategy also helped increase support for office automation in the rest of the plant. While the systems group originally had assumed that only administrative support personnel would use word processors, it discovered that a number of managers in the plant were also interested in learning to use this new technology.

Most members of the systems team were, nonetheless, dissatisfied with the two-track strategy. They felt that the expectations they had initially been encouraged to develop when they joined the team were not being met. As one said, "When I was hired in, I understood that we would be doing mostly creative types of things, and that we would be dealing with the latest and the best types of equipment. As it has turned out, we are stuck doing the same things traditional systems areas have always done. It is kind of frustrating."

Members were also disturbed at being asked to create what they saw as suboptimal systems: "Our hands are kind of tied. We know a lot of the things we do are not the best, and we don't have the luxury of time, or the financial backing, to acquire other things that we know we can do better. We probably don't have the political clout either. . . . "

Further, because of the systems team's multiple objectives—providing training to plant members on computer systems already in place, getting the interim systems up and running, and planning a long-term systems strategy—team members were often unclear about what they should do first. While they generally felt their time could most usefully be spent developing long-term systems, they had to balance this against other, immediate demands—for example, from a manager who was afraid that he had inadvertently destroyed a word processing file or from an accounting team member who needed training in the interim accounts receivable program.

Team Effectiveness

Despite all these frustrations, the systems team performed well. It scored well above average on most of our measures of team effectiveness—including the acceptability of team products, the quality of intergroup relationships, and member motivation and satisfaction. In addition, managers throughout the Fairfield plant generally were complimentary about the team's responsiveness to their needs.

The person most responsible for the systems team's effectiveness was its manager, Bob Jones. Jones skillfully shaped the group's composition, its task, and the quality of members' interaction to compensate for the difficulties described above.

Group Composition. Jones assembled a team whose members had complementary skills and responsibilities. Ellen Meyer, who had worked on office automation at corporate headquarters, had primary responsibility for designing, purchasing, and installing the plant's office automation systems. Peter Mack and Alex Andrews, who had strong general programming backgrounds, did the work needed to get the plant's business systems (such as payroll, general ledger, and accounts payable) up and running.

George Washburn, whose background was in manufacturing, focused on development of the computer systems that would support the machining lines. Jane Bolton, who had not previously worked in a systems area, was mainly responsible for training the rest of the plant in how to use the computer systems that the team was developing and installing.

Team members were different from one another but not too different to work well together. Indeed, the team was able to draw on the diversity of members' skills to compensate for the relative scarcity of external technical support. As one member said, "Everyone has their own specialty in their own area. If one person doesn't know, we know who to turn to for that answer. We can usually find an answer in the group."

Group Task. Jones was aware that group members were not happy at having to develop interim computer systems. Consequently, he often spent time in team meetings explaining to team members the significance of their work for the success of the overall plant start-up. He also gave them a great deal of latitude for managing their own projects. Members appreciated that. As one said, "I like Bob's attitude. He is willing to give the responsibility to the person to do the job, without constantly checking on [him or her]."

The nature of the work required team members to deal with users throughout the plant. These exchanges, coupled with the inherently feedback-rich nature of computer programming activities, kept members constantly knowledgeable about the results of their work and compensated for the lack of direct feedback from senior plant management. In the words of one member, "I think our main feedback is from users, and we do get that, on a one-to-one basis, constantly."

Group Process. Jones also was adept at fostering an atmosphere of openness and trust within the team. He was seen as willing both to share power and to be challenged by the other members of the team. One member said, "Bob has let us make the decisions as a team. [He] lets [us] reach a consensus rather than vote. . . . He may have definite ideas about something and spring it on the group and we say, 'Wait a minute Bob, we can't live with that and this is why.' And we listen to him and he listens to us."

In the systems team meetings I observed, when team members disagreed with Jones, they made their feelings known through good-natured but pointed kidding. Jones appeared quite comfortable receiving these gentle barbs. And his openness to criticism was emulated by other team members. One explained,

> There are a lot of times that we are under a lot of pressure trying to do things, but that still doesn't affect our working relationships. We are very open and honest with one another. If we have a complaint or gripe, no one is hesitant about saying it to one another and no one is offended by it. It is very easy for us to work well. You have such varied people here. Because we are all specialists in our own field, we have to call on each other when we are working on a project to get input and to get help. And everyone is good about that. I have found it a comfortable group to work with.

The availability within the plant of relevant training and group process assistance also facilitated relationships within the team. Most notably, five of the six members of the systems team were able to attend a five-week plant orientation and training program known as Core Skills. In this program, participants worked together to make a product using machines similar to those on the FCP's production lines. Although members of the systems group would not be working on production machinery after they finished the program, they, like manufacturing teams, required good communication and coordination among members to be effective. Moreover, the Core Skills course helped the team's work by teaching members about managing interpersonal relationships in a work team.

Conclusion

The role of a professional support team during the start-up of a team-based manufacturing plant is a difficult one. Such teams run the risk of being caught between managers at the plant level, who may not understand the need for technical innovation, and those at corporate headquarters, who may be threatened by such innovations. Further, the work of support teams, while necessary, is not central to the primary task of the organization—manufacturing.

These factors make it easy for technical support teams to be misunderstood, or at least to feel misunderstood. This is particularly true in a start-up, when disputes are not so much over current systems (whose effectiveness presumably can be assessed empirically) but over the likely future value of systems that are still on the drawing boards. Political support is critical in such circumstances to sustain innovative momentum. Thus, when the political protection of a support group disappears, as it did at the FCP when Barry Mackay was replaced by Alan Rasky, the group and its members can expect to encounter frustration and disappointment.

There are, however, compensations for members of support teams during a start-up. Precisely because no system is already entrenched, opportunities for experimentation and innovation are plentiful. The systems team at FCP exploited such opportunities, particularly in the office automation area. Also, the small scale of a start-up generally makes it easier for members to exert organizational influence and to accomplish individual and team objectives than it would be in a larger and more mature setting. As one systems member explained,

There are several layers of management that you have to go through [at corporate headquarters] to get a job done. You are just like a person without a face. And even though things are obvious to you about cost-benefit [ratios] and productivity gains that can be made, you have to go through a lot of crap to get it. . . . Since you are so project oriented, you don't get a feel for the big picture. Part of why I came to Fairfield was that I wanted the learning, the exposure, and I thought it would be good for my career. . . . Now some of the things that I am doing have given me a lot more exposure.

Overall, the chance to work as part of a team seems to be just as attractive for functional support staff as it is for those in manufacturing. Interdependence exists in the intellectual tasks for which support teams are responsible, just as it does for physical production tasks. The team organization allows for flexible and effective management of interdependent relationships in both cases. Further, professional work such as programming can be lonely, so functional team members appreciate the emotional support as well as the technical support they provide one another.

At the beginning of this chapter, I noted that senior managers in high-commitment work systems sometimes assume that functional support groups should be managed in the same way as manufacturing teams. The history of the Fairfield Systems Group suggests that, on one level, these managers are right. Professional support teams, like any team, need to be given a compelling task, appropriate recognition when they are successful, and adequate technical and process assistance. The problem lies in determining how to provide these contextual supports to a group whose members generally differ in background, perspective, and style from those in the dominant manufacturing culture. The history of the Fairfield Systems Group highlights the important role of the team leader in ensuring that these generic needs are met—and met in a way that both acknowledges and builds constructively upon the special needs of professional support staff.

Notes

1. For further background information on the FCP see Chapters One and Twenty-Five on the Fairfield Coordinating Group and the Compressor Team, respectively.
2. The scores for the systems team on our research questionnaire support this observation. The systems team scored below average both on the degree to which members felt the team was rewarded for good performance and on their perception of the amount of technical and educational support the team received.

11

Daniel R. Denison

꿈꿈꿈꿈꿈꿈꿈꿈꿈꿈꿈꿈꿈꿈

Airline Maintenance Group

"Maintenance control," he barked into the phone as he answered his third call in five minutes, "this is Harry." Two other calls were on hold. This call came from the pilot of a People Express plane approaching Baltimore-Washington International Airport. The pilot reported that one of his gauges was giving an abnormal reading. Was it safe? Could the gauge be wrong? What would the symptoms be if the gauge was right? Could this damage the engine? Could the gauge be replaced or serviced in Washington before returning to Newark Airport?

At the same time, waiting around the door was a group of three men wearing uniforms and hats emblazoned with the words *Butler Aviation.* They worked for the company with which People Express contracted for maintenance services. They were waiting for instructions from maintenance control on what to do about the APU, or auxiliary power unit, in one of the planes sitting outside at the gate. The APU was necessary to operate the plane's air conditioning system. It was a hot, humid August day at the airport, and this type of problem created a crisis of its own.

The Team and Its Task

When the phone rang in the maintenance control room at People Express Airlines, it could be nearly anything—a call from a local supplier with word that some spare parts had come in, an update on a plane that was being repaired, or a call from a pilot whose plane had serious mechanical problems and who needed to make an immediate decision to turn back, continue on, or land as soon as possible. Safety was the preeminent objective, of course, but many other factors entered into the decisions that the maintenance control team helped to make. Team members also had significant supervisory responsibility: they directed maintenance workers in their routine service and repair work as planes moved in and out of the airport. Beyond all these short-term activities, team members were also involved in long-term tasks such as major servicing of aircraft and special engineering projects.

The team described in this chapter consisted of four men who covered one of two eight-hour shifts each day. A similar team covered the other shift. On any particular day, two individuals were drawn from the team to cover the shift. The team had responsibility for covering their shift seven days a week, and shared resources to do so. If someone wanted to take a week's vacation, the others had to work extra shifts that week. Team members learned both from each other and from others inside and outside the airline. And, under most conditions, the team managed maintenance control without supervision.

The four men who made up this team were very different from one another. Harry, the oldest, was in his early fifties and had worked for many years in maintenance at Pan American. He was skilled at troubleshooting, but he was accustomed to the resources and management systems of a much larger, well-established airline. He had been laid off by Pan Am a year earlier and had been with People Express about four months. Terry, the youngest, had little airline experience. He was energetic and impulsive, and he seemed to thrive on crisis. He would swing into action and take control whenever a new problem emerged. The other two team members were somewhere in the middle; Larry and Bill were both in their middle to late thirties, and both had some previous airline experience. Larry was very sociable and often acted as the team's spokesperson. Bill was the most talented engineer of the group and liked working on special projects. Each working dyad that could be constructed out of this four-person team had very different strengths and weaknesses.

Most of the team's work took place in a small ten-by-twelve-foot room adjacent to dispatch—the place where pilots checked in to pick up their paperwork and weather reports before each flight. The room was equipped with three telephones, several radios, a number of technical manuals, and three or four chairs. In the back of the room was a blackboard with a column for each of the seventeen People Express aircraft. This board helped members keep track of each plane, its service schedule, and any repairs it needed. A short distance from the door to the maintenance control room, another door led outside to the planes and the gates. Butler's maintenance workers frequently came through that door with questions or problems for the maintenance control team.

The work that took place in the maintenance control room was fast paced. During busier times in the maintenance control room, the phone rang every two or three minutes, often before the previous conversation had ended. One of the two members on duty was always seated in front of that phone. The second member was more mobile; he helped answer the phone and direct maintenance workers when things were busy, or he worked on special projects if there were an hour or two when things were under control. Each day had cycles, which usually peaked at 10 A.M., 2 P.M., and 5 P.M., when nearly all of the People Express planes were on the ground at the same time. During these times the team was extremely busy, but between the peaks members were able to work at a more relaxed pace.

An additional responsibility of the team was to supervise the maintenance workers from Butler Aviation. This aspect of the job added complexity to the work because the maintenance control team had to manage the employees of that organization (with whom the airline contracted for maintenance services) to get its own work done.

Butler Aviation's traditional organizational structure and conventional hierarchy aggravated the dilemma of managing across this organizational boundary. Butler differed markedly from People Express, which emphasized self-management, the

development of individual skills, and high employee involvement and commitment. Learning the unfamiliar precepts of the
People Express organization while dealing with traditional Butler employees and managers was a trying and challenging effort
for the maintenance control team.

The team's larger and longer-term projects provided a
welcome counterpoint to the hectic job of staffing the phones
in maintenance control. For example, planes, like cars, must be
given periodic overhauls, and maintenance managers were personally involved in major tasks such as these. For example,
United Airlines in San Francisco did most overhauls for People
Express, and a team member frequently traveled there with a
plane that was to be serviced. Other assignments, such as re-
searching and revising maintenance procedures and specifications, sometimes lasted several months. These projects provided
a way for team members to become involved in more challenging and visible work. Most of the projects required juggling of
schedules, however, because some team members always had to
be on duty to take care of short-term responsibilities.

The work of the maintenance control team had a unique
and unusual character. First, it was fundamentally reactive work.
Despite the frequently hectic pace, members spent much of
their time waiting. The pulse that drove this team was the telephone. Anything could happen, and it was the team's job to respond. At the same time, the stakes could be very high. Even
though the final decision about in-flight problems was always
the captain's, the team's advice and decisions could mean life or
death to the passengers, pilots, and cabin crew. This combination of dependence, ambiguity, and limited formal authority
made team members uneasy. As one put it, the maintenance
control job was "99 percent boredom and 1 percent terror."

The Organizational Context

At the time I studied the maintenance control team, People Express Airlines was just over one year old and growing rapidly.
With 500 to 600 employees, the company was still relatively
small. In the past year, the company had flown 600,000 passen-

gers, and revenue for the previous quarter had been $35 million. The airline was already known as an innovator and had broken into the newly deregulated air travel market with prices well under going rates. Headquartered at Newark International Airport, the airline flew to about fifteen cities in the East and Midwest, many of which previously had only limited air service. The airline had a simple hub-and-spoke route structure with almost all flights either beginning or ending in Newark. This structure, along with other product innovations such as on-board ticketing, high seating density, limited cabin service, and direct reservations, allowed People Express to fly with a much lower cost-per-seat mile than the established carriers.

The company was also innovative in its approach to management (Hackman, 1984). All employees in the company were called managers—and they were treated that way. The company expected them to manage themselves rather than wait for direction and supervision from the bosses. This arrangement created a flat organization with high autonomy for groups and individuals. There was little conventional supervision. Each member of the organization was also a stockbroker, and profit sharing made up an important part of the compensation package for all employees.

The top management of the organization was a small group of managing officers, assisted by a small but growing number of general managers and team managers. There were three broad categories of "regular" employees: flight managers (pilots), maintenance managers, and customer service managers. Within these categories, individuals or groups rotated among jobs on a regular basis. Thus, a flight manager (FM) might get involved in administration or scheduling; a customer service manager (CSM) team would cycle between flying, ground operations, and staff work; and maintenance managers (MMs) would cycle back and forth between managing the day-to-day maintenance responsibilities and longer-term projects such as purchasing parts and fuel, maintaining Federal Aviation Administration (FAA) records, and finding ways to improve the efficiency and safety of the fleet. Wherever possible, People Express designed work to be done by teams.

These innovative ideas provided the maintenance control

team with a supportive work environment that demanded a high level of involvement. The organization also presented the team with a dilemma: many of the most innovative management ideas were applied to the CSMs and to the team managers rather than to the MMs and FMs. MMs and FMs had, in general, spent far more time in conventional airlines and military organizations and were accustomed to an ordered, hierarchical way of doing business. In the case of the maintenance control team, the situation was particularly complicated since members needed to use a conventional approach to management when they were dealing with the employees of the maintenance contractor, Butler Aviation, and, at the same time, they needed to learn to work within an innovative management system in their own organization.

Although part of the People Express strategy was to fly its planes more hours per day than did competitors, staffing in the maintenance area was lean: there were only twenty-five MMs altogether, with about one-third of those working regularly in maintenance control. Other MMs were involved with managing FAA relationships, purchasing parts and fuel, dealing with maintenance contractors, and getting new planes ready for service.

One of the more vocal members of the maintenance control team spent much of his time comparing his job at People Express with his previous position at a large airline. At that company, he said, there were "hundreds of people in maintenance." When a crisis arose, "People dove on it . . . they converged . . . incredible resources were brought to bear on the problem." He would not have believed that a maintenance organization could be run with so few people and so little hierarchy if he hadn't seen it work at People Express. He also greatly preferred the People Express system, primarily because of the feeling of accomplishment it gave him.

The Nature of Professional Support Work

Working in a support role in an airline—and probably in any other organization—is an inherently reactive activity. It was nearly impossible for members of the maintenance control team to be proactive in their work. This meant that the team members, despite the potential life-and-death nature of their work, had limited formal authority: they could only advise pilots. Furthermore, their work was not seen as being particularly central to the goals of the overall organization. As one member of the team put it, "If we do our job perfectly, no one even knows we're here." The team's influence was greatest during times of emergency, and the goal in these situations was always the same: to reestablish control over operations and return them to normal. Once control was established, the team was no longer needed. "The spotlight," as one of the team members put it, "was seldom on maintenance control—and when it was, it was usually negative." Doing their job well allowed others to remain on center stage.

This situation created an unusual attitude toward crisis within the team. It would be an overstatement to say that team members wanted crises to emerge, and all of them reacted with genuine shock and concern to any problem that posed a direct and immediate threat to safety. Nonetheless, it was clear to all that the most motivating part of the maintenance control job was a crisis. During crises, team members had their clearest purpose. Crises also gave the team its only real opportunity to shine and its only opportunity to formulate and implement a proactive strategy. An example will illustrate.

A few months before I studied the team, an aircraft lost an engine on a flight from Newark to Florida. The oil pressure dropped, and the engine incurred serious damage before the crew could shut it down. Safety on landing was not an issue, but the plane could not take off again. The situation was immediately reported to maintenance control along with the obvious question, "What should we do now?" The pilots and cabin crew returned to Newark on the next flight, but the plane remained on the ground in Jacksonville.

The Jacksonville Airport was not equipped to replace an engine, so other options had to be considered. An engine could be delivered to Jacksonville, but it would take several days and be expensive. The company could contract out repair of the engine in Florida, but that would be both expensive and time-consuming. The third option was for the People Express maintenance managers to solve the problem themselves.

The solution was to rent a truck, find a spare engine, and drive to Florida. Additional men flew down to help with the repair, which was completed in record time. The MMs were on site in Jacksonville changing the engine twenty-four hours after the incident. The team completed the repair more quickly and at lower cost than would have been possible if anyone else had done it. Because of the MMs' heroic around-the-clock efforts, everything had returned to normal.

While this episode was indeed a team effort by the maintenance managers, it is noteworthy that it was not carried out by the four-person team described in this chapter. The incident was reported during the team's shift, but only one of the team's members (who was skilled in engine repair) actually had been involved. The others needed to stay behind to cover the shift, answer the phone, and keep routine repairs and maintenance under control.

This incident shows how the members of the maintenance control team were able to use their skills and ingenuity to bring a difficult problem under control. It also highlights some of the dynamics of that team and its work: the team's essentially dependent and reactive stance, the excitement and opportunity that come with a crisis, and the difficulty of doing maintenance work as an intact team.

Lessons from the Maintenance Control Team

The maintenance control team proved to be a rich source of learning about group behavior. The chapter will close with a review of five lessons about work groups and organizational design that were highlighted by this team.

The Context of Professional Support. The first lesson is a general observation about the nature of professional support teams. As noted above, the work of the maintenance control team was almost entirely dependent and reactive. Members were experts, but they had limited authority. They even came to "like" crises because crises allowed members to be proactive.

With the telephone ringing and maintenance people

crowded around the door, the maintenance control team's services and expertise were always in demand. All of these transactions were, however, primarily one way; demands were made on the team, and it responded as best it could.

Beyond responding to the continuous stream of requests for help and advice, the team appeared to have very few interactions with the rest of the organization. Those interactions it did have with supervisors or management usually focused on two topics: resources (for example, the stocking of spare parts and supplies necessary to maintain and repair aircraft) and the assignment of work (particularly when it involved one of the longer-term assignments). Stocking spare parts and supplies involved a classic conflict of interest between the maintenance control team and the airline. The team wanted a large supply on hand to expedite repair and maintenance, while the airline wanted a limited selection in order to minimize inventory. Work assignment also was a contested area. Team members hoped that performing well would increase the chances that more interesting work would be assigned in the future—such as a week in San Francisco for an overhaul or assignment to an engineering project that could take several months.

Maintenance managers were quite conscious of status and position, and many counted on the possibility of promotion as the airline continued to grow. Yet they also sometimes felt as if they were invisible to senior management. Their minimal contact with senior managers, coupled with job duties that kept them out of the mainstream of activities in the company, left team members feeling (as do professional support staff in many organizations) that they received little support or recognition for their contributions to the firm.

Learning Two Management Systems. A second lesson from this team comes from members' struggle to manage the maintenance workers from Butler Aviation. This part of the job required the maintenance control team to learn and use two management systems. When dealing with the Butler maintenance workers, team members employed a conventional model of authority, much like the ones they had experienced when they worked for

other airlines. When dealing with their own organization, however, they needed to use a different system, which was both innovative and unfamiliar. To make matters more complex, there
were significant differences in culture among the different parts
of their own organization; MMs and FMs were more accustomed
to (and tended to prefer) a conventional approach, while CSMs
and higher management relentlessly experimented with innovative management systems.

This problem is a little like trying to learn a new language
while surrounded by people who speak the old language—it feels
good to revert and do things the old way. Trying the new way is
promising, and even elating at times, but still a little intimidating. The maintenance control team seemed to do best at resolving the problem when members took on the attitude of games-
men—that is, when they chose not to question the nature of the
two systems but simply tried to determine how best to use
them. Learning how and when to use multiple management
styles proved to be a complex and sophisticated management
skill that was difficult for the team members to master. Support
teams in other kinds of organizations encounter similar problems—for example, a team of computer experts that must relate
to both their colleagues in the information systems department
and the computer-illiterate users of their services.

Pooled Interdependence. The third lesson from this team concerned the use of pools as teams. Given the relatively low interdependence inherent in the maintenance control task, the airline could have chosen to design this work by creating a large
pool of maintenance control workers and then assigning them at
random to cover shifts. If this had been done, however, the
group's capacity for self-management would have been significantly diminished. The resource-based interdependence that
held this group together, even though it was a weaker glue than
task-based interdependence would have been, did provide at
least a modest basis for developing a real maintenance team.

The maintenance control team itself was designed as a
four-person pool—a collection of individuals with comparable
skills from which pairs were drawn to staff particular shifts. The

pool arrangement required substantial interdependence among the team members but seldom allowed them to work together as a group on an immediate task.

Thus, the team was something of a hybrid between an actual work team with a group task, face-to-face interaction, and high interdependence and a coacting work group with each member performing an individual task with little interdependence or face-to-face interaction. To illustrate, the classic example of a coacting work group is a bank of telephone operators, each performing the same parallel task with little interaction or interdependence. An example of a full-fledged work team is the tracking team described in Chapter Nine.

Since the task of maintenance control does not inherently require a team to accomplish the work, People Express could have handled the maintenance control function by using a large coacting group. Instead, the company created hybrid teams based on resource interdependence. This type of team is somewhat unusual and merits brief discussion. A hybrid team has four characteristics. First, interdependence is based on jointly managed resources—such as supplies, time, money, and people—rather than on shared task objectives. Second, although members may see one another regularly, the group as a whole meets together very infrequently. Third, members tend to identify, at least at first, with a set of individual role expectations, as they would in a coacting work group, rather than with the team itself. As a result, a hybrid team may not give much attention to the relationship between the team and its organizational context. At People Express, it was only after team members began to comprehend their interdependence with the rest of the organization that the group became proactive in trying to improve its context. Finally, commitment, membership, and group identity tend to be looser in a hybrid team than they are in a task-interdependent work team, although they are still stronger than in a coacting work group.

Hybrid teams, then, represent a design alternative that may be useful for professional support work in settings where neither coacting groups nor full-fledged task teams are viable. When well designed and well supported, a hybrid team may be able to provide many of the benefits of teamwork and still allow for flexibility in the deployment of individual team members.

Self-Managing Work Teams. Even though members of the maintenance control team did not often work together as an intact team, they did manage themselves. The team had enormous autonomy, and there was very little formal supervision of its work. The only time it called in its "supervisors" was when it had resource problems that it could not resolve or work around. The most extreme example was when planes had to be taken out of the schedule. In this case, the team had to inform scheduling, dispatch, and senior management so airline-wide coordination could be accomplished.

Self-management worked well for the maintenance control team and created a work environment that members liked. Team members expected that they would work together, learn from one another, and deal with maintenance and repair problems as they came up—all with a minimum of supervision. When a problem was beyond the team's control, they would enlist the help of others in the organization to take care of it. Most of the time, it worked just that way. Without the team design and without an emphasis on peer control, this level of coordination would have been difficult to achieve.

The experience of the maintenance control team suggests that self-management contributes to the success of a hybrid team design. Members' willingness and ability to share resources were directly related to their being allowed (*required* would probably be a better word) to self-manage. With a direct system of close supervision, resource-based interdependence alone would not have been strong enough to develop a sense of "group membership," "group task," or "maintenance control team." Given the autonomy that self-management provided, however, the relatively weak resource-based interdependence was enough to provide members a moderately strong sense that they were, indeed, working as a team.

Development over Time. The final lesson from the People Express maintenance control team came during the feedback session, when we presented the research findings to the team. This was also one of the few times the team met as a group. The quantitative data showed that team members viewed conditions within the team favorably and that they saw their organizational context as the source of most of their problems.

Despite the fundamental bias toward this type of attribution, members accepted the validity of the data, and the discussion slowly turned to the topic of "how to manage the organizational context." This discussion created among members a perception that they could influence and improve their context—but only if they acted as a group. They also realized that one way to change and improve the terms of a fundamentally reactive job is to be proactive in their transactions and negotiations with others in the organization. And this approach, they concluded, could help to create conditions that would reduce some of the dependence, ambiguity, and anxiety that they encountered in their day-to-day work.

Several months later, I ran into one of the team members in the hall and asked about the team. I was interested to learn whether members had become more of a team since the time I spent with them, or whether they were now simply a collection of individuals. His answer was clear: members now had a stronger team identity and operated more as a team than they had earlier. They had developed, he said, from a pool into a real team.

12

Mary Lou Davis-Sacks
Daniel R. Denison
Russell A. Eisenstat

Summary:
Professional Support Teams

Although the three teams in this section differed in many respects, they shared certain characteristics that distinguish them as professional support teams. Each team operated as a pool of experts waiting for a need to arise—a need to which it could apply its knowledge and skill. In so doing, it facilitated the work of those who performed the primary task of the organization. The tracking team generated reports on congressional deliberations for senior political officials in the executive branch of the federal government; the Fairfield systems team was responsible to its manufacturing plant for creating and maintaining the plant's computerized information system; and the maintenance control team coordinated aircraft maintenance activities for its company.

Special Skills

Each team was composed of people who had specialized skills and knowledge not widely shared in their organizations. This expertise was critical in making it possible for members to respond to special organizational needs. It also created problems for the teams because it differentiated them from the rest of their organizations. This differentiation sometimes created tensions, especially when team members and their clients disagreed about what the organization needed to succeed.

The expertise the teams needed could not be simply

195

bought off the street because some was organization specific and some required constant updating. Moreover, the teams often dealt with new and sometimes unexpected organizational problems, which sometimes made it impossible for managers to create clear performance guidelines for team behavior or to specify clearly what training members should obtain.

Thus, keeping member knowledge and skills current was a constant challenge that consumed considerable member time and energy. Partly because of the investment they made in skill development activities, team members sought and highly valued opportunities to exercise those skills. Showing what they could do was a major psychological payoff for the teams and their members. And they often became frustrated and listless when things were going so smoothly in the organization that there was little need for their expertise.

Distinctive Rhythms

The support teams we studied had a pulse or rhythm that clearly differentiated them from other types of work teams. Generally, members had little to do until others explicitly requested their services, or until some organizational triggering event occurred. In reflecting on life in these groups, we found ourselves using metaphors that suggested pent-up energy seeking release—such as "gathering storm clouds" or an "unmilked cow." Sometimes the tension of inactivity became so high that a team would create a crisis when none actually existed just so members could swing into action. Whenever an alarm actually did sound, the teams leapt to the challenge like fire fighters dashing for their engine. Little was more satisfying to team members than using their expertise to bring an interesting problem under control.

Despite the considerable differences in the work the three teams did, a generic work cycle characterized all of them—a cycle that differentiates professional support teams from others described in this book. This cycle has four stages: scanning, diagnosing, proposing, and handing off.

Scanning. At this stage, the professional support team lies in wait, antennae extended, for a problem to emerge.

Eventually, the team's client within the larger organization identifies the problem. The team may be either actively scanning the organization or passively waiting for the phone to ring. In either case, the dynamic is the same: waiting for a client to come up with a problem that requires the team's special expertise.

Diagnosing. Even though the client has presented the problem, the support team must reformulate it in members' own terms and technical language. Like a physician, the team often works with a set of symptoms from which members must develop an understanding of the underlying problem.

Proposing. In most cases, the team must produce a concrete proposal for action that the client can implement. This process involves considering various solutions and then agreeing on one that will be acceptable both to the team, because it is *right,* and to the client, because it looks as if it will *work.* The team must then translate the proposal back into a language and format that the client can understand and present it to the client for approval.

Handing off. One irony of professional support work is that someone else usually does final decision making about the teams' recommendations and the actual execution of the teams' ideas. Members often are not able to see the results of their work or learn why their proposals have been modified or rejected. Sometimes, a team must stand by and watch while its proposal is implemented differently than members ever imagined it would be—or, worst of all, set aside and never seriously considered.

Even though each of the teams we studied went through a cycle roughly like the one described above, the length of these cycles varied tremendously. The maintenance control team sometimes started a new cycle every fifteen minutes or so and often had multiple cycles going at the same time. These short cycles made up the bulk of the team's activity, even though the team also undertook long-cycle engineering projects on occasion. The Fairfield systems team was well along with work on a long-cycle project when its task changed radically. The plant manager who initially had given the team its mandate was replaced by someone who had a different view of what was needed. The team had to reframe its work in midcycle, which created considerable upheaval within the team and strained relations between the team and the new plant manager.

The federal agency tracking team also did not complete an entire cycle because what the team was supposed to monitor and report upon never happened. This team also differed from the others in that it was not charged with producing actual action plans; instead, it was to provide data and reports to those who would frame such plans. Despite the tracking team's being one step further removed from the action than were the maintenance control and systems teams, members of this team were equally committed to producing quality professional work, and they were dismayed when that work was prematurely terminated. Because professional support teams often wait eagerly for opportunities to bring their expertise to bear on organizational problems, they can become frustrated indeed when the work is terminated, interrupted, or redirected after it has finally got under way.

It is not unusual for professional support teams to carry on multiple cycles of varying lengths at the same time. All three of the teams we studied did so at one time or another, mixing long-term projects with immediate fire fighting. Although this mix can disrupt the normal rhythm of the teams' work, both long- and short-cycle projects do follow the basic four-stage process. Perhaps most significant, however, is that every cycle, whether long or short, ends with a hand-off to someone else. Whether the team's product is a repaired airplane, a report summarizing economic analyses, or a computer system, the team submits it to line managers for use at their discretion. If everything has gone well, no one even needs to be aware of the team's existence. This, obviously, can significantly limit the extent to which members are able to experience that special pride that comes from having seen an important piece of work all the way through to a successful conclusion.

Cultural Conflict

The professional support teams we studied were created specifically to serve as repositories of specialized knowledge and skills not otherwise available in their organizations. Members had both expertise and strong views about how it should be used: the tracking team knew just what kind of analyses it should do and what kinds of reports it should write; members of the maintenance control team had their own ideas about the decisions pilots should make in emergencies; and the systems team had clear opinions about the computer systems the Fairfield plant needed.

Yet members' expertise and the uniqueness of their professional skills also tended to create cultural conflict between team members and other organizational actors. When the professionals tried to explain their perspectives, they often seemed to others in their organizations to be speaking a foreign language. In the federal agency, for example, the technology and language of sophisticated economic analysis that were the stock and trade of the tracking team were less familiar to their political appointee clients. Moreover, the clients had little interest in the niceties of economic analysis. Instead, they sought concrete information that would help them achieve political objectives—aspirations with which the civil servants on the tracking team sometimes personally disagreed.

The systems and maintenance control teams experienced similar conflicts with their clients. Indeed, conflicts were exacerbated for these teams because both operated in organizations that sought, to the greatest extent possible, to use line personnel to perform tasks traditionally done by professionals. To team members, this practice seemed to devalue both their expertise and the importance of the team to the organization—a perception that occasionally prompted some defensiveness in their interactions with line personnel.

Cultural conflicts between the professional support teams and their clients were expressed in a variety of ways, ranging from merely symbolic disputes over how neat systems group members' desks needed to be to disagreement about major policy questions such as the role of advanced technology in a plant start-up. Team members took the conflicts seriously—whether over small or large issues—because they knew that having influence on their organizations required accommodation to line managers' needs and wishes. All three groups had to struggle constantly with an ongoing disparity between their considerable expertise and their limited authority.

More generally, all of the professional support teams we studied had to manage extremely complex relations with various other groups, both within and outside the organization. For example, the work of the maintenance control team involved coordinating relations between groups of maintenance workers employed by another company and the crews who worked for the team's own organization. Similarly, the systems team often had to arbitrate between the demands of corporate systems personnel and those of the local plant management team. And the role of the tracking team was quite literally to report the actions of one group (Congress) to another (a unit within the executive branch of government).

These activities require ongoing management of intergroup relations, and that, too, requires professional skill. Support teams typically are not trained in intergroup skills and, indeed, they may view such activities as outside the domain of their "real" work. That view is, perhaps, one reason why cultural conflicts between professional support teams and their clients sometimes get out of hand and can significantly impede accomplishment of the organization's work.

Conclusion: Seeking Balance

The three teams we studied were constantly adjusting the balance between their two competing identities: that of skilled professionals and that of organizational members. Both identities are necessary for team effectiveness since the tasks of professional support teams typically require both high professional expertise and good relationships with line organizational personnel. As we have seen, however, these two identities also sometimes pull professional support teams in opposite directions. Support staff gain and maintain their professional expertise through cross-training by their fellow group members and through their involvement with extraorganizational professional groups. These activities were especially appealing to members of the teams we studied because they provided a level of intellectual stimulation that often was missing from their day-to-day organizational activities. Yet such activities also risked further increasing the cultural barrier between team members and their organizational colleagues.

Maintaining an appropriate balance between the need for professionalism and the need for organizational integration requires cooperation between those who manage the support teams and those who manage the line organization. The contributions needed from line and staff managers are complementary. Because the path of least resistance for support teams often involves engaging in professional development activities at the cost of members' involvement in the organization, it is important for the managers of such teams to push members toward organizational engagement. Strategies for accomplishing this include rotating line personnel through the support team, rotating support personnel through line operations, physically locating the team so it is close to line activities, developing "cousin" relationships between support teams and line teams, and so on.

There also are things that line managers can do to increase the chances that the organization will reap full benefit from its investment in professional support teams. Probably the most important and the most difficult is for line managers to understand that such teams are valuable precisely *because* they have an approach that differs from the rest of the organization. Once that is accepted, managers can engage in a variety of activities to validate and constructively exploit those differences—activities such as including the support team in policy-making deliberations, contributing resources for the further development of team members' professional skills, and inviting support teams to take initiatives when the managers discover unmet organizational needs for which the team's professional expertise is relevant.

Part Four

PERFORMING GROUPS: PLAYING TO AUDIENCES

The teams in this section do not produce a service, a decision, or a tangible product as do the other teams described in this book. What these teams produce is a performance—be it musical, theatrical, or athletic. The client of the work typically is an audience (although in some cases the audience may be the team itself, as when members "play for the fun of it"). The idea of play, whether done for money or for fun, is key to the life and work of performing teams.

Also distinctive to these teams is their relatively unusual organizational context: the audience for which they perform is typically far more salient to and consequential for the team than is the formal organization within which the team operates. And leadership in performing teams typically has more to do with creating and coaching than it does with supervising and managing.

The first team examined, in Chapter Thirteen, is a professional string quartet. This ensemble had been together for many years, and members' routines had become so familiar and stable as to be nearly invisible to an observer. Rarely were disagreements, or any other explicit process discussions, seen in the life and work of the group. The quartet's pace of work was slow and steady, and the reviews that mattered most to members were their own. The quartet seemed the very model of a mature, successful self-managing team; yet there was reason to believe that there might be a hidden downside to the group—some issues unaddressed by members that might eventually threaten its viability as a performing team.

Chapter Fourteen explores group dynamics in a semiprofessional theater company. An arm of a municipal school system, this company produced plays intended mainly for audiences of children. We observed two casts during both the rehearsal and performance phases of their work. The clear differences we found between these phases, and between the dynamics of the two casts, generate some insights about group development, leadership, and the role of audiences in the life and work of performing teams.

The groups discussed in Chapters Fifteen and Sixteen are athletic teams whose "work" consists of competing against other teams on the court, ice, or field. The teams range from amateurs who play strictly for the fun of it to professionals whose livelihoods depend on the quality of their play. Chapter Fifteen compares two college teams: an intramural basketball team and a varsity baseball team. Athletes were attracted to both teams mainly because they enjoyed playing the game. The task of the teams' coaches, then, was to build upon that individual motivation to develop excellent *team* performance. The reasons why, unexpectedly, the leader of the intramural team was better able to do that than was the coach of the varsity team offer some insights into the special dynamics, and the special organizational needs, of teams whose members are there more to play than to work.

Members of the professional hockey team discussed in Chapter Sixteen, a first-level farm club of a National Hockey League (NHL) team, also were initially attracted to the game because they loved playing it. That motivation, while still alive, was now supplemented by concerns about sustaining a career as a professional athlete. Some members of the team were on their way up to the parent NHL team, others had played on that team and were now on their way down, and still others felt they had little prospect for career movement. The context of these individual dynamics was a complicated organizational structure in which the parent team, the local organization, and local businesses, fans, and press all affected what happened to the team and its members. Together, these external forces created great, perhaps insurmountable challenges for the team's coach. How he handled those challenges, and what happened to him in the process, raise some interesting questions about the role and behavior of the leaders of performing teams.

13

Tory Butterworth

‡⌐⌐‡⌐⌐‡⌐⌐‡⌐⌐‡⌐⌐‡⌐⌐‡⌐⌐‡⌐⌐

Detroit String Quartet

Jim's house was familiar to me. Located in a Detroit sub-
urb, it had been the setting for my weekly violin lessons
for almost ten years. Now I was there to observe a rehearsal
of the Detroit String Quartet (called the DSQ by its members), to see what I could learn from the ensemble about
how teams work.

Three members of the DSQ also played in the Detroit
Symphony Orchestra (DSO). The group was a part-time effort for them—something they enjoyed doing that also generated some additional income. I had seen the quartet perform half a dozen times, although always with the former
cello player, Mario. I had read reviews of their performances (invariably both favorable and incomprehensible
to me) in the *Detroit News,* and I had heard music circle
gossip about them while I was a high school youth orchestra member. But except for Jim, whom I knew first as a
music teacher and later as a friend, the musicians were unknown to me.

A bit uneasy about what was to be a new experience both
for me and for the DSQ, I arrived early. Jim greeted me
and showed me where the rehearsal would take place: a
large, comfortably cluttered living room with windows
looking out on a raised porch and a cheerful backyard.

Plants and upright lamps were scattered throughout. One end of the room held a television set surrounded by chairs and a coffee table. The other end, near the kitchen, was fitted with a table, chairs, and a couch along the wall. I decided that the couch would be a good and unobtrusive place for me to sit and to observe.

Jim and I chatted a bit while waiting for the rest of the members to arrive. As each came in, he introduced me. Jim himself was in his fifties, with black, slicked-back hair and a mustache and goatee. Members agreed that he was the idea man of the group, having originally conceived and created it, and the one who now did most of the organizational work needed to keep it running. He was enthusiastic about cooperating in my research, partly as a favor to me but also because he wanted to show off how well the quartet functioned.

Inez, the second violinist and the only quartet member not in the DSO, was first to arrive. In her forties and neatly dressed in a skirt and blouse, she was always organized and precise. When I asked to interview her about the group, for example, she chose to meet at her house just prior to a rehearsal and made a point of being punctual about beginning and ending the interview. David, the violist, also in his fifties, had gray, wavy hair. He often wore a serious, thoughtful look. He expressed great interest in the research, asking me several times over the course of my observations about the overall purpose of the study and the findings thus far. John, the cellist, came in last. Younger than the other members, he was the only one without a family. He clowned and joked frequently, and was kidded about his addiction to golf. John was the most recent member of the quartet, having been asked to join after Mario resigned. Although new to the DSQ, he had considerable experience with the string quartet repertoire from prior membership in other quartets.

After each member had briefly acknowledged my presence, they began chatting among themselves. Instrument cases were opened, stands were set up, chairs were moved, and music was sorted—all while members were talking, joking, and laughing. An air of ease and bonhomie pervaded the room. No questions were asked or instructions given: this all had happened many times before in the same way in the middle of this same living room. Throughout, Jim and his spouse played host and hostess. While he made sure there were enough stands and chairs, she offered coffee or tea from the kitchen. Then, when everything seemed in order, she disappeared into another part of the house.

Within ten minutes after John had arrived, the quartet was settled into position and ready to work. Members listened quietly while Jim suggested a schedule for the rehearsal. They would first run through the Debussey as a whole and then begin detailed work on each movement separately. They would work on one movement this evening and then two at the next rehearsal. The other three members nodded, adjusted their music and posture, and then the quartet began to play.

Observing from my overstuffed couch at the side of the room, I soon began to wonder what there was for me to see. The quartet's group process, like the music played, was of a piece: harmonious, flowing, and integrated in a way that made it nearly impossible to discern who was doing what. Decisions were made and executed almost invisibly, without explicit discussion. The group was managing itself continuously and seemingly effortlessly, there was no doubt about that. But I could not find in members' behaviors a clue as to how they were doing it.

Eventually I decided that this was something I could worry about later. For now, I thought, the thing to do was to sit back and let myself experience the quartet's product. So I settled into the cushions behind me and, with the breeze from the window wafting softly across my face, let myself be transported elsewhere by the ephemeral strains of Debussey.

"A string quartet is three people beating up on a fourth." This was the phrase most often quoted to me while I studied the DSQ. Its very lack of truth for this quartet provides insight into the group's unique nature. String quartets come and go, but the DSQ survived fifteen years with only one member change. And they were good. Not a world-class string quartet, they continually reminded me. But better than anyone would expect, given their individual playing competencies and the fact that the group was part-time for all members. Fifteen hours of observation as well as interviews and questionnaires from each of the members affirmed that what they told me was true. It has taken much further analysis, however, to begin to reach conclusions about how they achieved excellence as an ensemble.

Key Features of the Team

Invisible Management. The management of the quartet—both internal processes and relations with the team's external environment—happened almost invisibly. As an outside observer, I frequently saw evidence that tasks were accomplished without my knowing how, why, or by whom. When questioned, the members often expressed surprise that I did not know: they knew precisely who did what, and they took it for granted.

Jim, for example, performed the "secretarial" duties (his word) for the group—getting music, booking performances, making space arrangements, and so forth. Of course, he consulted with all members before accepting any performance or tackling a new piece of music. Other than that, however, the others wished not to be bothered with these details. Jim took the time to make these arrangements because he was the one in the group who cared most that they were done right.

Interpersonal relations in the quartet were extremely smooth, apparently because there had been so much work on them long before I arrived on the scene. For example, there had been problems (I did not learn exactly what they were) when Mario had been in the group. The quartet almost disbanded at one point and did not meet for several months. When Mario officially resigned after some time off, the quartet found a new cellist and resumed playing. In that case, it was a change of membership that brought the group back to smooth functioning. The group had not explicitly worked through the difficulties it was having at the time, nor were members much interested in reviewing them with me. My sense was that members felt some things in the life of the quartet were better left unexplored.

The low-key style of self-management also showed itself when one member got into the habit of arriving late for rehearsals. Another member was assigned to talk to the delinquent musician personally, so as not to come on too strong. The late arrivals soon stopped, and all members agreed that the problem had been resolved. Yet the incident also left a residue in the life of the group. John told me that he now arrived for performances earlier than he previously had felt was necessary to prevent Jim from getting worried and upset. If Jim's ability to play was reduced because he was upset, John told me, then the quartet as a whole would suffer. Arriving a little earlier than necessary seemed to John a small price to pay to eliminate that risk. Yet again, the members talked about none of this explicitly.

After hearing stories such as these, I eventually decided to ask the group specifically how often members worked on their own process. "Constantly," was the answer, and Jim in particular talked about all the time members spent discussing how the quartet could function better. But in all of my observations, I never saw any such thing happen.

What I did see looked very much like the positive result that one would hope such discussions would bring. For example, Jim would suggest a schedule for the rehearsals and the others quickly would agree to it. Or John would make comments on how a particular passage could be interpreted musically, and the other members would listen carefully and then integrate the ideas into their playing styles. During one rehearsal, a member turned to the others and simply stated, "I'm at your mercy" regarding a solo passage, explaining that if the others sped up the tempo during the solo he was sure to fumble. It was all very good-humored. It did indeed appear that whatever "process issues" the quartet had faced in the past had been worked through and had stayed fixed. There were none of the under-the-surface grumblings and twitterings that, in so many work teams, point to the existence of smoothed-over conflict or still-unresolved interpersonal issues.

Commitment to Excellence. The quartet had a clear and deep commitment to musical excellence. Commercial success was not so important, as I saw in a rehearsal for one of the group's light performances—those done primarily to make money or to please a friend. Jim reported that these performances, which might be dinner music or for an inauguration, were taken with good humor—and that the quartet charged all they could get for them. However, after watching the rehearsal for one such engagement, I concluded that members approached them quite differently than was the case for their serious music. Jim had received a specific request that the quartet play Pachelbel's *Canon* for a church service the quartet was doing for a friend. Jim cajoled the group into running through the piece once by telling them they would "not see it again until performance." John joked about the cello part, passing it around to show the group that it consisted of only one measure repeated throughout the piece. The tone of this part of the rehearsal was lighter, almost jocular. This became particularly clear later when the quartet actually got down to work, playing through the Debussey with great concentration, stopping frequently to repeat parts that were not quite right.

The quartet's commitment to the music appears to have derived, in large part, from members' needs to express themselves creatively in a small setting. Jim pointed out that string players in a large orchestra do not get much chance to be heard as individuals. Wind players do get to play solos occasionally and therefore "speak out" in the typical orchestral repertoire; except for the concert master, string players do not. And while wind players in the Detroit Symphony Orchestra do occasionally get together to play as ensembles, Jim reported that these groups do not continue for as long as had the DSQ—nor do they take the music as seriously.

It was true that the DSQ had a long and stable history—fifteen years together with only one member change. Jim commented that the quartet's stability must have been "close to a record," particularly for a group that "didn't make any money." He added that quartets that "get rich" from their work have more material incentive to stay together than did the DSQ.

All members of the DSQ earned their primary income through the Detroit Symphony Orchestra. (Inez, a former DSO member, was supported by her husband, a current member.) When the group was encountering interpersonal problems with Mario, it failed to meet for several months without any severe financial strain on the participants. John, after a bad experience in another ensemble, even went so far as to swear he would never become part of a quartet again. Yet he did decide to become a member, and the quartet continued to put in the time and effort necessary to perform well on what surely is one of the most complex group tasks imaginable. This, in itself, was an important demonstration of the group's commitment to its music.

Part-Time Membership. The part-time involvement of DSQ members in the quartet is a defining characteristic of the ensemble. Because each member had a stable financial base outside the quartet, the money they took home was pin money rather than primary income. Members did not have to rehearse constantly, see only each other, and work only together. Group parties and social contacts outside of rehearsals and performances were rare. Because members maintained friendly relations and, at the same time, kept some distance from one another, the quartet stayed on an even keel emotionally. In all, there was little pressure on the quartet and its members, and virtually all meetings were relaxed. In contrast, John described to me the "manic" nature of another quartet he was in. After one particularly bad rehearsal, all members of that quartet got up, packed up their instruments, and left without saying a word to each other. But at other times, the members would party together.

The part-time character of the quartet was one of its

strengths but also its biggest weakness. The DSQ could never hope to perform on the level of the world's greatest quartets since three of its four members also played twenty hours each week in the DSO. This not only took time away from quartet rehearsal, it also influenced the members' playing styles. After playing in a large string section, members' styles tended to become sloppy and harsh. Playing in a string quartet requires a delicacy and lightness that the DSQ found hard to produce. Both the advantages and the disadvantages of part-time ensemble playing were directly reflected in the life and work of the quartet.

Ingredients of Success

The DSQ was indeed a group that was greater than the sum of its parts. Rather than "three members beating up a fourth," it was four members working harmoniously, in unison, toward group goals. It was a successful group—despite the fact that members devoted only part of their professional time to the ensemble. What were some of the ingredients of the quartet's success?

A Shared Sense of Direction. First of all, members shared a clear understanding of who they were and what they were trying to accomplish, and they were individually and collectively engaged by their self-selected mission. The music they played provided the most important component of the group's direction. The music dictated a certain format, a style of playing, and so on. It is hard to imagine more engaging work or work that contributes more to a person's growth as a musician and as a human being. The task was infinitely challenging: nobody ever has given a perfect performance of quartet music nor will that ever happen. The work of the quartet also was intrinsically satisfying to members. The process of making music inherently fills many artistic, creative, and sensual needs. It supports one's sense of self, giving meaning and pleasure to life. Because music is an exclusively human activity, a musician can take pride in knowing that no machine can ever take his or her place. Even another human, or group of humans, could not render the exact shades of meaning the DSQ gave to their music.

The inward orientation of the DSQ reinforced the direction the music provided. Although other performing groups might strive for audience approval, the quartet continually downplayed this side of their work. Jim, as a music teacher, had emphasized the importance of a player's evaluation of his or her own music. He told me that I, as a student, knew my own playing best. Judges in musical competitions, he asserted, could never hope to know as much about how well I had done in performances as I did. This philosophy, at one level, was a way of overcoming stage fright and coping with inconsistent reviews. At another level, it reinforced the intrinsic pleasure of the music beyond the ephemeral joy of audience approval.

The DSQ picked an appropriate level of aspiration for its playing. Members knew they would never be a world-class string quartet, and they did not aspire to become one. They also knew that they could give some excellent performances of their music, and they continuously strove to do just that. If they had chosen a level of aspiration above or below their potential, their direction would have been neither as clear nor as engaging to members as it was. If the aspiration were too high, members would risk being continually downcast because of their failure to meet their own standards. If it were too low, they would not be challenged to stretch to be the best they could be. Either choice would have resulted in a group that was considerably less alive and less involved in its work.

Finally, the group had a clear and shared understanding about the kind of interpersonal relationships members sought. John told me that when he was asked to join the group, Jim explained the group philosophy: that they could run an ongoing string quartet and still "get along" together. John intimated that it was this philosophy that got him to reconsider his previous personal decision not to be a part of another quartet.

A Well-Designed Team. The Detroit String Quartet, quite literally, designed itself. The quartet had complete autonomy to decide the tasks it would perform, who would be a member of the team, and what norms of conduct would guide behavior within it. There was no supervisor or manager constraining those choices: the DSQ was a fully self-governing ensemble. The evidence I gathered suggests that, given their purposes, the members did a good job at designing their group.

The basic task of the quartet—making music—stands high on all three of the factors that Hackman and Oldham (1980) identify as critical for work motivation and satisfaction: meaningfulness, responsibility, and knowledge of results. The work was extraordinarily meaningful to the members, both because each person cared personally about making music and because it required a level of skill that most people do not have—and that those who do must constantly nurture. Moreover, playing a quartet is a "whole" piece of work and one that is consequential to the quartet members as well as to their audiences.

Members of the DSQ also experienced a strong sense of collective responsibility for the outcomes of their work. No one was looking over their shoulders to make sure they were playing right or working hard enough. Each member had made a personal commitment to his or her work—first by choosing a career as a professional musician, and then by deciding to become a member of the DSQ. And since the quartet was completely self-governing, there was nobody else to blame if a piece came out poorly—and nobody with whom credit had to be shared if it turned out well.

The third property of motivating tasks—knowledge of results—also was amply present for the DSQ every time the group rehearsed or performed. Once I asked Jim if it was clear to members when they had played better or worse. At the next rehearsal, after playing through the Debussey a second time, he turned to me and said, "That time was better." Then he turned to the group and explained what my question had been. The others nodded in assent, affirming a consensus that was so obvious to them it had not been necessary to make it explicit. Such immediate feedback both reinforced the group when it was successful and provided corrective information when performance was subpar.

The composition of the DSQ also helped members work

well as a team. Each member was a competent, committed, highly motivated musician. And because the Detroit Symphony Orchestra provided a ready pool of talent, quartet members did not have to look very far to find a suitable person on the one occasion when they needed a new member—when Mario left the quartet. Jim recalled talking extensively to John about the group's philosophy (that members aspire both to play music well and to get along well together) when the quartet was considering John as Mario's replacement. The conversation helped John understand that smooth and congenial social relations were among the goals of the quartet, and he made his decision to join partly on that basis. This contrasts with the situation of many other work teams whose members must contend with new members they did not pick—and would not have picked had they been given the opportunity.

Because years ago the DSQ had developed the core norms that guided team behavior and since then had enforced them on a more-or-less continuous basis, little on-line management of member behavior was required; everyone knew how the group operated and what behaviors were and were not acceptable. It was all implicit and hidden from view, however. While this made it harder for me, as an outside observer, to understand what was going on, it made it easier for members themselves to perform their work. Some group norms were, of course, dictated by the music. For example, members could not have switched who played the violin and cello parts even if they had wanted to. But even those issues for which the quartet had discretion were well under normative control. There was no question that the DSQ was a fully mature group.

Because the work involved constant and intense interdependence, the definition of member roles had to be both task appropriate and personally satisfying to individual members. Players were indeed constantly at the mercy of each other in their work. This fact forced the group to address questions of coordination and differences among members that could be ignored or glossed over in other kinds of work groups. Each player had to learn and cater to every other player's strengths and weaknesses for members to play together well as a quartet.

Members believed the folklore in musical circles that when ensemble members are not getting along with each other, it shows to the audience—that fights must be resolved in the dressing room lest the performance be affected. This aspect of the task made DSQ's goal—that members would not only play music but also get along together—not merely an added "group perk," but an essential part of their ability to perform as a team.

In sum, the design of the DSQ provided a stable platform for the quartet's development. Members did not have to spend time and energy motivating each other, teaching others how to do their jobs, or explaining to them the way the group works. They therefore had a greater proportion of their time available to use fine-tuning themselves as a team than would have been the case if their team design were less well suited to their work and their collective purposes.

A Unique and Supportive Context. The Detroit Symphony Orchestra provided a unique and supportive organizational context for the quartet—albeit not one that had any actual authority over the group and its work. Probably the single greatest contribution made by the DSO to the quartet occurred when the DSQ formed: the orchestra provided a ready pool of musicians where group members could casually feel each other out about the possibility of starting up a quartet and begin to select others who seemed most appropriate for the fledgling ensemble.

The DSO also provided members with a steady income, thereby making it possible for the quartet to function as a part-time group. When I asked John, "How come you work so well together?" he specifically stated that it was because the regular work of members, the income-producing work, was with the DSO. This, he said, took the pressure off so that the quartet could have the luxury of a slow, steady pace, free from the need to work eight- or ten-hour days for weeks on end to prepare for a concert tour. The DSO also allowed members to keep a certain distance from one another without having to expend much energy in doing so. This arrangement contrasts with another quartet members described to me. The musicians in that quartet, which was widely considered a world-class group, never saw each other outside of rehearsal or performance; they even would eat at separate tables in the dining car if riding on the same train. The DSQ did not need this kind of relief from one another because, in the course of their daily work lives at the DSO, they encountered many other musicians who played quite different kinds of music.

Finally, the DSO provided the quartet with help as a referral source—that is, in obtaining engagements to play. Thus, the quartet did not need to spend much time in marketing or in continually changing its product in response to economic cycles. The DSQ had many opportunities to play, to earn money, and to achieve the level of recognition it sought. Although many leads and referrals did come from the symphony, the choice about what to play, for whom, and where was always the quartet's own. Members could recall only one exception—the time Maestro Dorati (then conductor of the DSO) asked them to play. One just does not turn down Maestro Dorati, members reported. Otherwise, they felt free to play only those performances that fit their philosophy and schedule. They had real freedom to direct their time and effort internally, working on what was most important to them—their music. Such a benevolent environment certainly aided their creative efforts.

Conclusion

The features of the Detroit String Quartet discussed in the previous section—the group's direction, design, and context—come from the orienting framework for this project (see the introduction to this book). While these factors do aid in our understanding of the DSQ, there is another aspect of the group, not addressed in that framework, that is key to understanding the quartet as a performing team. For lack of a better term, I will describe it as *pace*, but it also could be described as rhythm or tempo. It was this factor, more than any other, that was essential to my understanding of the DSQ—and that most clearly points to what the DSQ has to teach us as a performing group.

Pacing and Performing. It was impossible to observe the DSQ and not be impressed by the quartet's slow, even pace and unhurried, unharried style. The group somehow had achieved a state of harmonious equilibrium both in its artistic efforts and in its management of group process. It was as if the group had an Eastern philosophy, as epitomized by the Chinese proverb, "The longest journey begins with a single step." Never in my observations did I hear members berate one another for not doing an adequate job, not being good enough (yet), or not being "there" (wherever "there" was) soon enough.

The inward orientation of the quartet, discussed earlier, was deeply rooted. Never did I observe the DSQ turning to audiences or critical reviews for confirmation of members' own sense of their collective worth, nor did I ever hear them compare themselves to other quartets to see if they measured up to the competition. Based on what I observed, the DSQ might, in members' minds, have been the only string quartet in the world.

Its unhurried pace and its freedom from external demands and comparisons helped keep the quartet on an even keel. Many musical ensembles do not have such freedom and cannot enjoy a relaxed pace. Instead, they place themselves at the mercy of people who may not be expert in what they do (such as audiences) or whose taste and preferences may be unreliable or at variance with the aspirations of ensemble members (such as critics and booking agents). Life can be hectic and unsatisfying for such ensembles. They may, for example, swing from euphoria one day to depression the next in response to criticism or audience reactions. Such swings can result in a rather manic life (as was the case for John's previous quartet), and they can compromise the long-term well-being of both the ensemble and the individual musicians.

The DSQ did not suffer from these problems. To illustrate, Jim described a DSQ performance at an event that included an ad hoc group of other musicians who were superior individually to the DSQ members. He felt the DSQ, as a quartet, gave a better performance than did the other group, and other members of the Detroit Symphony Orchestra who heard both performances shared his assessment. Yet critical reviews concluded the opposite. Jim said that he and the other quartet members were able to accept the praise from their DSO colleagues and keep the printed reviews in perspective because of their own stable sense that the DSQ had indeed performed well. In sum, members' internal orientation and self-generated standards, coupled with their realism about the quartet's strengths and weaknesses, allowed them to put outside opinions into perspective and maintain the pace and direction of the quartet—even if some listeners were occasionally less than pleased by what they heard when the quartet played.

In a world of quick fixes, filled with individuals, groups, and organizations continuously and hurriedly trying to better themselves, a slow-moving, ongoing, internally guided effort toward improvement stands out. How did the DSQ achieve its unique style and avoid the competitive pressures that pervade the world of professional musical performance? Most important, of course, was the enjoyment of the work itself. Making beautiful music was far more important to quartet members than critical or commercial success. This attitude allowed the ensemble to plug along at a slow, steady pace consistent with its aspiration of continual improvement coupled with harmonious group relations. Questions such as "How fast do we get there?" and "What are we getting out of this?" were not necessary to sustain the quartet's motivation. Members, individually and collectively, were not so concerned with the destination of their journey that they did not have time to sniff the roses and to explore some interesting-looking byways along the path.

Moreover, the DSQ was not forced to produce at a predetermined rate for economic reasons. It did not need to take on that one extra performance to make an extra dollar. *All* the money it made was extra. Members had total personal control over their pacing because of the financial platform provided by the Detroit Symphony Orchestra.

The pace of the quartet, its rhythm, cannot be designed into a musical ensemble—or into any other group, for that matter. There is no specific "cause" that will yield this particular "effect." Instead, it is an emergent quality, something that members themselves grow and nurture. Yet not all groups will be capable of developing the kind of character the DSQ had, nor will all contexts support the kind of group that the DSQ was. Consider, for example, a newly formed ensemble whose members have cut off all other sources of income to devote their full time and energy to becoming successful commercially, critically, and artistically. Such a group surely would not be able to enjoy the inner direction or afford the slow pace that characterized the DSQ. The performance conditions that the DSQ had—its sense of direction, the design of the group itself, and the stable and supportive context provided by the Detroit Symphony Orchestra—did not in any sense cause the quartet to develop the pace and style that it did. But those conditions surely did make it easier for the group to evolve in its own unique direction.

A Hidden Downside? Throughout this account of the Detroit String Quartet, I have emphasized the "harmony" of the group. Smooth interpersonal relations were a part of the direction of the group and freed members from having to deal with difficult interpersonal conflicts and process issues. It was easy to see the benefits of harmonious group functioning in the quality of the quartet's playing as well as in the quality of their experience as quartet members.

Nevertheless, there is something about the way the quartet managed its internal processes that raises an eyebrow. Members said they worked on group process "constantly," yet I never saw them actually do it. They described the "difficult" departure of Mario only in the most general terms, and they were unwilling to tell me about the events that led to his departure or how the departure itself actually occurred. How capable was this group, in fact, of managing truly difficult issues when they did arise?

The group was rarely tested on this score. Only Mario's departure was a life-threatening problem, and it was dealt with by temporarily halting the group. The problem of late arrivals, hardly a major issue, was dealt with by assigning one member to talk privately, outside the group, with the offending individual. Never did I observe or hear from a quartet member an account of a "process issue" being worked through in the group itself.

These data suggest that the gestalt of the Detroit String Quartet may have been a relatively static one—one not flexible in meeting changing environmental demands or member needs. Because the quartet's world was relatively benign during the time I observed it, I did not have the opportunity to assess how resilient the group actually was, to see whether it had sufficient reserves ready should a real crisis develop in the life or work of the group. Nor did I learn about the extent of the group's ability to engage issues that potentially could disrupt the harmony that was so important to it—that, indeed, it had identified as a key feature of the quartet's philosophy.

An event that occurred after I completed the research demonstrates how the group's philosophy determined not only how the quartet members lived together as a group, but also how the group died. Inez left the Detroit area (her husband had found a better job elsewhere), and the quartet was without a second violinist. Rather than face the difficult and anxiety-arousing issues involved in recruiting and training a new member, the quartet decided it was time to quit. As Jim told me over the telephone, members had put in fifteen good years of hard work together and now it was time to retire, relax, and enjoy other aspects of life.

In one sense, the members' choice to let the group die was a rational one for a team that had chosen to have a group life as free from conflict and anxiety as they could make it. I leave it to the reader to decide whether he or she would be disappointed with this same choice. Would going another round with a new member, with all its potential toil and conflict, have provided sufficient learning and future rewards to justify upsetting the quartet's steady state? Certainly it was in keeping with the quartet's philosophy that this was not, in fact, the path members chose.

Summary. The life and work of the Detroit String Quartet provides additional documentation of the importance and interdependence of a work team's direction, its structure, and its organizational context. Beyond that, however, the DSQ provides an excellent illustration of how a slow and steady team can succeed on its own terms. In an increasingly high-pressure and externally oriented society, the DSQ demonstrates that intrinsi-

cally satisfying work and team self-direction can result in outcomes that are of high quality both for those the team served
(in this case, its audiences) and for team members themselves.
That, in the end, the group chose not to exist rather than to
alter its mode of operating provides the final and ultimately
most convincing demonstration of the kind of life the team led.

Jim told me recently that over the years he had collected
some fifty reel-to-reel tapes of the DSQ's great and not-so-great
performances. He stated that he did not have much money to
leave his children but would instead pass on to them this collection of tapes. I cannot think of a better statement of the pride
he placed in the DSQ's work, nor of the benefits of this group's
work for generations to come.

14

Stewart D. Friedman

Children's Theatre Company[1]

Sally, founder of the Children's Theatre Company (CTC), is in her car on the way to a rehearsal of one of the company's shows. She is troubled by disturbing questions about the two casts in which she is currently working. "Why is it that no matter what I do, no one else in the CTC seems to have the kind of commitment that I do for our work? Will we get roped into doing any of those damn benefit performances again this year? Will the cast show up on time for this rehearsal? How will the new replacement work out? Will he learn his role soon enough to be ready for the first performance? Indeed, will the rest of us know the play when the first curtain goes up? Why did Ben quit anyway?"

The Children's Theatre Company created and performed plays, mainly for audiences of school children. The company performed most shows in a school gymnasium or auditorium, although it did occasionally perform for other audiences. Created three years before I studied it, the company was still getting settled.

Sally worked in the payroll department of the school system in addition to managing the CTC. Her heart was with the acting company, however, and she wished she could devote herself full-time to it. She was intent on getting the CTC established on a solid, professional basis. Most company members were either acting students or experienced amateurs who also

225

performed in other local theater groups. Pay was minimal—ten dollars to each actor for every show performed and nothing for rehearsals.

Primary responsibility for any given show was held by the producer-director. He or she conceived the show, cast it from among other CTC members, and then prepared it for production. The company was preparing two shows for the current season: *Gold for the Queen* and *Cinderella.* Sally was both producer-director of and an actress in *Gold for the Queen,* which had a cast of four. *Cinderella,* an original musical comedy adaptation of the folktale, was written, produced, and directed by Joe, another company member. Joe also acted in *Gold for the Queen,* and Sally was also a member of the four-person *Cinderella* cast.

This chapter is about these two casts and about their experiences in rehearsal and in performance before audiences. In the next few pages, I will sketch a picture of the lives of the casts in a series of short takes. First, we will see what life was like for the cast of *Gold for the Queen* during rehearsals. Then we will switch to *Cinderella* to see how things were different for a cast once actual performances got under way.

Rehearsal: Scenes from *Gold for the Queen*

The CTC held rehearsals at the school system's Cultural Arts Building (CAB) either in the large dance studio, in the "green room," or, as last resort, in a small, spare room sometimes used as an office. Sally complained, "That really upsets me. Why do we get second priority in the CAB just because, unlike the dance class, we don't generate revenues for the Arts Department? We make an important contribution to the cultural life of the school system!"

Only Sally arrived on time for the first rehearsal. When the other three cast members finally did arrive, she assigned players to parts. Each player had to play multiple roles, although never in the same scene. "This should be exciting and challenging for all of us," Sally said. "Costume changes between scenes will be frequent. I hope we have all the costume stuff we'll need."

After reading through the script, the cast blocked the show, figuring out where the players should move and when. Sally asked everyone, after blocking a scene, "How does this seem to you?" "They have some good ideas for stage directions," she observed. "It makes me feel good when everyone participates in deciding how we're going to do things."

Before the first rehearsal, I had met individually with all company members and secured their agreement to participate in the research. But my role was not yet clear, and they looked to me for commentary, for feedback. I did not give it. The players seemed to dislike having me there, just sitting and watching. They wanted me to participate, either as one of them or at least as a critic or coach.

Trying to arrange a time for the next rehearsal pained and frustrated Sally. Everyone seemed to have other, more important, things to do—a pattern that was replicated every time the cast tried to schedule a rehearsal. Over time, Sally became increasingly perturbed at members' tardiness. Not once did all cast members arrive on time. She always greeted late-arriving colleagues with a sidelong glance, but she never explicitly reproached them.

The plan was for players to learn their lines at home and then use rehearsal time to work out the nuances of delivery. However, certain players did not learn their lines as they had agreed to, so progress toward crystallizing the subtleties of each scene was slow and the rehearsals became tense.

Sally rarely made specific comments about how the players presented their parts in rehearsal. Instead, she would ask, "How does this feel to you? Is this OK?" The players made suggestions and altered their performance strategies ad lib. Sally encouraged creativity. She viewed rehearsals as a time for experimenting. For example, in an early rehearsal two players (one male, one female) in a scene actually switched roles to gain different perspectives on their parts.

Cast members spent considerable time during rehearsals

discussing nonwork matters, especially love relationships. Sally was single and Toni, the other woman in the cast, was divorced with two children (who often came with her to rehearsals). Joe was single as were each of the three men who, in turn, took the other male roles in the play. Conversations about unrequited love, the difficulties of dating, and problems with therapists were commonplace. Once, for example, when awaiting the arrival of a cast member, Joe began to cry while recounting the story of his lover's leaving. Sally gingerly hugged him and repeatedly patted him on the back.

The limits of my willingness to get involved continued to be tested. In one rehearsal, I was asked to join in a song. I declined, but the cast did talk me into playing bongo drum accompaniment to one scene. After this session, I decided to make a public statement about the limits of my role. I asserted that no longer would I participate in any way; I would observe and only observe. Cast members begrudgingly acknowledged the boundary I had drawn—but they continued to look to me for expressions of encouragement or dismay. I tried hard to remain unobtrusive, but their words and glances continued to be a strong pull to contribute somehow to the collective effort.

Two weeks into rehearsals, one of the players quit. He told me that the low level of professionalism (lack of adequate costumes, for example) was too frustrating for him. He had joined in order to expand his theatrical horizons but now felt that his work with the company would, instead, limit his horizons. Sally quickly found a replacement, but he also quit within two weeks. Among his complaints was the lack of clear signals from Sally about how things ought to be done. The next replacement did stay with the cast throughout its life.

The first performance was a benefit that Sally had reluctantly agreed to do. It occurred about five weeks after the first rehearsal. As the performance date approached, a sense of excitement grew among the players. They rehearsed more frequently and with greater seriousness, yet it was not altogether clear to them just what makes a show "ready." But it was clear that one day soon, when the curtain rose on the first performance of *Gold for the Queen,* the cast would finally get feedback from a real audience.

Performance: Scenes from *Cinderella*

Cinderella was Joe's baby. He conceived an original adaptation of the folktale, wrote the script and lyrics, composed the score, selected the cast, and directed the show. Joe had a complete concept of the show, and his direction about details of performance during rehearsals was specific and insistent. He knew exactly what he wanted in a scene, and if he did not quite get it, he worked with the players until he did.

Even after the cast had moved into the performance phase, Joe held special rehearsals to fine-tune various aspects of the show. For example, Joe discovered by accident that wearing his false beard lopsided had a humorous effect at one point in the show. He capitalized on that discovery in subsequent performances, and he kept experimenting with different ways of using the beard to realize the effect he was looking for. He also made adjustments in stage directions to accommodate differences in the facilities where the cast performed. I felt that the play was indeed ready for performance—but that it remained unfinished.

Whereas suggestions for improving *Gold for the Queen* came from all players, Joe kept a tight rein on *Cinderella.* Sally tried to make suggestions now and then, but with limited success. On one occasion, Sally gave Toni a suggested stage direction that would have changed how the movement was performed. Joe quickly intervened and changed the movement back to the way it had been.

Yet Sally was the CTC administrator, and Joe relied on her to handle logistics, arrange bookings, and obtain resources needed for the production. For example, *Cinderella* was first performed poolside in a public park using a prerecorded version of the piano part. Joe felt that the accompaniment was unsatisfactory and that a live piano player was needed. He convinced Sally of this, and she proceeded to hire a pianist who played for all subsequent performances.

Although there was some tension between Joe and Sally around the inherently blurry boundary between the responsibilities of the producer-director and those of the administrator, the real conflict within the cast was between Sally and Toni. Toni was a holdover from the previous season, and everyone assumed that something had happened to sour permanently her relationship with Sally—but no one knew what it was. Signs of the problem were obvious. During one performance-phase rehearsal, for example, Toni complained that she could not take a whole day from her work just to do one show that might be added to the schedule. "It's only a half-hour show," Sally responded. "Can't you take that much time off?" Toni was adamant, and the air crackled with tension. Another time Toni, who worked as a wallpaper hanger, was late for a rehearsal. Sally announced, sarcastically: "Probably she wallpapered herself into a corner."

Despite such flare-ups, commitment to the show was high. All members liked the show and enjoyed performing it. It was exciting and challenging for them to be in an original production that required singing and dancing as well as acting. No one was ever late for a performance, and no one showed any sign of wanting to quit. Audiences also liked the show. Because audience members were children, they were very expressive. When bored, they did not hide their yawns and restlessness; when excited, they jumped, laughed, and squealed. The *Cinderella* company got lots of jumping, laughing, and squealing as partial reward for its work. In addition, the cast occasionally received a letter of appreciation from a teacher or from a group of students. Such feedback meant more to Sally than it did to the players. Although they did care about their audiences' reactions, cast members wished they were playing to adults rather than to children.

Group Effectiveness

How effective was the Children's Theatre Company? The answer depends on whether one assesses the performances themselves or how the company and its members developed over time. It depends on whether one focuses on *Gold for the Queen* or *Cinderella*. And it depends on whether one examines the rehearsal or performance phase of each cast's life.

In rehearsals, there was no external review of the performance; there was no bottom line. Sally, as CTC supervisor, was supposed to approve each show, but, for both productions, this process was essentially implicit. And while it is true that the producer-director establishes standards and lets the cast know how well those standards are being met, there is no client or audience to turn to for feedback during rehearsals. The cast of *Cinderella*, continuously prodded by Joe to meet his high standards, felt better about its work during the rehearsal phase than did the *Gold for the Queen* cast. But both were bothered by the absence of feedback from outsiders—which is one reason why there was so much pressure on me to provide some.

Once performances began, there was plenty of feedback—and the audiences of both productions turned in positive assessments. Audience reception of *Gold for the Queen*, cast members reported, was positive but modest. Everyone involved with *Cinderella*, on the other hand, agreed that the show was a hit. Each performance surpassed audience expectations, as noted by one school principal who wrote to the cast: "You've outdone yourselves this time!"

Beyond the quality of its products—the performances—how well did the CTC do in developing its casts as strong, flexible teams? What was the impact of the experience on individual actors? At season's end, had the CTC become a stronger company, ready to start the next season from a higher platform than was in place at the start of the current season? Or did the company become weaker over the season, resulting in a diminution of members' willingness or ability to work well together on subsequent productions?

The CTC certainly did not begin strong. The previous season, the company had numbered between fifteen and twenty players, but only three of them returned the next year. Concerned about this, Sally had asked each member to sign a "commitment paper" in which the person formally agreed to serve as producer-director for at least one show and make every effort to be available for rehearsals. Unfortunately, her initiative had little effect; commitment remained low for most actors. Absences and tardiness were constant problems during the rehearsal phase, and two actors left *Gold for the Queen* before the cast finally jelled. Still, there was no direct evidence that performance suffered because of problems members had working together. There were interpersonal difficulties, to be sure—most noticeably between Sally and Toni in *Cinderella*—yet no one observing the performance of that show would have seen signs of such tensions.

Why not? Circumstances were, after all, fairly grim. For one thing, the casts never explicitly addressed or worked through the interpersonal and group process difficulties that plagued them. Even though members made angry comments to me about the lateness or absenteeism of others, they never said anything directly to the offending parties. Similarly, they never talked about the lack of explicit negotiation in *Cinderella* regarding the dual leadership roles taken by Joe and Sally—neither in the group as a whole nor privately with the two members. Should not this pattern of avoidance have impaired the casts' performances?

If the group had been meeting regularly, day in and day out, the problems no doubt would have taken their toll. But these casts rehearsed and performed on an occasional schedule, and work with CTC was not at the center of any member's day-to-day life. This may have provided a kind of buffer that kept the process difficulties from impairing the work of the group. On the other hand, neither cast showed marked growth as an *ensemble* during the season, and that may have been due to the fact that the cast "just existed," as one *Gold for the Queen* member reported.

Individual cast members reported, for the most part, that they were more satisfied than frustrated by their experiences in the casts. Indeed, the two members from *Gold for the Queen* who did become significantly frustrated simply quit during the rehearsal phase. One reported that he found the experience destructive: "There was no challenge for me; it hurt my performing ability." Those who stayed, however, generally had positive things to say. For Toni, participation provided an opportunity to broaden her performing experience and a flexible enough rehearsal schedule to make that possible. Joe reported that he participated in *Gold for the Queen* mostly as a favor to Sally—and to obtain from her the chance to have his own show produced. Sally liked having the chance to act, and she was proud, with *Cinderella*, that CTC had produced an original show of high quality. For Jim, in the *Cinderella* cast, "The chance to perform in a new situation . . . does a lot for me personally." Jeff, a cast member in *Gold for the Queen*, was perhaps most positive of all: "I find something new in the CTC—a lot more challenge than in the City Theatre. It's been very satisfying in my own development."

Each of the members of the Children's Theatre Company obtained something personally useful from his or her participation. Moreover, the company worked, in that competent productions were created and performed—even though the CTC's potential as an *ensemble* was not realized. Moreover, audiences were pleased with the performances they attended. Indeed, *Cinderella* audiences were enthusiastic about what they experienced. Overall, the CTC was a moderately effective group, albeit one that was unable to exploit fully its potential as a repertory company.

Design of the Casts as Performing Units

Can the structure of the casts explain their effectiveness as teams? I will explore three structural features: (1) the motivational structure of the group's tasks, (2) the composition of the casts, and (3) the core norms that guided behavior within the company.

Motivational Structure of the Group Task

The task for *Cinderella* was more motivating than was the task for *Gold for the Queen*, and, for both casts, the performance phase was more motivating than was the rehearsal phase.

The motivation of *Cinderella* cast members clearly was boosted by the play's being an original musical comedy adaptation, written and scored by one of the company members. More-over, the play required singing and dancing as well as acting, and these demands stretched members' skills. That the play would be engaging was obvious from the beginning. As Joe reported in recalling the first reading of the script, "Everyone loved it!" *Gold for the Queen,* on the other hand, was not an original production. It is a folktale too, but Sally's task in preparing the show was simply to copy the script out of a book. Everyone in this production played different parts in a series of vignettes, and it might be expected that this variety would have added to members' motivation. But the variety of parts to be played (and the frequent costume changes) merely required members to do more of the same thing—not nearly as motivating as doing *different* things (both singing and dancing) was for the *Cinderella* cast.

It was hard for both casts to sustain high motivation during the rehearsal phase. The absence of feedback from an audience was, of course, missed. But the rehearsal task inherently provides less feedback than does a performance. When a show is being performed, the sequence of action provides a more coherent context for cast members to use in evaluating their work than is the case in rehearsal—when there is typically much starting and stopping as a scene is prepared. Because there is no stopping once a performance begins, timing and coordination are critical. Even if someone goofs a line, the flow of the play must not be disrupted. The actors do make and recover from errors, of course—sometimes without the audience's even knowing what happened. But cast members recognize each error immediately, just as they recognize their level of success in recovering. Thus, in part because there is no turning back and in part because the consequences of mistakes are greater in front of an audience, performances provide far greater built-in motivation for casts than do rehearsals.

Group Composition

Both casts had sufficient talent to carry off their productions. There was, however, considerable heterogeneity among members in experience and expertise. The casts benefited from this heterogeneity, in that the scripts called for variety in character types. Moreover, the presence in the casts of experienced members enhanced the opportunities for others to develop as actors.

On the other hand, the more experienced members tended to have higher standards for the quality of the productions than did their less experienced colleagues. This discrepancy resulted in occasional impatience and frustration on the part of the more experienced members and created interpersonal problems within the casts. Unfortunately, the interpersonal skills of company members were not sufficiently well developed for them to solve these problems so that they stayed solved. The ongoing process difficulties both casts experienced and the loss of two members from *Gold for the Queen* during the rehearsal phase appear to be, at least in part, a result of this dynamic.

Gold for the Queen also suffered from small group size. While the four-person cast was able to perform the play by switching roles and costumes between scenes, members felt that the production would have been more professional if the cast had been larger and less switching had been required. Also, there may have been insufficient role differentiation in *Gold for the Queen:* Sally was both supervisor of the company as a whole and producer-director of that play; the result was a hub-and-spokes authority structure. In *Cinderella*, on the other hand, the division of labor between Joe, as producer-director, and Sally, as administrator, was, in some ways, beneficial. As Joe commented, "It's good to have a business person to support the artistic efforts."

Group Norms About Performance Processes

For both plays, norms became more potent as the casts moved from rehearsal to performance. Norms about absenteeism and tardiness are illustrative. These matters were a chronic problem for the CTC. During rehearsals, some members came early, others late, and others not at all. While everyone recognized this was a problem, no one did much of anything about it. They did not have shared expectations about behavior, and thus no agreement about how violations should be dealt with. Although one member might make a snide remark or cast a sidelong glance to another who was late for a rehearsal, it was clear that these were person-to-person acts not made on behalf of the group as a whole. The dynamic surrounding attendance was a specific and easily discerned example of the general absence of group norms during the rehearsal phase; both casts' approach to the preparation of the plays was relatively lackadaisical.

The discipline of performance did bring clear movement toward role and norm clarity. Failure to appear or appear on time for a performance has obvious and serious consequences. Members recognized that and behaved accordingly. When I asked one member, during the rehearsal phase, to give an example of a time when behavior in the group was particularly orderly, she responded, "It hasn't clicked yet; we're waiting to perform." It was true. After a show had been performed a few times, the cast did develop routines specifying who would do what upon arrival at the school—for example, who would greet the principal, set up costumes, talk with the children, and so on. Behavior in the plays also became more predictable; there was noticeably less experimentation and "sloppy" acting than was the case during rehearsals.

There were also differences in norm and role definition between the two plays. In *Cinderella*, Joe had artistic control and he was prepared to crack down if necessary to make sure that behavior was in accord with his expectations and standards. In contrast, Sally's preference was for as much improvisation as possible, for everyone to have a chance to have a say about the details of the production. The result was stronger group norms for *Cinderella* than ever developed for *Gold for the Queen* under Sally's relatively laissez-faire direction.

The one domain in which clear norms were not established in *Cinderella* was the division of labor between Joe and Sally. There were many occasions when Joe could have sought to establish more clearly "who is in charge here," but he did not. "With Sally," he said, "it is hard to separate roles." Because Joe did not confront the matter, the ambiguity persisted; Sally was at the same time Joe's supervisor (in her role as head of CTC) and his subordinate (as an actress in his play). So, even though norms about running the show were relatively well crystallized in

Cinderella, norms about the partitioning of leadership responsibilities were not.

Performance Context

Did the Children's Theatre Company generally, and its two casts in particular, receive external support to help members develop first-rate productions? Or did transactions with the environment impede the work of the company and make it harder for the casts to achieve and to sustain excellence?

Reward System

One of the most significant contextual features for a work team is the degree to which excellent team performance is recognized and rewarded. For the CTC, the reward system was quite different from what might be expected for, say, an industrial work team. Specifically, little recognition came from the casts' own organization, but highly salient rewards did come from sources outside that organization.

Organizationally provided rewards were few in number, small in size, and administered to individual members rather than to intact casts. In *Cinderella*, for example, Joe provided clear performance objectives and standards, and he overtly praised individual cast members when they achieved them. Sally, in directing *Gold for the Queen*, tended not to provide this kind of reinforcement. The small financial payment members of both casts did receive for each performance was simply for doing the performance, regardless of quality. There was no evidence that this compensation was significant for company members, other than as a symbol that this was professional rather than amateur work.

There were essentially no organizationally conferred rewards or punishments for the casts as intact units, in either the rehearsal or performance phases. Neither Sally, as CTC supervisor, nor Carol, the cultural arts coordinator for the school system and Sally's manager, provided any performance-contingent recognition or reward to the casts. CTC members were not surprised at the lack of recognition, but some resented it. When asked to talk about a time when a cast received some reward from organizational representatives, one member of the *Cinderella* cast responded, "Never, and we probably never will be. I resent it! The CTC has shabbily thrown together shows with little rehearsal. Now, CTC is doing an original, coherent show. It's got music, it's unique! No one would ever know. I would like more realistic, sincere appraisal, if there was someone above me who was knowledgeable enough to evaluate me."

The rewards that really counted for the CTC casts were those that came directly from audiences. Cast members not only immediately heard laughter or sensed boredom during a production, they also subsequently might receive letters, pictures, and poems from their audiences expressing gratitude and appreciation for a show. At the same time, it was unsettling to the players that their audiences consisted mainly of children. Children are tough for two reasons. First, they have a short attention span and limited social graces. Children make it quite clear to everyone when they are bored or listless. Second, they are but children. Their reactions, although more directly (and primitively) expressed, are not those of mature, intelligent adults—and the performers value their opinions less than they would value appraisals by knowledgeable adults such as the higher levels of CTC management, school officials, or colleagues outside the organization. However, as noted, the casts received mainly silence from these parties.

Ultimately, the major rewards for CTC members, individually and in casts, were recognition (which came almost entirely from extraorganizational sources) and the opportunity to develop one's skills (which was managed and experienced primarily by individuals). Although Sally promoted the CTC as a place to act and get paid for it, and although she talked more about contracts and money than about qualifications and artistic aspirations, the rate of pay was so low as to make the work essentially voluntary. Cast members joined and remained in the company mainly for personal and intrinsic reasons. This conflict, between external and internal rewards, was endemic to the CTC, and the company never satisfactorily resolved it. That, coupled with the paucity of group-level recognition, increased the difficulty of sustaining high levels of collective effort, especially during rehearsal phases when audience reinforcement was an expectation for the future rather than a present reality.

Other Contextual Supports

Clearly, other supports from the organizational context—ranging from educational assistance to information to mundane material resources—could have facilitated the work of the CTC casts. Unfortunately, such supports generally were unavailable, in short supply, or difficult to obtain.

For example, cast members reported that some special training or technical advice would have been useful on occasion—especially vocal and choreographic coaching for the *Cinderella* cast. Even though such assistance (for example, dance instructors and vocal coaches) was potentially available through the school system's Cultural Arts Program, the casts never sought it and the program staff never offered it.

Task-relevant information, including both guidance about objectives and more mundane information about performance conditions, also was scarce. The objective of the CTC, for example, was vaguely specified in a school system document as being to provide "theatre . . . of a high caliber of professionalism." While much discussion went on within the company about how that general objective should be operationalized, such discussions never involved representatives of the school system or its Cultural Arts Program. Neither did the casts have advance information about performance conditions (such as stage and lighting arrangements) or about audience characteristics. Because such data were neither provided nor actively sought, the casts sometimes were surprised by, and unprepared for, the circumstances under which they had to perform.

Finally, material resources were always in short supply. The second actor to quit *Gold for the Queen* did so in part because he found costume preparation inadequate. The production, he said, was plagued by "schlockiness," which (although he appeared not to realize it) was due directly to the CTC's chronic scarcity of money, materials, and staff assistance.

In sum, the broader organization did not actively impede the work of the casts, but neither did it provide support to help the casts develop the best possible productions, given members' acting abilities. In assessing why this state of affairs existed and persisted, we must examine the role and behavior of the CTC leaders. How was their behavior affected by the absence of organizational supports? What, if any, substitutes for such support did they provide?

Leadership

Both Sally, as CTC supervisor and producer-director of one play, and Joe, as producer-director of the other, had numerous opportunities to seek out organizational supports for the work of the company, build their casts as cohesive performing units, and coach individual actors. How did they use these opportunities?

Creating Favorable Performance Conditions

Both Sally and Joe generally accepted their organization as it was and did not take initiatives to improve the conditions under which the company and the casts worked. Although they recognized the limitations they faced, they never attempted to exercise influence upward in the organization to improve performance conditions. Their behavior, instead, reflected a can-do attitude, and they encouraged other company members to join them in making the best of a situation that was only marginally satisfactory for the work the company had to do. The one exception to this generalization was Joe's taking the initiative with Sally to get a piano player for *Cinderella*—but this occurred within the company, not between the company and its context.

The tendency to take performance conditions as given appears to have its roots, in part, in the leadership styles of Sally and Joe. It also reflects a more general norm in the theater world. During rehearsals for *Gold for the Queen*, the cast needed some special assistance. All agreed that the problem was better dealt with internally by the director. "In theater," one explained, "you don't use outsiders." While casts do need (and in major league companies often receive) help from choreographers, voice coaches, lighting consultants, and the like, these consultants typically are closely associated with the company. In the final analysis, it is the director who calls the shots. A director who asks for help outside the company runs the risk of violating cast members' expectations and, for this reason, directors may be reluctant to seek outside assistance even when it would benefit the production.

Building the Casts as Performing Units

Neither director took explicit action to build the casts into cohesive performing units with clear norms and high commitment to the collective enterprise. Sally did take one significant initiative to foster greater commitment to the CTC as an organization, yet her approach contradicted her espoused aims: she had all new CTC members sign a commitment paper without fully discussing what each person wanted to gain from the commitment he or she was making. When she subsequently spoke about the "commitment problem" at company meetings, her tone often was angry and experienced by members as alienating. Clearly, Sally's attempts to develop the company into a cohesive performing unit were unsuccessful.

She also had little success in building the cast of *Gold for the Queen* into a cohesive performing unit. Again, her aims were not realized by her behavior. By being highly participative and by encouraging all members to contribute suggestions about the production on an equal basis, Sally hoped to build collective involvement in and commitment to the production. Cast members, however, saw her style as impeding rather than facilitating the development of an excellent production. They wanted more and clearer direction from her, and they probably would have melded into a stronger cast if they had received it.

The cast of *Cinderella*, on the other hand, did develop into a more cohesive unit—in major part because Joe's intense interest in the show he had created rubbed off on other cast members. Joe did not engage in any explicit team-building activities, but his enthusiasm and his stronger, more directive style did foster member commitment to the cast and to the production. Even so, Joe avoided explicitly addressing issues that threatened the integrity of the cast—issues such as the continuing interpersonal difficulties between Sally and Toni, the ambiguity around leadership roles between Sally and Joe, and the chronic tardiness problems. Like Sally, Joe did not give explicit attention to building or to maintaining his cast as a performing unit.

Coaching and Leading Cast Members

Coaching and hands-on leadership are at the core of what directors in the theater are supposed to do, and both Sally and Joe did a lot of this. Again, however, there were differences between them. As noted earlier, Sally tended toward a laissez-faire or consensus style: she encouraged cast members to come to agreement about the best way to proceed. Joe, on the other hand, was not at all shy about actively leading the cast and coaching individual members. Indeed, he continued to coach them all the way into the performance phase; there was always something to be brushed up and refined. Finally, Joe was more effusive in providing feedback to cast members than was Sally. This not only contributed to the success of his production, but it also helped members develop their skills as actors.

Both Sally and Joe spent more of their energy as directors providing coaching than they did in the other two leadership functions—creating favorable performance conditions and building their casts as performing units. Overall, however, neither could be characterized as a highly active leader. The CTC had a significant need for strong leadership: neither the performance situation nor the company members were "set" at the beginning in a way that would ensure the production of great shows. There also were many opportunities for Sally and Joe to exhibit strong leadership; they were not significantly constrained by immutable organizational rules and practices. Yet neither leader took advantage of these opportunities to the extent they could have, and neither production turned out quite as well as it might have if they had done so.

Conclusion: The Uniqueness of Casts as Work Teams

Actors and the Special Task of Acting

The work of actors is far different from that of most people. Moreover, acting as a profession tends to attract people with certain needs and personal styles. Together, these factors can powerfully shape the behaviors that occur in theater casts. Consider first some of the distinctive features of acting as a job:

> *Unstable work.* An actor goes from one job to the next frequently, and each time there may be a new producer, a new director, a new work group, or a new location. Because one's next job is so uncertain, personal planning is severely constrained. As theater critic Vincent Canby observed: "The actor's life is a precarious one. Every role may be the last. Not until the name appears above the title can an actor feel there might possibly be some continuity of employment" (Canby, 1983).

> *Actor as other.* At work, the actor is on stage, enacting the words and feelings of someone else, another persona. The audience reaction, therefore, is to the enacted role, not just to the person acting the part. Rewards accrue to the actor for acting like someone else.

> *Instant feedback.* Recognition for performance is immediate and direct. The actor at work is completely exposed to public scrutiny, and audiences' reactions are highly consequential for the actor—both personally and professionally.

Not everyone is attracted to work that can be simultaneously so exciting and so lacking in security, so thrilling and so scary. What kind of person chooses this kind of life? My research on this question has extended beyond my nine months with the Children's Theatre Company and includes interviews with other actors, study of published literature on theater management, and consultations with clinical psychologists familiar with the life and work of actors. My findings suggest that there is some truth to the common view that acting attracts people who have both great sensitivity and high intensity—people who like to live on the edge. Beyond this, however, actors appear to have a unique complex of needs. More than most people at work, actors tend to seek (1) the evaluation and attention of strangers, (2) instant gratification, (3) emotional nourishment from audiences, and (4) a great deal of externally imposed structure on their work. By examining these needs, it may be possible to advance our understanding of the unique dynamics of theater casts as work teams.

Attention of Strangers. While most people seek recognition for the work they do, the drive to obtain it may be stronger for performing artists than it is for other workers. When actors perform they have the attention of many people with whom they are not close or familiar, people who may either praise or damn their work. An actor's task is to enact the emotions of another, using his or her own experience and imagination as sources of inspiration. The target of an audience's evaluation, then, is the actor's own emotional life.

Most workers are evaluated on a product or service that represents personal effort yet is a step removed from one's inner being. Most of us obtain satisfaction of our needs for love and attention in close relationships, not in more superficial work-related interactions. The performing artist, however, often seeks basic approval and acceptance through his or her work. Indeed, one expert in theater management has observed that "Many young actors are more interested in approbation than in the art form they presume to serve" (Langley, 1974, p. 6). It may be that, as the young actor matures, he or she learns—via the experience of taking on the emotional lives of others—more about his or her own emotional life. This exploration of one's inner life is akin to the psychotherapeutic process or a spiritual journey. For the performer, the experience is public.

Instant Gratification. The expression of the audience's response to an actor's performance is instantaneous. Applause, bravos, boos, laughter, tears, coughs, yawns, or even exit from the theater are among the direct and immediate forms of feedback the performing artist can receive. Whether a smash or a bomb, loved or hated, the actor knows it as he or she performs. Most forms of labor, by contrast, are evaluated, then either rewarded or punished some time after performance of the task. Gratification is delayed. The ability to tolerate delayed gratification is required in most jobs; not so for performers. In this sense they are more like children than mature adults. Indeed, actors pursue the emotional freedom of childhood. Swoozie Kurtz, a Broadway actress, said in an interview, "You just have to be not afraid to make a fool of yourself. Acting is like recovering childhood" (Nemy, 1986).

Audience as Source of Emotional Nourishment. Unlike the musician, who has an instrument to play, the actor's instrument is the self. Hence, that which the audience evaluates is a close reflection of his or her inner being; actors at work are both exposed and vulnerable. The audience, with whom the actor becomes immediately intimate once on stage, reacts to work of the heart. Indeed, it is said that to learn one's role is to know it "by heart." The performer-audience relationship is an affective one, and to receive applause and good notices is, for actors, to be loved.

Even though the actor's relationship with the audience is critical, the audience is not part of the organization to which an actor belongs; members of the audience are customers. For many actors in performance, recognition is more important than money as reward, so their extraorganizational relationship with the audience is more salient than their intraorganizational contacts. This is especially true in quasi-voluntary organizations like the CTC.

Externally Imposed Structure. An actor's behavior in a role is enormously constrained. He or she is told what to wear, where to move, how to move, what to say, how to say it, and what to feel (or, more precisely, what to seem to feel). Although the performer has some latitude in determining how to play a part, most actions are directed. Such constraints would create discomfort for most people, who tend to prefer more rather than less on-the-job autonomy; it typically is not a major problem for actors.

Evidence from the two casts I studied, for example, suggests that structure and direction are not merely tolerated—they are actively sought. Sally and Joe provided contrasting ways of dealing with this issue, she being laissez-faire and declining to provide structure, he being insistently directive and structuring. Nearly all cast members commented that Joe's style was more appropriate for the task of putting on a play, more what they needed.

Whereas for conventional work teams participation in decision making can be valuable and appropriate, the opposite may be true for groups of performers. Actor-director Dennis Hopper noted, "The director's the director; what he says, the actor better do. [As actor] you don't come to direct, that's not your business. . . . It took me a while to learn that" (Turan, 1983). The norm in theater is institutionalized: the director controls, the cast executes.

Evaluation: Preparation, Rehearsal, and Performance

The life cycle of theater casts is bisected at the first performance in front of an audience. The rehearsal phase is analogous to the gestation period of a fetus; the first presentation is akin to the show's birth. From the moment of conception to the time of the first curtain, the show exists in a protected environment. Outsiders are kept outside, and for a good reason.

Social psychologists have found that the presence of an audience, especially an evaluative audience, increases the likelihood that a person will exhibit well-learned behaviors rather than new ones. Thus, audiences facilitate the execution of tasks that actors have already mastered, but they make it harder for actors to learn new, unfamiliar tasks (Zajonc, 1965). For this reason, it usually is a good idea for a new task to be learned in isolation, but executed in public once it *has* been learned—which is exactly what happens in the theater.

One of the first steps in producing a play is for cast members to master their parts—that is, to memorize their lines. Each actor prepares privately. Then, when the cast convenes for rehearsals, the other cast members form an audience for each member. Assuming that each person has mastered his or her lines, this audience of colleagues should facilitate rather than impair performance. But at this point, the task changes: it is no longer a matter of individuals learning their lines; it is now the group as a whole learning how to execute the ensemble performance. Appropriately, there is no audience present while this group-level learning takes place. Only when the play is ready—when the group has mastered it—is it performed for an audience.

Thus, the typical arrangement for the creation and execution of theater productions makes a great deal of sense given what is known about audience effects. This perspective also helps explain why my presence during rehearsals disturbed the CTC casts and why they tried to pull me in and get me to participate in their work. Even though I tried hard to remain objective by not offering commentary, or even a smile if I could help it, I clearly was an outsider with the potential to evaluate how they were doing. Because they were still learning the group task at the time, my presence as an audience of one increased the difficulty of their work. On the other hand, they hardly noticed me at all once the casts entered the performance phase. Then, my role was fully appropriate: I was one member of an audience for whom the cast was performing (not rehearsing) a well-learned play.

Group Dynamics

In theater, fantasy prevails. By creating contrivances of emotional reality, plays allow audiences an opportunity to see their own inner lives, to view the lives of others, and, in the best outcome, to learn about themselves by comparison and introspection. As specialized work groups, then, groups of performing artists serve society by revealing the unbridled world of emotions within the protected confines of the stage. Audiences confront, and thereby better understand, their collective emotional life through theater.

The theory of group dynamics developed by Bion (1961) sheds light on how groups of performing artists play out fantasy themes. In brief, Bion posited that two parallel streams of activity go on in all groups. One consists of *work group activities* concerned with accomplishing the task at hand. The other stream consists of *basic assumption group activities,* which unfold without members taking much cognizance of time or of their "real" task. An example of a basic assumption group activity is one in which members behave as if their purpose were to manage the group's dependency on an authority figure; other basic assumptions involve so-called pairing activities and fight-versus-flight stances vis-a-vis threatening or anxiety-arousing objects.

Two concepts in Bion's scheme have special relevance to understanding groups of performing artists. The first concept, *valency,* refers to the capacity of individuals for "instantaneous involuntary combination . . . with another for sharing and acting on a basic assumption" (p. 153). Bion argues that group members with high valencies, such as actors, tend to be resistant to work group (task) activity. Groups of performing artists, then, are likely to be engrossed in basic assumption activities more than are other task-performing teams. Although the emotional bonds between members may be no stronger than in other kinds of work teams, overt expression of affection or dislike is much more common among actors.

The second concept, the *specialized work group,* ascribes to certain groups in society (such as the church or the army) a special purpose: the neutralization of particular basic assumption group functions—for example, dependency for the church, fight-flight for the army. The function of specialized groups is to prevent "obstruction of the work group function of the main group" (p. 157). Groups of performing artists, viewed as specialized work groups, may serve the main group (society) by coping with the basic assumption of flight, or escape, from the irrational and tumultuous world of emotions.

In the typical cast, then, one would expect to find considerable basic assumption functioning. The CTC casts illustrate this. For instance, awareness of time was greatly lacking. Never did all group members arrive on time to a rehearsal. (Paradoxically, good timing is essential for successful performance.) There were frequent references to the personal—that is, emotional, sexual, and financial—lives of group members during rehearsals and around performances. Various amorous adventures were described, interpreted, and recounted again in the context of other tales. Although such behavior rarely was germane to the task at hand, it often consumed more time than did the work itself. The performance process that a cast's director has to manage is like a seething caldron compared to the relatively tranquil emotional existence of other kinds of work teams.

These phenomena, and the other special features of casts that I have discussed in this chapter, pose a considerable challenge to theatrical directors. As we have seen, directors are the formal leaders of teams whose members have high valencies and whose function is to bring fantasy to reality. Thus, directors must be tender; they have in their hands cast members' raw emotions. They also must be strong, because the work is real work and because cast members need and seek structure and clear direction. The director must constantly manage the boundary between reality and fantasy, and, as we have seen in the casts of the Children's Theatre Company, that is not easy to do. Ultimately, to manage a theatrical cast is to find ways to be creative in "this hall of mirrors, this endless playoff between performance and reality [which] has always been the situation of the artist" (Leverett, 1985).

Note

1. The names of individuals, as well as certain other details, have been changed to protect the anonymity of the participants.

15

William A. Kahn

㲜坔㲜坔㲜坔㲜坔㲜坔㲜坔㲜坔㲜坔㲜坔㲜坔

University Athletic Teams[1]

The pitcher walked the batter, putting runners on first and third. He was noticeably agitated, nervously glancing over his shoulder at the head coach and at the sideline where another pitcher was warming up. The next batter hit a sharp line drive, caught by the second baseman, to end the inning. Storming over to the bench, clearly upset, the pitcher swore. Then, angrily, "How the hell can I pitch when all I'm thinking about is getting canned as soon as I get out there?"

This chapter is about two university athletic teams—an undergraduate varsity baseball team and a graduate intramural basketball team. Sports teams are essentially performing groups, in the theatrical sense, whose performances depend simultaneously on aspects of competition and cooperation within and between teams. Compared to professional athletic teams, university teams are unique for their emphasis on athletic performance as entertainment for the players themselves as well as (or rather than) for outside consumers. The dimensions of performance, simultaneous competition and cooperation, and the personal benefits of performance are integral to our understanding of such teams. They have analogs with nonperforming groups as well.

The Teams

The teams operated out of a private university's athletic department, which provided material resources, game schedules, and, for the undergraduate baseball team, management and transportation. The basketball team played in a league of graduate and professional students, loosely organized by the athletic department's intramural office. Besides scheduling games, the office provided gymnasium space and referees. Each team in the league was self-managing, handling its own member selection, performance strategies, and playing-time distribution throughout the regular season and play-offs. To join the league merely required getting players from an academic department together and turning their names in as a team.

The basketball team was relatively successful. It was undefeated during the season, although it lost unexpectedly in the play-offs to a team that it had previously defeated. The team's win-loss record was acceptable to those for whom it mattered—the players themselves—even though the final loss was (literally and figuratively) upsetting. Team members got along reasonably well and chose to play together again the following season (in which they did win the play-offs). The players found their experiences on the team personally satisfying and looked forward to playing each week. Their main reported frustration was the limited amount of playing time they could arrange.

The baseball team was more formally organized, managed by a coaching staff the athletic department hired. Players were talented undergraduates selected by the coaches. The baseball team's life cycle spanned a single academic semester and included practice games, the regular game schedule, and the league play-offs.

The baseball team was relatively ineffective. It lost over half of its regular season games and was soundly defeated in the first round of the league play-offs. The season was frustrating to the coaches, who made their feelings known verbally and with extra practice sessions, and to the players themselves, who grew increasingly despondent as their losing season progressed. The frustrations the team members experienced undermined their ability to work together. The pain of losing fueled debilitating anger and resentment, and both coaches and players increasingly expressed these feelings to one another as the season wore on. Individual players reported considerable dissatisfaction with their experiences as team members; the losses, coupled with their relatively poor relations with the coaching staff, did little to bolster their feelings of self-worth and achievement.

How can we understand what happened to these teams? The question seems simple and the answer straightforward given what we generally know about athletics: more skilled, better coached, more motivated athletes defeat those who are less so. Upsets occur, of course, but such is the nature of the game: balls spin and bounce crazily, and luck does not always favor those who are skillful enough to create or recognize it. So the wins and losses of the two teams should be explainable by comparing the skills, coaching, and efforts of members to those of their opponents, leaving some room for chance and circumstance. Yet these commonly used explanations may in fact be merely the symptoms of the teams' levels of effectiveness, not the underlying causes. We will have to probe deeper to learn why some teams are more skilled and better coached and why they work harder than others. That is what this chapter is about.

In analyzing these teams, it is important to keep in mind their special nature. Although performing teams, they have only token audiences (friends and die-hard sports fans), in contrast with theater casts and professional athletic teams. They operate in competitive environments, yet there are few tangible rewards of success; it is playing the game itself that attracts these members and sustains players' interest. Things operate differently for these types of teams, even compared to other athletic and performing teams.

Intramural Basketball Team. The basketball team consisted of nine graduate students and junior faculty members from the same academic department. Four had played varsity basketball as undergraduates; two also had been subsequently involved in coaching high school players. Members were generally quite skilled relative to the league in which they played, and the team had both physically larger individuals who played the center and forward positions and the smaller, quicker guards who had the running, dribbling, and passing skills necessary to guide the team's offense. Although, on average, team members were larger and more experienced than most of their opponents, there were also some players who did not have much knowledge, skill, or experience in organized basketball. They, like the others, were on the team to exercise, have fun, play the game, and win games. Such were the rewards for the basketball players. Playing well—and its correlate, winning—increased the joys of playing; it meant greater self-esteem, pride in the team, and a sense of achievement that translated into fun. They experienced these rewards within the private sphere of the team rather than in the public sphere of any audience or encompassing organization.

A junior faculty member who had a great deal of experience and skill in playing and coaching basketball organized the team. He took the lead in recruiting players, organizing a few preseason practices, and keeping members informed about the team's schedule. He became, in essence, the team's player-coach. His most important act, in consultation with some of the better players on the team, was to devise an offensive system. That system was based on the simple assumption that the better players should have the most scoring opportunities. Players were assigned roles within recurring patterns of movement: while one player brought the ball downcourt and passed, another player waited for the chance to shoot from a particular area of the court. The shooters were to shoot the basketball, and the other players were to set up those shots. During the games, when the player-coach was on the court, the players looked to him to run the offensive system. When he was on the sideline, the team looked to the most skilled players on the court for that leadership. When on the sidelines during play, the more experienced players made suggestions that typically reinforced the established system.

The offensive system worked partly on the premise that the better players had more playing time. Initially this premise was unspoken, but the team had an explicit discussion early in the season after one of the less skilled players expressed his dissatisfaction with his amount of playing time. Team members agreed that it was important to them to win their games, and that, in order to do so, the better players would have more playing time—particularly in the case of close games, when the team was not clearly winning or losing. Initially, the player-coach made all the substitutions. Midway through the season, he tired of that responsibility, and members of the team managed their own playing time.

The players implemented the offensive system in a less-than-ideal fashion during play. They did what they could, based on their experience and abilities, but the system was relatively complex; it was intended for a somewhat more advanced level of play. In their attempts to adhere to the offensive strategies of the system, the players focused on the mechanics of their individual assignments: "I have to get to that spot on the court and be ready to pass to that player over at that spot." And their specific foci meant that they did not always fully grasp the overall strategy of moving the ball around quickly enough to create openings for the better shooters.

The unintended result was that the system actively discouraged players from acting and reacting, unthinkingly, according to the instincts of the moment. Basketball is a fluid, dynamic game, characterized by constant motion as players create quick patterns of movement and stillness. It is an opportunistic game, like fencing, and it is played best by those who are able to create, perceive, lunge for, and defend open spaces. Such opportunities involve the coordination of five people per team—a complexity that, at some moments, enhances the grace and speed of the dance and, at other moments, encourages only stifled movement. For the basketball team, it was too often the latter.

More specifically, the system encouraged players to perform circumscribed movements and play specific, limited roles in ways that undermined individual and team creativity. The tendency was to bring the ball downcourt, set up a play for the best player on the court at the time, and wait for him to do something. That player was given free rein—but at the expense of the other players' individual expressions and imaginations. Yet it worked—at least during the regular season. The skill and height advantages of the team over its competitors were sufficient for the team to score points and move through the season undefeated. Many games were close, however, for three reasons. First, the players sometimes were not sure whom to turn to on the court when they had the ball and wanted to get it to the right person for a score. Second, when the better players were not shooting well, the team was unclear about how to compensate by sharing offensive responsibilities.[2] Finally, the fragmentation that the offensive system encouraged acted to undermine the defensive zone system. The zone system depended on the equal participation and coordination of all players (who were responsible for defending separate yet interconnected zones of the court). The players had difficulty making the transitions from the implicit hierarchy governing the offensive system to the more democratic interdependence of the defensive system. The team won its games on the strength of its offensive play—not its defensive play.

Varsity Baseball Team. The varsity baseball team consisted of approximately twenty-five undergraduate men, ranging from freshmen to seniors, rookies to veterans. Varsity baseball players in high school, they chose to attend a university that provided neither athletic scholarships nor a springboard to professional athletic careers. The players were, on average, about as skilled, knowledgeable, and physically gifted as their counterparts at opposing schools. Yet the team lacked the superstars that had propelled it to the league championship the previous season—including a pitcher who went on to achieve success in the major leagues. The team's mixture of rookies and veterans was balanced, and there were an appropriate number of members able to play the various positions.

The baseball players sought many of the same rewards as the intramural basketball players. They played for the joy of the game and the chance to express themselves physically. They played for the exercise and the fun of playing with others. Additionally, there was an external component to the rewards that the basketball players did not have. Being a varsity baseball player brought some measure of status within the undergraduate community and an audience at the games, as well as the occasional tangible reward such as a preseason trip to a warm climate. Winning brought external rewards as well, such as a league championship that meant trophies and a trip to the national championships.

The most salient reward for players, however, the one

that captured most of their attention throughout the season, was playing time. The team's coaching staff instituted a reward system that operated using the currency of minutes that players were allowed to perform in games. It was a merit system—one in which accounts and ledgers constantly were updated. Players who performed well were granted playing time, while those who had not recently "produced" (as defined by the coach) were quickly replaced in the lineup, often in the middle of a game.

The episode I recounted at the beginning of this chapter was not a unique incident, nor was it limited to the team's pitcher. The coach benched outfielders for missing fly balls and infielders for bobbling grounders. When he pulled players from the game, he often gave them no explanation. At times, he greeted them only with derision or sarcasm as they entered the dugout. The consequence of all this was that individual players often played entire games in a state of anxiety; on occasion, this anxiety spread throughout the team as all members waited to see who would be next to be signaled off the field. This dynamic between players and coaches, only occasionally present early in the year, became ever more pronounced as the team continued on its way to a losing season.

On organized athletic teams, short periods of unsettledness, as the coaches determine initial positions or overhaul slumping lineups, typically are followed by longer periods of relative stability. With that stability comes the opportunity for teams to jell and for players to grow accustomed to their roles and status levels on the team. On the baseball team, however, the inconsistency and unpredictability about who would play (and for how long) meant that players could never forget they were in constant competition with each other over playing time. Constantly worrying about one's production at the plate and on the field—for fear of being replaced by a teammate—limited the extent to which the players were able to relax, enjoy playing baseball, and perform up to their potentials. Team members spoke about how they were not having much fun, and they expressed their frustrations with the constant unpredictability and inconsistency that marked playing time allocations. They arrived late for practices and games, and they left early rather than linger—even after the games they won. The chatter that usually accompanies baseball performances often was noticeably absent. In its place was silence or, at times, quietly aired grievances against the coaches.

One way to understand the baseball team's losing season (aside from issues about athletic skills and abilities) is to consider the extent to which the players were too distracted by worries about being suddenly benched to fully concentrate on, or to become engaged in, their teamwork. The coach shaped the team into an aggregation of individuals, each of whom was reinforced for attending to his own performance. Members did make efforts to field the grounder and get the hit, of course, but there were signs that they were distracted from pulling together in what is at least nominally a team sport.

The signs existed at both individual and group levels. At the individual level were data about the cut-off throws: that is, the throw from an outfielder to an infielder, who subsequently decides whether he should relay the ball to the appropriate base (often home plate). As the season progressed, the outfielders increasingly ignored the cut-off men, preferring instead to hold the ball and then to try to throw it all the way to the base where they thought it should go. It was a generally less effective strategy than using the infielders, because the longer throws were slower and less accurate. One way to understand this is to recognize that the outfielders were eager to show that they, individually, were contributing to the team in ways that bypassed, literally, the actions of others. Or, perhaps, the outfielders were simply less trusting of their teammates and preferred to maintain control of the ball. Such distrust was partly a function of the way the reward system, by which playing time was given and taken away, encouraged the players to view one another more as competitors than as teammates.

At the group level were data about the effectiveness of the team as a whole. The most typical comment I heard about the team in interviews with both players and coaches was that when one aspect of the team's skills was dominating, the other was crippling. The pitching would be great and the hitting impotent, or vice versa. This comment symbolized the difficulty of working as a whole unit when the reward system was so explicitly individualistic. Players were simply too distracted to put together the different and equally necessary parts of their skills and abilities as a team. Recall as well that the intramural basketball team was able to work together in a well-defined, hierarchical offensive system but was less effective at managing the more democratic defensive system. That, too, showed how players who are rewarded for bringing only certain parts of themselves into their performances may become unable to perform as a single, whole unit.

Implications

The two university teams offer some special lessons about work teams. Athletic teams are unique among work teams because of both the athletic nature of their tasks and the primary motivations of their members—playing and winning games. They also are unique in their relative lack of the kinds of organizational supports that typically surround other work teams. These unique features suggest two factors that may be helpful in understanding the dynamics of these teams and of others like them: (1) play and playfulness, and (2) strategy and leadership.

Play and Playfulness. In studying the two university athletic teams, it became clear that any explanation of their behaviors and performances must somehow account for the inherent playfulness with which university athletes consciously or unconsciously approach their sports. It was clear that beneath the formal trappings of organized sports, the university athlete was akin to a child playing a game. This characteristic is a reflection not of emotional, intellectual, or physical immaturity, but of the simple attraction to and wonder at the playing of games—and the sheer enjoyment of doing so. Extracurricular activities occupied a special, if peripheral, place in the lives of the student athletes—the place reserved for the child's playfulness and imagination.

That playfulness was implicitly undermined, in different ways, on the two sports teams. On the basketball team, the relatively rigid offensive system, which was in many ways inappropriate to the nature of intramural athletics, stifled the freewheeling playfulness by which basketball players create ways to score points. On the baseball team, the harshness of the system by which the coach allocated playing time undermined the playfulness by which student athletes create ways of working together toward shared goals. The system was inappropriate to the nature and values of scholastic athletics. On both teams, then, there was some sort of system that did not connect psychologically with the wellspring of playfulness that attracted the athletes to the sport in the first place and that maintained their engagement with it.

Part of the data for this interpretation comes from observing expressions of playfulness outside of the game itself. On the basketball team, for example, the playfulness suppressed within the offensive system was expressed through the instructions, exhortations, cheers, and joking catcalls with which the sidelined team members followed the players up and down the court. The "bench jockeying" was funny and creative, playful relief from the intensity of the games themselves. Moreover, players sought each other out during the weeks between games to swap stories, jokes, and strategy—activities that helped minimize the differences between the roles they had during games. The vocal harmonies of the "bench jockeying" and off-court interactions built a sense of play and community that was often lacking on the court.

A great deal of comradeship and humor also characterized the interactions of the baseball players throughout the season, particularly late in the season when the coaches were constantly juggling positions in their quixotic search for winning combinations. The players directed much of this humor at the coaching staff. Through playful (albeit often hostile) humor, players banded together against the coaches' authority and behavior—for example, by mocking the coaches' pep talks. The humor and practical jokes also helped team members deal with the anxieties that stemmed from their competition with one another for playing time and positions and with their anger at one another for the team's ineffective performance. While these expressions of playfulness were functional in some ways, there was also something counterproductive about them. The psychological energy spent acting out against the coaches' authority and avoiding member conflict was, in some respects, energy not spent in banding together players and coaches against the opposing teams.

Of course, the athletes on both teams were not simply children, and they understood that their desire to win demanded that they compromise on the image of childlike playfulness. Two types of intrinsic rewards were operating here: those of playing and those of winning. These rewards formed a combination that was tightly interwoven and difficult to disentangle; the joy of the game is often the joy of success, for so often we like that at which we excel and we excel at that which we like. Compromises on the ideal of playfulness are necessary simply for the organization they bring and, for the most part, these compromises are acceptable to the athletes themselves. They become unacceptable, it seems, when the systems of organization suppress too much of the playfulness and spontaneity that are necessary and appropriate for playing and winning games. When the management system does not fit with the imperatives of the sport and the motives of members, the sense of play and all that it brings to the game—at whatever level of competition—is undermined.

The question remains: did not all athletic teams in these leagues face the same sorts of dilemmas and derive the same sorts of solutions? Yes and no. Yes, they faced the same dilemmas, but no, they did not all solve them in the same ways. Other teams in the basketball league, for example, managed to create structures flexible enough to satisfy the need to be organized without building in excessive rigidity. The team that won the play-offs, for example, had a few set plays, but often changed them midstream to use the better players as decoys and let whoever had the ball freelance his way to the basket. In the baseball league, other coaches found other ways to allocate playing time and motivate players. These included setting a starting lineup and then staying with it, making alterations only for strategic reasons (rather than to punish an individual who made an error), and relying far more heavily on positive than negative reinforcement of player and team performance.

Leadership and Strategy. A key function of leadership on an athletic team is to set game and season strategy. Those who call the plays are, in fact, the team leaders—whether officially designated as such or not. On the basketball team, the player-coach was the leader largely because of the offensive system he created. This individual also tended to lead the team in real time when he was on the court, helping shape the implementation of his offensive system in response to immediate circumstances. Yet when he was not playing (and occasionally even when he was), both the offensive and the defensive systems were run by anyone with enough confidence to call a play and help set it into motion. Typically, the better players did this, but anyone—particularly if he had the basketball—could initiate or redirect the process at any time. The team had a number of different leaders throughout the season, based simply on who was playing well and guiding the flow of the team's movements at the time.

On the baseball team, the coach, not the team, specified the strategies—which had different consequences for team leadership. The coaching staff directly controlled the offense: bunts, base stealing, hit-and-run plays, sacrifice flies, and even whether hitters swung at certain pitches were signaled by the coaches on the sidelines. The coaches also controlled the defense, partly through signals (for example, to purposely walk opposing batters) but primarily through the installation, by repeated practice, of certain plays to be performed in certain situations (such as double plays, cut-off throws, and pitch outs). The coaches had all the authority on the team, and by using that authority to dictate game strategy, they had all the leadership as well. The players on the field could demonstrate leadership only by showing character through hustling and spiritedness, or by rebelling against the authority of the coaches—for example, by clowning. They had little opportunity to influence game strategies, which are the currency of athletic leadership.[3]

The extent to which players had control over their plays

dictated the informal leadership that emerged on the teams. When possible, informal leadership emerged in the processes of implementing performance strategies. On the basketball team, leaders were those players who controlled the flow of the team up and down the court. On the baseball team, where there was little room for designing and implementing performance strategies, informal leadership emerged in setting the tone by which the team responded, verbally and physically, to the authority of the coaches and their systems. Different informal leaders emerged, depending on the psychological needs of the team. Some players led in acting out anger against the coaches, whether verbally (for example, through cutting humor) or behaviorally (for example, by sluggishness); others led by fostering commitment to and care about the team's performance. On both teams, the way game strategies were handled set the stage upon which informal leadership emerged. Because strategic leadership provided both opportunities for and constraints upon the emergence and expression of informal leadership, it is an important factor in understanding the differences in how the two teams operated.

Conclusion

Neither the basketball team nor the baseball team operated within the kind of rich and structured organizational context that characterizes most teams discussed in this book. Compared to the professional hockey team (see Chapter Sixteen), for example, the college teams had relatively few organizational structures and systems to support, constrain, or shape what transpired. The relative absence of an organizational context magnifies the importance of the two factors discussed above: play and leadership. It is clear from the two teams I have analyzed that play is a great motivator for university athletes (at least those in a school whose athletic program is decidedly amateur rather than pseudoprofessional). There are no real substitutes (such as financial or career rewards) for the intrinsic enjoyment of playing the games themselves. Even winning the league championship pales in comparison to the financial rewards and career possibilities that come from winning in professional sports.

The importance of the second factor, leadership, is also magnified by the absence of a strong organizational context. In university sports, team leaders—whether the conveners of intramural basketball teams or the coaches of varsity baseball teams—must provide virtually all the functions that would otherwise be handled by other aspects of their contexts (for example, by people with specialized roles or special authority). Leadership becomes more important in such informal settings. Perhaps this is one way to understand the relative success, and lack of it, of the basketball and baseball teams, respectively. The basketball team's player-coach offered guidance, support, and organization in ways that satisfied the minimal (though important) needs of the team for organizing. The baseball team's coach, on the other hand, used his authority in ways that undermined the players' abilities to perform—individually and as a team. In both cases, the absence of elaborate organizational contexts magnified these effects.

The general form of management on the two teams also is noteworthy. The basketball team was self-managing; the baseball team was manager-led. Is there a connection between the management structure and a team's success? That is, did the basketball team perform more effectively than the baseball team simply on the strength of its self-management structure? On the most obvious level, the answer is no. We can imagine a truly bad self-managing basketball team, underbounded to a fault, that encourages poor spirit, no leadership, spotty attendance, and chaos on the court. We can also imagine a superbly effective manager-led baseball team, headed by a coach who develops and maintains appropriate team boundaries, provides stability, builds individual skills and team spirit, and provides strategy-level leadership about overall goals and processes without undermining player abilities and confidence. Both self-managing and manager-led forms are viable options for sports teams, and either can succeed or fail.

In fact, a hybrid model may be required—one that has some features of both the self-managing model and the manager-led model. The basketball team's relative success was due partly to its ability to accept a system of movement designed by one of its members and to place itself under his direction. The team was self-managing but, within that frame, accepted the authority of a player-coach. The baseball team's lack of success was due partly to the players' lack of participation—their lack of voice—in designing and implementing team strategies. This team shows how difficult it can be for a team that is insistently manager-led to tap into players' creative and productive energies.

The different authority structures of the two teams did not occur by chance. It is no doubt true that the self-managing model is more likely to appear in intramural competition and that the manager-led model is more likely in intercollegiate varsity sports. However, the effectiveness of each model ultimately may depend on how open it is to incorporating features of the other form. Both teams needed acceptance of an authority who provided clear leadership and direction, and both needed to hear the voices and to release the energies of the players. While the level of attention that should be given to these imperatives surely varies across various kinds of sports and teams, the need for some measure of balance between them appears to be general.

Notes

1. I appreciate the collaboration of Jack Wood on the study of the varsity baseball team.
2. The team was upset in the play-offs because the better players were shooting poorly and the team had little idea how to compensate (either by changing their offensive plays or by working to let the other players shoot). In that game, the designated shooters continued to shoot and to miss, instead of adapting to the situation.
3. There was one clear exception. The catcher on the baseball team, as on most baseball teams, had a measure of authority. His tasks included calling the pitches that the pitcher would throw, helping to run the defense (for example, by calling out the cut-offs that should occur), and positioning the defense in special strategic situations. His authority was subject to that of the coaching staff, whose calls for certain defensive strategies and decisions about pitching set the stage for the catcher's leadership.

16

Jack Denfeld Wood

New Haven Nighthawks[1]

The National Hockey League has a rule that freezes team rosters on the second Tuesday of March, a few weeks before the play-offs. After that date, teams are prohibited from trading players or putting them on waivers, and there is a massive reshuffling of players as that deadline approaches. For a minor league team, it is chaos. Demoted major league players appear like apparitions in the doorways of minor league locker rooms. A few minor league players pack their bags and head up to the big time. A few pack their bags and head down to a lower league. Some pack their bags and head home. Most of the rest wait in fear. The tension is terrific. One regular player told us that he finally went to the coach during the roster freeze because his roommate, a solid contributor to the team, had been climbing the walls night after night out of fear that he would be sent home. The coach tried to reassure the anxious player, we were told, but was unable to guarantee him a place on the team because those decisions were completely in the hands of the parent organization.

A few weeks later, we attended a players' meeting. The meeting was after practice one quiet afternoon in the Coliseum's VIP bar shortly after the team had made the play-offs. The informal rule for these players' meetings was that the coach could attend as an observer only. He was there, watching, but the players did all of the talking.

The meeting turned into a series of little pep talks. The players took turns. "Come on guys, we can do it!" That sort of thing. It sounded like a high school locker room between periods. Except it did not ring true. The words were right but the passion and commitment were not there. Even players who had spoken contemptuously to us in private about playing on the Nighthawks took turns trying to be inspirational. But they were clearly going through the motions, appearing to be good team members. This was a team in trouble. What had gone wrong?

The New Haven Nighthawks play in the American Hockey League (AHL), a middle-tier league sandwiched between the premier National Hockey League (NHL) and the third-tier International Hockey League (IHL). At the time of our study, the Nighthawks were the AHL farm team for the major league Los Angeles Kings. Nighthawks players were drawn from the Kings' farm system.

At home, the Nighthawks play in the multimillion-dollar steel and concrete New Haven Coliseum. The games have a festive carnival atmosphere. Vendors hawk programs, pennants, peanuts, and pop. Fans mill excitedly around the beer and hot dog stands. A half hour prior to game time, the teams take the ice for warm-ups. The Nighthawks have never packed them in— a few thousand on a good night—but like most hockey fans, New Haven's are enthusiastic. Following a short post–warm-up locker room pep talk, the skaters reappear for the first period, to the ritual cheers and boos of the crowd.

Ice hockey is a heady, rough, and exciting game played with steel and wood and rubber on an inch-thick sheet of ice. Opposing teams battle nearly continuously for three twenty-minute periods, withdrawing briefly to rest between each period as the ice is shaved and a fresh skim coat of water is laid. Ice hockey penalties have names like *slashing, high sticking, charging,* and *fighting.* Drawing blood from an opponent increases a two-minute minor penalty to a five-minute major penalty. The crowd loves it. For the athletes, to play in the professional ranks is to achieve a lifelong goal.

The Nighthawks had an uneven season the year we studied them. They were near the top of the league early in the season, near the middle by mid-season, in the play-offs—but just barely—at season's end, and eliminated in the first play-off round. Many factors, of course, contribute to a team's degree of success. Spectators might assume that a team's record depends on the talent of the players and coach, but that is not the whole story. Talent is a necessary but insufficient guarantee of success. We found that player ability in the AHL, as in many other professional athletic leagues, was fairly evenly distributed—the Nighthawks had their fair share of strong players. And we found the coach, a former NHL player, to be knowledgeable and well respected by the players. A deficit in talent could not account for the team's mediocre finish. We had to look elsewhere for an explanation.

Who Were the Nighthawks?

To the audience, the team identity of the Nighthawks seemed obvious. The players all wore the same flashy red, white, and blue team uniforms. Fans and press conspired to see the Nighthawks as a tightly bounded team with a clearly defined identity. To an extent, so did management and the players. A peek behind the curtain, however, tells the story of a team different than the one performing at game time in the Coliseum.

The Nighthawks' season began in September with a two-week training camp, which was actually a two-week tryout. The players hated it. They were watched closely and evaluated constantly. It was make-or-break time for them. During the tryouts, coaches from the various levels of the Los Angeles system got together and assigned players to their respective home teams. Then the regular season—a grueling stretch that lasted until May—got under way.

Throughout the season, players came and went. The roster changed so frequently that the game programs could not keep up. Some players were moving up to the NHL in Los Angeles, some were moving down to the IHL farm team in Saginaw, and some were returning home to Mom and Pop in Canada.

Players never knew from day to day who would occupy the adjacent locker or who would disappear. This was especially true as the roster freeze approached, exacerbating the already high turnover typical of minor league teams. With a roster of twenty players, it is not uncommon for a minor league team such as New Haven to have over 100 personnel changes during a season. The tension on the team was thick and oppressive, though different subgroups of players—the promising rookies, the regular AHL journeymen, and the NHL veterans—handled the turnover in different ways.

The rookies worked the hardest and seemed least dispirited by the turmoil. Most felt that they were on their way up to the NHL and that it was only a matter of time and hard work until they made it. The AHL journeymen had a rougher time. These were players who hoped that they might play regularly in the NHL but suspected that they would wind up being minor league players for the duration of their careers. They felt as though they were standing still as they watched the talented rookies arrive, gain experience, and move up to the big league. They saw themselves being replaced by players sent down to New Haven from Los Angeles. And they feared, above all, being sent home.

Players sent down from the Kings had their own problems. They often were sulky with their new coach, sat apart from the other players, and performed lackadaisically on the ice. Two recent arrivals bitterly complained about the difference between playing in the "big apple" NHL and the "crab apple" AHL. The difference? It could not have been the money, because former NHL players generally had a very large and guaranteed salary regardless of the league in which they played. Perhaps it was the change in status, the demotion to the minor league, that took its toll on the motivation of the former NHL players and, in turn, on the effectiveness of the team as a whole.

As the play-offs approached, the New Haven Nighthawks looked like a team in trouble. Clearly, part of the problem lay with the structural rules, such as the roster freeze, that adversely affected the team's performance. Yet the other AHL teams played by the same rules, and some of them managed to do better than New Haven. Our research suggests that much of the problem for the Nighthawks was the result of two interrelated factors: the nature of professional ice hockey in general and the organizational context of the New Haven team in particular.

Professional Sports as Entertainment

Professional sports is big business—and the business is entertainment. Appropriately enough, the majority of the athletes on the Nighthawks were Canadian citizens who were playing in the United States on entertainer's visas. The Nighthawks resembled an itinerant troupe, and violent competition was their performance. Both individual athletes and the team as a whole performed for two sets of audiences, however. On the one hand was the "horizontal" (external and public) audience, consisting of opponents, the fans, the press, and local business sponsors. On the other hand was the "vertical" (internal and organizational) audience, consisting of teammates, the coach, local management (New Haven), and the parent organization (Los Angeles).

Figure 1 depicts the major relationships that the team and the players encountered. The two audiences, horizontal and vertical, pulled the team in different directions, with predictably disastrous consequences on team effectiveness.

The Horizontal Relationship: The External, Public Audiences. The work of performing on a professional ice hockey team has two facets—play and recognition. Hockey players, like professional musicians, dancers, and actors, develop an intimate relationship with their art when they are very young. "Play" is an integral part of both the vocabulary and the reality of performers. The primary motivation for little boys who play ice hockey is probably intrinsic enjoyment: the feeling of speed and freedom when skating, the exhilaration of playing outdoors, and the pleasure of strenuous physical competition. The budding relationship of the peewee hockey player with his sport entails an element of play, and play never completely leaves his relationship with the game of hockey—even as he turns professional. This part of playing the game, this part of the performance, is

Figure 1. Vertical and Horizontal Contexts of a Performing Team:
Caught in the Middle.

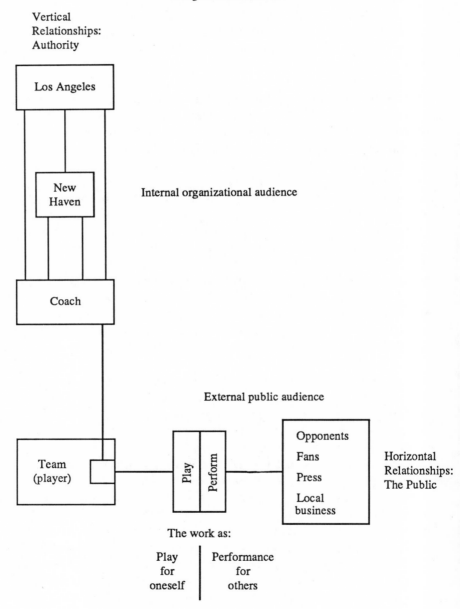

for the player himself: it's simply fun. As his career progresses, however, rewards become increasingly extrinsic as the player becomes ever more influenced by recognition and, finally, by money. Somewhere on the path between the pond and the coliseum something besides innocence is lost. The Nighthawks were part of a system in which one could see that loss taking place.

Recognition from the public—including opponents, fans, the press, and local business sponsors—was immediate and essential. But if gratification was immediate, it was also tenuous. The Nighthawks players skated on the edge of their self-image. The athletes were acutely aware of their opponents. They knew what provinces other players came from, how they played, and whether they had yet been in the NHL. They also knew that their opponents were professionals, whereas the fans, the press, and the local sponsors were not. You could not fake it with your opponents, and they would not be impressed by your uniform. The respect of opposing players was very important to the athletes we studied. Somewhat less important to the players were fans, press, and local businesses.

Nighthawks fans had their favorite players and were loyal when the team was winning but otherwise were fickle. They were also anonymous to the players. It was a one-sided relationship. Fans, complete strangers, would pass players on the street and address them by their first names. The players would not have a clue about who was speaking to them. From the players' perspective, it was a simultaneously gratifying and unsettling relationship. The relationship between players and press was different. It was a more mutual, personal relationship. Press and players usually knew one another, at least by name. Nighthawks players were highly sensitive to press accounts and frequently recounted to one another what sportswriters had written about the team. Finally, a few local businesses established even more reciprocal relationships with the team and its members. Some local businesspeople (such as car dealers or restaurateurs) developed long-term relationships both with the front office (through advertising) and with the players (through public relations promotions, or even part-time seasonal or full-time off-season jobs). These relationships tended to bind the players to the local community and thus to the team. They had a centripetal effect, but they were not enough to hold the team together. Centrifugal influences built into the organizational system, such as promotion into the NHL, tended to pull the team apart. We examine them next.

The Vertical Relationship: The Internal, Organizational Audiences. The structure of authority on this team included three distinct foci: the local ownership and management, the distant ownership and management, and the coach.

Local ownership and management was transient. In the public's view, the Nighthawks had been in New Haven for over a decade. But New Haven actually had been a revolving door for franchises as well as for players. The Nighthawks' parent organization nominally was the Los Angeles Kings. Los Angeles employed and paid most of the players and the coach. But a local New Haven businessman legally owned the team and provided the local management. Known as the "front office" in trade lingo, local management included the manager, trainers, secretaries, publicists, equipment, and so on. In addition, the local owner employed and paid a handful of players through what is known as a *hometown contract.*

Distant ownership and managent had also been transient. During the previous season, an arrangement similar to that between New Haven and Los Angeles had existed between the local Nighthawks' management and a different parent organization, the New York Rangers. That year, New Haven had been a Ranger farm team. The year following our study, Los Angeles bought out the local ownership and maintained the team for two years as sole owner. The year after that, Los Angeles and New York split the expenses of the team, with the head coach coming from the Los Angeles system and the assistant coach from the New York system. The Nighthawks still wear the same uniforms—the ones they have worn for almost two decades. But behind the scenes they have had an identity problem.

With each management change, the roster of players changed virtually completely. Behind the team front was a drama of individual mobility—a drama that had an adverse effect on team cohesion. The team not only had to manage the usual season-long loss of players and the pre–play-off player freeze through which all AHL teams suffer, but it also had to manage the on-again, off-again relationship with revolving parent organizations.

Basically, the New Haven and Los Angeles organizations had different interests, and the team was caught in the middle. Both wanted the team to win and draw large crowds, of course. But New Haven *needed* the Nighthawks to win, draw crowds, make money, and survive. Los Angeles did not. For Los Angeles the Nighthawks were a pool of talent from which they could draw promising players and to which they could deposit their wounded and their ineffectual. What was good for Los Angeles (the development of talent) was bad for New Haven (the loss of the best players and the arrival of injured or highly paid and disgruntled former NHL players).

Because hockey is a team sport, teammates must cooperate to win. But *professional* hockey is largely an individual enterprise. From a player's perspective, the primary competition may be with teammates for promotion off the team and into the NHL. That is a bit of a paradox, but it is built into the system. Players were contracted individually. Large differences in salary existed—$20,000 to over $250,000. Players were promoted or demoted individually. In a sense, the team functioned as a holding area for individuals on their very lonely journeys up or down. Player motivation was largely isolated from team outcomes since it was the player's performance as an individual that counted most. Whether the team won or lost was largely irrelevant for a player's career. A player could excel and be sent up; he could play in a mediocre way and remain on the team; he could be demoted to Saginaw; or he could be sent home. Internal team competition and cooperation thus assumed a fascinating and complex form.

For the Nighthawks, a clear line of authority ran down from Los Angeles to the coach. A second, more obscure line ran from the local owner through the front office to the coach. The coach sat in an unenviable spot. He, too, was caught in the middle. In addition to dealing with the usual individual differences on a team, the coach had the chronic problem of contending with subgroups of players in transition: those on their way up (usually the young and eager), those going nowhere (usually solid minor league talent), and those on their way down (the bitter, sulky former NHL players). He needed to win to keep his job. But the better he developed the talent at his command, the quicker they were promoted off the team, and the less likely he was to win. That is another built-in paradox. The better the coach does, the worse things get—unless *he* can get promoted into the NHL.[2]

Not surprisingly, the relationship between the coach and the players was complex. Recall the description of the player meeting—where the coach merely observed. He was seated off to the side of the room, and the players had unconsciously formed a loose semicircle to give the coach an unobstructed view of their meeting. They clearly were putting on a show, and this performance was for the coach. But there was something about the pattern of the discussion that seemed oddly familiar to me. Then it hit me. It had not changed. The basic dynamics were the same. The player-coach relationship on this professional team, composed of men in their twenties and thirties, had the same character as the relationships that many of us experienced with our college, high school, and peewee coaches. In some ways, apparently, the player-coach relationship never changes, never matures, even in as rugged and masculine a game as ice hockey.

Hockey is steeped in a culture of masculine competition and violence. At the professional level, the men play for keeps. So it was surprising to see men in their twenties and thirties relating to their coach like grammar school boys to a teacher or like competitive siblings to a distant and austere parent. But that is what we saw—in the players' meeting, in the locker room, in casual conversation, and on the ice. For his part, the coach was locked into the complex role of parent and disciplinarian.

The parent-child dynamic between the athletes and the coach may have been rooted in each player's childhood. Professional hockey players begin to play the sport when they are very young children, at a time when dependency characterizes relationships with adults. The authority dynamic of this relationship may have begun in the childhood relationship between boy and coach and continued essentially unchanged through adolescence and into adulthood. The dependency relationship between professional Nighthawks players and their coach simply may have reflected a fundamental developmental pattern—a pattern perhaps found in other professions where skill acquisition follows a similar process.

Stability and Rhythm. Historically, the best professional hockey teams have had stable and talented three-man lines and defensive pairs, such as the Boston Bruins' famous "Kraut Line" of Milt Schmidt, Eddie Bauer, and Woody Dumart in the late 1940s. Members of these famous combinations played together for years and sometimes even for decades. They knew intimately each other's moves, idiosyncrasies, strengths, and weaknesses. Partly due to AHL vulnerability to NHL demands, and partly due to life within the Los Angeles–New Haven system, the Nighthawks coach never kept players together on the same line long enough for them to become comfortable with each other's play. Indeed, the coach switched players around so often on the Nighthawks that no player knew for sure who would be on his line until he found himself on the ice. Different combinations were continuously tried and discarded in a vain search for a line or pair of defensemen that clicked. The right combination was never found, and instability plagued the Nighthawks for the entire season.

The rhythms of professional ice hockey, like the rhythms of other performing teams, consist of alternating periods of intense activity and rest. We saw this pattern in a number of guises: the daily pattern of a two-hour practice followed by free time; the weekly grind of practices, games, and road trips (half speed, full speed, and then boredom on the bus and in motel rooms); the yearly pattern of the job (training camp, regular season, play-offs, and a second job over the summer); and, perhaps most poignantly, the lifelong pattern of an ice hockey career that begins before a player has entered kindergarten and that ends, often involuntarily, when he is in his early thirties.

Playing professional hockey is not the glorious life that it may
have seemed to the little Canadian boy chasing his friends across
the cold black ice of a frozen, lonely, and nameless provincial
pond.

Minor league professional hockey teams are buffeted by
destabilizing and centrifugal forces. The organizational and contextual factors we have mentioned—the annual NHL player
freeze, the large turnover inherent in the farm-team system, the
complex Los Angeles–New Haven web of ownership and authority, the traditional dependency dynamic between player and
coach, the evolution of an athlete's motivation from intrinsic
physical enjoyment to extrinsic recognition and money, and the
centrality of individual (as opposed to team) rewards—all have
made divergent demands on the players and coach and have
combined to exert a destabilizing effect on the New Haven team.

Conclusion: The Coach as Pivot in an Organizational System

The Nighthawks coach occupied a pivotal position in the New
Haven system. He controlled, or attempted to control, the performance of the team in much the same way that a conductor
of a symphony or a director of a repertory theater supervises
the performances of his or her players. He attempted to medi-
ate the divergent demands placed on the team by brokering
among the players, the parent organization, the local ownership,
and the public (fans, press, and local businesses). But he was
clearly caught in the middle of an unhappy system. The Nighthawks coach could do little about New Haven's powerful and
destabilizing organizational context. He was acutely aware that
he was an employee of the Los Angeles system and that he held
his job at their sufferance.

The hands of the New Haven coach were tied by the personnel requirements of Los Angeles' NHL team, the Kings, as
well as by Los Angeles' contracts with the individual Nighthawks players in the larger organizational farm system. He had
little say over the composition of his own team. The formal reward system—at least money—was clearly in the hands of Los
Angeles. He could work within narrow limits on the motiva-

tional structure of the task, praising the players and controlling playing time, but control over larger issues like team composition and salary rested squarely with Los Angeles. The New Haven coach exemplified the classic middle-manager bind. He had exclusive responsibility with little or no authority. His decisions were local and tactical but not strategic. He had to operate, however, in the middle of a strategic system—a system in which Los Angeles called all the important shots and jealously guarded its authority. The results were predictably unfortunate for the New Haven coach. He was fired.[3]

Could a new coach do better? In subsequent years, New Haven's performance with a new coach and a new team has been equally disappointing. Given the organizational system described in this chapter, crafting changes to improve team performance presents a formidable challenge. Improving team performance would be especially difficult since it would necessitate intervention in the broader organizational context of an established professional farm-team system. Yet some remedies do come to mind. The Nighthawks organization could be streamlined, for example, to permit a single line of ownership and authority. With streamlined ownership, the parent organization, Los Angeles, might have greater legitimate interest in the success of its New Haven farm club as a local enterprise and might be more willing to provide it the support, resources, and stability needed for team effectiveness.

Another AHL team, one more successful than the Nighthawks, illustrates an even better remedy. In addition to streamlined authority, the team has an explicit dual track for players' careers. The team is built around a core of talented players who are on extended local contract. These players do not expect to move up or down. They are guaranteed a good salary and a place on the team for as long as they want to stay; they have job security if they work to become a winning team and to help the other, principally younger players develop their skills. That team wins in part because it has a core of experienced and talented players. But there are other reasons it wins.

The team is free of the disharmony engendered by the multiple authorities that characterize farm-team organizations similar to New Haven's. The team is more cohesive; it is less rent by the kind of internal competition that pervaded New Haven. And player motivation is high. The players on this team are happy because they have stability, a good job, and a community for their families. Spectator motivation is high: the fans are happy because they have a team that wins whose membership is recognizable from year to year. The coach's job is more manageable because his relationship with the parent organization is simpler, his relationship with the players can be closer, and he has the opportunity to build an integrated team over time. In short, the team as a performing unit benefits because it has a core of talent, more integrity, more stability, and higher morale. And it wins. It is hard to believe that such a farm team would not, over the long term, benefit the parent organization as well.

One must not be too optimistic, however. Organizational changes such as those described above are hostage to the primitive and largely unconscious influences within the culture of competitive sports. These cultural influences chronically and subtly hinder team performance and probably are impossible to overcome. As with other professional sports in North America, the larger culture of professional ice hockey has woven profound limitations into the fabric of the sport. The imagery in the local newspaper's report of the firing of the Nighthawks' coach powerfully illustrates the heavily unconscious weight of this culture and provides an implicit and sober warning to would-be consultants and organizational change aficionados:

Hawks: [coach's name] axed

He was primarily a thinker, a person who would spend his time dabbling with the analytic processes of running a professional hockey team. . . . He was an Ivy-covered coach in a beer-stained league. An intellect in a reactionary world. [After some modest success the first half-year he had the job], the next two years proved fatal for [the coach]. . . . He asked questions. Unfortunately, he didn't have the answers, and so he lost his job. . . . No successor will be immediately named. The Kings' organization, its phone lines and mailboxes already loaded with applications from those who smelled [the coach's] blood, will whittle the list to about two dozen candidates . . . (*New Haven Journal-Courier*, May 29, 1985).

Notes

1. Since the completion of this study, the ownership, coach, and player roster of the New Haven Nighthawks have changed completely; my observations and conclus...us are limited to the original participant organization, team, and personnel. I thank the management, coach, and players of the New Haven Nighthawks, without whose cooperation the research would not have been possible. I also thank Bill Kahn for his camaraderie and perceptiveness during the fieldwork and for his helpful comments on earlier versions of this chapter.

2. That had recently happened. Shortly before we began our research (in midseason), the previous New Haven coach had been promoted to Los Angeles. He subsequently lost his NHL job.

3. Following the 1984–85 season, the Nighthawks' coach lost his job. Two consecutive seasons without a play-off spot had done the trick. In the local sports page, the Los Angeles general manager was quoted as saying that the coach had been "a very hard-working man. . . . But we felt we needed a change and the coach is always the first to go" (*New Haven Register*, May 29, 1985).

17

Tory Butterworth
Stewart D. Friedman
William A. Kahn
Jack Denfeld Wood

꿈꿈꿈꿈꿈꿈꿈꿈꿈꿈꿈

Summary: Performing Groups

The preceding chapters offer varying portraits of groups dedicated to creative, artistic, or athletic performances. These teams conduct performances that are at once processes and products—the means for achieving ends and the ends themselves. Their tasks are inherently ephemeral, spontaneous, and unrepeatable. Their work mixes presentations to audiences with intragroup presentations. It includes elements of both work and play, thereby bringing a paradoxical flavor to group life.

Much of our synthesis revolves around the twists and turns of the notion of *performance.* In our separate chapters, we struggled to construe the teams' task performances simultaneously as work processes, as work products, and as staged entertainments. Such entanglements make these teams special. That their tasks *are* their performances clearly sets them apart from both industrial and artistic teams that produce distinct physical artifacts—a canvas, a shoe, a computer. With no canvas or paint to preserve their efforts, the means becomes the end, yielding products immediately captured by audience-consumers. The performances are plays, in both senses of the word: performing groups "play," and they do so on more or less theatrical stages.

The nature of performing groups is inherently shaped by the nature of the performing task. The people we studied played music, acted on stages, threw baseballs, and shot pucks or basketballs. They communicated with one another within their performances in the languages of those performances: musical phrases in the string quartet, stage cues in the theater, pucks passed on the hockey ice, balls thrown on the basketball floor and on the baseball diamond. Communication in such languages meant self-expression as well. Observable performances were many things at once—necessary actions directed toward explicit goals, interpersonal communications to synchronize member behavior, and the self-expressions of individuals working (playing) in concert.

At yet another level, performances were manifestations of internal group processes. The words *harmony, tempo,* and *rhythm* characterized not only the string quartet's music but also the way members ran their group. Competition between hockey players for promotion also showed up on the ice, when players chose between passing (teamwork) or shooting the puck (standing out). External performance parallels internal group process, reflecting the process-as-product nature of the performing group's task.

Rhythm and Cycles

These parallel processes were particularly salient in the rhythm of the groups' lives. Performing groups set a certain rhythm to their tasks, contending with the cyclical highs and lows of their days, seasons, and individual lives. The groups we studied varied in the length and magnitude of these cycles: in some, such as the string quartet, cycles were slower and more even, while in others, such as the professional hockey team, cycles were shorter with greater highs and lows. Each performance had its own rhythm, according to its purpose: practices and rehearsals started out low-key, gradually building in energy and tension until "opening night."

Such rhythmic variation is expressed, concretely and vividly, in performances—in the intensity and pacing of the game, in the dialogue, and in the musical phrasings. Intensity builds until released in the catharsis of performance, enabling highs in performing groups not often found in other work groups. Energy then spent, team members experience the low points of daily performance cycles, on the bus trip home or the morning after a performance. The cycle is repeated, on a larger scale, during the seasons themselves. Performing work teams build intensity throughout their seasons, husbanding energy throughout formation and rehearsal to focus on increasingly more central performance, and then they retreat to periods of inactivity until the cycle begins anew.

Performers' careers are also cyclical. Team members often begin their art or sport as children, in the energy and innocence of youth: playing, throwing, acting. They then join groups of increasingly skillful, dedicated performers and move through the ranks toward the high point of their careers. At some point, performers begin to lose their skills; they become too old to perform and finally retire. For actors or musicians, retirement can be near the ends of their lives, with the fortunate remaining active into their eighties and nineties. By contrast, the professional careers of hockey players are over when players are in their thirties. The length of these cycles is a function of the tasks performed. One can play the violin or a part on stage long after three generations of hockey players have come and gone. Members of performing groups are (often painfully) aware of these career cycles, realizing that they participate—in ways more explicitly observable than in traditional work teams—in an unforgiving progression in which the effective continuously replace the ineffective. Actors, musicians, and athletes must prove, over and over again, that they deserve their roles by passing public tests—tests whose criteria are known and observable.

Work and Play

Throughout our discussion, we have used the words *work* and *play* almost interchangeably. For performing groups, the terms are indeed virtually synonymous. Actors play parts, musicians play instruments and pieces, athletes play games. This is different, obviously, from other kinds of jobs; factory workers do not "play" assembly lines, nor do executives "play" management (although lawyers and physicians "practice" and have "practices"). The tasks of performing groups, although considered as play, are very much work. The beauty and grace of stirring performances—on musical, theatrical, and athletic stages—are products of disciplined practice and hard work, the learning of specific skills and ways of combining them that ultimately lead to creativity and spontaneity.

The domains in which such work is done, however, are those of play, and they evolve out of the child's playfulness. We assume that playfulness is for oneself, intrinsically satisfying. Work is for others, a deliberate activity that requires discipline. We work for something: money, praise, prestige. Performing groups exist at the intersection of work and play. Their members must somehow reconcile that they, as adults, are working at tasks that are closely identified with children's activities. How they do this influences both the ways they define and execute their tasks and their relations with one another, with authority figures, and with audiences.

Authorities and Audiences

Members of the performing groups we observed continuously defined and redefined the nature of their tasks in attempting to balance the seemingly contradictory demands of working at playing. On one hand, the performers had jobs to do; that is, there were expectations of, and responsibilities for, the completion of various tasks and duties, regardless of whether there were tangible compensations. For the professional performers, the expectations were great and varied—outlined in detailed contracts. For the amateur performers, there were fewer expectations, perhaps simply because of their limited commitments of time and energy.

All were in some ways subject to the control of formal authority. The child's relative freedom was replaced by the adult's responsibility and discipline. No longer could a group member decide when to wander on or off the field or stage or to simply stop one game and play another. On the other hand, actors, musicians, and athletes had opportunities to work together on tasks that could be graceful, harmonious, and sensual. They were games, those tasks, built on fantasy and imagination. Yet they also contained elements of danger; performances were subject to the thrilling risks of missteps before real and critical audiences. Performing groups were constantly living, on some level, with the tensions inherent in their work-play mandates.

Performers play for themselves, for their director or conductor or coach, and for their audiences. All these constituencies provide immediate feedback (recognition, reinforcement, or retribution) based on their own criteria for successful performances. There is considerable likelihood that members will receive contradictory feedback from these different groups—feedback that can heighten their concern about whom, exactly, they are playing for at any given moment.

In the final analysis, of course, performers play for themselves—for their own enjoyment and for their careers. Yet that enjoyment and, indeed, the progress of careers are inevitably affected by the reactions of audiences and authority figures. Public audiences are neither as knowledgeable nor as objective as are performers and their group leaders. Audiences tend to exaggerate both brilliant flourishes and glaring mistakes. They are fickle and have transient, ephemeral relationships with performers. Still, audience opinion does influence performers' own assessments of their success. And some audiences clearly matter more than others, often because they control future opportunities—or just because team members care more about what certain audiences think.

Regardless of the compositions of audiences, they remain central (if unacknowledged) to the performing groups' reason for being. This was evidenced quite powerfully by the tendency of some performing groups to place us, as researchers, into audience roles. We were an additional audience and, in some ways, were more threatening than their typical audiences. We observed our groups offstage—a time and place of safety and protection, informality, and practice. Our presence blurred the boundary between on-stage and off-stage, violating formerly private spaces and confusing the distinction between rehearsal and performance.

The groups reacted to us in different ways. The theater

company coped with an academic observer by urging him into a participant-critic role and soliciting feedback and advice. In some sense, the theater company was attempting to diffuse the anxiety of being watched offstage by cajoling the observer into joining the group and offering the role of "interested observer." The string quartet dealt with its anxiety by ignoring the observer during rehearsal: one member told her he had simply forgotten she was there. Some of the professional hockey players were interested in the observers; others merely tolerated them—perhaps reflecting the degree to which different athletes were accustomed to being observed. The university athletes—both varsity and intramural—were generally indifferent to the observers, an indifference that probably was a function of their own lack of dealings with audiences generally.

Rewards and Roles

Some of the internal dynamics of performing groups can be traced directly to the presence of audiences. Audience approval can create tensions between the individual and the group, between being a "star" and a "team player." Although the potential for such tensions exists within most types of work teams, they are highlighted for performing groups by the glory audiences offer—glory conferred directly on stars and reflected only indirectly onto team players.

Performers make choices, consciously and unconsciously, between performing their roles in ways that enable them to stand out or to remain solidly within the collective. The intrinsic satisfactions differ; standing out fulfills the childlike wish for specialness and attention, while being a team player brings the joy of being part of something bigger than oneself, camaraderie, and the intimacy of peers. These choices also are influenced by potential extrinsic rewards. Performers may be rewarded individually (for example, individual promotion onto stages and fields of greater prestige) or collectively (for example, group rewards of "gigs" or postseason tournaments). Ultimately, being a successful performing group simultaneously yields collective rewards and individual rewards.

Success for a performing group requires that individuals assume explicitly formulated roles within more-or-less orchestrated plays. Role frameworks, specifying assignments about who plays what part, position, or instrument, bring order to the constant (and fleeting) reciprocal interdependencies that characterize the work of performing groups. They also ensure the continuation of the groups in the face of member turnover, while striking the appropriate balance: members are at once replaceable (in the roles they play) and irreplaceable (for the ways they play their roles).

Leaders and Lessons

The work of performing groups is orchestrated by their directors, conductors, or coaches. Some groups (for example, the repertory theater company and the professional athletic team) have central authority structures that coordinate group performances in relatively imposing, directive ways. The consequent relationship between leader and group in such cases echoes the dependency of the parent-child relationship, with leaders often becoming the single most salient feature of a group's context.

The relationships that develop between leaders and performing group members are, in part, a function of the underlying childlike nature of the groups' activities. Internal group dynamics may come to resemble family relationships, as performers act out sibling rivalries and seek parental approval. Performing groups without central authority structures (for example, the string quartet and the intramural athletic team) are self-managing teams that must counterbalance their childlike playfulness with their parental structures of order and control. These groups emphasized internal rather than external frames of reference, repeatedly insisting that they played for themselves rather than for audiences or critics. Members were both performers and audiences, both children and parents. They escaped the cycle of group-leader dependency that is characteristic of other performing groups.

As we have seen, performing groups are unique in many ways. Yet they highlight rather than contrast the issues faced by work teams generally. All working groups have some rhythm to their tasks and to the careers of their members. All working groups deal, at varying levels of awareness, with the tensions between individual and group interests, and they institute reward systems designed to balance those interests. Perhaps most fundamentally, all working groups deal with the tensions between work and play and between discipline and spontaneity, and they deal with the demands of various audiences for whom they perform. Performing groups are unique because these issues lie at the center of their existence.

Part Five

HUMAN SERVICE TEAMS: TAKING CARE OF PEOPLE

The teams examined in this section serve clients who are in need of some kind of therapy or rehabilitation. They differ from other teams in this book in that people, rather than ideas or things, are processed. Human service teams are composed mainly of professionals such as nurses and psychologists, and their effectiveness depends on the degree to which clients are better off for having received members' ministrations—not always an easy judgment to make.

The human service teams we studied operated in institutions such as hospitals and prisons. The special characteristics of those institutions—and of the clients who come there for treatment or rehabilitation—posed a number of management challenges for the teams. Particularly salient and difficult was the need for the teams to manage *intra*group relations among members from different professional disciplines, while simultaneously carrying on complex *inter*group transactions with clients and with other teams in the institution.

The first team reported, in Chapter Eighteen, consists of operating room nurses. Members of this team had two chronic problems. First, they were always subordinate to the surgeons they assisted in the operating room—a dominance relation that many of the physicians seemed intent on keeping quite salient. Second, the work of the team, while routine in some respects (for example, counting instruments after an operation), could be very emotionally demanding (for example, dealing with life-threatening situations and reassuring patients and their families). One might expect that team members would decide collectively how to deal with these matters and then support one another in doing so. Yet the nursing team was more a pool of talent than an interdependent team; the group as a whole dealt only with internal matters such as assignments and scheduling. The rest of the time, individuals or subgroups were away interacting with nonmembers. It is instructive to see how the nurses used their group to help members manage, and recover from, the emotionally stressful experiences with which they routinely had to contend.

The team examined in Chapter Nineteen had a quite different type of client: convicted male felons incarcerated at a federal correctional institution. This team, which included a variety of professional and managerial staff, had virtually complete control of the lives of inmates on its unit. Members were charged with both fostering the rehabilitation of the team's clients and controlling their behavior—objectives that, on occasion, conflicted with each another. The special challenges for this team derived from its closed and tightly bounded institutional environment and from its clients being both dangerous and often more interested in gaming the team than in being helped by it. How the team used a special group technique called "teamming" to deal with these challenges offers some insights into the ways groups can provide human services even in difficult institutional environments.

The last chapter in the section, Chapter Twenty, examines two mental health treatment teams—one a short-term admissions team, the other a long-term therapy team. Both consisted of professionals from a variety of mental health and social service disciplines. Like those in the correctional institution, these teams had to simultaneously help and control their clients. However, the differences in team members' professional disciplines were both more pronounced and more difficult to manage than was the case for the correctional teams. For example, experienced team members from relatively low-status disciplines such as nursing routinely had to take orders from new and inexperienced team members from a higher-status discipline such as medicine. Also, the teams' boundaries were constantly in flux, partly because staff continuously flowed across them for training purposes and partly because patients were viewed as members of treatment teams and allowed to participate in many team meetings. The permeability of the teams' boundaries, coupled with the cross-discipline tensions among members, posed real threats to their ability to serve their clients well.

18

Daniel R. Denison
Robert I. Sutton

Operating Room Nurses

"What's the job of OR head nurse like?" we asked Janet a few minutes after seven o'clock on a Monday morning. By noon we were starting to get the picture. She had explained a surgical technique to one of the nurses in her group and ordered another nurse to end her break and provide assistance with a coronary bypass operation. She had assisted a surgeon in one operation—doing exactly as he said. Later, in the hallway, she teased this same surgeon about being a "macho dude," and a couple of minutes after that she was in the nurses' lounge complaining about him, referring to him as a "jerk." By noon, she was tired and angry, and she started to resent the two researchers who kept following her around asking questions.

That afternoon, the members of her team gathered for a staff meeting. The atmosphere was somewhere between the mood in a locker room at halftime and that of the morning after storming the beach at Normandy. They had a full agenda (of which we were a part) but had trouble staying on track because of the emotional stress of their morning's work. Consequently, the meeting moved back and forth between releasing tension from an exhausting morning and planning how the group could better manage its work, its schedule, and its resources.

The operating room suite at St. Joseph's Hospital is busy and tense. More than 50 operations take place each day in this 558-bed teaching hospital in Ann Arbor, Michigan. More than 100 surgeons use the hospital's 20 operating rooms to perform operations ranging from five-minute tonsillectomies to five-hour coronary bypasses. Each patient must be prepared for his or her operation, wheeled from the "pre-op" area into one of the operating rooms, operated upon, and then moved to the recovery room. The schedule for operations is tighter than those of many manufacturing organizations, and there are literally life-and-death consequences of the work.

People who work in the operating room suite repeat the same cycle over and over: they join a new surgical team, perform an operation, and then disband. Each of these temporary teams consists of a surgeon, an anesthesiologist, a scrub nurse (one who remains sterile throughout the operation to provide direct assistance to the surgeon), and a circulating nurse who provides secondary support such as doing paperwork and getting supplies. Other members may include residents, technicians, and an occasional administrator.

We spent a week observing group behavior in this exciting and intimidating setting. Although we spent much of our time watching these temporary teams in action, our research focused on the permanent teams that supplied nurses for operations. One of our permanent teams of surgical nurses staffed each operation conducted at St. Joseph's Hospital. Each of the thirty nurses in the operating room was a member of one of these four teams.

The observations we made, the interviews we conducted, and the survey data we gathered focused on one of these teams, known as Team Two. Team Two consisted of eight women: two head nurses, five registered nurses, and a surgical technician. The members of Team Two specialized in four areas of surgery: one head nurse coordinated open heart and thoracic surgery while the second head nurse coordinated urology and ear, nose, and throat operations. Some team members had special knowledge about one of these areas, but each member of the team tried to develop the range of skills required to serve as both a scrub nurse and a circulating nurse in all four specialties.

Our week of research taught us much about the design of Team Two's work. We also discovered that the design of work for surgical nurses is only part of the story. In addition to the time they spent operating on patients in temporary surgical teams, the members of Team Two also took part in at least three other kinds of important interactions: "time-outs" with surgeons present, time-outs with each other, and times with patients and their families. Each kind of interaction, or *social region*, had different norms and required the nurses to respond to a different reference group. After describing the design of work, we will discuss these four social regions in the operating room suite, thereby providing a more complete picture of how organizational life unfolded for the members of Team Two.

The Design of Nursing Work in the Operating Room Suite

Work design had been a central concern among the nurses at St. Joseph's operating room suite for several years before our observations. A work design innovation implemented about two years before our study changed the operating room from a traditional design to a team approach (see Spurr, Ehnis, & Feldkamp, 1981). Below, we describe the organization of the operating room nurses before and after the redesign.

Before the Team Approach. Prior to the innovation, there had been no intermediate level of organization between the operating room administrator and the nurses assigned to operations. Head nurses had little authority or responsibility for supervising other nurses. For example, although the head administrator obtained input from the head nurses, she wrote performance evaluations for all of the nurses who worked in the suite. And in the suite's haphazard process of specialization, scrub and circulating nurses trained only for those specialties that they found most interesting.

To schedule operations, the administrator had relied on

input from the nurses combined with her prior experience and intuition. Each afternoon at about 2:30, she made decisions about how long each of the fifty operations scheduled for the next day would take, which nurses would be best suited for each operation, and how many would be needed for each operation. This seat-of-the-pants method had worked well when the operating rooms had only ten or twenty patients per day. But with over fifty patients per day there was chaos every afternoon at 2:30 as twenty-five or thirty nurses crowded around the administrator's office. This system was, of course, highly dependent on the personal skills of the administrator.

A number of factors combined to increase the pressure. As patient load increased, so did the number of scheduling errors. The nurses complained that the process was capricious, and they were often unhappy about their assignments. In addition, the operating room was performing increasingly complex operations, which required nurses to have more specialized training and knowledge. Thus, although some nurses had been trained for complex operations, the match between the nurses' skills and those that surgeons needed often was less than ideal. As a result of these pressures, the administrator felt considerable stress while making the daily assignments. Moreover, she often was interrupted during the day because so many scheduling problems occurred.

These difficulties prompted the operating room administrator to seek the advice of a member of the hospital's human resources staff—an organizational development specialist familiar with the principles of job design and autonomous work groups. The administrator, the human resources manager, and a task force composed of operating room nurses worked together to redesign nursing work in the operating rooms. The team system we observed was the result of those efforts.

The Team Approach. Under the new system, there were four teams consisting of six to ten members. Each team was supervised by a pair of head nurses. These head nurses had responsibility for scheduling the team's operations and evaluating the performance of each nurse on the team. Team One specialized in obstetrics and gynecology, cardiovascular medicine, neurology, and general medicine. Team Two, as noted above, specialized in open-heart surgery, thoracic surgery, urology, and ear, nose, and throat operations. Team Three specialized in orthopedics, plastic surgery, and eye surgery. Team Four was the float team and did not specialize in any particular type of surgery. Team Four had no head nurse; the operating room administrator retained responsibility for scheduling this team's work and evaluating its members. Because of concern that this design would lead to too much specialization, each nurse on Teams One, Two, and Three worked on operations performed by another team for one week every ninety days. This rotation helped nurses maintain familiarity with procedures required for operations outside of their specialty.

Our interviews with administrators, surgeons, and nurses all indicated that the redesign had been a success. Scheduling was much smoother, mainly because coordinating six or ten nurses on one team was far easier than orchestrating the activities of thirty. The operating room administrator reported that she had more time for other tasks and that her greatest single source of job stress had been eliminated. And the doctors we interviewed reported that the quality of nursing had improved.

The new design also fostered the professional development of nurses through cross-training. In the old design, nurses picked up new skills by working with their head nurse or through outside training. In contrast, the team approach required that each nurse learn the full range of skills needed in his or her group. Teams and head nurses shared responsibility for nurses' acquisition of skills. This system achieved a higher level of skill for each individual and a greater depth of skill within the team, which was particularly useful when someone was needed to be on call. Once nurses were cross-trained, there were many more options for who could assist in emergencies.

All evidence we gathered indicated that the nurses were pleased with the redesign. They liked having more control over when and with whom they worked. Indeed, the two head nurses in Team Two gave members considerable responsibility for scheduling their own operations. All eight members agreed that the statement on our survey, "The supervisor or manager responsible for our group has a participative or democratic style," was "very accurate."

Each Team Two member we spoke with reported that she liked both her job and her fellow team members. The team was well above the national average on survey measures of overall job satisfaction and satisfaction with social relations at work. Typical remarks included "We are a group of people with diverse backgrounds who work together well" and "The best thing about the group is that there is little conflict."

The lack of turnover was perhaps the best indicator of satisfaction among members of Team Two. Turnover among operating room nurses historically had been 30 percent per year before the redesign. Yet there had been no turnover at all among the members of Team Two during the eighteen months since the redesign had been implemented.

We could not obtain objective evidence about the performance of Team Two, but a surgeon who regularly conducted coronary bypass operations with team members reported that, of the four hospitals where he regularly performed the operation, these nurses were the most knowledgeable and most efficient. He also reported that, since the redesign, their skills in assisting him had increased steadily.

Despite the success of the redesign, the members of Team Two did report three problems. The most frequent complaint was that the team was too small; members reported that they were constantly overloaded. Several nurses complained that they had fewer and shorter rest breaks than did members of the other three teams. Second, although members reported receiving sufficient feedback from one another, they complained that neither doctors nor hospital administrators let them know how they were doing.

These first two problems showed promise of resolution. The team already had acquired two new members by the time we completed our research and had asked several doctors with whom they worked to give them more feedback. But a third problem, lack of autonomy in the operating room, was far more difficult to resolve. The nurses complained that they were "slaves" and had to do whatever doctors asked. Our survey data confirmed that their perceived autonomy was low in comparison to other properties of well-designed jobs, such as task meaningfulness and feedback. This third problem is more difficult to overcome because standard surgical procedures and occupational socialization (for both physicians and nurses) mandate that nurses do whatever doctors ask. Nurses are appropriately expected to follow procedures (such as holding clamps or handling the instruments) that doctors request. Nonetheless, as we discuss later, the nurses in Team Two often felt oppressed by doctors and could point to concrete instances when doctors indeed had made unreasonable demands.

The Four Social Regions Encountered by Team Two

We began our study of Team Two armed with what Steinbeck (1951) called "mental provisioning," which led us to focus on the opportunities, demands, and constraints the nurses faced when they were doing their jobs. Our interactions with hospital administrators and the members of our own research team, as well as the theoretical and methodological perspectives used in this study, led us to look for certain clues about the causes of the nurses' doing their work well or badly. "Doing the work," in our initial view, meant assisting with surgery in an operating room. Yet in following the nurses around and talking with them about doing their jobs, we discovered that our emphasis on what occurred in the operating rooms was too narrow.

In fact, the nurses' workday was filled with important interactions that occurred outside of the operating rooms. These interactions also seemed to be an important part of doing their jobs. To use Kurt Lewin's (1936) terms, members engaged in locomotion among several regions that each placed different psychological demands on the nurses and had different rules for behavior. As mentioned earlier, we identified four social regions that appeared to have distinct psychological boundaries and behavioral rules: time spent in the operating room, time-outs with surgeons present, time-outs with each other, and time spent with patients and their families.

We found that expressed emotions were among the most reliable and vivid indicators of the clear boundaries among these four social regions and that these emotions helped reveal the distinct norms about how members were expected to behave within each one. The discussion below analyzes these four social regions in terms of display rules (Ekman & Oster, 1979) and norms about expressing emotions.

In the Operating Room. At first we were surprised by the norms of emotional expression in the operating rooms. The first time we entered the room where a coronary bypass operation was being done, for example, we were surprised by the loud rock music blaring from the speakers, the smiles on the faces of the surgical team, and the constant joking. Denison observed one surgeon who joked and told a series of funny stories as he performed the complicated task of cutting the veins out of a patient's leg—veins that would be used to bypass clogged coronary arteries. Similarly, one reason that Sutton almost passed out during a tonsillectomy was that he became very upset when the surgeon laughed, joked, and talked about "what was on the tube last night" while blood from an unconscious child splattered about.

Such joking appeared to serve two important functions. First, the operating room can be a tense place; after all, mistakes made here can have severe consequences. Joking is a classic psychological means for reducing tension (Freud, [1905] 1960). Second, despite the pressure for perfection in the operating room, many surgical tasks are routine and boring for both doctors and nurses. Just as production workers use banter, laughter, and joking to make their work go more quickly (Roy, 1959), operating room staff rely on laughter and jokes as a source of variety. Indeed, we believe that the surgeon whom we saw conduct six tonsillectomies in an hour and a half was bored with his job. He spent a great deal of time joking with us because we were a new source of entertainment.

Nurses in this social region had to follow different norms of emotional expression than did the surgeons, and nurses had much less choice about which emotions they could express.

They also could not laugh and joke as much as the doctors and could do so only with the doctors' permission. The surgeons often gave subtle but strong cues to manage the ebb and flow of expressed emotion. One example occurred during a coronary bypass operation at the critical point when the repaired heart is literally shocked back to life (defibrillation) as the patient is removed from the heart-lung machine that has kept him alive during the operation. The head surgeon looked around the room and gave everyone a very serious look. The nurses, interns, and technicians responded by looking somber and attentive. Then the circulating nurse turned down the radio that was blasting out "Hotel California," a popular song by the Eagles. This instance illustrates the use of expressed emotion as a "control move" that influences the behavior of other organization members (Rafaeli & Sutton, 1987). That serious look by the surgeon was a powerful cue that changed the behavior of everyone in the operating room.

As with all other activities in the operating room, nurses who did not follow doctors' wishes about emotional behavior often would be sanctioned. For example, two nurses began talking very quietly between themselves after two of the surgeons started swapping stories about the Detroit Tigers. The head surgeon responded immediately by aiming a nasty glare in their direction and bellowing, "Come on people, let's keep it down in here!"

With Surgeons Present. The time the nurses spent talking and joking with the surgeons outside of the operating room had different rules than did the time spent on the job in the operating room. The absolute authority that surgeons held and exercised in the operating room was unnecessary during these time-outs, which Van Maanen (1986) defines as gatherings at which some of the ordinary norms of the workplace are suspended. Thus, time-outs provide greater freedom of emotional expression than is available during work time. Indeed, we watched nurses in Team Two initiate joking and friendly conversations with surgeons, and even offer mock insults, during nonwork times.

Anthropologists have observed that joking serves the

function of maintaining a satisfactory relationship between people who have social ties that might generate hostility (Radcliffe-Brown, 1952). In the present case, some of the tension generated in the operating room—where doctors have total authority over nurses—was released when nurses teased doctors. For example, Sutton overheard a conversation during such a time-out in which the nurse repeatedly referred to the doctor as "your highness." This kind of disrespect would never be permitted in the operating room, but the joke may have helped reduce tension so that the two parties could work well in the operating room where the doctor really was the king.

With Other Team Members. Another type of time-out, with very different rules for the display of emotion, took place when doctors or administrators were not present. These interactions sometimes occurred in the halls or in operating rooms after the doctors had left, but they most often took place in the nurses' lounge or in the hospital cafeteria. There was some joking and banter, but the dominant theme, as one nurse told us, was "to get together and bitch about everything." We heard the nurses complain about hundreds of things during these time-outs, including the incompetence of doctors and orderlies, the unending sexual harassment of one particular doctor, the difficulty of their jobs, and the burden of instrument counts—the requirement that all instruments be counted to ensure that none was left inside the patient or stolen. Such "bitching" was confined to settings where only nurses were present. We never observed it during time-outs on the job or when doctors were present.

With Patients and Their Families. Most of the patients that the nurses on Team Two encountered were unconscious. As a result, there usually was no need to change their behavior just because a patient had entered or left the operating room. There were exceptions, however. Some operations, like tonsillectomies, required that the child be anesthetized in the operating room just before the surgery began. Thus, the circulating nurse had to keep the child calm and occasionally had to help physically restrain the child.

Nurses in Team Two sometimes encountered worried family members who were waiting outside the operating room. In such instances, the nurses were invariably supportive, offering assurances that things were going well and often praising the surgeon's competence and explaining the details of the surgery. In addition, we noticed that even when a nurse was very busy or had not taken a break in hours, she would take the time to get information about a patient's progress if family members asked. There were only warm smiles at these times. There was little joking and never any sign of cynicism.

Expressed emotions also served as control moves in this fourth social region. Nurses who were warm and supportive of patients and their families reduced the anxiety of these worried people. In addition, acting warm and supportive toward these people made the nurses' jobs easier to do. If a child who was about to be "knocked out" became hysterical, the operation took longer and the doctor was likely to become irritated at the nurses. Similarly, families who became hysterical or started complaining were an additional source of aggravation. By the appropriate management of expressed emotions, nurses were able to head off such potential problems.

Endemic Tensions Revealed by the Displayed Emotions

The four sets of norms described above required members of Team Two to make abrupt and frequent changes in the emotions they expressed to others. Our observations of these shifting emotional expressions, coupled with evidence from the other data sources, revealed a pair of tensions that the members of Team Two faced and that we suspect are endemic for most operating room nurses: (1) the need to control nurses' actions versus nurses' needs for autonomy, and (2) the need to "bitch" and release tension versus the need to get the work done. We discuss these tensions next.

The Need to Control Nurses' Actions Versus the Need for Autonomy. The struggle for control was a constant, subtle tension between doctors and nurses and between administrators and nurses. The work redesign had increased nurses' autonomy considerably, but they still felt that they were pushed around too much. There were some cases in which doctors clearly exceeded their authority, including one in which we observed a doctor chasing a head nurse down the hall in an unsuccessful effort to grab her derriere.

Nurses acknowledged that doctors had superior knowledge of surgical technique and that they should be in charge in the operating room. But the nurses complained bitterly that surgeons abused this legitimate power by restricting nurses' autonomy in ways that damaged their self-esteem and performance. And nurses continually contested the gray area between the appropriate prerogatives of expertise and the unnecessary oppression used to keep nurses in their place.

We mentioned an incident earlier in which two doctors started joking and talking but then reprimanded two nurses for engaging in a quiet conversation. We suspect that this reprimand was used primarily to put down the nurses. It is, perhaps, possible that the nurses' conversation did distract the doctors and increase the chances they would make mistakes. Yet rock music blared in the background and the doctors themselves were joking loudly.

An ongoing battle between nurses and administrators, especially the operating room administrators, centered on what constituted "nursing work" and what constituted "nonnursing work." The battle often was about instrument counts. Nurses saw this task as boring and degrading—very much at odds with the expectation that they were supposed to be responsible and autonomous. Nurses felt that they were careful to keep track of instruments during operations and that any counting done after the operation was a job for orderlies. And because nurses performed instrument counts after the doctors had left the room, the activity provided a prime opportunity for bitching rather than productive work.

This example seemed to us to be in the gray area between reasonable and unreasonable constraints on the nurses' autonomy. Administrators and doctors felt the instrument counts were necessary because such counts lowered the risk that patients would get infections and reduced the chance that patients would sue the hospital and the surgeons for malpractice. Administrators and doctors did not trust orderlies to do this important yet tedious task, so they insisted that the nurses do it.

The Need to Release Tension Versus the Need to Get the Work Done. We described earlier how time-outs that included only other nurses were characterized by "bitching." This tension release helped nurses express their frustrations so that, when they returned to the other three social regions, they would be less likely to act bitter or cynical. However, the work redesign meant that the time nurses spent with one another also had to be used to plan their work—a price they paid for their increased autonomy and responsibility.

As a result, there was a constant tension between "the need to bitch" and "the need to do our work," a tension that was most evident during Team Two's weekly staff meetings. The nurses constantly struggled about what the agenda for these meetings should include: some members wanted to complain and others expressed a need to "get on with the planning." This problem was compounded by one member who was very active in both planning and bitching—and who held the opinion that the group could and should do both at once.

From one perspective, the display rules for times when the nurses were free from the demands of doctors, administrators, and patients haunted staff meetings because the rules hampered the nurses' ability to get their work done—especially their ability to schedule operations and engage in continuing education. On the other hand, nurses did not get many time-outs together. They were under constant pressure, and they needed opportunities to vent their feelings if they were to function at their best in the other three social regions.

Our Own Emotional Reactions: An Additional Source of Data

We have already discussed the lessons learned from our observational, interview, and questionnaire data. In addition, we learned a great deal from an additional, and less traditional, data source— our own emotional reactions. Indeed, we developed the metaphor of a "divining rod" for our investigation of Team Two: strong emotional reactions on our part often pointed to lessons about the team's design and social regions. This approach follows Berg's (1985) argument that anxiety in a research relationship can be a useful source for learning about the organization one is studying. Two incidents that occurred during time-outs that usually were only for nurses are illustrative. Both episodes left us feeling like rejected and unwelcome visitors. Both also taught us valuable lessons.

The first episode occurred during lunch with one of the head nurses. She had been working all morning to juggle a schedule that contained too many operations for her tiny team to staff. As soon as we sat down, Sutton starting asking interview questions about how long she had been with the team, how many operations they were working on that day, and so on. The nurse responded with a nasty tirade about how everyone she encountered—the doctors, the director of the operating room, her subordinates, and now us—was putting pressure on her. She said she did not have time to deal with us and wanted to be left alone.

Our anxiety about being the target of such hostility forced us to think about the setting and ourselves. In retrospect, we believe that there were two reasons for this nurse's flash of hot emotion—and both of them had to do with us. First, we were interrupting her time-out. Most days, she would have been able to use her lunch break to vent her emotions and receive social support from other members of the team. The anger that she expressed at Sutton appeared to be typical of the emotion that she and other nurses expressed during time-outs after a stressful morning. Second, we were men. She had spent much of the morning being pushed around by male surgeons, and she was in no mood to respond to the demands of another group of men.

The second episode took place in the nurses' lounge. Nurses and doctors had separate lounges in the operating room suite and usually retreated to their respective lounges during breaks, between operations, or before leaving for the day. We conducted several interviews there. Denison approached a nurse from another team whom he had met the day before and asked what she had been doing that morning. This was not an attempt to start a formal interview. He merely wished to engage in an informal conversation with a member of another team. Denison hoped that, by doing so, he could learn a bit more about life in the operating room suite and the nurses' work within it.

She replied with an icy stare that seemed to last forever. She finally replied "D and Cs" (dilation and curettage). Another icy stare followed. Denison blinked and retreated quickly. In retrospect, there appeared to be, in this refusal, two messages that were similar to the first: (1) don't bother emotionally distraught nurses during time-outs and (2) sometimes nursing is women's business.

The consistency of these two episodes helped crystallize our understanding of the dynamics of the operating room. Status and gender were almost perfectly confounded, creating great tension for the women we studied. Escaping from men, complaining about men, and providing each other social support were essential parts of their day. Some nurses enjoyed the novelty of our presence and the attention they received from us. But these two incidents, along with several other, less dramatic episodes, made us aware that we—as male intruders—often took some opportunities for psychological relief away from these nurses.

Conclusions

We learned some lessons from this research that may apply to the design and management of nursing work more generally. For one thing, we learned that many of the work redesign principles originally developed for use in production and manufacturing firms can be applied as well in health care organizations. Team Two used, to good advantage, work design for teams rather than for individuals, participation in decision making, cross-training, and work rotation. We also learned that surgical nurses have a complex and varied set of rules about what constitutes appropriate behavior, and that these rules change drastically depending on which social region the nurses occupy.

These lessons were not, however, all that we learned from

this research. Two other lessons emerged unexpectedly. First, we learned a conceptual lesson about expressed emotions. Psychologists know that tasks vary in the mental demands they place on the people who perform them; some tasks require more cognitive complexity than others. This research taught us that jobs also vary in affective complexity—the extent to which they require the display of a wide range of emotions. The nurses in Team Two had to be skilled in displaying a variety of emotions—and acting sincere about it—no matter how they really felt. They had to follow surgeons' sometimes subtle and sometimes blatant cues about emotional expression in the operating room; they had to act warm and caring with patients and their families; and they had to know how much they could get away with in teasing surgeons during time-outs. Only during time-outs with each other could they begin to release their personal feelings. In other words, these nursing jobs have a great deal of affective complexity. Little theory exists and little research has been done on this concept, but we believe it holds promise for understanding the demands of many human service jobs.

Second, we learned that our own emotional reactions are an important source of data, and this lesson has served us well in our subsequent field research on topics ranging from organizational birth to organizational death. Our experience confirmed Berg's (1985) assertion that the researcher's anxiety can offer lessons about self as well as setting. Displaying a neutral and accepting demeanor to the emotionally charged people we studied in the operating room was a bad idea, despite what we had learned from the literature about how to conduct interviews (for example, Survey Research Center, 1976). How could we be neutral when a nurse bragged about how she saved a kid's life? We felt happy too, and we let her know it. How could we be accepting when the head nurse began to yell at us? We felt hurt and angry—and, when she saw that we felt that way, it may have helped her trust us a bit more.

19

Addie L. Perkins
David J. Abramis

Midwest Federal Correctional Institution

"Mark! Mark! Let's get outta here. They're coming. . . . We're caught, man. Oh God, we're caught." Mark jerks awake, perspiration covering his body. His recurring nightmare has happened once again. His mind replays the scene again and again until it takes on nightmarish qualities and forces him to wake up. Funny, it always seems to happen just before a teamming session.

*   *   *

"Where's Mark?" calls one prisoner to another. "He's being teammed," is the response. It sounds a bit strange. *Team* is rarely used as a verb outside the prison walls of the Midwest Federal Correctional Institution. But within the walls of the prison, in Unit 1, Mark is being teammed.

*   *   *

Six staff members sit in a small meeting room in the dorm. The group consists of a unit manager, a psychologist, two case workers, and two counselors. Collectively, they are responsible for all aspects of the lives of inmates in their unit: physical and emotional well-being, prison employment, educational planning, inmate finances, coordination (with family, federal agencies, and parole boards), rewards and punishments, and a miscellany of other tasks associated with day-to-day prison life. The challenge for the staff teams is to create, maintain, and supervise all of these programs, to meet a large number of federal bureaucratic requirements in a highly regulated but dangerous environment, and to attempt to rehabilitate some of the toughest customers in the world.

The team discusses each inmate just prior to his arrival. The unit manager facilitates the session, although any one of the team members may begin the discussion by identifying the next inmate and prompting for a full report of his activities and progress in each of several critical areas. Each staff member is encouraged to contribute whatever information is available regardless of whether the inmate is officially assigned to his caseload. All aspects of the inmate's behavior are discussed, including emotional well-being and adjustment to the prison, physical and psychological health and stability, infractions or insubordination, dorm citizenship, personal maintenance, and relationships with staff and other inmates. The inmate's work detail, attendance record, and productivity are reviewed and possible reassignments, if appropriate, are discussed. If the inmate is in an educational program, his progress and possible next steps are outlined. Medical issues are considered and custody issues resolved. Finally, any pending court dates, parole board hearings, or bureaucratic paperwork are discussed. At the conclusion of the discussion, the team has a general idea of the inmate's status in virtually every aspect of his prison life.

The inmates at Midwest Federal Correctional Institution (hereafter called FCI) are a heterogeneous lot. There are 750 of them, all adult males. They range in age from eighteen to seventy-one. Some have as little as a second-grade education while others hold graduate degrees. Virtually every ethnic group and region of the country are represented. Almost half are repeat offenders who have spent the majority of their lives in institutions. Sentence lengths range from three months to over seventy years, averaging about ten years. Overall, the inmates are a savvy bunch and have a sometimes lethal mixture of formal education, street smarts, and common sense. They should not be underestimated.

When most people think of human service work, they think of caring for people who are needy, poor, helpless, worried, or depressed. And the people served by the Midwest FCI staff teams certainly have those characteristics. They also happen to be tax evaders, armed robbers, kidnappers, murderers, rapists, racketeers, bank robbers, larcenists, drug dealers, and a slew of other types of federal criminals.

Mark's Case

Mark Sullivan (a pseudonym) is a tall, thin, attractive young man in his mid-twenties with thick, sandy hair and startling blue eyes. Mark has an interesting history. Born into a middle-class background, Mark was the darling of his community. He was bright, athletic, charming, and well mannered. In high school he was all-state in basketball his junior year and seemed to have an athletic scholarship at the state university in the bag.

Unfortunately, things began to take a turn for the worse the summer after his junior year. That's the summer he "started hanging out with the college boys" and was introduced to drugs. At first, Mark refused any substance whatsoever, but after being bullied into trying marijuana and finding it harmless as promised, Mark quickly moved on to other drugs to keep up with his newfound friends. Well into his senior year, his grades and athletic prowess began to suffer. When the state scholarship eventually was denied him because of rumors about his drug involvement, Mark went to pieces. Drugs became a method of revenge and a way of life. It was not long before his drug habit far exceeded his financial resources. Initially, Mark turned to petty crime—stealing things from his home and money from his parents' wallets. But as pressures at the local college and in his personal life mounted—bad grades and a pregnant girlfriend—Mark began to depend more heavily on drugs "to get through the day." This, of course, required additional money.

Mark decided he needed "a big score to set [himself] up for a while." Brainstorming with two friends, he decided to hold up the local liquor store whose setup they knew quite well. The three developed a "foolproof" plan that somehow did not take into account a silent alarm system tied to the local police station. Mark's recurring nightmare plays out the scene where the police arrive while the robbery is in progress and catch the three partners in crime in the act. The trio was jailed and subsequently convicted of armed robbery. Mark never imagined he actually would be sent to prison. As a first-time offender, he assumed he would be paroled, not incarcerated. But he was sentenced to ten years in a federal prison and was sent to Midwest FCI, where he was placed in Unit 1 because of his history of drug abuse.

Mark says he only has nightmares the night before a teaming session. These quarterly sessions upset him because they force him to face the reality of his incarceration and his loss of freedom. Mark has been at Midwest FCI and in Unit 1 for about two years, so he is very familiar with the teaming process. He has been taking college courses while at Midwest FCI and now wants to take additional courses at the local community college. He also feels that he has been working in the laundry long enough (a punishment for a previous infraction). He wants a job either in the kitchen or outside doing grounds maintenance—two of the most coveted work details in the prison. Taking courses at the community college would require that his status be changed from *in-custody* to *community custody*. This is a very serious step that the team takes only after careful consideration.

The team makes its decisions on custody requests during teaming sessions. Well beforehand, Mark began to have informal discussions with each member of the unit team. He tried to convince the psychologist that he had been a model inmate, that he had been attending all of his group and individual counseling and therapy sessions, and that he had not been prone to violent behavior in at least six months. Mark's goal was to get a verbal commitment from the psychologist to support his case. He also talked informally with his case manager and counselor— again explaining his model behavior in the dorm, on work detail, and in his classes. In preparing for the teaming session,

Mark used any ammunition he could find: calling in favors, information, blackmail, ingratiation, and charm. He gamed the staff as best he could before they met to act on his requests.

Teamming Mark

In Mark's case, the staff spent about fifteen minutes in discussion, primarily around the custody decision. The staff focused on the warden's posture on granting community custody. The unit manager explained that the warden generally demands that the inmate have a spotless record for at least twelve to eighteen months prior to the request and that he be relatively "short" (that is, with only six months or fewer before parole or release). In Mark's case, while he generally had been a good inmate, he did have a blemish on his record: a particularly violent fight with another inmate five or six months before. That resulted in both inmates being sent to solitary confinement (the hole) for two days. While Mark's record has been spotless since then, the infraction was too serious for him to expect the warden to overlook it. The team decided that Mark's request would be denied at this review but reconsidered at a subsequent teamming session. In the meantime, something would be worked out for a transfer from the laundry detail. Members discussed current openings and what might be appropriate for Mark, but decided to delay a decision until his views were heard. Finally, the team spent a few minutes discussing Mark's attempt to influence the outcome of the custody decision, reiterating what a con artist he can be when he really wants something.

The case manager then called Mark into the room and seated him at the table. The unit manager began by complimenting Mark on his extremely good behavior during the previous ninety days. He noted that this was in direct contrast to his behavior five months ago when he did not seem to be getting along very well with anyone. Mark thanked the unit manager for the compliment and explained that five months ago he was very upset because his wife had just informed him that she was filing for divorce and was moving the family to Detroit. The discussion then proceeded as follows:

Psychologist: Why didn't you tell us about the divorce at your last teamming meeting?

Mark: I wasn't ready to talk about it then.

Counselor: Well, you know that not telling us didn't help your case any. That's one reason you weren't transferred out of the laundry detail. Your behavior didn't warrant a better assignment. You even spent two days in the hole.

Mark: Yeah, I know. I was in a bad way then.

Unit manager: Well, I'm glad you're getting back on track. Your behavior has always been pretty good. I'd hate to see you messing up now. I see here that you're asking for community custody so you can get a job working outside the gate and take courses at the community college. You're working in the laundry now?

Mark: Yeah, and I want out of there.

Counselor: Where do you want to work?

Mark: Well, me and Mr. B [case manager] were talking yesterday and we thought the kitchen would be good or doing, you know, yard work.

Case manager: Mark, we didn't agree on that. I told you we could talk about it today. That's what we agreed on.

Mark: Yeah, right, right.

Counselor: Do you have any special skills for working in the kitchen or the yard?

Mark: Who needs special skills? I can cook and I can cut grass. No big deal. (General laughter)

Case manager: I checked today and right now there are no openings in the kitchen. And you don't have the right custody to work in the yard.

Mark: Well, that's what I wanted to talk about today. What about changing my custody? Then I could go to school like we talked about, right Doc? And work in the yard too.

Case manager: Watch him, Doc. He'll put words in your mouth too. (General laughter)

Unit manager: Well, since everything hinges on the custody request, maybe we should talk about that. Mark, the staff and I have agreed that your case is not strong. The warden would not approve a request for community custody so soon after your trip to the hole. Only your previous record prevented you from being busted down to out custody. We can come back to the custody issue in your next review if you like, but right now I don't think we stand a chance. (Case manager makes notation in file.)

Mark: Damn, I was afraid of that! (Silence) What do I have to do to get out of the laundry?

Case manager: We'll keep our eyes open for a spot somewhere else for you. Something should come up in the next week or so. It may not be the kitchen, though.

Mark: OK, I'm ready to take almost anything. (Case manager makes notation in the file.)

Psychologist: Since you can't take courses on the outside, what can you do inside?

Mark: I don't know.

Counselor: Have you taken all of the computer courses the center offers?

Mark: Well, I'm not sure. There was this special programming class I wanted to take at the community college. They don't have it here.

Unit manager: Well, you won't be taking that, so what else can you do?

Mark: I don't know. Maybe there's something else.

Case manager: I'll check with the education department to see if there is anything else you can take. In the meantime, I'll check to see if Mr. C would be willing to take you on in the computer center. Maybe you can get some more experience that way. But remember, I'm not making any promises.

Mark: Hey man, that would be all right. (Case manager makes notation in the file.)

Unit manager: OK, that takes care of the custody issue, education, and work detail. What else?

Case manager: Mark, you have to tell me what happens with the divorce and if you want your payments to stop going to your wife. Also if there is any paperwork we need to fill out for a court date.

Mark: I'll let you know.

Unit manager: Any parole board dates or whatever before the next review?

Case manager: None that I can see.

Psychologist: Mark, I see you're signed up for the two groups starting next week. I think you could really get something from them. Your attendance wasn't so good for your last group. I'd suggest you improve your attendance for these two groups so you can get certified and stay in this unit. How did you like the last group?

Mark: It was OK. But some of the guys weren't, you know, serious. It got to be a joke after a while.

Psychologist: Yeah, I heard about that. We'll try to make sure that doesn't happen again. Just make sure you show up. The first group starts next Tuesday and the second group on Wednesday.

Mark: Next Tuesday. OK, Doc. I wanted to talk to you about some ideas I had for a group. Can I come talk to you?

Psychologist: Sure, just stop by my office after your work detail this afternoon.

Unit manager: OK, Mark, we couldn't recommend the custody you wanted, but Mr. B is going to work on getting you a new work detail and getting you into more programming courses. You are signed up for two groups, but it won't do you any good unless you go and get certified. Anything else?

Mark: I'll get my custody next time, right?

Unit manager: No promises.

With that, Mark is asked to sign the forms the case manager has completed indicating the review has taken place and specifying the outcomes. Mark leaves and the staff begins discussion of the next inmate.

The Prison

Midwest Federal Correctional Institution is an isolated, self-contained entity. It is a small, self-sufficient community with its own dining facilities, laundry, educational system, chapel, medical and dental units, social system, and culture. Each inmate is assigned to one of eight units or dormitories in the prison.

Each unit has its own staff team. Most teams consist of a unit manager, a psychologist, two case workers, and two counselors. Teams have strong loyalties to their units, and team members and custodial staff visibly and actively support one another. Unit staff are protective of their ability to maintain order and discipline, and they resent having to take on an inmate or staff member who may disrupt the status quo. Relationships between units have a moderate we-they flavor.

Because FCI is a medium-security prison, visitors are permitted on a regular basis, inmates may make collect calls to outsiders from public telephones in the dormitories, and weekend passes are available for inmates whose sentence times are short. In addition, many groups from the surrounding community are permitted to hold meetings and provide services and entertainment for the inmates. The warden and many administrative and custodial staff live on the prison grounds or in the vicinity of the prison.

There are four categories of prison staff: management, custodial (security and control), human services, and maintenance. Interdependence among the four groups is essential to ensure that the prison functions with the staff, not the inmates, in control. Federal regulations govern much of the staff's activities and interaction with inmates.

Inmates are integral to the functioning of the institution. Indeed, the prison could not operate effectively without their cooperation; they outnumber staff members three to one. Many inmates perform administrative duties to supplement a staff greatly reduced by budgetary cuts. In many respects, the prison represents a cooperative agreement between staff and inmates.

The Focal Team

The Unit 1 team was an adult drug unit. Unlike some of the other units at FCI, it had a complete staff and a manageable work load. Both inmates and staff coveted the unit. Each inmate had his own room in the unit, and the building was the most modern one in the institution. The dorm was air conditioned and had the most up-to-date conveniences, equipment, and facilities. All inmates in the unit had a history of drug abuse. To remain there, they had to participate in rehabilitation programs and maintain model prison citizenship. The greatest catastrophe to befall an inmate in Unit 1 was to be reassigned to another unit where living conditions resembled those of a massive army barrack. This served as a great incentive for good behavior.

Team members in Unit 1 had worked together for one or two years, and their identity as a group was clear and strong. Collectively, they had responsibility for the 100 inmates in the unit, 50 in each of two dormitory wings. Each case worker and counselor was responsible for the inmates in one of the wings. The unit manager and psychologist had direct responsibility for all inmates in the unit.

The warden appointed unit managers within federal guidelines and regulations. The unit manager had ultimate accountability and responsibility for the effective functioning of the unit, including not only maintenance and custody of inmates but also the coordination and development of staff. He was the top manager in the unit and reported directly to the assistant warden.

The psychologist was an integral part of the team. Unlike other team members, he reported functionally to the chief of psychology and indirectly to the unit manager. He had responsibility for the day-to-day psychological well-being of the inmates and shared responsibility with his teammates for their physical maintenance. His duties included all those of a traditional clinical or counseling psychologist. While serving in one unit full-time, he provided part-time assistance to the other units. He also conducted developmental seminars for the benefit of the staff. In Unit 1, the psychologist often served as second in command. While the unit manager worried about technical details, the psychologist assisted with group process issues.

The two counselors were primarily responsible for individual and group counseling, developing visiting lists, inspecting mail, serving as dorm officers (supplementing the custodial force), and solving specific inmate problems by coordinating with other departments throughout the institution. The two case managers had responsibility for all administrative paperwork affecting inmates, including intake summaries, progress reports, parole commission reports, and release forms. In addition, case managers provided some group and individual counseling.

The custodial staff consisted of one guard in each unit. These individuals were responsible for security and control, and technically were part of the unit team. Because of other responsibilities, however, they rarely participated in the most frequent group activity—teamming. They reported directly to the guard captain and indirectly to the unit manager.

Teamming

Team members' roles and interdependence are most clearly demonstrated during teamming—the quarterly review of each inmate that is required by law. The teamming process is one of the most critical, regulated, and time-consuming aspects of the team's work. Members spend at least 50 percent of their time preparing for, participating in, and following up on teamming sessions. If the teamming process works well, it achieves the following outcomes: (1) inmates' needs are properly identified and serviced, (2) paperwork is completed on a timely basis, (3) housekeeping standards are maintained, (4) federal guidelines are met, and (5) the staff—rather than the inmates—remain in control of the unit.

During teamming, the team reviews each inmate's past conduct, prison employment, custody level, parole status, financial situation, family status, health, and educational activities and plans. The unit manager facilitates the sessions and solicits input from all team members. The psychologist offers views about the psychological well-being of the inmate and makes suggestions about appropriate group and individual counseling. The counselors orally review information regarding results of counseling sessions and day-to-day maintenance issues. The case managers provide information from observations during daily contact and counseling sessions, and they keep track of any reports that are due. They also complete all paperwork resulting from the teamming session. After soliciting the views, explanations, and preferences of the inmate, the team develops a formal maintenance plan for the next ninety days, usually by consensus. The unit manager settles any disputes, but most sessions are fairly routine.

Members must come prepared if the staff is to have an effective teamming session. Typically, they make contact ahead of time with other prison departments to check on inmate status and behavior—including education, vocational training, medical, work detail, recreation, custody, psychology, and prison administration. Team members maintain almost continuous contact with these departments; such contact is essential for the team to review ten to fifteen inmates each session and to hold two sessions per week.

The high degree of interdependence between inmates and staff complicates the teamming process. The relationship is symbiotic, but it also is fundamentally a parent-child relationship. Staff members must be aware of inmates' tendencies to use information garnered from continued close proximity and daily interaction to play one staff member off against another. Many of the inmates resent their perceived loss of manhood and actively seek ways to gain control of the environment. While friendly relationships can and do exist between staff and inmates, staff members can never forget that Midwest FCI is a federal prison and that the inmates are convicted criminals.

The Team's Organizational Environment

The prison system is a highly regulated environment. Federal regulations mandate many of the procedures and processes and much of the paperwork. Definitions of roles and duties provide limited flexibility. The warden may make recommendations about hiring, transfers, and promotions, but the final decision is made elsewhere. Moreover, external agencies partly determine the pace of the work. The Department of Justice and the Bureau of Prisons require reports on a certain schedule; otherwise, the warden and unit manager determine the work pace. The unit manager determines acceptable and unacceptable staff behavior within guidelines set by the warden.

As opposed to teams in other human service settings, the teams at Midwest FCI are much more likely to go by the book because of the extreme penalties for disobedience. Externally, the Department of Justice and the Bureau of Prisons promptly suspend, investigate, and (if charges are substantiated) terminate anyone accused of an infraction of the rules. Internally, an infraction could place other staff in danger and, ultimately, threaten the entire institution. For example, the dorm meeting rooms and staff offices all have glass windows that must not be covered. A staff member seeking privacy might be tempted to cover the windows, but this seemingly innocuous act would be a serious infraction because guards would be unable to maintain visual contact to ascertain safety. An inmate might then feel confident enough to take advantage of the situation by taking the staff member hostage, thereby endangering everyone.

The potentially hostile environment requires strict adherence to the myriad of prison rules and regulations, particularly during times of prison overcrowding. Yet 90 percent of the time everything runs smoothly. The staff can become lulled into a false sense of security and become lax. It takes only one brief period of laxity and one enterprising inmate to create a volatile situation.

Influences on Team Effectiveness

Unit 1 functioned more effectively than most other unit teams at Midwest FCI. They had high scores on our research measures of team effectiveness, and members reported in interviews that they perceived the team to be effective. Other staff in the institution concurred. The Unit 1 team got its work done well, on time, and with interpersonal processes that built rather than undermined the team's performance capabilities. And individual members generally reported that their own needs were more satisfied than frustrated by work in the team. The only area of concern we discovered had to do with external relationships. While within-group relations were strong and healthy, relations with prison officials, staff members outside the unit, and other unit teams were less trusting.[1]

The unit manager and team members set high standards for their collective performance and were willing to expend great effort to get the job done well. While being realistic, the team was generally positive about the inmates, willing to go the extra mile for them. Team members viewed the team as becoming increasingly effective over time. Being well perceived by others also enhanced the group's positive self-image, strengthened members' commitment to the team's work, and perpetuated their effective performance.

Three general factors appeared to contribute to the effectiveness of the Unit 1 team: the design of the team (its task, composition, and norms), organizational supports for the team (rewards and resources), and team leadership. We examine these in turn.

Team Design

The Team's Core Task. The work of the team was intrinsically meaningful, in large part because what the team did was so consequential for the inmates they served. And, although the team operated in a highly regulated and structured environment, there was some task-based autonomy: the group had latitude about how it operated so long as it did not violate federal regulations or the warden's directives.

Feedback on the group's actions was usually immediate—albeit often unpredictable. Any number of crises requiring seat-of-the-pants decision making might occur during the course of a given day. A decision made concerning one inmate had implications for many others. When the team made an unpopular decision, the displeasure multiplied rapidly as other inmates in similar situations became incensed. Effective management of this instantaneous feedback was crucial. An element of danger always existed, which made even the simplest decision something to be given careful consideration.

Team Composition. Effective decision making in the prison environment required a moderate level of knowledge and skill. Federal rules and regulations had to be clearly understood and interpreted appropriately to avoid violations. This requirement was relatively easy to fulfill. Knowledge of human behavior and people-management skills also were crucial, however, and presented more of a problem when staff were selected. Because team composition was vital, it was managed quite deliberately. When an opening occurred, prospective members were carefully screened and selected within the constraints of civil service regulations.

At the time of our study, the Unit 1 team seemed to be of precisely the right size and mix of skills for the type and volume of work they had to do. Team members got along very well. The unit manager was long tenured and thus relatively familiar with federal rules and regulations—and with the warden's style of management. In addition, the psychologist and counselors had academic training and experience in human behavior and its management.

Federal regulations and guidelines mandated training for team members. Other training was offered on an as-needed or as-available basis. Some training took the form of one-day in-house seminars on topics such as drug typologies, psychological disorders, or developing effective communication skills. Some limited opportunities for outside courses also were available. Most team members, however, were expected to come on board with the requisite knowledge and skills or to develop them on the job.

Team Norms of Conduct. The Unit 1 team developed strong group norms about what constituted acceptable and unacceptable behavior. Because the consequences of ineffective behavior were so severe, the team strictly enforced adherence to group norms—especially those having to do with interactions with inmates.

The prison environment causes inmates to develop dependencies on the unit staff, but an inmate who seeks to control his environment seeks to manage or minimize this dependency. Several strategies can accomplish this control. Most of them involve developing a special relationship with a team member to obtain special favors or opportunities. Continued proximity facilitates this, as it allows the inmate to determine how best to motivate the staff member. By learning how to meet the needs of the team member, the inmate is in a better position to have his own needs met. The inmate then begins to game the staff member. The team member may find himself providing small favors ("Get me a job in the kitchen"), larger favors ("Call my mother and ask her to send me $50"), and even illegal favors such as bringing in or taking out contraband items in exchange for compliance or in response to blackmail. Such actions endanger the entire unit team because other inmates quickly become aware of such relationships and begin to make demands. Therefore, the relationship between staff and inmates is an area in which very clear expectations of behavior exist. The staff explicitly discusses violations and severely reprimands violators.

The result at Midwest FCI was a system bounded at both the unit level and the prison level. Each unit became an entity unto itself, with its own culture, climate, and social system. Having no infractions or inmate disturbances in the unit was a point of honor, and the team oriented its norms specifically toward maintaining order. The team prodded negligent staff members gently, and sometimes not so gently, with feedback or negative reinforcement until their work met acceptable standards.

Organizational Supports

Rewards. The major reinforcements the team received were intrinsic—the pats on the back members gave each other for a job well done or the prods they applied to one another when things did not go well. These rewards derived directly from the design of the work, discussed above.

Rewards to the team from external sources were scarce. Sometimes the warden put a gold star on a piece of work he particularly liked or made some public announcement about the team's good performance. Government auditors from the regional prison system evaluated the team and its work semiannually and summarized their findings in an audit report. A good audit report contributed to the unit's reputation and was valued by team members. There also were some rewards administered to individual team members—rewards such as being promoted, being selected "Employee of the Month," or being offered the opportunity for additional training as recognition for good performance. But these, too, were relatively rare.

It was fortunate that the team had meaningful work, autonomy for carrying it out, and feedback that flowed directly from the work itself. Without the intrinsic reinforcement that came from performing such work well, it surely would have been difficult for the team to survive a system that provided extrinsic rewards so sparingly.

Other Resources. Resource availability was a problem within Midwest FCI, even in Unit 1. Although we found no evidence of performance problems directly attributable to scarcity of resources, team members did feel that the resources available to them were not commensurate with the quality and efficiency of their work.

The resource most valued by team members was information. For example, it was important for the team to know in advance about any proposed changes in federal regulations that would affect inmates so the team could prepare for its new responsibilities or requirements. Other valued resources included equipment, materials, and opportunities for training. Education provided staff cross-training, which was needed both for good team functioning and for individual advancement. Equipment and materials were both valued and scarce. But their scarcity did not appear to significantly impede the work of the team.

Leadership

The most effective units at Midwest FCI, and particularly Unit 1, had unit managers with good managerial skills. The Unit 1

leader commanded the attention and respect of top management, staff, and inmates. He was considered to be a no-nonsense
manager who went by the book but was fair. He was task-oriented, but with fairly well-developed humanistic skills. Rarely
flustered, he instilled trust, confidence, and loyalty in his team.
Moreover, he managed the team in a way that drew heavily on,
and made appropriate use of, the special knowledge, skill, and
experience of the team members—both individually and collectively.

The Unit 1 manager also was organizationally savvy. He
was always cognizant of the most current federal rules and regulations and was adept at interpreting them in ways that facilitated the work of the team. He also knew how to manage upward, and he usually was successful in obtaining critically needed
resources from top management and in preparing work that
would garner the warden's approval. In one instance, the warden was known to be resistant to granting community custody.
The unit manager was able to provide the right ingredients to
make a special case for an inmate while simultaneously gaining
commendation for the work from the warden. This inspired
confidence in both the staff and the inmates. The staff were impressed that the unit manager knew his way around the institution, and the inmates became increasingly confident that the
unit manager could and would go to bat for those who deserved
special attention.

The psychologist on the unit team shared some leadership
responsibilities with the unit manager. In an environment where
people-management is critical, a psychologist with knowledge of
human behavior is a real asset in managing behavior and in training others how to do so. In effect, the staff psychologist in Unit
1 became the informal assistant unit manager, thereby greatly
increasing the leverage of the unit manager.

Special Challenges for Correctional Teams

The cards are stacked against unit teams in correctional institutions in a number of ways. Their clients are unwilling, difficult,
and conniving. They operate in an insecure, confining, nonprivate

work environment. Members' jobs are low-status in society and mostly invisible to the public eye—unless, of course, the team makes a serious mistake that brings unwelcome attention to the team and to the prison. Prison riots and high recidivism rates are always on the front pages of newspapers, while prison successes go unreported.

Despite these problems, many unit teams are quite successful—at least by traditional prison standards. Working in a fairly routinized but potentially hostile environment, these teams somehow are able to meet the basic needs of their client group while simultaneously maintaining control and equilibrium. The best ones also establish a cooperative relationship with prison management, and they earn the respect and cooperation of their clients, the inmates.

How do they do it? Our research at FCI suggests a number of conditions that foster team effectiveness. First, team performance obviously is enhanced by having a full complement of staff—enough people to do what needs to be done. The most effective teams we studied always felt stretched, but not overloaded with work. This is an obvious point, perhaps, but it also is a condition all too rarely met in U.S. prisons. It also is important for the team to have a full complement of skills and the right mix of skills. Key among these is the ability to deal interpersonally with a highly specialized and difficult client group. In addition, teams need adequate information—about their clients certainly, but also about the rules, regulations, and constraints of their organization and the broader prison system. The culture of prisons, being institutions that withhold and confine, sometimes increases the difficulty teams have in obtaining the information they need to do their work well.

Strong, skilled leaders are also vital to the effectiveness of these teams. Leaders need to be task-oriented to be sure, but they also must have well-developed humanistic skills. They must be able to instill trust and loyalty in their team members and yet retain control. They also must be organizationally savvy—able to obtain resources in an environment in which they usually are scarce, and able to exercise influence both laterally and upward in the organization to create performance conditions that foster team effectiveness. These qualities are, of course, attractive in any team leader. But they may be harder to find and cultivate among individuals who have selected employment in a prison system than would be the case for individuals in, for example, a fast-paced, fast-growing business concern.

Group effectiveness also depends heavily on members' intrinsic motivation and on their ability to manage their groups' norms and relationships in an environment characterized by scarce resources and scarce rewards. The intrinsic motivation is developed partly through professionalism fostered by individual training and partly through the team spirit engendered by the task and by team leadership.

Having significant control over the work also is fundamental to the success of unit teams. Such control takes several forms—such as setting the pace of the work, having discretion about inmate-related decisions, and selecting the team's own internal processes. The problem is the amount of control a team has over its own affairs. In prisons, both regulation and the nature of the organization and its clients limit that control. Conditions in prisons can foster the burnout that is so common in the helping professions. Burnout tends to occur when responsibility for consequential decisions about people is high (such as determining how much longer an inmate must stay in prison), when control over the decision is low, and when there is little social support from co-workers and supervisors. Thus, it is important to design and manage prison organizations in ways that foster both team autonomy and supportive relationships within and between teams.

Finally, if teams are to be effective in a prison environment, organizational conditions and leadership practices must explicitly accommodate the symbiotic and dangerous relationship between the team and the inmates. Leaders must promote proactive management of the team-inmate relationship so that all stakeholders benefit—inmates, team members, and the broader society. It would be easy for the relationship to tip dangerously toward overcontrol of inmates—thus preventing rehabilitation—or toward undercontrol—thus increasing the physical danger to which inmates and staff are exposed. But, as the Unit

1 team demonstrated, at the Midwest Federal Correctional Institution, that relationship *can* be managed.

Note

1. However, there may have been some underlying mistrust among Unit 1 members. Of the seven research questionnaires that team members returned to us, only three identified their team. We are not sure what prompted this apparent concern about confidentiality, but it was more pronounced for this team than for others we studied at the prison.

20

Robert Bruce Shaw

Mental Health
Treatment Teams

"Name? Purpose of your visit?" The man asking the questions appeared tired from the heat and humidity. He wrote down the information I gave him and allowed me to pass through the twelve-foot walls surrounding the facility. Inside, the red brick buildings were, without exception, very large and old. A few people walked slowly across well-kept lawns. Some sat silently on benches. I turned off the main road and eventually found the unit where patients are admitted. Using a master key, I unlocked a series of doors and walked down one brightly lit hallway after another. I was struck, on entering ward F-4, by the smell of disinfectant. As the door closed behind me, I noticed a small woman walking in my direction. She smiled broadly and asked, "Do you have any cigarettes? Are you a doctor or a lawyer?" Before I could answer she added, "I'm Barbara. Do you want to play pool?"

Over the next several days, I learned that Barbara was in the hospital because of emotional problems due in part to her use of drugs. She had a history of getting high on PCP and wandering incoherent through the city's streets. Men had raped her on a number of occasions. Often, she had become agitated to the extent that someone summoned the police. Barbara had entered the hospital four times over a three-year period: she would come in when the strain of her life became too much for her or those around her, stay for five or six weeks, and then leave. Her current hospitalization began when the police brought her in at her family's request.

Soon after her arrival, Barbara sat in the ward activity room with fifteen other people. The head nurse, a woman with twenty years of experience, opened the meeting by asking the man sitting next to Barbara how he was feeling and if he had any requests. Ed whispered that he was feeling better—not as down as he had been in the past. He added that he would like to go home over the weekend. A brief discussion followed with patients and staff making observations about Ed and his condition. A number of people complained that Ed never said anything to others on the ward. The nurse then introduced Barbara, noting that this was not her first visit to the hospital. Barbara looked at the floor and said she had nothing to say.

Each patient, in turn, became the focus of attention as the head nurse went around the circle asking the same question: "How are you feeling today?" Some patients talked a great deal while others appeared more asleep than awake. Near the end of the session, one patient angrily responded to her questions by stating, "I'm sick of your attitude. You act like you know what is going on with us and you don't. Why don't you stop acting like you know it all? Why don't you stop pretending you're better than us?" The session ended after one hour with the staff moving to another room to debrief the meeting, review patient requests, and discuss upcoming ward activities. They decided, among other things, that Ed should not go home over the weekend.

A group discussion occurs every morning on Barbara's ward. Subgroups of ward staff, which I will refer to as *treatment teams*, also meet once a week to create therapeutic plans for the teams' patients. Members include a psychiatrist, a psychologist, a social worker, a nurse, and any number of psychiatric nursing assistants. Patients, family, and other staff also attend when the team needs their views. In some units, the team meets around a table in a rather formal manner. Reviews begin with a staff member, usually a psychiatric resident, giving a brief summary of a patient's condition and therapeutic history. The case is then opened to group discussion. On average, the team reviews four or five patients at any one meeting, with the psychiatric resident (or whoever is the designated team leader) facilitating the discussion. The general level of discourse in the meetings varies from one week to the next. Some meetings are intense with individual staff members vehemently arguing in favor of one plan of action over another. Other meetings are so boring that some of the staff fall asleep. Contributions to a plan's development are usually based on a staff person's disciplinary training ("As a social worker, I think Barbara's problem is due to . . . ") and interactions with patients ("I saw Barbara today and she told me . . . ").

Team members review the effectiveness of the interventions attempted since the plan was last revised. If necessary, they develop a new treatment strategy, and some proposed revisions are very specific. For example, someone might say, "Let's try putting Barbara on a new medication." Others are general: "We need to encourage her to be independent of her family." A plan emerges that everyone in the group can support, and the team leader records it in the hospital files. The team also reviews what it needs to implement the new plan effectively. For example, the team almost always informs ward staff and family members of changes in a patient's therapeutic plan.

The entire staff on a ward also meet once a week to discuss the progress of patients. These meetings are led by a ward administrator who is not a participant in the planning sessions held by treatment teams. Here, teams have an opportunity to explain the strategy they are following with their patients. The ward administrator asks each team if it would like to discuss particular patients; he also names those whose cases he would like to review. These meetings can be tense because an individual who has considerable power in the hospital is evaluating the team members. For example, ward administrators and other staff often criticize teams for what has proven to be an ineffective treatment plan. Moreover, team members, to varying degrees, also compete with one another, and arguments among group members mark some meetings.

Most patients on a short-term ward are released from the hospital after three or four weeks. Some, however, are transferred to a different type of ward—a ward designed to provide more extensive and long-term therapy. Barbara was transferred to such a unit after eight weeks on a short-term ward. Once on a long-term ward, she found that team activities became even more important as a focal point of therapy. Twice a day, four times a week, the members of her team (staff and patients) met to discuss general issues related to patient well-being. Each Monday, teams also met to comment, as a group and in a public forum, on the behavior of the ward staff. Following this meeting, everyone on the ward engaged in a general group discussion. On Tuesday and Thursday, team members participated in a group psychotherapy session. Each Friday, team members again came together to provide ward staff with an opportunity to comment on patient behavior. A combined ward meeting followed this meeting. Thus, on a typical day in a long-term ward, Barbara spent three to four hours interacting with other individuals in group events. This degree of daily involvement in ongoing team work might continue for years depending on her progress.

The Hospital and Its Teams

Regional Hospital (not its real name) has many of the characteristics of a small town. Its 100 buildings are dispersed over 300 acres of land. In addition to administrative and residential structures, Regional has a church, a library, a restaurant, an auditorium, a laundry, a machine shop, and a garage. Nearly 4,000 full-time employees staff these facilities, and almost 10,000 individuals from the nearby metropolitan area enter Regional each year for some type of psychiatric service. Within this complex system of buildings and people, one finds many different groups at work. The hospital has groups, for instance, that counsel alcoholics and others that work with troubled adolescents. Some staff groups work exclusively with Hispanic patients while others care for the elderly. Supporting these types of teams, and the team concept in general, is important at Regional because group designs are thought to improve the overall quality of psychiatric care (see Shaw, 1985).

Within most wards, treatment teams are responsible for the care of patients. Teams are staffed by a chief (usually a psychiatrist), a medical doctor, a psychologist, one or two social workers, five or six registered nurses, eight to ten psychiatric nursing assistants, and a variety of student interns. Collectively, these individuals develop and put into action a therapeutic program for each of Regional's patients. Teams report to a ward administrator, who is ultimately responsible for the patients on his or her ward. Team members also report to their functional supervisors, such as the director of social work. The functional departments are responsible for training, supervision, and appraisal, but the treatment teams are the basic units for providing therapy. Teams within Regional have either a long- or short-term focus. Short-term teams work with patients upon their initial entry into the hospital. Individuals can remain on the short-term wards for up to six months, although the average stay is about two weeks. Long-term teams specialize in the treatment of chronic disorders. Patients remain on these wards for two years or more before leaving the hospital or transferring to another, perhaps more suitable, unit.

Treatment teams at Regional also oversee the training of student interns, who become members of a team as part of their formal education. The most important interns at Regional are psychiatric residents who work for six months as full-time members of a team. Other interns in the fields of medicine, social work, psychology, nursing, and religion also participate in team activities. Some hospital staff view participation in these activities as tantamount to on-the-job training. A social worker commented, "The team experience is very important in the development of the interns. They learn about the ward and how it operates. They also learn about disciplines other than their own and the role those disciplines have in our overall treatment philosophy." Interns assist in the development of patient treatment plans. From their first day on the ward, they attend team meetings and volunteer opinions. Frequently, however, interns remain quiet because they feel their knowledge is inadequate relative to others on the ward, but they become more confident and verbal over time.

Still, the veteran members of the teams I observed—members who possess a great deal of education and experience—had questions about their own knowledge and skills. The teams at Regional did have low scores on the items in our research questionnaire that asked about the level of knowledge group members possessed. One practitioner, who had worked for years in the field of mental health, told me, "We recognize our limitations. I would be disappointed if people said that we knew all there was to know about mental disease. People who believe we have all the answers are lying to themselves and the patients we work with." Another said, "We never forget our mistakes. We can't because the consequences are so extreme. When a treatment plan fails, we see the patient stagnating on the ward for months on end. And those who do improve often come back after a short period of time in the community. Sometimes we just don't know enough to help our patients."

At Regional, treatment teams, in addition to their therapeutic and training functions, serve an important social need. Employees, particularly newcomers, are encouraged to talk openly with team members as a way of managing the stress that comes from working and training in a mental health institution. My own feelings as a researcher gave me some insight into what it is like to work in such an environment. I intended to live in one of Regional's residential units as I collected research data. I found, however, that I wanted to leave the facility at the end of each day and on weekends. Even apparently minor features of the institution, such as most doors being locked, began to bother me. I soon moved off the grounds in an attempt to lift my spirits.

My psychological reaction to the institution was similar to that of patients and staff. I talked with nurses who described the strain of working with individuals who verbally and physically assaulted them. Others noted the frustration of interacting with patients who fail to show signs of improvement despite a great deal of staff effort. (Some of the older patients at Regional have lived in the institution for thirty-five years.) Moreover, most of Regional's patients were poor and had little hope of gainful employment once they left the institution. One staff member observed, "This can be a very depressing place to work. People who can't survive in society often end up here. We patch them up and send them back into the environment that scarred them in the first place. The larger problems remain the same. Sometimes I feel like I am applying Band-Aids to the critically wounded."

Effective Team Behavior in a Mental Health Facility

Treatment teams must confront a number of dilemmas as they struggle to accomplish complex work in a difficult setting. In exploring these dilemmas, I concentrate on group and organizational factors that affect team outcomes. The findings are based on in-depth observations of two teams—one short-term and the other long-term—within the hospital. In the sections that follow, I examine mission clarity, task design, group boundaries, and leadership, and their influences on group performance. In general, my conclusions emphasize the critical role of the organizational context in determining how, and how well, treatment teams perform.

Clarity of Mission. Mission clarity is a major issue in a hospital like Regional. The most obvious service the hospital provides is therapy, and publications distributed by the hospital indicate that its purpose is to rehabilitate those with mental disorders. Indeed, almost every hospital activity is cast in terms of its therapeutic import. A second service the hospital provides is training student interns. Most disciplines within the facility have a training program and a large number of students in residence; the hospital derives a great deal of prestige from its training programs. A third service is basic mental health research. Regional has developed a variety of new therapies and techniques over its long history.

These three primary tasks often are complementary. Training and research, for instance, contribute to the quality of patient care by bringing additional funds and personnel into the hospital—including researchers who are at the forefront of their disciplines. Still, the hospital's primary tasks can also conflict. A researcher who experiments with new and untested techniques may not help, and risks harming, the patients with whom he or she is working. Training and therapeutic responsibilities also can be in conflict. For example, one nursing assistant complained, "We sometimes do things that benefit interns but not patients. Many people will tell you that patients always come first but it is simply not true. That bothers me."

Many of the problems the treatment teams encountered derived from the tension between therapy and training. The flow of trainees through the ward occasionally compromised team effectiveness. Indeed, the flow was so constant that permanent staff tended to refer to interns by function—the medical student or the nurse intern—rather than by name. Training also confused disciplinary roles within the teams. One employee noted, "A problem on this team is that the roles of the social worker, medical student, and resident are blurred. On this team you cannot count on the social worker knowing a patient's family history. Such a blurring is planned in order to give the trainees an opportunity to learn important skills."

The training of interns influenced interpersonal relationships among staff and patients. Group members noted that their teams went through a period of adjustment whenever a new trainee joined the ward. On my first day of observing the long-term team, three new nurse interns joined the staff. One of the patients commented that it was very difficult to share personal feelings with so many new people in the meetings. Similarly, patients were more anxious after a new group of psychiatric residents replaced a familiar set of residents.

Clearly, the two purposes for the teams—intern training and patient care—sometimes conflicted with each another. But some Regional employees were even unclear just why teams were being used in the hospital and how they related to the institution's mission. Some group members said that having two teams on each ward promoted closer patient-staff relationships. However, no one I talked with was aware of an optimal patient-staff ratio or had a strong view about the number of people who ideally should be on a team. My curiosity aroused, I asked a long-term employee in the hospital training section why two teams were on each ward. The reason, he said, was simple: each ward was responsible for training two psychiatric interns, and each had a team so each could have his or her own staff. Yet none of the team members I asked ever mentioned this rationale; they focused instead on the role of the teams in providing patient care. Team members were reluctant to address explicitly the trade-offs they were making. Instead, they avoided the tensions that arose from their conflicting responsibilities by downplaying one or more of the purposes that teams legitimately served in the hospital.

Treatment teams face a dilemma in being expected to realize conflicting goals. Two of the most important benefits associated with a team design are improved treatment plan quality and implementation—both of which are therapeutic advantages. Teams that want to realize these benefits must exhibit certain characteristics—for example, stable team boundaries—that may conflict with the demands of other goals, such as training interns. This conflict does not mean that group designs are inappropriate in the training of interns. In fact, the ability of teams to socialize new members effectively is impressive. It is important to note, however, that a design that promotes effective training or research may not be the same design that promotes effective therapy. At Regional, the training of interns resulted in a group design that sometimes hindered the provision of therapeutic services.

Most hospitals provide a variety of services, some of which are explicit and some of which are not. In general, Regional staff members were reluctant to confront either the trade-offs among the different services or the members' disagreements about the priorities of these various activities. Some individuals at Regional believed that treatment teams were mainly in the business of providing therapy, while others believed they were primarily for providing custodial care. Still others believed that they existed mainly to satisfy administrative requirements. Yet group members tended not to discuss—and sometimes seemed not even to recognize—such basic differences. Ideally, a team would both uncover and learn how to manage the tensions that arise from the fact that a hospital inevitably has multiple legitimate missions.

Task Design. Treatment teams need to be clear about their task priorities. If they are not, development and implementation of a coherent treatment strategy will be nearly impossible, member frustration is likely to increase, and performance surely will suffer. The difficulty the Regional teams had on this score derived directly from the tension between the custodial and therapeutic aspects of mental health work. When I explored this tension with a staff member on the short-term ward, he told me that his team believed in using drugs to stabilize patient behavior. He stated, "Unlike some wards, we act quickly to calm patients down." Other members of the same team, however, spoke with conviction about the importance of patients remaining independent of the hospital and its staff. Still unsure about the team's philosophy, I asked a team member to explain. He said, "This is an admissions ward and our function is clear. We know we are here to deal with patients when they first come into the hospital. Our identity is clear and we know what we need to do. There is more ambivalence on a long-term ward."

The short-term staff seemed to be saying, indirectly, that they were not in the business of providing therapy. This team was very successful; on our research measures, it was one of the most effective in our entire project. And it appears that its success was due, in part, to the team's ability to define its task objectives clearly. A hospital employee with long tenure summed it up this way: "The teams that have problems in this facility are those which do not understand what it is they are supposed to accomplish. We have short-term admissions teams that try to provide intensive therapy. That is not what they were set up to do, and they consequently fail because of a lack of resources and skill."

The staff on the long-term ward, on the other hand, agreed that their first priority was to provide each patient with an appropriate form of therapy. Still, mental health is an ambiguous concept, and techniques available for promoting it often are of unknown effectiveness. Therefore, staff were pursuing an inherently obscure goal with necessarily limited knowledge.

One way to respond to this double-barreled challenge is to specify only the broad, general outlines of a treatment philosophy and allow teams to develop their own strategies within those outlines. One administrator did just this, arguing that having great autonomy was the best way for team members to become competent mental health professionals. Consequently, some team members spent a great deal of time trying to decipher what the ward administrator viewed as a legitimate therapeutic strategy.

Newer team members sometimes were frustrated and unsure about their ability to help patients. As one said, "I often feel that we are lost as a team. We are not sure what we are doing and the ward administrator is unwilling, or unable, to help us." Another added, "There were times when the ward administrator was very critical but not very helpful. We could have used his help because we were not sure how to deal with the patient. He only told us that we were doing a bad job. We needed more than that. We needed guidance."

The ward administrator would clarify his perspective only when the team moved in a direction he thought unproductive. For example, one resident believed interventions of a religious nature would benefit patients. The administrator, reacting to this approach, said, "I have requested that the hospital chaplains leave therapy to us and, in turn, I have agreed that we will leave religious counseling to them." As head of the ward, the administrator was trying to strike a balance between an approach that was too general (allowing his staff to do whatever they deemed appropriate) and one that was too rigid (telling his staff how to act in every situation).

Another way to deal with the ambiguity and uncertainty of mental health work is to follow a very narrow, very safe strategy and focus one's energy on compliance with all administrative regulations. The rationale is that if a team does everything the regulations require, then surely there can be no substantial complaints about its task performance. But complaints there are, such as this comment from a member of the short-term team: "We have too many people looking at what we do—the Central Office of Quality Assurance, Joint Commission of Accredited Hospitals, work surveys, peer reviews, supervisory reviews, and so on. Most of the attention we get focuses on the records we keep. We end up spending too much time making sure the records are up to date and within regulation. We end up treating the records and not the patients." Another member added, "We frequently get bogged down in administrative details when we should be dealing with patients' problems. Important emotional issues are glossed over while we spend entire sessions discussing what I see as trivial administrative issues."

In sum, a treatment strategy that is too general may be difficult to implement, but one that is too narrow or too rigid may not adequately address the complex nature of mental disease. Constructive discussion of this tension within a team can foster more effective team behavior, as illustrated by this team member when he described one of his group's successes: "We had a patient who was not responding to our treatment plan. As a team, we talked about the problem and decided that our usual approach, the approach we preferred, was not working. We then debated various alternative approaches and decided to try something different. A behavioral approach was tried and it worked wonderfully. It was a great success because that was not our area of expertise."

Group Boundaries. On the short-term ward, the names and photographs of the training staff were posted on a bulletin board. I was surprised to find, however, that my official team list was different from that on the board. I asked one of the staff about the apparent discrepancy; he laughed and told me that people had changed teams or left the ward while the bulletin postings had remained the same. Within a few weeks, I realized that others were also confused about team membership. In fact, some did not view the treatment team as a group at all. A psychologist told me, "I have a hard time answering your questions because I don't see the team as a group. I see the entire ward as a group. We don't have a strong sense of identity; we are more members of a ward than we are members of a team. Our team task is very narrow: we get together once a week to develop treatment plans."

Even those who saw the team as an intact group gave me different lists when asked to name other members of their group. One staff member noted, "We do not have a lot of cohesiveness on our teams because of shifts in personnel. I would prefer more stable assignments which would build cohesiveness. At the present, we need to know about the patients on both teams and consequently don't learn enough about the patients on any one team. Shortages and shift work force us to operate in this manner."

The issue of group membership surfaced in another way. On the short-term ward, patients were not seen as members of the team. None of the staff mentioned patients when listing members of their group. On the long-term ward, however, patients were an integral part of the treatment teams. Staff on that ward, when asked to list members of their team, often named patients before naming their fellow employees. One person asserted, "I see the patients as part of our team. Without them, we wouldn't have a team." As team members, the patients took an active role in creating a therapeutic milieu that enabled them to recognize and manage the conflicts that brought them into the facility. Although they did not participate in the development of specific therapeutic plans, they were asked to reflect on the behavior of their fellow patients, of the staff, and of the group as a whole. And they reflected on the activities of the ward in general.

The different status levels of patients on the two teams I observed were undoubtedly related to the different tasks the teams performed. Because patients stayed on the short-term ward relatively briefly, viewing them as members of the team would only further weaken already tenuous team boundaries. Also, because the short-term ward did not provide in-depth therapy, the involvement of patients in the team was less important than it was on a long-term ward.

Team membership on the long-term ward was much more stable. Patients on that ward developed close ties to each other and to the staff. To exclude them from team membership would have been a missed therapeutic opportunity. These differences highlight the interaction between the teams' goals and the establishment of an appropriate team boundary. Each of the teams I observed sought to create, often unknowingly, an optimal group boundary, given its resources and objectives. As we will see below, that goal was not easy to accomplish because of inherent ambiguities in the tasks of the treatment teams.

Leadership Issues. Like most groups, the teams at Regional struggled with the exercise of power and authority. These matters, difficult enough by themselves, were intertwined with issues of member expertise and the status of functional disciplines in the hospital. Consider, for example, the practice at Regional of putting psychiatric interns into positions of authority on treatment teams. This practice makes sense in helping interns develop the skills needed to become competent professionals. But it also illustrates how the training function in particular, and status differences in general, sometimes can override the therapeutic function. The same phenomenon existed for psychiatric residents: they were in a position of running wards without having any experience working on them. Senior staff were required to report to individuals who knew almost nothing about the ward and its practices. Not surprisingly, problems emerged. As one veteran team member related, "We had one resident who would not incorporate our suggestions into the treatment plan. Even when she was wrong, she remained dogmatic. I persisted in making my points and was thus seen as an unrelenting critic. On several occasions, we went to the ward administrator to settle our differences. I had to stand up to her because she was making wrong decisions."

There was experimentation in the hospital to try to remedy the problem of inexperienced leaders. In one ward, the administrator removed a person from the team leader role and appointed a more experienced member as leader. Unfortunately, the new leader (a psychologist) proceeded to dominate the group to the extent of intimidating the interns, so the ward administrator then eliminated the role of team leader entirely. He explained, "The interns do not know enough to lead the group and yet we can't put them under the supervision of someone who will not allow them to develop their own skills. My compromise is to have a leaderless group." But even that arrangement was not satisfactory; there are times when a treatment team really does need a formal leader.

However, many team members did not want to be governed by a formal leader. One person told me, "I like more informal leadership. A designated team leader takes away from the team concept." One of the teams I observed wanted to involve every team member in the development and implementation of treatment plans. A social worker reported, "Some wards do not allow the psychiatric nursing assistants to write notes on the records. We believe that even the lowest nursing assistant can deal with patients and contribute to patient treatment records. We encourage them to get involved." Another person reinforced this view in explaining why she liked her team so much: "This is a very democratic team. The ward administrator has the same rights within the team as the nursing assistants. Some wards have a rigid caste system. We are open with each other. We can discuss our needs, feelings that we have about our jobs, and even our own personal lives. We are not afraid that someone will do something negative if we are honest."

Full participative decision making, whereby each staff person has an equal say in the development of treatment strategy, does give everyone voice in policy formation, and it may increase morale. Moreover, those lowest in the organizational hierarchy have a great deal of information about patients and they play an important role in implementing whatever plan is developed. Their commitment to a plan surely will be higher if they help create it.

But full participation can be an inefficient and ineffective use of team resources in resolving complicated issues. Hierarchical distinctions may indeed be necessary in some situations if a group is to benefit from the full expertise of its members. To illustrate, I talked with one team member, a nursing assistant, who felt patients should be "mothered." She was not convinced the approach her team was following was the best, even though her group had spent some time discussing the strengths and liabilities of various therapeutic perspectives. Eventually, a senior team member told her she was undermining the group's strategy and asked her to comply with the treatment plan.

Some people in a treatment team do have more training and experience than others and often are better qualified, at least in certain areas, to guide the development of a treatment plan. A medical doctor with an understanding of therapeutic theory and practice, for example, is usually in a better position to develop an effective plan than is a nursing assistant who believes in the power of mothering.

The two Regional teams were participative, but only to an extent: the psychiatrists on the wards retained the power to overrule any individual or group decision. The teams did recognize that certain individuals had expertise that was especially needed for certain problems or decisions—for example, prescribing an appropriate medication or dealing with a type of disorder with which the team had little experience. These teams frequently deferred to particular members who had special expertise for a given problem and, on occasion, even called in outside experts for consultation.

Sharing power in a multidisciplinary team can cause problems in another way. Most mental health disciplines have an area of expertise that is legitimated in the larger hospital environment, and professionals from one discipline often resist being in a group dominated by one or more members from another, higher-status discipline. Psychologists, for example, often feel the power they have in a mental hospital is less than it should be given their expertise. When working with other psychologists or with patients and their families, psychologists are empowered and relatively autonomous. Working on treatment teams at Regional was different and, in some ways, less satisfactory to them. Because these teams were dominated by psychiatrists (often merely student residents), it was clear to everyone that the medical profession controls mental hospitals. One psychologist, describing the role of his profession in the institution, summed it up: "We are all guests in the psychiatrists' house."

Task groups that encourage employee participation can threaten traditional disciplinary distinctions and reporting relationships. Commitment to treatment teamwork is often lacking because employees identify with their professional disciplines. They have good reason to do so because they are evaluated and rewarded through their disciplinary programs, not by their ward or team administrators. Thus, there is little incentive at an organizational level to view oneself primarily as a team member. In addition, employees who prefer to remain autonomous, or who believe in following a formal chain of command, may not enjoy working in a participative group. Several nurses quit one of the wards, apparently because they did not want to share with other team members the power that traditionally inheres in the nursing role. Nor were they comfortable explicitly negotiating responsibilities with other team members, as is necessary in self-managing teams.

Members of different disciplines are inclined to compete with one another for power. Consequently, they are less likely to work cooperatively in the group. Treatment teams often are stifled by precisely that which they are intended to rectify—the antagonistic stance that mental health disciplines have toward one another. The desire to sustain professional distinctions and perspectives can be so strong and so embedded in an organization's history that it undermines team effectiveness.

Conclusion

It clearly is possible to design and manage treatment teams in a mental hospital in a way that promotes their effectiveness, but it also is quite difficult to do so. In many ways, Regional Hospital, despite being a very team-oriented place, did not support its work groups. Multiple task demands made it hard for them to focus on their main work. Constantly shifting staff assignments undermined the development of group boundaries. Disciplinary factions and a rigid organizational hierarchy made it hard for members to identify with their teams, become committed to them, and self-manage within them. And although teams had ready access to organizational resources, formal organizational rewards were provided based on individual rather than team performance. Also, feedback on performance was given to individual employees, not groups, through their respective disciplinary programs. These practices tended to undermine the importance of teams as the basic service-providing units of the organization.

Treatment teams are curious entities in mental health organizations. They are intended to facilitate open communication between patients and staff and among different mental health professions. However, the various organizational groups jealously maintain their fundamental divisions, often leaving teams in a precarious position. People do agree on the need for patient and staff participation in the development of treatment plans, and this belief allows staff members to feel better about their roles in the hospital. Staff and patients can point to the existence of teams to demonstrate the importance of therapy—for example, "We need a variety of perspectives in order to come up with an appropriate therapy for each of our patients." Multidisciplinary teams are tangible proof that psychiatric service at Regional is more than custodial care. Those in positions of power can also point to the existence of multidisciplinary teams to illustrate the sharing of power among professional disciplines within the facility. Even those in positions of relatively little power, such as the nursing assistants and patients, can feel that, as team members, they have some say in what happens within the institution. Issues of intergroup conflict, domination, and control are thus muted to some extent.

Treatment teams, for all their advantages, threaten many traditions in the field of mental health. For example, bringing patients into a team that explores group-level dynamics blurs the rigid distinction between patients and staff. Asking employees to work together to develop a multidisciplinary treatment strategy challenges the well-defined hierarchy that places doctors in positions of almost uncontested power. And inviting teams to examine both their own goals and those of the institution raises the whole issue of organizational control. Thus, to do their work well, treatment teams must address and struggle to resolve a number of issues fundamental to the mental health field—issues that have burdened that field since its inception.

The dynamics of treatment teams point to a more general tension that exists between work groups and the organizations in which they operate. Specifically, the relationship between work groups and organizations often is characterized by a fundamental ambivalence based, in part, on the positive and negative consequences of using teams to accomplish work. Organizations and their leaders find work teams desirable because they are the most effective, and perhaps only, means of accomplishing certain kinds of complex tasks. Yet, work teams can become quite autonomous and powerful—to the point of challenging standard operating procedures and the authority of dominant individuals and groups within an organization. Organizations, to varying degrees, fear the development of competing groups and ideologies, and often take steps to prevent groups from challenging the status quo. These steps may appear relatively innocuous, even unintentional, but they have the cumulative effect of eroding the power and, in some cases, the effectiveness of work groups.

Some limits on the autonomy and power of groups clearly are necessary if an organization is to meet its task demands, control competing internal factions, and survive as an entity. Organizational researchers often examine the tension between individual and organizational needs. In the case of work groups, this tension is more pronounced because groups are more powerful than individuals. Organizations and their groups often exist in a dynamic relationship that is simultaneously supportive and distrusting. Albert Memmi (1984, p. 68), in his analysis of provider-dependent relationships, captures what may be a fundamental tension between organizations and their groups:

> In one of his works, Henry Moore, the great sculptor, has depicted a mother gathering her children to her and, at the same time, pushing them away. It is easy to see from the way her progeny are behaving that if she didn't push them away, they would devour her. A provider has to defend herself from her dependents. If she does defend herself, however, she appears to be doing something scandalous, becomes the object of accusations and, before too long, violence. If she doesn't defend herself, she perishes in her role as provider. . . .

21

**Addie L. Perkins
Robert Bruce Shaw
Robert I. Sutton**

᠁᠁᠁᠁᠁᠁᠁᠁᠁᠁᠁᠁᠁᠁᠁᠁

Summary: Human Service Teams

Differences among the several human service teams we studied are pronounced. Surgical teams, for example, use highly programmed technologies and are under severe time pressure; lower-status members of these teams are rarely asked their opinions about how the work should be accomplished. Correctional and mental health teams, in contrast, employ many poorly understood technologies and are under little moment-to-moment time pressure; all members of these teams contribute their opinions about the work.

Yet the differences among these teams are not nearly as striking as the similarities. Specifically, three endemic tensions were evident across the teams we studied: (1) struggling for control; (2) providing efficient versus high-quality service; and (3) balancing client needs and team member needs. This summary chapter describes these tensions and derives from them five questions whose answers may be useful in guiding the design and management of human service teams.

Struggling for Control

Members of human service teams often feel that they are fighting for control over their work—to keep both the work and other people from getting the better of them. It is a common view that power is not a zero-sum game; increasing the influence held by one group need not decrease the influence of others (see, for example, Tannenbaum, 1968). Yet members of the teams we studied generally did not hold this view. Instead, they experienced themselves as more or less constantly engaged in contests for control—with teammates, with other individuals and groups in the organization, and with representatives of the institutional environment. These contests cannot be eliminated in human service work. But the following three questions suggest some ways to minimize their negative effects—both for the quality of service to clients and for the quality of the work lives of team members.

Question One: How can the team be designed so that the internal hierarchy does not interfere with the quality of service provided? Each of the teams we studied had a clear status hierarchy. Surgeons were the masters of the operating room teams, unit managers had highest status in the correctional teams, and psychiatrists were clearly in charge of the mental health treatment teams. The quality of service each of these teams provided occasionally was impaired because higher-status members asserted and enforced their views while failing to solicit or consider the opinions of lower-status members—members who, for some aspects of the work, were more knowledgeable. This problem occurred frequently in the operating room where surgeons usually ignored the opinions of knowledgeable surgical nurses. And it was especially pronounced in the mental health teams, in which psychologists and social workers with years of experience had to defer to psychiatric residents who were new to the hospital and its practices.

Designing teams so that lower-status but knowledgeable people can be heard is difficult. One mental health team attempted to accomplish this by eliminating the role of leader. This did not work. Sometimes a formal leader really is needed— and an informal status system is almost certain to develop in the group in any case. A better way to deal with the problem would be to help the team develop norms and process skills that enable members to efficiently assess members' expertise for various problems and then to weight their inputs in accord with that assessment. Something along these lines occurred when the operating room nurses became teams. The new teams were facilitated by an organizational development consultant who met with them once each week. Members who had greater expertise than the head nurses in assisting with certain operations were encouraged to take primary responsibility for teaching those skills to less knowledgeable team members. The authority structure of the team was left firmly in place, however, and the head nurse was encouraged to exercise her authority for issues that previously had generated petty and self-serving conflict in the group—issues such as deciding when nurses could take vacation days.

Question Two: How can the team be designed so that members follow well-developed procedures for serving clients, yet retain a measure of autonomy in their work? Each of the teams we studied was bound by fairly rigid procedural rules. Correctional teams, for example, risked severe sanctions for their institutions, and even the loss of their own jobs, if they did not follow strict legal procedures. Similarly, members of surgical teams who deviated from approved medical procedures risked malpractice lawsuits and, possibly, the lives of their patients.

Human service managers may resist giving teams autonomy when independent thought and action can place the organization and its clients at risk. The controversy around surgical instrument counts is a case in point. The nurses were required to take the time to count every instrument after each operation. They disliked this work because they viewed it as beneath them and because it required them to spend time alone in the operating room counting bloody instruments before they could take a break or move on to the next operation. Yet the cost of leaving an instrument in a patient was very high, so the hospital insisted that the nurses follow a strict procedure to account for all instruments. Similarly, the mental health teams were required to follow a set of administrative guidelines so rigid that some staff complained that the records received better treatment than did the patients.

The challenge in designing human service teams, then, is to find ways to ensure that they follow critical procedures—

without undermining team autonomy. One way to accomplish this is to distinguish those aspects of the work that do not require strict procedures (as is the case, for example, in conducting long-term therapy) and give the team autonomy in those areas. This approach would provide something of a balance: low team autonomy for critical procedures of high consequence and high autonomy in other areas. This was done for the surgical nurses. When the teams were redesigned, there was no increase in autonomy regarding key surgical procedures, but teams were given substantial freedom in choosing new team members and in managing their work schedules.

Question Three: To what extent should the clients served by the team have influence on how they are treated? The clients of all three teams we studied had some measure of influence on their own treatment. Surgical patients had the least; typically, they merely discussed the planned procedures with medical staff and then signed informed consent documents. Mental health patients had the most influence. The staff viewed them as legitimate team members and encouraged them to help plan and carry out their own treatment.

Yet questions about the amount of influence clients should have did create tension in all three settings. Surgical patients, for example, sometimes were viewed as not having sufficient expertise to participate in decisions about their treatment. Mental health patients were viewed by some team members as people who could not think for themselves (if they could, it was argued, they would not be in the institution). Prison inmates were viewed as constantly gaming staff to improve their lives. When, for example, one inmate came up with an elaborate argument about why he was now ready to do yard work and take community college courses outside the prison, team members laughed openly and joked about his skill in twisting facts to help his cause.

Ideally, the amount of influence a team grants its clients would depend on their ability to choose which services they need. But the cases we examined here suggest that team members often decide to limit the influence of the people they serve for two reasons that have more to do with themselves than with their clients' capabilities. First, by restricting the influence of clients and keeping their status low, team members enhance their own power and status in the social system. Second, team-work is less complex and more efficient when members do not have to take clients' ideas and suggestions seriously. Restricting the autonomy of clients enhances that of the team. Moreover, this tactic helps team members manage the anxiety-provoking aspects of providing services to other human beings, particularly in settings such as a hospital or correctional facility where cli-ents are highly dependent on staff. The downside of this com-monly used strategy, of course, is that the clients may become depersonalized in the process and the quality of the treatment may suffer.

Providing Efficient Versus High-Quality Service

A second tension faced by human service teams is between working efficiently and working effectively. Members of the surgical team, for example, talked about how tight their sched-ule of operations was, and they complained that such schedul-ing often caused them to miss breaks. Time pressures placed obvious stress on the team—stress evidenced by within-team bickering, teasing of doctors, and expressions of hostility toward the researchers. Nevertheless, members of each team also talked about the importance of providing the best possible service. Mental health staff, for example, debated endlessly about the most appropriate treatment regime for each patient.

The problem is that providing human services efficiently and providing the best possible care often place seemingly in-compatible demands on the team. The mental health teams and the nursing team treated this as something of a "dirty little se-cret." Pressure to process people almost in a productlike and uniform manner conflicted with members' desire to see each person as an individual and to provide him or her with care spe-cifically tailored to his or her own needs.

Question Four: How can a team be designed so that members are able to balance competing pressures for efficiency and quality service? Any complete answer to this question would require specific knowledge of the human service technology used by the team. Yet we did observe two general types of response in the teams we studied. The first was denial: team members often refused to acknowledge that there was a trade-off between the efficiency and the quality of the services they provided. In the nursing team, for example, the schedule sometimes required nurses to work when they were tired or assist with operations for which they lacked experience. Despite this, nurses, doctors, and administrators all claimed that providing top quality health care was their only objective, and that they never behaved in ways that would compromise its achievement. Denial also was evident in the mental health teams: virtually every activity was portrayed in terms of its therapeutic benefit even though teams sometimes used strong and therapeutically irrelevant drugs to control patient behavior, and even though they allowed inexperienced interns to make questionable decisions about patient treatment.

A second response to the tension between efficiency and quality was for the team to alternate between the two aspirations. Members would work for a time to provide the best service of which they were capable, and then, when the need for efficiency became pressing, they would try to process clients as quickly as they could. Alternation was evident in all three types of teams we studied. In the correctional institution, for example, teams collected as much information about inmates to be "teammed" as they could, but they also made decisions under time pressure based on information members knew to be incomplete. Members of mental health teams sometimes spent enormous amounts of time trying to learn about their clients and experimenting with therapeutic techniques, but at other times they treated patients almost as objects—merely following administrative guidelines or using expedient techniques to keep behavior on the wards orderly.

These two strategies, denial and alternation, are in some ways adaptive. If members of human service teams worry too much about their inability to provide efficient and high-quality service simultaneously, anxiety and depression may develop and impair a team's ability to achieve *either* objective. Denial and alternation increase the likelihood that members of human service teams will be able to sustain their motivation and maintain their own psychological well-being over the long term.

These strategies also are insufficient, however. The designers of human service teams must take other steps to help members cope with the incompatible demands they encounter in their day-to-day work. One possibility is to legitimate the strategy of alternation—to acknowledge explicitly that alternation is necessary but also to encourage members to decide collectively and deliberately when a switch should be made. In the teams we observed, alternation occurred unconsciously and therefore created unanticipated problems for the teams and their clients. By legitimating the management of the efficiency-quality tension as part of the real and necessary work of the team—something now being done in some human service organizations—the team can reduce the frequency and severity of such problems. And, in the bargain, the team can reinforce the autonomy it has to manage its own work.

Balancing Client Needs and Team Member Needs

The clients served by human service teams need emotional support. Mentally ill patients need a supportive social environment in addition to insight about the causes of their problems. Surgical patients need assurances that their operations are safe and that they will recover. Prisoners need reinforcement for socially responsible behavior. Yet team members also require emotional support. The constant barrage of demands and problems they face can lead to hostility toward and cynicism about the very people they are seeking to help.

Question Five: How can teams be designed so that members can provide genuine emotional support and hope to clients, and at the same time cope with their own feelings of hostility and cynicism? Team members in all three settings occasionally did become cynical about their work and about their clients. Nurses assisting with coronary bypass operations, for example, expressed doubt that their patients would subsequently refrain from health-impairing behavior such as smoking and eating foods high in cholesterol. And members of teams in the prison were openly cynical about the likelihood that their clients would be rehabilitated. Nor were such feelings restricted to clients: psychologists in the mental health institution often expressed hostility toward the psychiatrists with whom they worked, and the surgical nurses sometimes felt contempt for the doctors they assisted.

Removing the forces that generate cynicism would be difficult in the organizations we studied. The socialization of doctors encourages them to treat nurses as inferior. And there really are sound reasons to mistrust prison inmates and to have doubts about the prospects of mental patients on a long-term ward.

There are at least two ways of coping with this problem. First, team members can be encouraged to vent their negative feelings at times and in settings where their clients cannot be harmed. The nurses used this strategy explicitly. Time-outs in their own lounge allowed nurses to express feelings about doctors and patients—feelings that would have been destructive if vented elsewhere. Staff meetings to which mental patients and prison inmates were not invited served a similar function in the other two organizations. By having a protected time and place where team members can express their feelings and support one another, members can tend to their own needs without placing their clients at risk.

The second solution to the problem of cynicism is more difficult to implement, but more powerful. Even if the structural causes of cynicism and hostility cannot be eliminated, team members can be made aware of the forces that generate such feelings and can work together to develop ways of managing those forces appropriately. Sometimes this will involve negotiating with other groups, as happened at the hospital when nurses met with surgeons to address the surgeons' treatment of them during operations. In the mental hospital, the multidisciplinary teams developed norms that supported a comprehensive examination of each case, taking into account the role that different groups (staff, patients, families) had to play in treatment strategies. Despite members' continuing frustration about "applying Band-Aids to the critically wounded," these teams worked hard and with some success to avoid negative stereotypes of the people they served. And that success, in turn, contributed positively to the psychological well-being of team members themselves.

Conclusion

One theme appears again and again in the human service teams we studied: members felt a continuing and aching insecurity about their ability to serve their clients well. Members of the mental health teams expressed these feelings openly, constantly worrying together about the seeming futility of their efforts to help some of their clients. Teams in the correctional institution felt chronically hampered by their lack of power to help inmates rehabilitate themselves and by their inability to make accurate predictions about inmates' future behavior. And in the operating room there was a constant fear that surgical procedures might do more harm than good and that patients could die because of imperfect technologies.

Such concerns surely are heightened when team members feel they have limited influence on the behavior of their co-workers and clients. For this reason, leadership strategies that foster the autonomy of human service teams and help members feel that, within limits, they really *can* make a difference may be among the most potent and useful interventions that can be made to improve the effectiveness of such teams.

Part Six

CUSTOMER SERVICE TEAMS: SELLING PRODUCTS AND SERVICES

Customer service teams provide services to clients. But unlike the human service teams discussed in the previous part, these teams do not seek mainly to improve the physical or psychological well-being of their clients. Instead, their objective is to provide service of sufficient quality that customers, who have a choice of providers, will continue to do business with the teams and their organizations. Regardless of whether such teams are actually called sales teams, selling is a large part of what they do, and therefore members must be especially attentive to and concerned with customers' satisfaction with their services.

Customer service teams live and work on the boundaries of their organizations. In many cases, members spend more time with customers than they do with other employees of their own firms. Because the demands of customers may conflict with organizational policies or practices, these teams often must navigate a narrow course between the wishes of their clients and the requirements of their employers. This can make life at work stressful for team members, and sometimes results in organizational labels for the teams (for example, that the team is "effective" or that it "cuts corners") that can be both enduring and self-reinforcing.

Two of the teams studied, reported in Chapter Twenty-

Two, sell and deliver beer to retail outlets, bars, and nightclubs. Management viewed one of these teams as a fine team, with both good sales figures and a good attitude; the other was viewed as constantly deviating from organizational policies and practices—probably, senior managers thought, because it was poorly led. What management did not take into account were the very different sales environments in which the two teams operated. The "good" team operated in a stable and prosperous region where standard company procedures happened to work very well, while the "bad" team had an unpredictable and highly competitive region where strict adherence to company procedures almost certainly would have resulted in poor sales performance. The ways the two teams dealt with their different environments and the response of the organization to their distinct strategies provide insight into some of the special problems with which customer service teams routinely must contend.

The other two teams, described in Chapter Twenty-Three, were located even farther from company headquarters. They were teams of flight attendants who did the bulk of their work literally up in the air, tending to safety and service for airline passengers. These two teams were also labeled differently by their organization: one was viewed as a model of what a team of flight attendants should be, while the other was characterized as lacking either the skill or motivation required for first-rate cabin service. What is particularly instructive about these teams is the fact that events very early in their lives—a favorable assignment for the "good" team, the termination of one member of the "bad" team—appear to have shaped what happened both to and within the teams throughout their entire histories.

When a team is not physically around the organization very often, as is typical of customer service teams, managers have little direct information about what the team is doing or how well it is doing it. This can result in a characterization of the team that is consequential for its future life and work—and one that is relatively unlikely to change. How this happens and what its consequences can be are seen vividly in the dynamics of the customer service teams discussed in this part.

22

Richard Saavedra

Beer Sales and Delivery Teams

Another round of beer was put before us. The mugs were impeccably chilled; the beer was served at *the* designated temperature; the head of foam was healthy. The attention to detail was impressively noticeable. "This organization," began Mr. Bruer, the president and owner of Maltshire Beer, "is about people. Our logo is a diamondlike structure of four individuals. It stands for people helping people up and outward at Maltshire Beer." Mr. Bruer sipped his beer and continued, "If people don't help and support each other, then nothing works."

The logo, which is on all employees' uniforms, is strikingly similar to another group structure: the diamond formation used by military fighter pilots in parade maneuvers. The formation is a tactic that is ever so dependent on precision teamwork and having complete trust in the abilities of the flight leader. Bruer is a retired military pilot, an avid aviator, and a very active promoter of NASA's space shuttle program. The analogy, then, is no coincidence. This is a people-oriented organization, both as a means (sales and delivery) and as an end (the customer).

361

A Nice Place to Come Home to

By any organizational standard, Maltshire Beer is a progressive company—in organizational structure, management, and physical layout and equipment. The facilities, for example, are modern, spacious, and attractive. Amenities abound: employees have a furnished lounge with projection TV, VCR, stereo equipment, Ping-Pong tables, and a large, well-equipped bar with Maltshire beer continuously on tap. In addition, they have individual lockers, a swimming pool, and a weight room. As a finishing touch, the pictoral organizational chart is prominently displayed in the lounge area. The chart is in the shape of an inverted pyramid with the CEO at the bottom. Instead of depicting individuals and their positions, it shows a series of work groups and their tasks—with sales and delivery teams at the top of the chart.

If this introduction conjures up images of a Holiday Inn, well that it should. For the two work groups that are the foci of this chapter, the contextual features of this organization make it a nice place to come "home" to after spending all day out on a sales route. These two teams live "out there" in the extraorganizational environments that will serve as the organizing framework for the description that follows.

Maltshire Beer divided its franchised distribution area into nine sales regions, and nine all-male sales and delivery teams of varying sizes and compositions serviced these areas. The president, sales manager, and chief financial officer carefully chose the two teams I studied to represent two very different kinds of teams—different both in performance effectiveness and in performance strategy.

The two groups were at the extremes of the distribution of teams at the company. One team was considered the company's best (henceforth referred to as the Topdogs); the status of the other team (henceforth referred to as the Underdogs) was not specified but it was clear from the nodding and looks among top managers that this group was a problem for the organization. As we will see, even though differences between these two teams related more to situational factors, the senior managers' view was that personal characteristics accounted most accurately for the performance differences they perceived.

Group Task Design and Management

Sales teams were responsible for marketing and distributing Maltshire Beer products to all accounts in their sales areas. Team members shared a powerful purpose: sales commissions. Specifically, members' commission checks came from total team sales. Management assigned each team a commission rate based on the sales volume and the number of accounts in its region. The team leader then set a rate per case for each member based on sales and seniority. Rates and the average number of accounts per employee were largely equivalent, however. The bottom line was that everyone had to pull his share to achieve sales goals and earn commission checks.

Group members typically operated alone or in pairs on their sales routes. The team leader coordinated backup assistance, contingent on overall work load. While members carried out the tasks on their routes in a generally independent manner, final sales volume was based on the sum of the members' combined efforts. The group's task, then, required members to pool their resources.

Specialization of member roles was an integral facet of groups at Maltshire Beer. Each group included a team leader or supervisor, an assistant team leader, driver-salesmen, route assistants or "juniors," and a coil cleaner or draft maintenance man. Sales routes rotated among group members for any of a variety of job-related or personal reasons; the group made such decisions. Occasionally, members were reassigned to another group in a different sales region. This occurred if the area became too routine or boring to an individual who wanted more stimulation or if another team needed the particular talents of an employee to strengthen sales in its area. Reassignment decisions were the prerogative of management.

Management left the pace and procedures used in carrying out the work to team members. Juniors who received on-the-job training were commonly told to observe and work with different driver-salesmen and to take the better points from each. Thus, members were encouraged to develop their own styles of work—whatever worked best for them.

The president saw the teams as self-managing mini-distributorships. He contended that group members should try to figure out the best way to do things while following a set of guidelines set forth by the brewery and the distributorship. For example, decisions about product changes or new product development rested solely with the brewery. Bruer and his sales manager, on the other hand, determined team sales goals and basic performance requirements. Together, the constraints the brewery and the distributorship imposed significantly limited the amount of autonomy and flexibility the sales teams had in the field.

The two groups I studied, then, were partly manager-led and partly self-managing. The team leader's role was to coordinate contingencies for the sharing of work and monitor members' performance. The president and sales manager selected team leaders solely on the basis of their sales records. Bruer firmly believed that effective leadership leads to good performance. He defined "effective leadership" as the ability of the team leader to motivate his men to exercise greater effort and aggressiveness in seeking new accounts and beer placements. According to Bruer's philosophy, if a team was performing below par, then it was time to change its leader.

Team-Environment Relations

Environmental factors strongly influenced sales revenue and operating practices for teams at Maltshire Beer. Market characteristics such as stability and predictability explain the *client* aspects of the environment. Organizational policies about product marketing and point-of-sale advertising are the fundamental *organizational* aspects of this environment.

Market Characteristics. Market stability and predictability directly influence sales revenue and operating procedures. Market stability refers to the volatility of the sales environment. Markets are volatile when retail purchasing policies, customer-induced competition, and requirements of special interest groups change frequently. It is hard to make predictions about sales volume or to know ahead of time how to ensure good sales in a volatile environment.

The characteristics of the markets serviced by the Underdogs and the Topdogs were remarkably different. The Underdogs operated in a volatile market—one consisting primarily of bars, convenience stores, and military accounts. Moreover, their sales region was in an area of the city in which commercial zoning had peaked: market growth was minimal. The Underdogs faced two major obstacles. First, the group had heavy competition from other product distributors; its region was very much a buyer's market, with retailers fostering competition among distributors and carefully comparing their promotional policies. For bars and military accounts in particular, product adoptions and sponsorship depended on product discounting and advertising. Second, the Underdogs had to conform to mandated purchasing policies related to alcohol sales at military posts—a situation peculiar to their sales area. In general, the Underdogs found themselves in a sales environment that was turbulent, unpredictable, and very competitive.

The major retail customers for the Topdogs, on the other hand, were large supermarket chain stores and popular nightclubs. The region was both stable and conducive to increased sales over time. Moreover, the region itself was an area with high market growth potential. For the Topdogs, changes in the environment occurred gradually, predictably, and usually in an agreeable direction.

Product Marketing. Both teams I studied had an unwavering commitment to quality—quality of product and quality of service. This commitment appeared to be the direct result of brewery and distributorship policies developed to compete with other breweries and distributors.

To ensure product freshness, a team had to follow beer rotation procedures carefully, always stocking older beer on top of newer beer and never leaving beer unrefrigerated for more than three days. Product quality was checked by four quality control inspectors, each of whom was a product and service expert with between fifteen and twenty years of experience at the company. The inspectors advised the sales manager of any negligence they found, and he, in turn, relayed the report to the responsible team leader.

To ensure quality service, a driver-salesman could never allow an account to run out of beer. He was never to offer inducements to accounts for the purpose of increasing sales, nor was he to leave an account without first receiving payment for delivery. Finally, team members were never to service accounts in dirty uniforms or trucks.

Such policies reflected the pride and confidence the Maltshire organization had in its products and the company's driving commitment to differentiate its product from other beers. It is unclear, however, to what extent retailers or the public were fully aware of what a Maltshire driver-salesman went through to ensure product and service quality.

Point-of-Sale Advertising. A team member had personal leverage on sales when he was managing a one-on-one transaction with a retail customer. That is when interpersonal sales strategy is crucial. A key aspect of such interchanges is providing retailers with point-of-sale (POS) advertising, such as lamps, calendars, clocks, and posters that carry company advertising. While Maltshire's competitors used POS advertising liberally to influence sales, Maltshire believed that the product would sell itself. Consequently, POS items were scarce and their use was highly regulated by the company.

The Topdogs dealt mainly with middle managers in the retail organizations they served. Customer demand and product cost strongly influenced these managers, and they had little interest in POS items. A few convenience store and bar owner-managers, however, did request POS advertising from time to time, and the ability of the team to meet these requests was consequential for the amount of product space and visibility Maltshire beer received in these establishments.

Because of the nature of its market, the Underdog team received many more requests for POS items than did the Topdogs. Moreover, these requests were more clearly linked to sales for the Underdogs than they were for the Topdogs. Yet the Underdogs had little discretion in providing POS items because management retained such tight control over their distribution.

The retail account manager clearly was vital to beer sales. To maximize sales, he made decisions continuously about matters such as POS advertising, account management procedures, delivery schedules, and storage policy. Even though a team's actual work experience in the region surely should have informed decision making about such matters, a team in the field had little say about them. They were, instead, codified in company-wide policy enforced by management.

Summary. I have discussed three aspects of team-environment relations: market stability and predictability, product marketing, and point-of-sale advertising. To the extent that organizational policies and practices dovetail with environmental demands, teams should encounter few built-in sales problems. If, however, there is significant variation in the environment, then team performance strategies must be tailored to fit the needs and expectations of retailers in different regions. If this is not done, then a team is unlikely to be competitive. The emphasis, at Maltshire, on standard, company-wide policies and procedures made it difficult for teams to tailor their services to idiosyncratic client needs or requests.

Topdogs Versus Underdogs: Team Profiles

Our research questionnaire showed that the two teams studied had strikingly similar profiles on almost all of our measures of task and interpersonal behavior. A significant difference between them was observed on only one variable, which I will discuss later. It is curious, therefore, that Maltshire management perceived there to be major differences between the two teams. Were these differences real, or were they merely imputed to the groups by management?

Work Strategies: Scanning and Planning. Because of the uncertainty that characterizes sales environments, assessing the environment and developing sales strategies based on that assessment are indispensable to sales team effectiveness. Yet at Maltshire, company policies and task requirements significantly limited the latitude teams had to accomplish this. Customers further limited teams' degrees of freedom. Specifically, the stores, restaurants, bars, and nightclubs served by Maltshire teams had to approve all deliveries, signs, and promotions.

The interaction between a driver-salesman and his retail customer is the only area in which a performance strategy will, in fact, make a difference. If a store manager liked a Maltshire team member's interpersonal style and was satisfied with both the quality of his work (for example, proper merchandising and clean signs) and the quantity of product provided (for example, not allowing the store to run out of beer while still maintaining a conservative storage stock), then the manager was likely to maintain the account at its present level and, possibly, increase it in the future. Managing the relationship between Maltshire Beer and its accounts was, at once, the driver-salesman's only real area of autonomy and his point of greatest leverage in affecting performance outcomes.

At times, autonomy was a double-edged sword for Maltshire driver-salesmen: company and brewery requirements and constraints had to be carefully weighed against competing and, at times, contrary requests or demands from clients. When organizational and client demands conflicted for Maltshire teams, the team leader made the judgment call. In the view of team members, successful decisions indicated effective leadership, and decisions that backfired were attributed to faulty leadership. Furthermore, because performance strategies were wholly attributed to a team's leader, he was held completely accountable for their consequences by the organization.

Environmental scanning and assessment were among the major strengths of the Underdogs. Norms supporting the active scanning of both organizational and extraorganizational constraints were especially evident. This team strove constantly for self-sufficiency and control over its environment. To achieve this, the group developed its own procedures for managing client transactions. Members got the job done despite company rules and they learned effective ways to cut red tape for military accounts. The team was independent and competitive, but members did not always toe the line of company policy. The team's stance in the field was: "If it will help the sale and not hurt the company, do it." This strategy was the team's way of countering the inattention to the client environment that characterized both the brewery and the distributorship.

It was common, for example, for a competing distributor to buy several kegs of beer for a bar, restaurant, or nightclub to "sample." Salesmen kept the establishment stocked over a weekend, during which the owner could sell the product at 100 percent profit. *Maltshire Beer does not believe such tactics are necessary: the beer will sell itself.* Sometimes a beer distributor would offer to "redecorate" a bar with new hanging lamps, pool table lamps, posters, wall clocks, and calendars in return for exclusive use of the distributor's product. *Maltshire Beer believes customer demand will eventually triumph.* Or a purchaser for a nightclub or military officers' club might request special delivery service in return for a favorable purchase. *Maltshire Beer will not compromise its standard operating procedures.* Others, however, did.

How did the Underdogs handle such behavior by competitors? For one thing, the team hoarded clocks, calendars, and lamps originally intended for company-approved customers. They used such perks to pacify particularly demanding customers who threatened to close an account if they did not get the POS products they requested. Although this practice was a form of misappropriation of company property, it was also critical to team survival in the Underdogs' glitzy sales region. Second, the Underdogs often made covert deliveries on members' own time to insistent purchasers or picky nightclubs. Third, the team sometimes bought one or more kegs as a present for a special client's private weekend party. Finally, team members sometimes left a store without collecting for their delivery. This enabled a store manager to begin selling the product to help with a cash flow problem; the salesmen returned and collected later in the day.

Yet even in the thick of a clandestine operation, the Underdogs always adhered to Maltshire Beer's quality control procedures. These measures were sacred and were the source of the fierce Maltshire pride. All purchases were made with the team members' personal funds; the vouchers, however, were falsified.

For the Topdogs, performance strategies were very different. In this team's region, managers of stores, restaurants, and bars frequently provided specific guidelines for beer delivery (time, place, and frequency), beer storage, merchandising practices, advertising, payment, and product displays. Complying with these requirements was highly consequential for maintaining and developing these accounts. The problem was that client mandates often conflicted with the company's standard operating procedures. The Topdogs' response when this happened invariably was to follow company-specified procedures: "They're there for a reason." The norm for this team was to do what the company said. Extra service was not provided, requests for special favors were denied, and customers were not given unauthorized promotional products.

Leadership: Participation and Decision Control. Because Maltshire teams were mixed between manager-led and self-managing designs, and because the president was so insistent that good leadership creates effective team performance, leadership processes in the two teams require special description and comment.

For the Underdogs, the team leader coordinated both task and social activities. He did not allow criticism to be exchanged among members, but insisted that he handle all problems himself. Even though this team was very self-sufficient in its interactions with its environment, it also was very dependent on the leader. For example, member feelings of inequity about shares of the overall work load were directed exclusively to the team leader. If he saw those feelings as legitimate, he would immediately call a team meeting to discuss and resolve the problem. If he felt they were not legitimate, then members had to continue to suffer in silence. Members often agreed with the team leader just to avoid problems. The Underdogs' leader maintained that his style of working with group members made their jobs easier and that he bothered them as little as possible. And that was true as long as members abided by his rules. This was *his* team and he ran it as *he* saw fit. In short, this team leader was control-oriented and often rather autocratic.

Unlike the Underdogs, the Topdogs managed their task and interpersonal functions as a group, with the team leader serving mainly as a coordinator and the moderator of group discussions. Although members easily could have shrugged off such responsibilities, which were, after all, the formal responsibility of the team leader, they did not. Instead, they worked collaboratively to try to make their team as effective and harmonious as they could. The team leader encouraged and supported such efforts.

The Topdogs' leader understood that at Maltshire the team leader was supposed to call the shots for the team, and he took his role responsibilities very seriously. However, he personally preferred to use a participative leadership style, and he encouraged members to challenge him or raise questions about his decisions. At the same time, he was concerned that his attempts to be consultative might be misconstrued as being soft or uncertain. He resolved this tension by charting a middle course: anything and everything was open for group discussion. He listened carefully to what members had to say, but in the end he made the final decision for the group.

Group Composition and Group Processes. The Underdogs had the largest sales area to cover and the largest volume to manage in the entire company. With nine members, it also was the largest team in the company. In fact, it was the consolidation of two teams under a single team leader. Reflecting on the responsibilities of his men, the leader observed, "There's too much work for one person, but not enough for two."

Because of problems with communication in such a large work group, the team experienced difficulties carrying out its planned strategies. Members reported that between 5 and 10 percent of the time actual practice fell short of plans. When management developed long-term contingencies for teamwork in the field, confusion arose about who was supposed to be where, when, and why. Members had trouble remembering the details of how responsibilities were to be rotated for some aspects of the work.

The Underdogs' heterogeneity of membership also made it unique among Maltshire teams. One member characterized the team as being "four young and crazy guys and four older, serious guys." The four younger members were a close-knit subgroup. They worked and played together. They also had common views about their team leader, the meaning of their work, and their futures at Maltshire Beer. The younger members were out to prove themselves. They worked to the hilt, and they had the full respect and approval of their team leader. They referred to the leader as their "stepdad" and indeed they viewed him much that way.

The older driver-salesmen, on the other hand, had been at their jobs for ten to sixteen years and felt they did not have to prove themselves to anyone. Whereas the younger members were playful, happy-go-lucky, and ready to conquer the world, the older members were more task-oriented, valued job security, and liked to spend more time with their families. This group was not close-knit: only two of the four members stuck closely together.

The team leader clearly favored the younger members, whom he called his "wild bunch" or "second family." He believed them to be more industrious, more eager, and more responsive to his leadership than were the older members who, he said, "just want to go home." Three of the older members expressed dislike for the team leader, who reported that the feeling was mutual. He acknowledged that he would gladly trade them in for three "green kids," and the four younger members said they would feel little remorse if the older members were in fact replaced.

The two subgroups competed for the team leader's favor: older members asserted that some of the young members played up to the team leader and that he, in turn, had pets whom he helped at the expense of other members. Clearly, the existence of the subgroups and the team leader's personal preferences negatively affected the cohesiveness of the team as a whole. Overall, however, the leader reported, his team "got along" 75 to 80 percent of the time.

The Topdogs' composition and group dynamics were quite different. The team had seven members, who had very similar levels of knowledge and skills, who used essentially the same performance strategies, and who exhibited comparable interpersonal styles—especially regarding the use of humor. The Topdogs represented an intermediate position both on demographics and on members' tenure and experience in the company. And members got along well. I found no serious problems or unexploited opportunities involving their effort, talent, or development and implementation of team performance strategies. Nor did I observe competition among members for the favor of the team leader.

However, the Topdogs, as a group, expressed greater dissatisfaction than did the Underdogs with the weighting process by which the team assessed and used the potential contributions of different individuals. Because the talents and expertise of Topdog members were generally equivalent, the team had no basis for objective discrimination among members' suggestions— even though they recognized the need to weight differentially these inputs during problem solving. Because of their homogeneity, the Topdogs dealt with questions about performance strategy by consulting other teams. By contrast, the Underdogs rejected consultation from outside the team, relying instead on wide-ranging member talents, experience, and options—as well as on their leader, who enjoyed his role as gatekeeper.

Because the Topdogs were so productive and because individuals were able to be open with each other about both personal and business matters, members derived a great deal of satisfaction from their team membership. The team managed to achieve a good balance between productivity and amiable, supportive relationships. Their supportive and enjoyable relations enhanced members' ability to work together.

Environmental Influences on Team "Personalities." Since the two teams operated in such different sales environments, it is useful to consider whether the properties of their sales regions influenced the behaviors members exhibited at work. There does seem to be a relationship. As noted above, the Underdogs' volatile sales environment tempted members to behave in ways that violated the standard operating procedures of the company. Such risk taking resulted in the team behaving in unusually political ways toward company management. And, to protect his camp, the team leader was a strong advocate of active situation scanning and strategy planning. He also kept a close watch on his men, making sure they were always well prepared for their work. By taking care of both business and personal matters internally, the team sought to avoid scrutiny by top management.

Bruer disliked and distrusted this team's cloak-and-dagger profile and attributed it exclusively to the team leader. He commented that one day the Underdogs' leader would go too far and that he wanted to be there to nab him. The political dynamics between Bruer and this team often were counterproductive: Bruer would "get" the team leader by denying the team's request for a higher commission rate, while the team leader would "get" management by pointedly ignoring company policy even when there was no particular reason to do so.

The guarded "personality" of the Underdogs stood in marked contrast to that of the Topdogs. The Topdogs were Maltshire's team. It was the leading sales team, the team that never fell short on inspection, the team that interacted smoothly with retail customers, the team that never had interpersonal problems. In short, this team was successful, dynamic, and attractive; members had a winning style and they wore it well. While it seems clear that the team's stable, responsive sales environment contributed directly to its style of operating, top management did not entertain this possibility. Instead, Bruer attributed the Topdogs' sales record completely to the qualities of the team and its leader.

Team Strategy and Task Effectiveness

Having examined the team profiles for the Topdogs and the Underdogs, a critical question remains: How did they actually do? The three criteria assessed in our research project were task performance (in this case, sales), team health, and individual satisfaction. With respect to team health, the Underdogs were less well off than were the Topdogs. On the other two criteria, our research measures showed that the two Maltshire teams were approximately equally effective—although they accomplished this in very different ways.

The Topdogs and the Underdogs encountered very different obstacles to effectiveness, and each developed its unique way of overcoming those obstacles. Overall, the Underdogs developed and insistently used a *proactive* strategy in dealing with both its customers and the Maltshire organization. The Topdogs relied on a more *adaptive* strategy. Both teams were served well by the strategies they evolved.

Underdogs. As noted earlier, the Underdogs operated in a turbulent and unpredictable sales market. To survive, the team had to develop operating practices that were flexible and responsive to sudden or unexpected changes in the behaviors of its retail customers and competitors. With this strategy, the Underdogs were able to forecast and take advantage of new opportunities, as well as to regulate existing client relationships. The team's large size and the changing nature of its market required unusually strong coordinative direction by the team's leader. He was not at all shy about providing it, but many times he neglected the needs of individual group members or he subjugated them to the needs of the group.

The team leader's power, coupled with the Underdogs' motivation to improve task performance, resulted in high vigilance within the team regarding the equity of member work efforts—especially between the two subgroups. This system of maintaining the team, while apparently necessary given the power dynamics within the group, also increased the reliance of the team on the team leader's negotiation abilities, problem-solving skills, and vision. And the Underdogs' leader did draw well on his considerable sales experience to position the team favorably in a dense and competitive sales jungle dominated by powerful retail customers.

How a team is led is consequential not only for performance outcomes but also for member motivation and satisfaction. The Underdogs, as a group, reported significantly higher "internal work motivation" than did the Topdogs. Internal motivation means that members feel a sense of personal satisfaction when they learn they have performed well, and feel bad or unhappy when they discover they have performed poorly. Because their sales environment was volatile, and because the team leader helped the team to do whatever had to be done within broad limits to compete in that environment, the Underdogs invented and implemented their own performance strategies. This approach apparently increased the degree to which members felt directly responsible for performance outcomes—and self-motivated to adjust them when they did not generate the outcomes the team expected.

There were, without question, problems in the design of the Underdog team. As we have seen, members were able to overcome most of them and turn in good sales performance. Yet the consistently negative evaluations received from top management clearly dampened team performance. Moreover, relations in the group and intermember cooperation often suffered when performance slipped. It is known that team processes are affected by managerial evaluations and by performance outcomes. The effect was heightened at Maltshire, however, because individuals' commission checks depended directly on total sales revenue.

Topdogs. The Topdogs operated in a generally stable and predictable environment. This team managed its business by adapting or conforming to trends in its market. Because its sales environment was so benign, the Topdogs' reliance on prepared work strategies did not have a significantly negative effect on revenue. Indeed, reliance on standard customer management procedures appeared to give the team the time to develop more comprehensive and effective strategies for coordinating among members. This team had the time to fine-tune its internal work processes.

Because of the Topdogs' reasonable size and its slow-changing market, the team leader's behavior was generally supportive and consultative. Members reported that they experienced a good balance between the amount of attention given to group versus individual goals. And, of course, group processes surely were enhanced by the fact that top management let it be known to all that the Topdogs were the leading sales team in the entire organization.

Conclusions

Trail Markers. Traditionally, psychological research from both social and organizational camps has focused on cause-effect models of group performance. A great deal of the work from this tradition subscribes to and advocates a tightly coupled linkage between hypothesized causes and observed effects. Although simple cause-effect models have been useful in guiding thinking and experimentation, it may now be time to depart from convention. Traditional "maps" have prompted designers and researchers of groups to follow certain roads—roads that, by virtue of being tried and tested, have come to be exceedingly well traveled over the years. The Maltshire teams suggest an alternative.

We have examined two teams, with essentially the same task, that evolved noticeably different ways to be effective. These teams varied markedly in their makeup, leadership, and group dynamics—as well as in the characteristics of their sales regions. Despite these complex and divergent sources of influence, the teams turned in performances that were remarkably comparable. Given their respective environments and structures, the two teams employed work strategies that, while contrasting, were compatible with the trail markers or characteristics of their clients. They affirm that there is no one best way for a group to be effective.

Inferences from Preferences. Although the Topdogs and the Underdogs were roughly equivalent in effectiveness, the organization—especially the president—viewed them as conspicuously different. Why? In general, Bruer made dispositional, as opposed to situational, attributions about the causes of events. An attribution is a retrospective causal explanation for why past incidents occurred as they did. Bruer was apt to assign the cause for an outcome such as success or failure to a team rather than to some feature of the situation. This tendency is so common that it has been called the *fundamental attribution error*. Actually, it is not as much an error as it is a reasonable perception, given the kind and amount of information a person has.

A team may, for example, attribute fluctuations in its performance to changes in the client environment. These *external* attributions are reasonable, given the detailed information that the team has about its environment. A manager like Bruer, on the other hand, is not privy to such information because he has no contact with the field. Moreover, he believes not only that client environments are comparable across teams, but also that they are relatively stable. It comes as no surprise, then, that he suspected that the causes of performance fluctuations were due to variations in factors *internal* to the teams—factors under the willful control of the teams and, especially, of their leaders. The caution to team designers and managers is unmistakable: be careful about inferences and attributions, because appearances can be deceiving when they are gathered from any single perspective.

Liable Leaders. To complicate matters, Bruer believed that leadership is the main factor that affects team performance. In keeping with his ideas about how teams and team leaders are supposed to act, he invariably attributed shortcomings in achieving sales goals or accomplishing modifications in operating practices to the relative incompetence or insubordination of the leader of the team having difficulty. Because the Topdogs acted and achieved without incident or plea for assistance, Bruer viewed their leader as effective. Because the Underdogs complained of inequitable commission rates given their brutally competitive client environment, and because they resorted to unorthodox performance strategies that did not conform to company policy, he considered them unmotivated and poorly led. A consideration of the starkly different markets of the two teams never entered into Bruer's analysis.

Environmental Imperatives. The external environment of the Maltshire distributorship was enormously powerful, both in affecting realistic sales potential and in conditioning the kinds of strategie. that a group needed to use to succeed. A group may require a substantial degree of latitude to operate effectively in its client environment, and if an organization has groups that operate in dissimilar environments, it is perilous to develop and enforce standard operating procedures. An analysis of client environments for sales groups surely should precede discussions about how teams should operate or decisions about the kinds of data that are needed to explain variations in performance outcomes.

Unregimented Capability. To succeed in their work, the Underdogs actually had to deceive and, in some sense, beat the organization—suggesting that the team had insufficient legitimate autonomy. The team was strongly motivated to use members' ingenuity to succeed because of the clarity, importance, and public character of bottom-line sales figures. Not only were team members' billfolds hostage to sales figures, but so were the team's reputation and its standing relative to others in the company.

The fundamental tension between cross-team standardization and team autonomy is a fundamental one for any organization in which team performance is highly consequential for organizational effectiveness. Just where and how does an organization draw the line between insistence on core, shared standards and values and the provision of sufficient autonomy for teams—autonomy they need to adapt to the uniqueness of their external environments and capitalize on their special internal resources?

Teams at Maltshire Beer ostensibly achieved coordination through standard operating procedures. From the perspective of top management, there were no game plans or performance strategies for teams to devise; team decisions were to be merely tactical. In this model, the real test of team leaders was their ability to make judgments about implementation in real time and keep members motivated and aligned with corporate standards. Management's pervasive insistence on product and service quality was indeed a positive feature of the work design at Maltshire. But management made a basic error by limiting the autonomy it gave the teams to do what needed to be done to achieve service and sales objectives.

As we have seen, the two teams handled their limited autonomy differently, and that difference appears to reflect the preferred styles of the respective team leaders. The Underdogs were under the direction of a capable and directive *strategist* who developed and implemented innovative performance strategies. This team dealt effectively with instability and uncertainty in the client environment—but ineffectively with organizational policies. The Topdogs were under the direction of a competent and fair *tactician* who closely followed organizationally developed and mandated procedures. This team dealt effectively with the stability and certainty in its client environment and epitomized the organization's model of what a sales team should be.

Both strategies worked in that both teams turned in good sales performances fairly consistently. Yet one wonders how much of the real potential of either team was actually realized. What could team performance at Maltshire have been if management had provided a better balance between centrally provided direction about goals and nonnegotiable quality standards on the one hand and decentralized autonomy for teams to manage client relations within those boundaries on the other?

Coming Home. Retailers have been serviced. The equipment is clean. The accounting is complete. The day is done. It is time to unwind and to have a cold Maltshire beer. It *is* tough work, and Maltshire Beer *is* a nice place to come home to after spending a day in a rigorous and demanding environment. When the work is done, the niceties of the physical space where teams debrief, regroup, and relax create an atmosphere of lightheartedness and calm.

Maltshire Beer is roughly the sum of its nine sales and delivery teams. With its dispersed and quasi-autonomous teams, the organization is a loosely coupled system when it is in its operational mode. When teams return to their base, however, the organization resembles a tightly coupled system as seen in the high reciprocal interdependence both within and across teams. To the observer, such social interaction is more important than the sum of the sales activities of individual teams and individual members. The cozy and entertaining home base provides a place for members to cohere—as teams and as an organization.

Providing a home is a critical ingredient of the organizational stew at Maltshire. The physical plant is a forum for the psychosocial integration that is necessary for maintaining core, shared standards and values. And it fosters the technical integration that comes from informal exchange of data on operational tactics and the idiosyncrasies of customers. In its design and focus, this is indeed a people-oriented organization.

23

Susan G. Cohen
Daniel R. Denison

Flight Attendant Teams

Team One

Kate and Dave were returning to the Newark hub of People Express Airlines after their overnight in Pittsburgh. They had checked into the Pittsburgh city station and the city manager informed them that an in-flight coordinator was going to observe their flight. Mindy, the in-flight coordinator, joined Kate and Dave and enthusiastically said, "I'll be joining you for a support ride." Kate smiled and said welcome, but her voice had an edge to it. When Mindy turned away, Dave rolled his eyes and Kate laughed.

Mindy, Kate, and Dave had been in the same training class for new customer service managers (flight attendants) when they all had joined the company about a year earlier. Mindy had become an in-flight coordinator—but she was not quite sure what this meant. For their part, Kate and Dave resented receiving feedback from another customer service manager. A "support ride," Kate explained, was just another term for a "check ride." She had resented check rides in her former job as a flight attendant for another airline and felt that an airline that believed in self-management should be different.

The third customer service manager assigned to the flight was new to the airline. She had just completed training,

382

and this was her second flight. Dave and Kate asked her to serve beverages so they could concentrate on collecting revenues (the airline used an in-flight ticketing procedure). It turned out that there was a discrepancy in their figures, so they spent most of the flight time checking the books. The beverage service was not completed, and some of the passengers complained about the lack of service.

At the end of the flight, Kate and Dave asked Mindy for her feedback. She said that she was late for a meeting in Newark and that she would get back to them. When they met two weeks later, Kate and Dave had flown several flights and could barely remember the specifics of this particular leg. Mindy said that basically they had done a good job, but they could have been more enthusiastic. She also suggested that they split up the beverage service, beginning one cart in the center of the cabin. Arguing that ticketing was their first priority, the team dismissed Mindy's suggestions.

Team Two

"These guys are great!" Gerry said as we walked down the hallway to meet the members of the team for the first time. Our first encounters with teams we study are often awkward; the teams are uncertain why they are being studied and not quite sure how to deal with a researcher who wants to observe. But it was easy with Team Two. We talked excitedly about the team and the airline for almost an hour before it was time to leave on an Albany overnight followed by a Jacksonville turn—airline language for an early evening trip to Albany, a stay overnight before returning to Newark, followed by a round trip to Jacksonville.

The flight to Albany was crowded, but the team boarded and seated the passengers quickly. Eileen greeted them at the front door, Karl helped stow their bags midcabin, and Harvey stayed in the back to encourage passengers to come all the way back and fill up the seats in the rear. They were friendly and helpful and appeared very professional.

Once everyone was seated, the show began. All of the team members obviously enjoyed the attention they received from the passengers, and they saw their work as something of a performance—for the researcher as well as for the passengers. Karl did the announcements and quickly put everyone at ease with a combination of humor and professionalism. We felt like guests on this flight rather than passengers.

En route to Albany, the time available to ticket and to serve beverages to passengers is only about forty minutes, and this flight had a full load of 118 passengers. To pull it off, Harvey started in midcabin serving beverages while Eileen started ticketing at the front of the plane. Karl followed her down the aisle with the second beverage cart. They had invented this method of ticketing and serving beverages so that they could ticket and beverage everyone, even on short flights. It worked. Team members flew down the aisle taking money, issuing tickets, and serving drinks, and they finished selling the last ticket just as the pilot announced, "We are now beginning our descent into Albany."

A day later, on the longer flight to Jacksonville, the team did a more relaxed version of the same in-flight task, but this time they added a few extras. Since the flight was two hours long, they took time for extended conversations with their passengers. Karl, Eileen, and Harvey seldom stopped talking. In addition, since they had more than enough time to finish ticketing, they used a second beverage cart to serve passengers in the back—the smokers—a second drink.

These two teams are both customer service manager (CSM) teams at an airline designed and managed to foster high employee commitment and participation. CSMs worked in self-managing teams on board the aircraft to provide cabin service and ticketing and to ensure passenger safety. In addition to this work, similar to that performed by flight attendants on other airlines, CSMs also worked regularly on the ground, checking bags and directing passengers to their flights, and often they had staff responsibilities (such as marketing, revenue accounting, or reservations) as well. CSMs usually worked in teams of three, which were formed as a part of a team-building process that occurred during their initial training. Team members stayed together, working as a unit in ground operations, in staff work, and in flight for an indefinite period of time. This chapter examines the two CSM teams sketched above—one highly effective and one relatively ineffective—and attempts to identify the factors that explain the differences between them.

The Two Teams: Wunderkind and Dyad

Both teams were part of People Express, which at the time of the research was a young and rapidly growing airline. The company used a number of innovative management practices such as stock ownership, profit sharing, cross-utilization, and self-management (Denison, 1985; Hackman, 1984; Reimer, 1984). Teams were relied upon to make decisions and perform work wherever possible, and there was an explicit recognition that productivity depends as much on teamwork as it does on individual effort. These management practices stood in stark contrast to those of traditional airlines, where performance typically was controlled through the standardization of jobs and a strict division of labor.

We will refer to the two teams we studied by the pseudonyms Wunderkind and Dyad. The Wunderkind team had a reputation throughout the company for both its sociability and its effective performance. It was, in fact, picked for the study as a model team, exemplary in performance and attitude. Its inflight service was exceptional, and it always completed on-board ticketing, even on short, crowded flights. Its beverage service was quick and efficient, and it provided a second service on all but the shortest flights. The team members were unbridled in their enthusiasm for their work, the company, and each other. In one member's words, "Our group's performance always exceeds the expectations of our passengers and fellow managers. We have an excellent turnaround time [and] good passenger relations."

The Wunderkind team consisted of two males and one female, all Caucasians in their late twenties. At the time of the study, they had been together about fourteen months; this was the only team that they had been a part of at People Express. In addition to being effective at work, they also socialized and even took vacations together. They exemplified the spirit of People Express in their claim that "The group that plays together stays together."

The Dyad team was unusual in that it had only two permanent members. This team originally had been a three-person team, but one of the original members had left the company, so the team now required a "rotating third" for each trip. The Dyad was composed of a twenty-seven-year-old Asian-American female and a thirty-one-year-old Caucasian male. Both members had worked for People Express for about twelve months. Before joining the company, Kate had worked as a flight attendant for another airline and Dave had worked in the mental health field. This was the second in-flight team for both members; they chose each other after they gained some experience working together in flight and on the ground checking in customers. Although the Dyad was able to complete ticketing and beverage service on long flights, it usually did not complete all services on short flights with full passenger loads. The Dyad also had occasional difficulties adapting to and including the rotating third member. The in-flight coordinator, who was familiar with the performance and working styles of the CSM teams, evaluated this team as lacking enthusiasm for customer service. Nonetheless, passengers generally expressed satisfaction with the team's performance, and the researcher who observed the team saw members respond efficiently and professionally to a medical emergency.

Both teams performed the same work for the same organization and had been with the company about the same length of time. Members were all about the same age, and members of both teams freely selected one another as teammates. Still, the teams differed dramatically in performance. What are the reasons for this difference?

Group Size. The most obvious difference between the two teams is the number of permanent members. The Dyad functioned as a two-person team and required a rotating third for each trip. The Wunderkind was the correct size for its in-flight work. Did the Wunderkind perform better simply because it was larger?

The Federal Aviation Administration (FAA) mandates that three flight attendants must be on board Boeing 737 aircraft for safety reasons. At People Express, the work load for cabin crew was higher than at other carriers operating the same equipment because CSMs had to collect fares in addition to their safety and service responsibilities. In addition, the Dyad always had the further burden of coordinating with someone relatively new. Thus, its small size may have contributed to its performance difficulties. Yet size alone cannot explain all the differences between the Dyad and the Wunderkind.

For one thing, previous research on work teams suggests that group size should be adequate to do the work, but no larger—and, indeed, that it can be advantageous for a group to be slightly smaller than what the task technically requires (Wicker, Kirmeyer, Hanson, & Alexander, 1976). There was evidence of this in the Dyad: members often exerted extra effort to compensate for the lack of a third permanent member. Moreover, members said they enjoyed coaching new CSMs and that only on short flights was it difficult to incorporate a new person and still get the work done. They did not feel that the size of the team impaired their performance.

That size alone does not explain the differences we observed is also attested to by the fact that the Wunderkind performed better than many other three-person teams at the airline. Even if size were a contributing factor to the performance and attitude differences between these two teams, it could not have been the only, or even the primary, factor.

Group Process. Behavioral scientists traditionally have attempted to explain differences in group effectiveness by examining the characteristics of the interpersonal processes that occur among members. Steiner (1972), for example, in his classic model of group process and effectiveness, contrasts the potential of a work group with its actual performance and attributes the difference to something called *process loss.* This tradition persists, despite the relative absence of supporting evidence, and often constitutes an assumption, rather than a hypothesis, in group process research. Our comparison of the Wunderkind and Dyad teams does not support this assumption. In fact, it may be quite wrong; both teams were characterized by excellent interpersonal processes.

The members of the Wunderkind team knew what to expect from one another on board the aircraft. They had excellent communication skills, and their coordination seemed effortless. They would decide how to divide up tasks at the last minute with only a glance, a smile, or a hand signal. While one made an announcement about a delay, the second would comfort a child flying alone for the first time, and the third would help mid-cabin customers place their luggage in the overhead compartments.

Early in the team's history, the Wunderkind would meet after the day's work to discuss how they could coordinate better and work more effectively. They enjoyed figuring out ways their work could be done quicker, easier, or better. It was clear from their joking and laughing that they enjoyed working with one another. In their own words, "Our communication is the best. There is no jealousy on the team. We are at home with each other."

Members of the Dyad also coordinated their efforts quite effectively and had excellent communication skills. In their own words, "When one of us is tired or not feeling well, the other fills in. The best thing about our team is our capacity to communicate." During the in-flight medical emergency that one of us observed, one CSM administered oxygen to the potential heart attack victim, the second informed the cockpit, and the third took care of the rest of the cabin. This division of labor took place with a minimum of conversation; yet eye contact and other nonverbal communication suggested that they had jointly determined this approach.

Dyad members were also friends outside the job, and they too had taken trips together for fun. In individual interviews, each member stressed how much he or she liked working with the other and how they could resolve problems just by talking them out. For example, they differed in the type of schedule that they preferred. Dave wanted weekends off to spend time with family and friends, while Kate wanted weekdays off so she could take advantage of the flying privileges enjoyed by airline employees. They resolved this by being flexible in how they bid for trips each month, taking into account the specific activities that each had planned.

In sum, the Dyad appeared to have excellent interpersonal processes—an observation that members' responses to items on our research questionnaire affirmed. Both teams had high scores on the "interpersonal process" index we constructed, and their averages did not differ significantly from one another. The only reasonable conclusion to reach from our data, both quantitative and qualitative, is that an excellent group process is not sufficient to distinguish between an effective and an ineffective team—and that improving relations among members brings no guarantee that improvements in team performance will follow.

Work Design. If neither size nor interpersonal process is sufficient to explain the differences between the Dyad and the Wunderkind, then where does one look for a better explanation? One other possibility is the design of the team's work. Theories of work design and performance (for example, Hackman & Oldham, 1980) posit that jobs that provide challenge, autonomy, and knowledge of results will prompt higher work motivation for most people than will jobs that do not have these properties. Can we explain the differences between these two teams by the differences in how their work was designed?

At first look, it would seem that the answer must be no, because both teams performed exactly the same set of in-flight tasks. Yet it also is clear that the two teams differed greatly in how they *experienced* that work. The Wunderkind team just plain enjoyed flying. As one member said, "I guess we're just 'stews' [stewards or stewardesses] at heart." They viewed short flights as opportunities to beat previous records for speed and efficiency. They were proud of their ability to sell tickets and provide beverage service to 118 passengers on a thirty-eight-minute flight from Newark to Boston. They liked interacting with customers and took advantage of any opportunity to talk with them. The team members felt that their task required much autonomous decision making and that task feedback was immediate and tangible. One member reported, for example, that the team knew immediately whether or not ticketing revenues balanced and how customers were reacting to the service.

The Dyad, in contrast, did not find in-flight work motivating. Indeed, they perceived cabin duties as trivial, routine, and demeaning. As one stated in an interview, "The work aboard the aircraft is not intellectually challenging. We feel like we are $25,000-a-year garbage collectors." The Dyad viewed most of the work as predetermined by either FAA requirements or company policies and, as a result, felt that the decisions they made as a team were either cut-and-dried or of little consequence. The team enjoyed receiving feedback from customers but felt that this did not occur very frequently. Consequently, members seldom took advantage of extra time in flight to talk to customers. The Dyad was thoroughly bored with the everyday routine.

Even though both teams performed the same basic task, one perceived the work as challenging and exciting while the other perceived it to be routine and trivial. This basic discrepancy between the Dyad's and Wunderkind's perceptions of the task is borne out by their responses to our survey: the Dyad averaged substantially lower on the measures of task design than did the Wunderkind.

To explore the reasons for the teams' differences in task perceptions, we independently evaluated the in-flight task. We found the collection of tasks that made up the in-flight work of CSMs—providing cabin services, ensuring passenger safety, and collecting revenues—to be moderate in motivating potential. The work was a mixture of the routine and the unexpected. Interacting with passengers was unpredictable, added variety, and helped to break up the monotony of repetitive in-flight subtasks. The potential for emergencies created uncertainty, but emergencies rarely occurred. To handle a large number of passengers on a short flight was a demanding task, even though the specific duties were relatively simple for experienced crews. Thus, there was considerable ambiguity in the work itself, which gave a crew a good deal of latitude in how it defined and interpreted the work. The two teams we studied used that latitude very differently: the Wunderkind focused almost exclusively on the positive aspects of the work, while the Dyad consistently focused on its more routine features.

Why? One possibility is that the perceptions of the task, and the set of internalized norms that supported those perceptions, acted as self-fulfilling prophecies in both the Dyad and the Wunderkind teams—albeit in different directions. The Wunderkind defined flying as exciting, and team members worked to keep it that way. They viewed short flights as a contest and worked to improve their efficiency. Members of the Dyad team, in contrast, accepted their inability to complete beverage services and complained that company policy should require four CSMs on short flights. The Wunderkind team maximized the opportunities for customer feedback, while the Dyad felt that feedback was out of members' control and defined away those opportunities that did present themselves. Even though the formal duties of these two teams were essentially the same, they acted as if they had entirely different jobs. The question then becomes: What created this fundamental difference in the two teams' perceptions of their essentially identical work?

The Teams' Early Histories

To say that the difference in the two teams' performance can be explained by differing perceptions of the task only begins to unravel the mystery of the performance gap between them. Was the key in the personalities of members? Were the Wunderkind simply more enthusiastic and positive people? Was it their situation, or was it their position in the organization? Our data show few differences in such factors and suggest an alternative possibility—differences in early histories of these two teams at People Express. For the Wunderkind, early experiences quickly fulfilled members' hopes and expectations, and members internalized the excitement of contributing to this new airline. For the Dyad, on the other hand, early experiences demonstrated that teamwork and in-flight performance would not be rewarded, and team members soon became unwilling to exert the extra effort the company sought. A negative spiral developed—a spiral in which members' perceptions reinforced the negative features of objective reality, thereby further strengthening those perceptions. Here is how it happened.

One in a Hundred. At the time of our research, the airline interviewed about 100 candidates (and scanned many more applications) to select a single customer service manager. This "one in a hundred" knew that he or she was special. People Express hired customer service managers for their enthusiasm, managerial talents, service excellence, and desire to learn and grow. Members of both the Dyad and the Wunderkind were told during recruiting and training that virtually unlimited opportunities were available to those who pursued them. Members of both teams believed in self-management, teamwork, and an organization whose number one precept was "service, commitment to the growth of people." They all wanted to contribute to the growth of this exciting new airline, but some things happened early in the lives of the two teams that set them on very different courses.

The Wunderkind. The promise of unlimited opportunity was quickly fulfilled for the Wunderkind team. After flying together for about five months, the team was selected to start up the airline's new city station in West Palm Beach, Florida. It was up to team members to do whatever was necessary to open the station and get service started between West Palm Beach and Newark. Members negotiated with government officials, personnel from other airlines, and senior managers at People Express. They selected contractors and bought supplies. They consulted with airline staff who had opened other city stations, but it was up to them to tailor the operational systems to the particular requirements of West Palm Beach.

Opening a new city station was a unique, exciting, and challenging opportunity for the Wunderkind. It also was a great success. The entire company was aware of the team's achieve-ment. Indeed, top-level managers, when asked for an example of an excellent team, frequently would mention the Wunderkind. Members felt recognized and rewarded for doing excellent work, and this feeling carried over to their in-flight duties and their perceptions of the in-flight job. They also were confident that their good performance would lead to other challenging op-portunities—and it did.[1] The Wunderkind succeeded at what Tracy Kidder (1981), author of *The Soul of a New Machine,* called "pinball"—winning one game allowed the team to play more. Success in West Palm Beach provided the team with rec-ognition and future opportunities. The People Express promise of ongoing personal and professional growth was a reality for the Wunderkind. They found that to be true early in the life of their team, and their subsequent behavior helped make it be true thereafter.

The Dyad. A key event in the early history of the Dyad team also had a strong influence on members' perceptions of their work and of the company—although in a negative direction. This event was the firing of Steve, their original third teammate. Eight months after the firing, Kate and Dave were still flying as a team of two with a rotating third. The matter was still very much on their minds; indeed, when approached to participate in the research, they initially wondered if we were including them in the study *because* of Steve's firing. They described the events as follows.

Kate, Dave, and Steve had reported to the crew room at the usual check-in time. They were scheduled for a double over-night and would not be home for four days. A note in Steve's mailbox asked him to see the managing officer in charge of hu-man resources. Scheduling assigned a standby CSM to replace Steve on the trip so he could meet the managing officer imme-diately.

Kate and Dave were concerned because there previously had been some problems with Steve. He sometimes came on too strong with passengers and, on occasion, he lost his temper with other CSMs. Recognizing that these problems had affected the team, Kate and Dave had worked with Steve to help him learn how to handle difficult situations more appropriately. In their minds, his performance had clearly improved, and the three of them felt proud to be a team. Kate and Dave viewed Steve as very dedicated to the company.

When Kate and Dave returned from their trip, they heard via the grapevine that Steve had been fired. Steve was bitter and felt that he had been unfairly treated. No one had asked Kate or Dave for their views about Steve's performance, nor were they involved in any way in Steve's counseling or termination. Kate and Dave asked to meet with the managing officer to discuss what had occurred, but she told them that the firing had nothing to do with the team—that it was purely an individual matter.

This experience had a powerful impact on the work perceptions and attitudes of the Dyad. First, it suggested to them that teamwork was not important to the company. The managing officer told them that Steve's firing had nothing to do with their performance as a team, and it seemed to be true. No one had shown any interest in their evaluation of Steve's work, even though they were the only managers in the company who had worked with him on a daily basis. It especially upset them that although Steve's performance—and the performance of the whole team—had improved recently, those in charge acted as if this were irrelevant.

Second, Kate and Dave felt that management had given Steve no recognition for his dedication to the company or his willingness to work at a staff job during his free time. Kate and Dave both wanted to have staff opportunities because they sought to increase the variety in their work and obtain some relief from the routine of flying day in and day out. Moreover, working staff was one of the ways that one could advance in the company and get more interesting work to do. Still, Dyad members were not willing to give up all their free time just to work in a staff job. Steve's experience reinforced their unwillingness to sacrifice their time off to pursue staff opportunities.

Dave also commented that he once had the chance to be in a staff position after three months of flying, but that he turned it down because he felt he needed more in-flight experience. He now regretted that decision because of the lack of current opportunities. Dave and Kate both felt they had suffered because of their early dedication to flying the line. This feeling, combined with Steve's treatment after he had volunteered to work staff in his free time, caused Dyad members to hesitate about getting more involved in and committed to the organization.

As time passed, the work of the Dyad increasingly involved regular line flying. Dave and Kate felt almost invisible. Both reported that those in positions of authority neither recognized nor rewarded good performance. Those CSMs selected to be team coordinators, they pointed out, generally had worked full-time in a staff area prior to their selection. Kate and Dave concluded that opportunity depended upon whom one knew rather than on how one performed. Visibility, friendships, and ceaseless work seemed to them to be the main criteria for advancement—and they resented it.

In sum, the buffet of opportunities for personal and professional growth espoused by People Express had turned out to be a false promise for the Dyad. As a result, they perceived the work they actually did as increasingly routine and nonchallenging—setting in motion a downward spiral just as powerful as the Wunderkind's upward spiral of fulfilled hopes, positive attitudes, and exemplary performance.

Conclusion

Our data suggest that the widely differing perceptions and attitudes of the Wunderkind and Dyad can best be explained by what happened in the early work histories of these two teams. The Dyad's early experiences taught members that the airline would not recognize or reward teamwork and good in-flight performance. The Wunderkind's experiences, in contrast, taught them that good performance would not only be rewarded but lead to a virtual explosion of opportunities and successes. This difference led the two teams to develop widely differing perceptions of the job itself and of the reward structure of the airline—perceptions that became, over time, self-sustaining.

What can these two teams teach us about factors that influence the performance of other types of work groups? For one thing, our findings confirm the view that looking exclusively to the internal interaction process of groups to understand and explain differences in task effectiveness can be misleading. Moreover, group interaction process does not appear to be a very promising point of intervention for attempting to improve performance. The two teams we studied, despite their very different levels of performance, had equally good internal communication processes and positive interpersonal relationships among members. But that clearly was not enough for the Dyad team.

A second lesson is that one should not focus exclusively on the structure of the actual task when trying to understand work team effectiveness. How a group views its task often is as important as the objective design of that task. Moreover, the perceived instrumentality of task behavior for obtaining other valued outcomes, beyond the work itself, also was a key motivator for these two teams—as the "expectancy theory" of work motivation suggests (Lawler, 1973; Vroom, 1964). Expectancy theory, although designed to explain individual rather than team behavior, aims our attention toward the future—the same direction that members of these two teams looked each day as they decided how much of themselves to put into the work.

The most important lesson we can learn from the Dyad and the Wunderkind, however, has to do with the way early organizational experiences can generate self-fulfilling and self-reinforcing cycles of team success or failure. A team that believes it will be successful in an organization behaves in ways that make it so. It develops the positive task perceptions and productivity norms to make it successful. A team that believes that opportunity will not be forthcoming no matter what it does will not generate much effort, nor will it capitalize on the opportunities that do present themselves. A downward spiral will set in. Such cycles are hard to change—particularly in customer service teams that spend most of their time in contact with customers rather than with other members of their organization.

Note

1. While the future fulfilled members' expectations, it also led to the breakup of the team. One year after our research, one of the members was the training representative on the task force that planned the airline's inauguration of international service; the second member was in the first group of CSMs qualified on the Boeing 747 and worked the company's first flight to London; and the third was chosen to work in a new city station the company was opening.

Richard Saavedra
Susan G. Cohen
Daniel R. Denison

24

Summary: Customer Service Teams

Customer service teams at both Maltshire Beer and People Express Airlines balanced between customer demands on the one hand and organizational requirements on the other. At both organizations one team was viewed as performing very well, and one was not considered up to organizational standards. In this summary chapter, we review how these teams managed the conflicts they experienced, how they came to be labeled as good or poor teams in their organizations, and what these teams have to say about the design and leadership of customer service teams more generally.

Competing Demands

Customer service teams must tailor their work to the needs of their clientele. Most customer service teams perform their work at the customer's convenience and often at the customer's location. Usually no member of management is present when the team is working with the customer. The teams we studied did their work far from headquarters: at bars, clubs, or liquor stores for the Maltshire teams, and literally in the air for the flight attendants (more properly, customer service managers or CSMs) at People Express. But even for teams that operate geographically near the home office, the customer encounter is almost always a private one between a member of the team and the customer.

For this reason, such teams have considerable discretion in how they manage their relations with customers.

At the same time, however, management expects customer service teams to operate in accord with overall organizational directions and constraints. Thus, the customer service managers were expected to provide especially friendly and attentive service to passengers, but they were prohibited from pleasing customers by passing out free drinks. The beer sales and delivery teams were expected to vigorously sell Maltshire products, but they were constrained in distributing point-of-sale advertising items. While in the field, a team may try hard to behave in accord with the dictum "The customer is always right." There may be trouble back home, however, if the team pleases its customers and sells its products in ways that deviate from how managers think it *should* be done.

Customer service teams operate precisely at the intersection between the company and its clients and often serve as something of a buffer between them, mediating or smoothing over conflicts. Customer teams are, after all, the first to receive feedback about what customers like and dislike about the organization's products and services. They are the first to hear what customers think the company should change or do differently— and even what customers think about competitors' products and services. At the same time, they know much better than do customers what the organization is trying to do—what its niche in the market is, and how it seeks to meet customer needs.

Ideally, a customer service team would exercise influence both in the field and at headquarters to create a good match— to create conditions in which the organization can succeed by serving its customers well. It is not uncommon, however, for a customer service team to experience competing and irreconcilable demands from customers and the organization. The customer may want something that the organization cannot or chooses not to provide, or the organization may insist that the team follow policies or practices that customers do not like. These conflicts create real tensions for customer service teams, especially when a special favor necessary to make a sale contravenes organizational rules.

It is not difficult for a customer service team to do well

when operating in a predictable and beneficent environment (such as an "easy" sales territory) or when organizational policies provide just what customers want. A team's mettle is tested, however, when the environment is demanding and organizational policies are at variance with customer demands. That is when the ability of the team to wield influence with customers, with its own organization, or sometimes with both simultaneously can spell the difference between excellent and poor performance.

Consider, for example, what is required of a customer service team when the environment is unpredictable and/or constantly changing. In such cases, teams must constantly adjust their performance strategies and may have to make repeated requests for organizational support. This occurred in some sales regions at Maltshire, but managerial policies and practices were so firm and stable that negotiating exceptions was nearly impossible. Transactions with customers at People Express, on the other hand, were rather predictable: customers, once on board an aircraft, rarely made extraordinary requests, and the unexpected events that the CSMs encountered were, by and large, ones with which the teams were experienced. The main problem the CSMs faced was not so much a capricious external environment as it was rapid change within their own organization. Considering both the customer and organizational environments in which they worked, teams in neither organization enjoyed optimum performance conditions. Yet all four teams we studied did manage, for the most part, to turn in acceptable performances.

Sometimes, however, acceptable performance is virtually impossible to achieve, and the teams we studied did encounter such situations. How, for example, can a team convince customers that what they *think* they want is not what they really need (a not uncommon sales strategy when you cannot deliver what customers are asking for), especially if competitors are eager to provide exactly what the customers are asking for? Or what do you do if for reasons entirely out of your control you cannot deliver what the organization has offered? The Maltshire teams had to contend with competitors who offered below-cost kegs of draft beer in exchange for having an exclusive product line in one region—something that the Maltshire distributorship explicitly prohibited its teams from doing. And the People Express CSMs regularly had to deal with the fact that their passengers were going to miss connections or be late for meetings because of maintenance or weather problems wholly out of the teams' control. Even though the ability of group members to deal persuasively with customers is important, team performance sometimes depends on factors about which the team by itself can do very little.

Labels and Spirals

It is not always easy to determine just how well a customer service team is performing. Performance feedback for the People Express CSMs, for example, was generally ambiguous. There is no agreed-upon metric for assessing the quality of service provided on board an aircraft—and no ready means of gathering such data even if an appropriate methodology were available. At Maltshire, on the other hand, a reliable, numerical measure was right at hand—the net sales of each team. The problem here was that this measure captures only a single, short-term aspect of the overall service provided by sales and delivery teams. And while the quality of the team's work did significantly affect sales, so did changes in the sales environment.

In both organizations, then, team members and their managers had many occasions to make their own assessments of how well a team really was performing. This was done in both organizations, and it resulted in labels for each of the teams we studied. One team at Maltshire was labeled as a high-performing team, and the other was labeled as low-performing; the same was true for the two groups of CSMs at People Express. In all cases, the labels stuck and affected the teams' subsequent life, work, and performance.

At People Express, one of the teams (the Wunderkind) had the opportunity early in its life to take responsibility for opening the station at a city where the airline was about to begin service. Members worked hard, the start-up of the new station was a great success, and the group was labeled by others in the organization as a successful CSM team. Not surprisingly, team members were happy to be so characterized and came to view themselves the same way. They increasingly found interacting with customers on the aircraft, which was their regular duty, to be engaging and intrinsically rewarding; they confidently expected that by continuing to work hard and do well they would earn opportunities both for more special tasks and for personal advancement in the company. In contrast, the other CSM team (the Dyad) was not given any special opportunities to show what it could do. Worse, one of its members was fired early in the life of the group. This group came to be viewed as a problem team, and that label, too, was accepted both by team members and managers. Eventually, group members became cynical about the degree to which the organization truly valued and supported group work, and they increasingly experienced their in-flight duties as routine rather than challenging. As one put it, a CSM is "just a $25,000-a-year garbage collector in the sky."

In effect, a self-reinforcing spiral developed for each of the People Express teams, one positive and one negative. While these two teams performed basically the same work, their early organizational experiences powerfully influenced how they subsequently perceived that work—as well as their expectations about what might be in store for them in the future. These experiences might have been countered in either case if the team had been given work assignments that altered members' perceptions and expectations. But once management labeled the teams in a way that was consistent with members' organizational experiences up to that point, the spirals were firmly established. The label "effective" for the Wunderkind reinforced members' motivation and commitment, while being labeled "ineffective" only served to remind members of the Dyad of their perceived mistreatment by the organization—and reinforced their view that a team could not get ahead at People Express merely by working hard and serving customers well. Subsequent assignments were generally consistent with each team's label—further fueling these spirals.

Labeling also occurred at Maltshire Beer, but not as much on the basis of teams' early experiences as on the properties of their sales environments. Managers at Maltshire believed that if a team followed company-specified procedures, healthy sales would be ensured. They did not recognize that different markets actually required performance strategies tailored uniquely to customers in each region. Any deviation from company policy was viewed as cutting corners and showing disloyalty to the company and its product. One Maltshire team had a beneficent sales region in which standard company policies and procedures worked well; team members went strictly by the book, and sales invariably were among the best in the company. The other team worked in an unstable, difficult region where competition was intense. To perform well, this team resorted to performance strategies that were customized to customers' needs—but that deviated on occasion from company policy. Managers, in reviewing the teams, noted that both teams had good sales records, but that one clearly was more loyal and committed to the company. Management labeled this team as "effective" and the other as "ineffective." As was the case at People Express, these labels affected life in the teams, member perceptions, and subsequent management behavior vis-a-vis the teams.

Conclusion

Customer service teams face multiple and difficult challenges. They operate on the boundary of their organizations and therefore must balance between competing and often conflicting demands from customers and their own managers. To succeed, they must tailor their service strategies to customers' needs and to the imperatives of the external environment; but, at the same time, they must follow organizational directions and remain within organizationally specified constraints.

Because customer service teams spend most of their time in the field, managers have relatively few direct data about what the teams actually do. The absence of such data invites managers to label teams based on whatever data they *do* have. Once a team is labeled "poor" or "disloyal" or "ineffective," there is little to prevent members from breaking the rules in the future if they feel they need to—or merely want to. Such behavior is, after all, what everyone expects of them. Gradually, members' own expectations, experiences, and behaviors come into congruence with how their teams have been labeled. And that, as we have seen, can set in motion self-reinforcing spirals of ever increasing or ever decreasing motivation and performance.

Managing customer service teams is a real challenge. Managers want to help teams succeed in their work with customers, but they also want to make sure that the teams, whose work they can rarely observe, affirm rather than undermine organizational values and strategy. One managerial strategy for accomplishing this, of course, would be to implement procedures that allow teams to be checked closely and continuously. This approach, we believe, ultimately would be self-defeating. To put a customer service team under constant scrutiny surely would create more problems than it would solve.

More promising, in our view, is a three-pronged management strategy. First, teams would be given more, rather than less, autonomy in carrying out their work and they would be held fully accountable for work outcomes. In effect, teams would be self-managing—actively encouraged to tailor their performance strategies to the imperatives of the customer environments they encounter. The only limits on team behavior would be those organizational directions and constraints that are absolutely inviolate—for example, adherence to service objectives critical to the firm's competitive strategy and honesty in financial transactions involving the company and its customers. What would *not* be specified would be the specific means by which organizational directions were pursued—details such as specific procedures for dealing with customer problems or opportunities.

Second, customer service teams would be charged with actively managing the boundary between customers and the organization. Such teams, perhaps better than anyone else in the organization, are able to discern trends in customer needs and preferences. And they, perhaps better than anyone else, are in position to communicate with and educate customers. Rather than having to balance between customers and the organization, customer service teams could perform critical intelligence-gathering and communications tasks that are, in many sales-driven organizations, sometimes overlooked.

Finally, managers of customer service teams would take special care in formulating and communicating their expectations about the behavior of their teams and in recognizing excellent and poor team performance. The experiences of the teams at People Express and Maltshire Beer demonstrate the considerable power of symbols and labels in affecting team behavior and performance. By attending to the symbolic content as well as the substance of their interactions with customer service teams, managers could increase the chances that the teams for which they are responsible would, over time, enter into self-reinforcing positive cycles of behavior and performance.

Part Seven

PRODUCTION TEAMS: TURNING OUT THE PRODUCT

The teams we discuss in this section directly create the core products of their organizations. Such teams begin with a set of raw materials and use tools and technology to transform them into outputs. In contrast to task forces and top management teams, the members of production teams do not serve as the representatives of other groups. In contrast to professional support, human service, and customer service teams, production teams typically are more involved with creating the product than they are with delivering it to end users.

The objectives of production teams typically involve the predictable and efficient creation of high-quality products. Consequently, these teams tend to focus on ways to minimize unexplained variations in the production process through increasingly standardized operating procedures. Teams exercise initiative in pushing back the frontier between the uncontrollable and the controllable. Unfortunately, as we shall see, the internal logic of the production process can lead to the pursuit of efficiency for its own sake and, ultimately, to a distancing from the needs of the final customer.

The three teams we examine in this section were at quite different points in their life cycles when we studied them. The first team, discussed in Chapter Twenty-Five, was created to produce parts for air conditioner compressors in a new manufacturing facility of a large industrial concern. But before production could begin, the team itself had to be produced. When our observations began, there were only a few people, some technology, and a challenging mandate from the organization that required members and their managers to create a self-managing production team that would use state-of-the-art manufacturing technology to produce parts at a quality level unprecedented in the corporation. By examining the processes by which the team was created and the dynamics that developed both among team members and between the team and others in the organization, the chapter provides some unique insights into the special problems and opportunities of teams that perform production work.

We observed the second team, described in Chapter Twenty-Six, throughout its entire life cycle: from formation through dissolution. This team was an airline cockpit crew, and its life spanned only four days. In that period of time, the team was formed from individuals who had not previously worked together. It developed relations with several other groups, the most important of which was the cabin crew with which the cockpit team worked throughout its life. The team repeatedly generated its product—the use of aircraft and technology to transport people from one place to another, sometimes routinely and other times in decidedly challenging circumstances. Eventually, the team disbanded and its members returned to the pool of pilots in the airline, where they remained until once again formed into teams to repeat the whole process. Although at first glance a cockpit crew might seem to have little in common with the industrial work groups that one usually thinks of as "production teams," the processes this crew went through recapitulate in a compressed time period, and in a highly visible way, group dynamics that are generic to production teams.

The last team in the section, discussed in Chapter Twenty-Seven, looks most like a traditional production team. This team manufactured parts of semiconductors (specifically, it added one or more electronic layers to silicon wafers) using sophisticated manufacturing technology. This team was something of an innovation in a fairly traditional production facility where technology, supervision, compensation, and staff support all had been designed to support individual work rather than teamwork. The struggles of this team and its managers to develop true teamwork in this organization illuminate a number of the issues that must be dealt with if production teams are, in fact, to develop synergy—and not operate merely as an aggregation of individuals doing their separate jobs in a social context.

25

Russell A. Eisenstat

Compressor Team Start-Up

When the first members of the compressor team interviewed for their jobs in the summer of 1981 they were taken on a plant tour. There wasn't much to see. A vast empty space separated the offices in the front from those in the back of Ashland Corporation's Fairfield Components Plant (FCP). Over the next year, somewhere in the midst of this un-broken expanse of cement floor, they would have to create Fairfield's first manufacturing team. The task was daunt-ing. As one team member later explained, "I don't think the reality hits you until you get here. You don't realize how barren it is. In the standard new plant start-up you take all of the policies you have in an existing plant and you move the books over here and you recreate from those documents. But . . . in Fairfield, none of those documents transferred. You had to create all of those documents and then build your procedures off of those. When you walked in, it was totally blank."

As the above quotation suggests, in a real sense the prod-uct of the compressor team during start-up was not compressor parts per se, but rather a set of organizational capabilities—the ability to machine and assemble parts at the quality and quan-tity levels needed for Ashland's new line of Q-15 air condition-ers.[1] The production of this set of capabilities occurred in two stages. During the first, individuals at the corporate and plant

411

levels developed specifications for some critical team components, including its technology and team design. During the second stage, the members of the compressor group themselves had to determine how to integrate these components into an effectively functioning team. As we examine the start-up of the compressor team, we will see that the successful completion of these two stages depended on effective use of a number of strategies for facilitating plant, team, and individual learning.

Phase One: Defining the Pieces of a Solution

Although the members of the compressor team may have felt at times as if they were starting with a totally blank slate, in fact, a great deal was already determined when they began their work. Before the first member of the line was chosen—indeed, before the Fairfield plant was even purchased—the Ashland corporation had already created a generic solution to the problem of how new manufacturing lines were supposed to function. The solution was a fifty-two-page set of requirements for all new manufacturing lines—the "Process Control Audit Checklist." The first version of this document had been written in the early 1970s to summarize federal regulatory requirements for new manufacturing lines. Over the years, the checklist had grown into a set of detailed standards for virtually every aspect of a line start-up. The table of contents of this document specified sixteen areas of concern, including requirements for operator training, process documentation (sheets containing complete operating instructions for every machine on the line), preventive machine maintenance programs, and inspection of parts at all stages of the manufacturing process.

The corporate project team responsible for coordinating the development of the Q-15 air conditioner line developed the technology to produce compressor parts. Members of that team spent a number of months visiting both domestic and international vendors searching for the technologies that would allow them to produce parts of the extremely high tolerances necessary for the Q-15 compressor.

Another group—the start-up team for the Fairfield Components Plant—developed the organizational design for the compressor team. Originally this team had planned to structure manufacturing teams in Fairfield in the same way they had designed them at the Ashland plant in Ridgeway, Pennsylvania. In Ridgeway, groups of manufacturing teams were organized into approximately 200-person "businesses," which also included support staff in areas such as personnel, finance, training, and machine maintenance. Both support staff and team managers reported to a business manager.

When the FCP start-up team visited Ridgeway, members discovered that even though support personnel had been decentralized to the business level there, manufacturing teams still found it difficult to get the functional resources they needed. Consequently, to improve manufacturing teams' access to functional expertise, the Fairfield top management group decided that teams in the plant would include four exempt support personnel who would report directly to the team manager. One of these team advisors would be a resource for human resource functions (training, organizational development, and personnel), a second advisor would be responsible for administration (finance, systems, and materials), a third for technical support (quality control), and a fourth for manufacturing support (manufacturing engineering). Over time, these advisors would train machine operators (known in Fairfield as *associates)* to take over their functions, and each advisor would move on to another job—perhaps as an advisor or manager for a second manufacturing team.

Phase Two: Putting the Pieces Together

Initial Attempts at Integration

Tom Cutler, the first manager of the compressor line, was charged with somehow creating a functioning manufacturing team out of a fifty-two-page list of requirements, a set of machines, and an abstract organizational design. Cutler, who originally had served as financial comptroller for the Q-15 team, had no prior experience in manufacturing. He was, however, eager to develop his skills as a line manager, and he became deeply immersed in his new job. In the spring of 1981, he supervised the delivery of the first machines for the line. Over the summer, he hired four team advisors, formed them into a core group, and began to work with them to figure out how they could meet the specifications in the quality audit checklist.

This was not an easy task. While each advisor had some relevant prior experience, none had worked in all of his or her new areas of responsibility. Consequently, each member of the core group needed to work closely with more specialized personnel in the central support areas of the plant to fulfill the manufacturing, administrative, quality, and human resource requirements of the team start-up. In many cases no one was available to provide help since the central support areas themselves were still being staffed.

Relationships between the core group and the quality support group were particularly difficult. Only by working well together could these groups expect to pass the quality audit. Yet both the permanent director for quality and the manager of quality were relatively recent arrivals at the plant. By the time the quality group was fully staffed and operational, the compressor team already had begun to develop quality systems on its own. A member of the quality group explained that, at that point, they had to tell the compressor team, in effect, " 'What you have done is no good.' Machine capability studies were only going to be done on certain key dimensions. And we said, 'No, you have to do it on every dimension.' A machine that is going to be run on five different parts was only going to be tested on one. We said, 'No, you have to do it on all.' [Cutler] got somewhat defensive and said the central quality group doesn't establish his quality goals, he does. And I said that is not my understanding."

Because of frictions with the quality group, Cutler and his advisors intensified their efforts to develop their own team quality systems. Cutler tried to keep the advisors focused on their key objectives while simultaneously giving them substantial freedom in deciding how to go about achieving those objectives. Despite his best efforts, the team began to fall behind schedule. According to one advisor:

Tom's approach was you were given the freedom to do it as you will and progress at your own speed in this evolving team concept. Tom accepted that you are a responsible adult, now do it. But a lot of things were slipping through the cracks. The total program was being developed, but a lot of the little programs that supported that were being overlooked . . . like getting gauging in here to inspect the parts that we had gotten in and had sat on the shelves for three or four months. Getting the inventory to actually put in the proper zones out here. Putting in a financial tracking system to see where we stood on expenditures against forecasts. Those kind of little things. Pieces of the total team picture.

The Change in Team Management

During the Christmas holidays in 1981, Fairfield's plant manager decided to remove Tom Cutler as manager of the compressor team. Cutler became a consultant to the plant manager for special projects. The new team manager was Bill Munson, who previously had managed a manufacturing team in another Ashland team-based plant in Jacksonville, Florida. The official explanation for the change in managers was that Cutler was at too high a salary level to be serving as a team manager and that his appointment to that post had always been a temporary one. But the unofficial word was that Cutler "had some problems fitting in the job, pulling the team together."

When Munson took over as manager in January, the team was approaching a critical deadline—its first scheduled shipment of compressors to Ridgeway in March. The compressors were to be tested in Ridgeway to ensure that the FCP was a satisfactory source of compressors for the Q-15 air conditioners. The team also had to be ready to go into the daily production of compressors by the beginning of August—a move that required certification by the corporate quality group that the line had met all specifications in the process control checklist.

As 1982 began, the compressor team had two major hurdles to surmount before it could meet these deadlines—debugging a new technology and debugging a new organizational design.

Debugging the Technology

As of the beginning of 1982, the machine delivery and installation process was substantially behind schedule. The major reason for the delay was that machines had to meet rigid quality specifications before they could be accepted for installation. For example, Fairfield would not accept a machine if it produced 3 or more parts in 1,000 that exceeded blueprint tolerances by more than 70 percent. Even after the machines arrived in the plant they had to be installed and then retested to make sure they still met these specifications. The installation and testing of the machines were a major preoccupation of the compressor line in early 1982; that work complicated all of the other work the team had to complete.

Debugging the Organizational Design

The compressor team was the first implementation of the new team organizational design to be used throughout the Fairfield plant. For the first time, the team manager, the team advisors, and the associates had to negotiate their roles. These negotiations did not go smoothly.

Advisor–Team Manager Relations. Relations were particularly tense between the four advisors and the new team manager. According to one advisor:

> We had finally gotten to the place where the team had been together for four months. . . . You start to build relationships, you had gotten used to everybody, you had done your groundwork knowing where everyone was coming from, and it was time to move onto the next stage of development. Then they announced that Tom would not be the team manager and that Bill would take his place. Which was a total surprise, no one saw it coming. Bam, here it is. That kind of left everyone in shock. . . . We had all been handpicked by Tom . . . and [then they] moved Tom out and moved in Bill.

To deal with these concerns, Munson brought in a member of the plant organization development department, David Finch. Finch facilitated a series of meetings between Munson and his advisors during which each side listed its fears, hopes, and expectations for the other. The advisors were particularly concerned that they not be judged as incompetent by the new team manager. For example, the advisors said they hoped that Bill "will help us to do it better without judging us." And they were afraid of "a lot of pressure and criticism [and] being judged as a failure."

Both sides felt that the meetings with Finch helped clear the air, but relationships remained tense between the advisors and Munson—partly because of his management style. In contrast with Cutler, Munson monitored their work quite closely. As one advisor explained, "It upset people that Bill came in and all of a sudden started to ask questions and demand answers. It upset me that all of a sudden I am being held accountable for all of these things that I didn't have to answer [for] on a daily basis before."

Other advisors wondered whether Munson, who previously had supervised only hourly employees, understood how to manage professionals such as themselves. These concerns only intensified when associates (the machine operators) began to join the team in the early months of 1982.

Integrating Associates into the Team. Two associates joined the team at the end of February, two in March, and one at the end of May. Although these associates were expected to eventually take over most of the advisors' duties, they first had to learn how to operate their machines. The training was particularly difficult for three of the associates who had no prior machining experience. One of them described her work during this period: "I was scared. . . . I looked at the [machine]. My god, I am never going to learn how to do this. . . . I immediately tried to set up for the compressor body. And I was up there on that machine with those wrenches and lead hammers trying to pound away to learn how to [run it]. I pounded my knuckles. I used to get so frustrated that I could scream."

In theory, the technicians who installed the machines were

supposed to teach the associates how to produce parts, but the technicians were more comfortable relating to industrial engineers than to hourly employees. As one of the associates explained, the technician "goes flying through and says push this and this and this and expects me to understand it. The guy told me that he never taught anyone to run one of these who didn't have a background in it." Consequently, the task of training the associates fell on the team advisors, although some of the manufacturing engineers in other parts of the plant did lend a hand.

The training process created difficulties between associates and advisors. Most associates assumed that the advisors' first priority was training. For example, one associate told me, "Sometimes we have had problems getting help from one of our advisors, and we don't take that so lightly, because to me I look on it as their job to do things for us, and to help us." In contrast, the advisors felt caught between their training responsibilities and their other obligations, such as creating team work systems and supervising the delivery of machines. Some advisors felt that the manufacturing team design may have created better jobs for associates than it had for them: "I am concerned about professionals getting what they need as well. My concern is that you may be so isolated that you won't be able to keep up with what needs to be done beyond the team. . . . I expected to do some training, but not all of the training. . . . With everything else that needs to get done, I have concerns there."

One consequence of this tension was a social split between advisors and associates. According to one associate: "There is this group of associates, and then there are these people up there who are there to help us. And if we need them, we talk to them. And if we talk to them and they don't talk to us, we bitch. We bitch to each other, but we should be bitching to them. . . . When we are out there on the line, that is how it is. When we are in a team meeting we are all a team. When we are out there on the line it seems like it is [just] us, and it seems like they are in there in the air conditioning."

The Pieces Finally Come Together

As spring progressed, these internal differences began to moderate. Henry Bunyon, the oldest and most technically skilled of the associates, played a crucial role in the healing process. Bunyon usually finished work on his machine before his peers and spent the rest of his day helping the other associates get their jobs done. He not only helped on technical tasks, he also played a vital role in encouraging associates to have a voice in team decision making equal to that of the advisors. One associate observed, "At first I sat back and I observed behavior . . . didn't do much or say much, just listened to people and got to know them. After about a month, I really started talking to Henry Bunyon, the first one I trusted. He said that if we were frustrated, we should bring it up in a team meeting or talk to Bill Munson about it. So I started talking to Bill."

A second unifying factor was the group's position as the plant's first manufacturing team. Others at the FCP often made team members feel that the whole plant's reputation was riding on how well they managed their team start-up. Members complained to each other about being in a "glass fishbowl." As one explained, "All these expectations were out here, and I have to live right up to these. . . . We were all in the same boat. Every single one of us."

As the March deadline for shipping the first compressors approached, this sense of shared responsibility helped the group coalesce into a functioning team. An associate reported later, "We were supposed to [ship our] first compressors for reliability tests and were having a tough time getting it done. And then everyone jelled together. . . . Nobody said no, everybody said yes, and we worked and got it done. It was smooth, and people [were] in a good mood. People worked long hours. It had to be there, and we did it. The advisors and everyone. There was no difference, they were out there working hand and hand with you, getting their hands just as dirty as you were."

On March 9, the compressor team shipped its first parts to Ridgeway to begin the source approval process. On April 12, the team sent a second set of parts to be tested for reliability. Both shipments were on time.

Work continued through the spring and early summer in preparation for the quality audit. A month or so before the audit, members of the team let it be known that they felt they were receiving a great deal of advice from individuals in other areas of the plant, but little hands-on help. In response, the plant manager announced that the quality audit should be the entire plant's top priority. Thereafter, every morning at 7:30 the compressor team would meet for a few minutes and assess what needed to get done that day. The word would then go out to the rest of the plant. Any employees who had slack in their schedules, whatever their area of expertise or organizational level, would come out to the line and serve as an extra set of hands—typing process documentation, gauging parts, or doing whatever else needed to be done.

The results of the audit, when it finally came at the end of July, were extremely positive. One of the auditors stated that he had never audited a team that had created process documentation, preventive maintenance, and training systems of such a uniformly high caliber. On August 6, Alan Rasky, the plant manager, received the following memo from corporate headquarters: "Based on audit performed by Walter Steel of Operations Quality and Bob Jackson of Ridgeway, you are authorized to begin production on the Compressor Line. Congratulations—sounds like some excellent work has been done."

That same week the compressor team completed our research questionnaires. Results showed that members of the team felt that their work was of high quality and that relationships were acceptable both within the team and between the team and other groups in the plant.

The questionnaire scores could not capture the shared sense of triumph that members felt at having overcome their earlier differences and having become a unified and effective team. As one associate put it, "We surprise ourselves with how much we have learned in a short time. I surprise myself. . . . We work as one, not as separate individuals." An advisor agreed, saying that he felt the best thing about the compressor team was its ability to "work together as a group to accomplish goals. If someone needs help, it's there."

Why Was the Compressor Team Start-Up Effective?

The main task confronting the compressor team during start-up was development of the behavioral skills and the written policies that would allow it to become a successful manufacturing team. The audit report and the compressor team members' own evaluations of their work suggest that they largely succeeded in this task.

A crucial reason for this success was that the team functioned during start-up as an effective organizational learning system. The start-up of the compressor team was in some ways similar to previous Ashland line start-ups, but it was unique in other ways. A large number of manufacturing teams had started up within Ashland before. The compressor team, however, was meant to move the state of the art one step further in both technology and team design. Thus, those responsible for managing the compressor team faced a dual learning challenge—on one hand, to maximize the transfer of useful knowledge from past manufacturing team start-ups; on the other, to facilitate the process of trial-and-error learning needed to integrate this particular set of individuals, this new technology, and this organizational design into an effectively functioning team. The strategies they used to meet these challenges are discussed below.

The Audit Checklist

The most tangible embodiment of the lessons from past Ashland start-ups was the audit checklist. This checklist specified the set of systems that had been found to be most important in managing previous manufacturing line start-ups. In addition, the team objectives specified in the checklist served as an implicit source of feedback to guide learning during the start-up period. The checklist provided a clear standard for identifying both those areas that were progressing satisfactorily and those that required remedial attention. As one of the advisors explained: "The fifty-two-page quality document said, 'Here are the things that we want you to satisfy ahead of time.' It took us a year to work toward those. But we had direction from beginning to end. All we had to do was go back to the document and say, 'Did we answer this question, did we answer that question?' "

Significantly, while the checklist provided a highly detailed statement of objectives, it left the team a great deal of autonomy in deciding how it would meet those objectives.

For example, the checklist required that the team develop systems for ensuring that operators received machine training, but it did not specify what those systems should be. The checklist provided lots of room for innovation—but innovation within a clearly defined structure.

Team Design

The design of the compressor team, like the audit checklist, was the result of an extended organizational learning process. Because of the difficulties manufacturing lines had experienced getting functional assistance in traditional Ashland plants, functional personnel were decentralized to the "business" level at Ridgeway. The start-up team for the FCP, in turn, learned from the experiences of the Ridgeway plant and decided that cooperation would be further enhanced if functional resources were decentralized even further—to the teams themselves.

Not only was the design of the compressor team a result of corporate learning, it was itself a means of facilitating learning within the team. Specifically, the team was set up to maximize the ease with which support personnel could transfer skills to associates. The role of manufacturing team advisors was to provide support to the associates on the line and to help them get the support they needed from central functional areas. Consequently, the members of the compressor team, while often lower in the organizational hierarchy than many of those they asked for help, felt that they had a strong and valid claim on plant resources. When this support was not forthcoming, team members felt empowered to take the action necessary to get it. For example, an associate on the team explained that, "For a while, folks in quality [said] they had their job to do and had a hard time fitting us in. But we had a meeting and straightened that out."

Team Leadership

The most direct action taken to transfer learning from past Ashland team start-ups was Alan Rasky's selection of Bill Munson to be the team's second leader. Munson was able to draw on his experience managing the start-up of a similar team in Jacksonville to develop an appropriate strategy for managing the development of the compressor line.[2] In the early days of the start-up Munson was quite directive. Although his style created some resentment on the part of his four advisors, it also proved to be effective. According to one advisor, "Bill became quite instrumental in getting us back on stream. This isn't meant to be a commercial. One of his real strong points is to identify a real area of need and push the buttons to get it through. He stepped on a lot of people's toes, some advisors' toes, and pissed some people off. But the end result was that we got the stuff in place, we have the programs in, and we have come a long way in the last eight months."

By the time I observed the team, the skill level of the group had substantially increased, and Munson was allowing advisors and associates to take more and more initiatives. According to a compressor team associate, "It is coming along just about right. [Bill] pretty well had a handle on us at first. But now he is letting us get off and stumble and fall once in a while."

The team also benefited from the informal leadership of Henry Bunyon. Bunyon's technical and interpersonal skills gave him credibility with the team advisors and with the team manager, as well as with his fellow associates. Bunyon used this credibility to convince team members that because associates were as committed to (and as important for) team effectiveness as were the team advisors, they deserved an equal voice in team decisions.

Additional Learning Resources

The Fairfield corporation also made available to the compressor team a number of other resources that facilitated team learning. First, Ashland's top management allowed sufficient time for the start-up of the compressor team—more time than was typical for the introduction of conventional manufacturing lines. Also, production workers were hired earlier than usual in the start-up process to allow them time to develop the necessary technical skills and interpersonal relationships.

Finally, the Fairfield plant made available to the team substantial managerial and group process assistance. For example, when Munson was having difficulties with his advisors he was able to draw in a consultant from the central organizational development group without delay. The team also was able to draw informally on the expertise of others in the plant, including the plant manager and the director of manufacturing, both of whom had experience with previous manufacturing team start-ups.

Creating the Motivation for Learning

Even with these resources, the trial-and-error learning necessary to start up the compressor team successfully did not come easily. During the course of the start-up the first team manager was replaced. Moreover, relationships often were strained—relationships between team manager and advisors, between advisors and associates, and between the team and support staff in the functional areas. Further, the technical task of producing parts to such high-quality specifications with an unfamiliar set of machines was difficult enough that members often found themselves agreeing with the associate quoted above who "used to get so frustrated that [she] could scream." Thus, it is doubtful that members of the compressor team could have developed the knowledge and skill necessary for a successful start-up without an extraordinary level of commitment to their jobs.

The major factor that led to this commitment was a highly motivating group task. The team had been designed so that the emphasis would be on group performance rather than on narrow functional accomplishment. Advisors reported not to a central functional department but to a team manager whose primary responsibility was turning out manufacturing parts. The team had control over all of the resources necessary to produce compressors—and it was fully accountable for the results of its work.

It should not be surprising, then, that the compressor team became most energized when members were working collaboratively toward achieving a specific overriding task, such as shipping the first compressors to Ridgeway for source approval. At such times, "Everyone jelled together . . . nobody said no; everybody said yes."

Perhaps because of the strong mobilizing effects of these team tasks, the team had a tendency to organize its work so that it progressed from crisis to crisis. As one team advisor put it, "[We] wait until the deadline and then run around like a chicken with his head cut off trying to solve the problem. Rather than a lot of preplanning, rather than trying to get it done ahead of time and making sure that crises don't come up. I think Americans like crises."

While the team's task orientation may have created some inefficiencies, it paid off motivationally. Team members rated their jobs as providing more autonomy and feedback and as being generally more engaging and involving than did most other groups in our research project. Compared to other teams we studied, members also felt better rewarded by the organization for doing a good job, more adept at determining who was best qualified to perform a particular task, and better at generating creative performance strategies.

These positive aspects of team design led to an extraordinarily high level of commitment on the part of members. According to one associate, "People felt a responsibility to get things done, wouldn't go home. That can get the company in trouble when people are here ten, eleven hours a day. People weren't working overtime. They didn't want the money, they just wanted to get the job done. Instead of getting ready to leave half an hour before the bell rings, everyone was here early and leaving late. So now they tell us we have to go home, and they are having a harder time getting it all done."

Conclusion

At the beginning of this chapter, I suggested that the start-up of a new manufacturing team can be thought of as a production task. In closing, it is worth noting that many of the learning strategies used in the compressor team start-up themselves represent effective adaptations of standard production techniques. For example, just as process documentation is used in a mature manufacturing line to capture in detail the lessons previously learned about how parts are produced, the audit checklist was used to capture in an equally detailed way lessons about how previous teams were "produced." Also, just as inspection procedures ensure that parts are produced to specification on a manufacturing line, the corporate quality audit ensured that the compressor team met the specifications of the audit checklist during its start-up.

By using the best of production theory and practice to produce a production team, the Fairfield Components Plant created a unit capable of learning—not merely by copying the most successful elements of previous teams, but also by synthesizing those elements into a genuinely new and more effective whole.

Notes

1. For more information on the start-up of the Fairfield Components Plant see Chapters One and Ten on, respectively, the plant operating committee and the plant computer system group.
2. Conversely, Cutler's lack of relevant manufacturing experience was a significant impediment to his effectiveness as the compressor team's first manager.

26

Robert C. Ginnett

Airline Cockpit Crew[1]

The flight planning room was more hectic than usual as Greg Webber worked his way through the maze of pilots who were trying to check the weather forecasts and radar summaries mounted on the wall. The huge frontal system that had extended from Canada through central Florida had finally moved off the East Coast but not without leaving the operation in shambles. Aircraft that had been due in at 1800 the evening before had not arrived until 0330 in the morning, so everything from routine maintenance schedules to gate assignments was now being arranged creatively. Even now at 0545, as Greg reached the counter and sorted through the paperwork for his crew, he saw that the hectic activity of the previous evening was going to carry over into the early morning. Not only was it the first day of the new monthly crew lines, but his flight had been assigned two different captains. As a flight engineer for only two months, he could count on learning something new every trip, but this was not what he had expected.

Across the room he saw Tom Hartman. At six feet two inches, the former football player was easy to find, even in the uniformly black-jacketed crowd. Tom was talking to another captain whom Greg recognized only by the four stripes on his coat sleeve. As he approached with the weather summaries and flight plans, he heard Tom telling

427

his peer that he was sorry they had called him in from reserves so early in the morning and in all this weather only to discover they did not have a trip for him. As the other captain turned to head back to the counter, he said, "Don't worry about it, Tom. As screwed up as things are here this morning, I'm sure I'll be able to pick up a trip." Tom could only nod and laugh.

"Hi Tom. Was that the other captain?" asked Greg.

"Yeah, they called the poor guy in off reserves for our flight. I don't know how it happened, but I'm going," Tom replied.

"Great, I got all the paperwork. Do you know the first officer? It's supposed to be somebody named Bill Runyon, but who knows this morning. I've never met him."

"Neither have I," replied Tom. Not knowing the crew members you were to fly with was the norm rather than the exception the first part of each month. That Tom and Greg had flown together once before put them into a small minority among the crews. As Tom glanced over the flight plan, he said, "Why don't you see if you can find Runyon. I want to check this weather one more time."

Greg managed to locate Bill Runyon, who was thumbing through the "hot read file," and together they walked over to the weather charts and met Tom. After a short exchange of pleasantries, Tom led them out of flight planning and down the hall to the briefing room where they would meet their cabin crew.

Four flight attendants were sitting around a table in one corner of the room as the cockpit crew arrived. The room smelled of coffee and was brightly illuminated—almost too bright for that hour in the morning. But compared with the black February sky and the north wind rattling against the windows of the briefing room, the contrast was welcome. As Tom approached the four young women, he asked, "Are you all going on the four-day?"

"Yep," responded the woman farthest from Tom. She had volunteered to be the lead flight attendant for the first day—the team leader. "Hi, I'm Tom Hartman. This is Bill Runyon, our first officer, and Greg Webber is our flight engineer. Maybe you could introduce yourselves so I get to know who you are."

None of the cockpit crew had ever flown with any of these flight attendants, but three of the four attendants had worked together as a team for several months. After the introductions, interrupted by several glances toward the windows to see if they were going to survive the lashing from the wind, Tom spoke again. He stood next to the table where the flight attendants sat drinking their coffee. Consistent with his loosened tie, open collar, and cowboy boots, he seemed very relaxed and comfortable.

"OK, let's get started here. I'd like to talk to you a little about what we're going to do. Our first objective is to be on time. That might not be possible because of the weather but we're going to try. While we're talking about this, I'd like you all to stay down when I turn the sign on in this weather."

"How is the weather?" asked the same attendant who had spoken before.

"Well, right now it's not really, really bad; but until we get up to about five or six thousand feet it's probably going to be bumpy. And also the same on the way down. I'll give you ten minutes on the no smoking sign on landing. And I'll do that on every leg whether we're real full or whether we're real light. That's a long time, but I do that so you can make a good safety check and be in your seats well prior to landing. So ten minutes again, make sure you do a good safety check and then go ahead and get in your seats. The reason I do that is I had a fed [FAA inspector] riding with me one day and he was real upset because he could hear the crew back there rattling around below five hundred feet. So when that sign comes on, whatever you're doing, stop at that time and put everything away and get in your seats. And also, sometimes it takes a little bit of adjustment to get used to because I guess a lot of captains don't do that. But I'll give you a good ten minutes unless for some reason we get vectored in and we're coming in early and then we'll have you come up and we'll tell you."

"Does anyone have a copy of our schedule for this trip?" asked another attendant. The flight engineer handed her a scrap of paper with the trip schedule printed on it.

"Oh yeah, how about the flight time to Washington?" asked the lead flight attendant.

"Ah, going to D.C., it says forty-one minutes. Coming back from D.C., it says thirty-eight minutes. And today with the winds being what they are, there'll be single runway operations, so I think we'll probably take a little longer, so you'll have a little more time. If we have any problems throughout the flight, I'll let you know what our intentions are up front, what we're going to do and our destination, if that changes. By the same token, if you guys have any problems back there, either with a passenger, or if something doesn't look right, let us know. You guys have been around enough, if it doesn't sound right or whatever, please come up front and we'll let Greg go back and take a look at it. It could be something important. And even if a passenger says something's not right with the airplane, let us know, OK? You know on another company's flight the other day, a passenger told the flight attendant that he saw part of the airplane fall off in flight, which in fact it had. And her answer to him was, 'Yes, the captain knows about it.' In fact, the captain didn't know about it. So even if a passenger says something, some of them are really pretty knowledgeable. And also we'll send Greg back to look at it just to give them a warm fuzzy feeling in their stomachs that somebody comes back and says everything's OK."

"OK," responded the lead.

"OK. Ah, you guys can board whenever you're ready. No need to ask us up front. And the same way, you can bring up the stairs after the people are on board, you don't need to ask. In both of those cases, if we don't want you to either board or bring up the aft air stairs for whatever reason, mechanical, whatever, we'll come tell you. Ahhh boy, on the other side of the coin, don't let the ground people rush you. If you guys aren't ready to board and they're trying to hurry up, have 'em come talk to me."

"OK, thank you very much. Would you like the door open when you taxi?"

Tom paused briefly and then replied to the question. "Yeah, I like it open and I'll tell you why. Because that way if we get a real quick taxi, I can look back and kind of pace ourselves so that we're not pulling on the runway then with the tower expecting us to go right away and you guys aren't ready yet. So if I can look back there and see, I can tell the tower we need a couple more minutes. And when you are ready, just stick your head in and let us know that you're ready."

"OK, great," replied the lead attendant once again.

"Is there anything that we all up front could do to make it easier for you? Anything that you guys like in particular?" asked Tom.

The lead flight attendant looked around the table and then said, "I think you've covered everything, right guys? Oh, do you know what gate we're at?"

"No, I don't. Why don't you check the monitor and let the rest of the crew know," replied Tom. "If there are no other questions, then we'll see everybody down there."

It was now 0638 in the morning. In less than one hour, three pilots had come together to form a crew. Under the direction of a legitimate authority figure, the captain, the first and second officers had formed their initial impressions of how they would work with this leader and each other as a crew to carry as many as 150 people at a time into the air in a Boeing 727. A crew that had never worked together before would now start to work without any time for "practice" and would have to perform effectively in a complex system for the next four days.

While the early moments are significant in the transition from a collection of strangers to an integrated crew, particularly when subsequent behaviors reinforce the initial impressions, these early behaviors do not stand alone. As with other aspects of group interactions, the behaviors of a flight crew vary over its life. Unfortunately, it is not possible to record all of the behavior of this four-day trip in one chapter. It is important, however, that the events this crew encountered beyond the initial formation process be presented in some detail. This detailed description will illustrate the range of situations a flight crew can experience. The experiences of this flight crew should add a small but somewhat unique facet to our understanding of how groups work.

Day One

The first problem the crew faced was unusual: there was no airplane for them to fly. It was not that the "wrong" airplane was at their assigned gate, but that there was no airplane there at all. Because of the adverse weather during the previous night, the normal gate assignments had been shuffled around. A ground crew had towed the aircraft that was to have been theirs away from the gate late at night to make room for another arriving flight. With the arrival of the arctic cold mass, the ground crews could not get enough of the tow tugs started to reassign the aircraft to their proper gates for the morning lines. So, after several calls to operations, Greg decided to walk over to the maintenance desk to see if he could help. In the meantime, Tom and Bill had discovered that the airplane was parked about a quarter of a mile away on a maintenance parking ramp. After learning of the difficulty with towing operations, Tom and Bill decided it would be easier if they just walked over and taxied the plane back to the gate. Hiking across the ramp in a minus-forty-degree windchill factor to start a cold airplane was not the way either of them had planned to begin the trip. But with Bill working the flight engineer's panel and Tom starting the engines, they soon were able to taxi the aircraft to the gate and begin boarding.

Preparation for the first flight in any aircraft always takes the longest time. Not only must the crew make all the normal preparations (checking the flight plan, the weather [for departure, en route, at the destination, and at any required alternates], fuel requirements and load, weight and balance, communication and navigation equipment, system performance on run-up, and arranging for clearance from Air Traffic Control [ATC]), they must also review the aircraft log, which contains a record of maintenance performed on the plane. The log also contains a listing of any open maintenance items that might either preclude the flight or limit the performance of the aircraft. On this particular aircraft, the log indicated that one pack (one of two redundant systems that control cabin temperature and pressure) was inoperative—although maintenance personnel had not placed the required placard on the gauge. The captain asked the maintenance manager to put a placard up there "so that I can remember what's wrong." The performance of the aircraft would be limited beyond a certain altitude, but that would not be a problem for the day's trips.

Tasks during this busy period are divided among the three crew members. Generally, the captain completes the flight log, handles any unusual situations, and directs the other crew members so that cockpit preparations are made in a timely manner prior to "push"—the time when the parking brakes are released and the tug pushes the aircraft back from the gate. ("Push" is the event that determines whether a flight has departed on time.) Additionally, the captain must prepare his side of the cockpit (the left seat) for flight and test all emergency warning devices. During these preparations, and for the duration of the flight, the captain is in full command of the aircraft and crew.

The first officer also must prepare his side of the cockpit (the right seat), since he will fly the airplane on alternating legs of the trip. In addition, he will usually obtain the clearance from ATC, and he must perform (or verify) the calculations necessary to determine whether the aircraft's weight is under the limits (including fuel, baggage, and passengers) and whether that weight is correctly distributed in relation to the aircraft's center of gravity. These calculations are also critical for determining the appropriate elevator trim (adjustment) for takeoff.

The aircraft systems are the responsibility of the flight engineer (FE). Although the FE is often a certified commercial pilot, he does not actually fly the plane. Rather, he sits sideways in the cockpit facing a panel that allows him to monitor and control the various subsystems aboard the aircraft, including hydraulics, electricals, fuel, engines, and environmentals (cabin pressure and temperature). His preflight duties include a visual check of the entire outside of the aircraft (the "walk around") and testing the remainder of the systems. He also serves as a backup in rechecking many of the settings and calculations the other two crew members make. At the captain's discretion (or, on some occasions, the first officer's, should he be the pilot flying), the flight engineer reads the various checklists and ensures compliance.

After waiting an unexpected twenty-five minutes for maintenance to replace the captain's broken oxygen mask, Flight 728 pushed—one hour and twenty-two minutes late. Given the weather and the number of canceled flights from the previous night, most of the passengers seemed relieved that the flight was going to go at all. Tom and Bill had decided jointly that Tom would fly to Washington and that they would alternate from then on. The engine start and taxi were routine: Greg operated the panel and checklists, Bill started the engines and communicated with the ground controller in the tower, and Tom taxied the aircraft. The cockpit design determines many of these activities. For example, only the FE can reach the controls for the auxiliary power unit (APU), and the captain is the only one who can taxi a Boeing aircraft since the nose gear steering wheel is located on the far left side of the cockpit.

By takeoff time the weather had warmed up to fifteen degrees but the wind was still high—out of the west at twenty-five knots gusting to thirty-five. Takeoffs in a reasonable crosswind are not too difficult in an airplane the size of a 727. As long as the runway is not slick, a crosswind correction with the ailerons will hold it while the wheels are on the ground, and once the wheels come up, the pilot can correct any drift of consequence relatively easily. Takeoff was routine, as was the flight to Washington. Trips of this duration maintain a rather high degree of task attention since there is little time spent purely at cruise. On this particular trip, most of the time was spent either climbing to cruise altitude and departing New York Center (the air traffic control region) or descending and entering the Washington Center.

The landing at Washington was somewhat challenging. Landings require more pilot skill than takeoffs even under ideal conditions. But the winds at Washington National Airport were similar to those in New York—in both direction and intensity. The automatic terminal information service (ATIS—a recorded message giving airport information) and the tower were reporting traffic landing on runway 36 (due north), which was indeed the runway the three previous aircraft had used. However, once we turned onto final for runway 36, the tower reported the wind from 290 degrees at thirty knots gusting to forty. At that point Tom asked Bill to request runway 33, which would decrease the crosswind angle from seventy to forty degrees. This change would require Tom to move his approach over to the east side of the Potomac River and then to bank sharply to the left at the edge of Bolling Air Force Base to line up with runway 33. Not only did Tom fly the approach smoothly, he put the main gear down without a bounce just past the runway numbers, leaving him with almost the entire runway to stop. While not qualifying as a "squeaker," the high quality of his airmanship did not go undetected. From the time the nose gear touched the runway until the aircraft was parked at the gate, both Bill and Greg had each complimented Tom three times. They also noted that his decision to request the shorter runway with the wind advantage must have been right, because the next four aircraft to land made the same request.

The return flight to New York also was without incident. However, shortly after taxiing to the gate, a maintenance employee came up to the cockpit and told the crew that the right main landing gear strut was leaking badly and would need to be serviced. Maintenance estimated the repair to be at least a two-hour job, so the next scheduled leg, to Boston, was canceled. Tom got the entire crew together to explain what was happening and told them to check back with him in the briefing room in two hours. Tom, Bill, and Greg walked to the crew lounge where they spent the time talking with other pilots about topics such as winter maintenance problems, company policy, and which airline was about to buy which other airline. They also agreed that trying to figure out the new bid package for next month's schedule was virtually impossible.

After maintenance serviced the strut, the next flight (a trip back to Washington) was boarded, much to the satisfaction of the crew. If that flight had been canceled, they would have been required to remain in New York—and, since that was their home station, they would have forfeited their per diem. The winds were continuing to die down so the trip back was the least eventful of the day. They arrived in Washington at 1600. While the flight attendants went into the terminal to close out their accounts, the cockpit crew briefed the oncoming crew about the minor uncorrected maintenance items and their experience with the right main strut.

At 1645, the entire crew left the airport and boarded the van for the ride to the motel. During the ride, the captain formally relinquished authority for the group, saying that the lead flight attendant was in charge of all social activity for the evening. Apart from arranging a meeting time for the next morning's departure, he abided by that statement. Although he participated as a regular group member and was frequently asked for his opinion during the evening, he made no decisions for the group. The entire crew—both cockpit and cabin—had a beer together in the bar, went to dinner together, and then went to a pub and listened to Irish music for about an hour.

By ten o'clock everyone decided to call it a night and return to the motel. Fatigue had set in. The work day had started at 0545 and had ended at 2200. They had flown for less than three hours, but they had been together as a crew for sixteen hours and fifteen minutes.

Day Two

The second day started at 0600 in the motel for everyone but Greg, who had caught the 0530 van back to the airport. He had called ahead and found that the liquids on the overnight aircraft had not been drained, and since the temperature had been below zero, he wanted to get there early to make sure there were no problems. The crew appreciated walking into a heated airplane, and they let him know it. The first two flights, from Washington to New York and then from New York to Columbus, Ohio, were uneventful. In fact, the weather had improved so much that the next leg, from Columbus to Sarasota, offered something the crew had not yet experienced on this trip—boredom. The scheduled flight time was two hours and twenty minutes, and the majority of that time was spent above 30,000 feet.

Perhaps the biggest challenge for the crew at long-range cruise is to remain sufficiently attentive. If there is no significant weather en route or at the destination, and if there are no mechanical problems with the aircraft, all the crew has to do is navigate and monitor the aircraft's performance. The autopilot holds the altitude and heading constant and keeps the aircraft properly trimmed. ATC monitors the flight's progress along the assigned route and altitude and keeps the crew advised of any other aircraft in the vicinity. The crew checks in with each control center as they enter the center's airspace, and they may, from time to time, request a more direct routing if conditions permit. The flight engineer and at least one of the flying crew members monitor fuel consumption and time en route. While there are other responsibilities that the crew must manage at cruise—such as balancing the fuel load and monitoring the temperature in the cabin—there is generally more time than there is work.

Cruise, therefore, is a time for discussions. The topics vary widely, from technical aeronautical topics to the latest sports news. It is not uncommon for crews to discuss how some aspect of the aircraft works, particularly if it is associated with a current maintenance problem. Company policy and management (or the perceived lack thereof) are always fair game, as are the latest load factors and profit sharing estimates (or anticipated lack thereof). Jokes abound, and since the cockpit is predominantly a white male environment, sexist and ethnic jokes are commonplace. It is often a time, as on this flight, when crew members ask about each other's backgrounds. Bill had learned to fly in the Air Force and spent his military time flying C-130s. He then had moved on to two commercial airlines, both of which had gone bankrupt. Greg had come from a civilian background, having graduated from Embry-Riddle Aeronautical University; his early experience was flying Metroliners for a commuter company. Tom had been a fighter pilot in the Air Force until coming to the company. He still flew F-4s with the Air Force Reserves.

On long cruises, especially when the passenger loads are light, flight attendants may come up into the cockpit to talk with the cockpit crew. Because space is limited, the pilots always outnumber them. Even though some general deference to the captain's authority can occasionally be noted, the flight attendants seem comfortable talking with the cockpit crew. On this flight, the lead flight attendant came up about an hour into the flight and suggested to the captain that he make an announcement about twenty minutes before he turned on the fasten-seat-belt sign so that people could get up and go to the bathroom. She said that otherwise, "People will sit through the whole flight and then just as the fasten-seat-belt sign comes on, they'll remember they haven't been to the bathroom yet. Then you get a whole group of them lined up in the aisle just as you begin your descent." Tom thought it was a good idea and said he would be sure to do that both on the way to Sarasota and coming back. He thanked her for making the suggestion.

Planning for the descent marks the end of cruise and is most often initiated by a call from ATC advising the crew that they can descend to a lower prescribed altitude "at pilot's discretion." Although Tom could have descended immediately, experience coupled with a concern for fuel conservation dictated that he stay as high as he could for as long as he could while still complying with the restrictions the controller specified. Greg already had received information about the Sarasota weather, winds, and runway in use from ATIS. He noted this information on the landing card for the pilot flying, along with the "go-around EPRs" (the exhaust pressure ratio based upon temperature, altitude, and humidity), so the engines could be increased to their maximum safe performance if the landing had to be aborted. Bill continued to handle the communications while pulling out his copy of the descent and approach plates that specified normal approach procedures for Sarasota.

The landing in Sarasota was uneventful. The push from Sarasota was delayed because somehow a few overbooked passengers managed to make it onto the plane only to discover there were no seats for them. Once the counter staff had taken care of them, the airplane departed and the flight back to Columbus was routine. By the time the crew checked into the motel for night two, it was obvious that everyone was fading. Again, the whole crew ate dinner together and then returned directly to the motel, ready for sleep at 9:30. So much for the myth of the wild and exciting lives of airline crews.

Days Three and Four

Day three began with a routine flight back to New York punctuated only by a severe case of Monday morning confusion by ATC. After instructing the crew to keep the speed up at cruise, ATC then instructed them to slow down to maintain proper spacing. Then, as they entered the New York area, the ATC center they were leaving told them to contact New York Center on an incorrect frequency. This prompted the receiving controller to inform Flight 662 that they were on the wrong frequency.[2] After getting the correct frequency, ATC first instructed Flight 662 to speed up and then decrease their forward speed while descending rapidly—a simple feat for a rock but not an easy maneuver in a 727.

Once again in New York, the airplane proceeded to fall apart on the ramp. One of the right inboard flaps had lost a roller and the number one engine had developed a major fuel leak. The flap roller was fixed in about thirty minutes but the fuel leak took four hours. The next leg was canceled and the crew arranged to be back in time for a Chicago departure at 1325.

After boarding the Chicago passengers, clearance delivery issued a thirty-minute gate hold for flow control into Chicago, and dispatch would only provide a "3585 Release." Each flight requires a release from a dispatcher that must also be signed by the captain. A 3585 Release is conditional (because of weather or other circumstances) and requires further clearance once en route. In tandem, these two bits of data were evidence to the crew that the weather in the Chicago area was indeed getting worse. After they departed New York and reached cruise altitude, Tom turned to Greg and asked him to stay in touch with the flight service stations en route so he could monitor conditions.

Murphy's Law of Weather took over. O'Hare was getting strong winds and heavy snow, which forced the airport to go to single runway operations. When one of the country's busiest airports drops its arrival rate down to eighteen per hour, stacks build all over the Midwest. At 1420, Flight 663 was put into a stack, and the crew went to work. Tom, who was flying, computed the turns and legs for the stack and began flying the pattern. He asked Bill to get out the approach plates for the two alternates (Milwaukee and Columbus) and to see what the winds were on their primary runways. He asked Greg to start working on the fuel available and the fuel required to the two alternates. Bill said that the winds would be acceptable at either of the alternates and Greg reported the results of a whole series of fuel calculations. After reviewing all the information, Tom turned to the rest of the crew and said, "If we make the decision before eleven [thousand pounds of fuel remaining], we can either go to Columbus or Milwaukee. Does that sound good to everybody? Does everyone agree with that?" Bill and Greg both nodded and confirmed the decision.

Now everyone paid particular attention to ATC instructions to other aircraft, to try to gauge the time they would have to remain in the stack. Since all planes in the stack were on the same radio frequency, it was possible to listen and get a good idea of when they would be cleared out. But as Flight 663 descended through the stack, something new began to happen. The United flight that was two ahead of them was not cleared into Chicago but instead went into a new holding area. The crew decided that if that happened to them, they would head back to Columbus (which was a company station, while Milwaukee was not) for more fuel. At 1600 ATC did direct Flight 663 into a new stack, and the default decision became the active plan. Bill requested vectors to Columbus, and within a few minutes ATC had provided the course. Bill found the new course on the map, Tom flew the vectors and told the lead flight attendant what was happening, and Greg explained the situation to the passengers. At 1650, the plane arrived in Columbus and was refueled.

Just as the tug started the push back at 1820 to begin another try for Chicago, Tom turned to the crew and said, "Well, things have been a little unusual so let's just take our time and do a good job." That set the stage for a very deliberate flight back to Chicago through another entire series of stacks beginning over Fort Wayne, Indiana, and continuing for an hour and fifteen minutes. At 10,000 feet, Tom turned the landing lights on. Snow was everywhere. The visibility was reported to be one mile with a ceiling of 800 feet. The winds were from 320 degrees at twenty knots with gusts to thirty-five in snow and blowing snow. At about 900 feet, the ground lights first became visible, and the high-intensity strobes at the end of the runway appeared shortly thereafter. Braking was reported fair to poor, which was verified after Tom had eased the 727 down between the two parallel rows of white lights. Finding the taxiway was even more difficult since the plowing crews had their hands full just keeping the single runway operable. Bill first noticed the faint blue glow from under the snow and said, "I think that's it." It was, and the remainder of the taxi was completed without incident. Tom's crew roundly praised him for his flying. He turned to them and said, "I think everybody deserves a beer for that job." It was after 9 P.M. when the crew left the airport for the motel.

Once again, the evening was marked by fatigue, which carried over to the next day. Day four included a long trip from New York to West Palm Beach and back. The conclusion of the final leg also marked the termination of the group's life. Just as the crew had come together easily, termination was handled as a routine event. Tom thanked Bill and Greg and then went back to thank the flight attendants. Each of them gave him a hug before he departed. Greg and Bill were both commuters from Florida and had scheduled jump seats back home that evening. Because Greg had a tight connection, he asked Bill if he would mind taking the paperwork in for him. He thanked Bill for sharing some of the tips learned in his days as an engineer, and then headed in for his connection. Bill was last off the aircraft and said good-bye again to Tom as they passed in flight planning. From the time this group formed until it terminated, eighty-five hours and thirty minutes had elapsed. Of this total time, forty-eight hours were required duty times, which included report times and delays due to weather or mechanical problems. Actual block time (total push-to-park times) was twenty-three hours and fifty-six minutes.

The Design of Effective Cockpit Crews

In this eighty-five-hour period, we witnessed the entire life of a work team—a real team that performed interdependent tasks within an organizational context. We can learn many lessons about group behavior from cockpit crews, but one is particularly salient: very little time is devoted to forming and building a team in the traditional sense. How is it that airline crews can come together so quickly and then perform such an important task so effectively? The answer to this question cannot be found either in group development theory or in airline procedure manuals. Rather, the answer lies in the tension between the attraction of standardization and the never-ending need for a team to deal with new and complex situations in nonstandard ways.

The argument for standardization is appealing. If the entire behavioral repertoire of a cockpit crew could be choreo-graphed, then each flight could be performed like a well-rehearsed ballet. Indeed, most routine portions of a flight are very much like this; so, too, are the well-practiced emergency procedures such as those for an engine fire on takeoff. In these cases, the behaviors of each crew member are so standardized that the men or women who play the roles are much like interchange-able parts in a machine. Pull one first officer out, replace her with another, and the crew continues to function as effectively as a ballet company on its three-hundred-fiftieth performance.

As compelling as this argument for standardization is, it misses the point that crews rarely run into problems during rou-tinized portions of the flight. Real problems happen when the crew encounters new, unusual, and confusing situations. Because there are no standard procedures to handle such times, they are the ones for which good teamwork is critical. This does not mean that standardization is bad. It simply means that even with the best of procedures, crews still must be built into com-petent performing units.

Two factors that significantly affect how, and how well, a crew develops are the supportiveness of the organizational con-text within which the crew works and how well designed the crew itself is (Hackman, 1987). Organizationally, crews need a context that supports and reinforces competent task work dur-ing line operations. The context should include (1) a reward system that provides challenging objectives not only for safety but also for organizational criteria such as on-time performance and fuel efficiency; (2) an education system that provides train-ing and consultation to supplement members' task expertise; and (3) an information system that provides the data needed to assess the performance situations and evaluate alternative strat-egies for handling them.

In addition, crews must be well designed as performing units. Among the design features that appear to be associated with team effectiveness are the group task (it should engage and motivate members) and group composition (it should provide the right mix of members who have ample task-relevant skill). A third class of factors, group norms, should actively support continuous situation scanning and strategy planning. Some of these factors are, for better or worse, built into crews by the very nature of the work itself or the cockpit technology. Others may be "imported" from the culture of flying or the culture of the organization to a particular crew. An example would be a norm that "Decisions by the captain are not to be questioned"—a norm that can get a crew into real trouble if the captain is wrong.

Even though design and contextual factors, such as those mentioned above, constrain much of the potential variation in crew performance, large and significant differences in crew behavior still exist. This is where the leadership provided by the captain (and other crew members) comes into play. The remainder of this chapter discusses the kinds of behaviors on the part of captains that can foster effective crew formation and development.

The Key Role of the Captain

The crew we have described in this chapter was a particularly effective one. A key reason for its effectiveness was the leadership the captain provided. In countless interviews with airline pilots, one statement was repeated again and again—namely, some captains are especially good at building and managing a team, and others are not at all good at it (see also Helmreich, Foushee, Benson, & Russini, 1986). While virtually none of the pilots I interviewed could articulate *what* an effective captain does, they said they could tell *whether* the captain they were to fly with was effective or not in just a few minutes.

Tom was an effective crew leader. The behaviors that made him effective were apparent in his initial briefing. My research has shown that effective captains consistently exhibit these behaviors. They include (1) explicitly discussing tasks that require coordination between the cockpit and the cabin, (2) defining and expanding crew boundaries, (3) explicitly setting norms for crew behavior, and, most important for airline crews, (4) appropriately managing the dynamics surrounding the authority inherent in the captain's own role. A captain balances the authority dynamic by demonstrating his competence, on the one hand (thereby supporting traditional dependency upon the captain), and, on the other hand, by actively engaging the crew in the work of the team (which tends to offset the traditional dependency). For details on how captains accomplish this (and for data on how such behavior contrasts with that of captains rated as less effective in the development and management of their teams), see Ginnett (1987).

The process of team development for cockpit crews is quite different from that described in traditional models of group development. Whether one prefers a psychodynamic approach (such as Bion, 1961) or a fixed developmental sequence of "forming, storming, norming, and performing" (Tuckman, 1965), it is difficult to see how all of these processes could occur in the formation of a flight crew. In the short ten minutes during which a cockpit crew moves from individual introductions to a team capable of performing interdependent work, even a superleader would be hard pressed to guide a group all the way through these steps of group development.

The reason traditional group development models apply poorly to cockpit crews lies not so much in the nature of the group (although that does play some part) as in the nature of the context. Much of our understanding of group formation and development has emerged from the study of learning groups or therapy groups (Ginnett, 1987; Gersick, 1988). Such groups import little from the organizational context; nor are they highly dependent on the organization for what they need to get their work done. The opposite is the case for cockpit crews. They form with an already well-developed task definition—that is, they all come to work knowing what they are going to do and possessing the necessary individual skills to do it. And they are part of an organization that provides most of the resources and information they need for their work. Furthermore, the organization is embedded within an environment of other agencies and organizations that further define and augment individual and collective tasks.

Even though the particular collection of individuals in a given crew may never have worked as a team before, when they come together, they step into a preexisting "shell" (Hackman,

1986a; Ginnett, 1987) that predefines much of what is expected of them as a team. This shell includes not only the context and design factors described by Hackman (1987), but also a set of expectations about the roles of each individual in the crew. It is as if the definitions of the captain, the first officer, the engineer, and the rest of the crew (and, to some degree, the boundary of the group as a whole) are already in place before any particular individual enters the setting. Although shell definitions are not rigid (they are more like definitions drawn with "dotted lines"), the shell does powerfully shape crew behavior.

It is this mechanism, the shell, that allows the crew to develop so quickly. When a captain begins his briefing, he is not really starting from zero. If he works for an airline that encourages and supports crew effectiveness, all the contextual work that has gone before him in laying the groundwork is already in place. All he has to do is affirm the imported shell—fill in the dotted lines—so the crew can proceed with what they have come to expect (see Figure 2). That only takes a few minutes. It is in those first few moments that the captain breathes life into the shell of the forming group.

Tom did more than merely affirm the shell. He took the time to expand the shell. He gave the crew a larger definition of tasks, boundaries, norms, and authority dynamics with which to work. Such a larger definition, while providing the potential for more effective crew work, is quite fragile. In fact, the expanded definition is, itself, a new dotted line of how the group will work. Just as the dotted line of imported definitions for all forming crews requires some work by the leader, so does the expanded shell require reinforcement. The congruence between what the captain says in the briefing and how he *behaves* in the briefing provides some of that reinforcement. Even more important is how he behaves during line flying. If he supports the expanded definition of crew work that he created, the dotted lines will fill in and more effective crew work will result. But if he should behave in a manner inconsistent with the expanded shell, its newly formed and fragile outer boundaries will collapse.

Effective teamwork does not just happen—it takes effort by everyone, especially the leader. Less effective crew leaders in

Figure 2. A Visualization of the Imported and Developed Portions of the Shell.

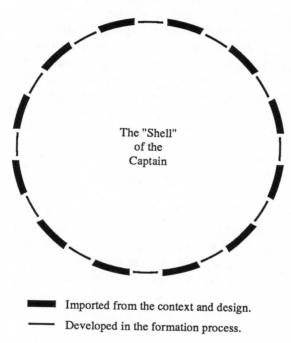

The "Shell"
of the
Captain

▬▬▬ Imported from the context and design.
───── Developed in the formation process.

my research (Ginnett, 1987) neither affirmed nor expanded the preexisting shell. Instead, some abdicated, leaving the crew with only the unconfirmed dotted lines they had imported. Even worse, some captains actively undermined the imported shell, causing it to collapse before the team ever really got a chance to perform.

Conclusion

The most important lesson to be learned from airline cockpit crews is that their rapid and efficient formation process is a function of the shell that each crew member imports—and much of that shell originates in the organizational context. This point has often been missed in other research because, as noted by

Hackman and Morris (1975), we too often control those variables that make up the shell. It should be clear from the data in the case in this chapter that so-called "storming" did not occur at all—which is probably a good thing for those of us who were passengers—and that "norming" was mostly imported. The concept of the shell provides a better model for understanding group formation and development in organizations than does that provided by widely taught models that posit fixed developmental sequences. If we are to understand groups in the real world, we need to pay close attention to the organizational contexts in which they work.

Notes

1. Preparation of this chapter was supported by Cooperative Agreement NCC 2-324 between NASA and Yale University.
2. Although FCC regulations prohibit the use of profanity on the radio, a few controllers in the New York area have mastered the fine art of implied profanity. This particular controller was a specialist in the implied "you dumb son-of-a-bitch."

27

David J. Abramis

Semiconductor Manufacturing Team[1]

Raymond, the team advisor, and I walked up to the team, each of us outfitted in a sterile white robe and wearing a shower-cap–like device over our heads. Six similarly dressed team members were distributed around three sides of an open-ended, rectangular work area, with a large handmade sign reading "Datron Team" posted at the end. All I could see were backs: each member was facing away from the interior of the work area, hunched over his or her work station. Raymond asked for members' attention, and everyone stopped working and turned around. He introduced me to each person, and I explained who I was and asked the team's permission to observe. We joked a bit, and the novelty of the situation reduced our mutual discomfort. No one objected to my observing, but neither did anyone seem very interested in finding out much about me or what I was doing.

The members turned back to their work stations, and I began to watch, notebook in hand. Each team member focused on his or her own work, passing completed parts on to the next member. Every few minutes one would say something to another, usually related to the work. After half an hour or so, one team member asked another if she

449

would like to switch positions for a while. The other member agreed, and they switched. I began to wonder: Are these people bored out of their minds? More important, is this really a *team?*

The recipe for work teams at Chiptronics was simple:

1. Take one traditional assembly line production operation.
2. Divide employees who work next to each other on the assembly line into groups of three to seven people.
3. Redesign the physical technology so most groups of employees can stand close to each other in U-shaped configurations.
4. Rename supervisors "team advisors."
5. Tell the supervisors that they now manage teams as well as individuals.
6. Provide employees with feedback about the performance of their teams in addition to feedback about their individual performances.
7. Say to everybody, "Now you work in teams."

Although the formula was simple, the results were impressive. Productivity increased. Employee interest and involvement in the work deepened. Workers did a better job of monitoring their own work and taking corrective action when called for. There was more communication among employees, and people reported that they had more and better data to use in making decisions.

Like so many recipes, however, the creation of teams at Chiptronics was not as simple as it appeared to be. This chapter discusses some of the challenges the members and managers of one team at Chiptronics faced. This team, called Datron, provides a diverse array of behavioral examples that illustrate both the benefits and the problems of teamwork in a production operation. The chapter begins with an overview of the Chiptronics plant, followed by a detailed description of the Datron team, and concludes with a discussion of the main lessons learned from the Chiptronics teams.

The Chiptronics Organization

There is no doubt that the town of Borman, where Chiptronics is located, is in the real West—complete with desert, sagebrush, and heat. Life is quiet, the air is clean, and some of the best skiing in the United States is only a short drive away. The cost of living is relatively low, as are wages. People are middle-class and generally conservative, both in religious beliefs and in politics.

Chiptronics is a semiconductor manufacturing firm with headquarters in California and additional manufacturing facilities in the Northwest, Southwest, and Midwest. Borman was the first Chiptronics plant to use teams to manufacture semiconductors. My observations took place on the first production line to institute teams, while they were still relatively new. Thus, the issues I discuss are very much those of teams in their early stages of life—teams in transition in an organization that was still learning how to use them as the basic unit for accomplishing work.

Teamwork in Borman was the baby of production manager Pete Townsend. Pete was a hard-nosed, tough-looking fellow with a dash of teddy bear. His trademarks were a bone-crushing handshake and the certainty of a southern preacher. His subordinates liked him, but it was hard for them not to fear him at the same time. Pete felt considerable pressure, both internally and from headquarters, to increase the productivity of his lines. While he was confident that using teams could improve productivity, at first Pete did not realize just how much organizational support they would require. After teams were created, he put considerable production pressure on them and their leaders. And produce they did—but they also produced some unanticipated organizational problems as by-products.

Despite the problems Pete and his colleagues encountered during implementation of the team concept at Borman, teamwork subsequently spread to other manufacturing lines in the plant. And a great deal of organizational learning occurred as the teams were being fine-tuned—learning that eventually resulted in some significant changes in the organization itself. Plant management now believes that teams have been funda-

uted to the experienced meaningfulness of the work. It also was true, however, that the product of the team's work did not have any obvious or direct significance for team members, nor were most members aware of how Chiptronics customers used the product the team was helping to make. When the Datron team completed its operations, wafers simply went on to the next team and that was the end of it as far as team members were concerned.

Team autonomy was quite low. Production procedures and processes were specified in clear and complete detail, and members were expected to follow them faithfully. Moreover, the technology fixed or constrained many aspects of the work: there was one right way to operate most of the production equipment. Members did have limited autonomy to decide who would perform which subtask on a given day, to allocate member resources to subtasks (which was critical when a bottleneck in the production process developed), and to schedule breaks and informal team meetings. But generally these decisions were checked and approved by the team advisor, who made most decisions he viewed as truly consequential himself. Although one of the reasons for instituting teams at Chiptronics was to encourage employees at Borman to become involved in improving the production process, the Datron team had no involvement in analyzing the process or in developing better production methods. These matters were exclusively the province of plant engineering and equipment maintenance staffs.

Knowledge of results was high. The technology automatically provided feedback about results for many subtasks, and members were able to tell in the course of a day how well they were doing. In addition, the team received feedback about the number of acceptable products it had produced at the end of each day. Members also received feedback about individual performance, and errors were traced back to the team members who made them.

The Team

Although members of the Datron team did not have much knowledge about the technical aspects of their work or the final products they were helping to make, they nonetheless were good at doing their jobs. There were differences among them in skill, due largely to members' varying tenures on the Datron team or at Chiptronics. The team dealt with these differences by having more experienced members help others learn the various jobs on the team.[3]

Datron team members also were diverse in national origin and religious preference. Moreover, two members were cousins and sometimes brought family conflicts to work. This created some difficult challenges for the team. Management dealt with the family conflicts and disputes about religion by recomposing the team when it became clear that team members were not going to resolve the problems themselves. Certain members were transferred out of the team and replaced with other plant employees. This move satisfactorily resolved the "cousin" problem. And while it did not entirely eliminate disputes about religion, it did significantly soften their intensity and disruptiveness to the work.

The problems that derived from differences in national origin had mainly to do with members' difficulties in understanding one another. The matter was more consequential for the social life of the group than it was for its work because the rigidly programmed technology did not require extensive or complex communications among members. The team itself resolved most of its communications difficulties, largely through the efforts of two gregarious members who were not easily put off by language barriers or cultural differences. These members took it upon themselves to promote group norms of patience, tolerance, and helpfulness. Their willingness to take the initiative, coupled with their social skills, kept national and cultural differences from undermining the life of the Datron team. Even so, the most skilled team members (who also happened to be native English speakers) were frustrated because they had to exert additional effort to understand, be understood by, and assist teammates from other countries.

Overall, members of the Datron team were moderately skilled, moderately diverse individuals who basically did what they were asked to do at work. They did not ask many questions, take many initiatives, or have high expectations for what life at work would hold for them. They did the job and seemed rather surprised on those relatively rare occasions when a manager asked for their views about how things should be changed. This moderately compliant stance turned out to fit well with the style of the team advisor.

Leadership

Datron clearly was a manager-led team. Raymond, the thirty-three-year-old team advisor, had responsibility for three production teams and the authority to make all important decisions for them. Raymond was not shy about using his authority, particularly for decisions he believed were consequential for the quality or quantity of the team's performance. While he sometimes did present members with choices (for example, who would perform which subtask on a given day, or when would be a good time to take a break or have a meeting), he usually made his own preferences clear. The team typically went along with Raymond's wishes.

Occasionally, Raymond took the team off the line for some team-building activities—usually based on some exercise he had learned in his own management training, such as using a ball-passing game to explore within-team communications. In this game, a member can speak only when he or she has possession of the ball; the member then passes the ball to the team member from whom he or she seeks a response. This exercise surfaced issues about interrupting and turn-taking in communications that Raymond thought to be important to good team functioning.

Overall, Raymond's leadership was soft-spoken, but strong and firm. Team members liked him and got a boost when he complimented them or gave them a reward—such as movie tickets or an extended lunch break. The feeling was reciprocated: Raymond liked the team and its members and wished he could spend more time with them. However, the day-to-day demands of his job required him to be constantly on the move among his teams, to keep after an unceasing flow of administrative work, and to attend numerous meetings with other team advisors and senior managers.

Raymond did have some help in leading the team—the team coordinator. This person had responsibility for real-time coordination among team members, for assisting Raymond, and for handling routine questions and problems when he was not available. Although team members elected the coordinator, there was little prior discussion among members about who it should be—and certainly no campaigning for the job. Everyone assumed that the member who was most senior and most skilled should have the job, and that person was elected.

There was some confusion about the role of the team co-ordinator—confusion that created tension within the group (and in other groups at Borman as well). Just how much responsibility and authority coordinators had never was completely clear to team members—nor to the coordinators. The Datron team coordinator liked the responsibility, but she also reported that the job seemed to have been created to get more work out of her without giving her any real authority. Team members generally liked receiving the coordinator's help, but they objected to this "nonleader" telling them what to do. The ambiguity was never resolved, and when we returned to Borman after a year for our second round of observations, the position had been eliminated from all teams.

Organizational Context

The Datron team was tightly linked to other people and groups in the Borman production operation. Horizontal links with the teams that preceded and followed Datron in the production process were well-defined. And despite a modest buffer in the production process—wafers completed by one team accumulated on a cart before going to the next team in the line—any time a given team had serious production or quality problems, other teams up and down the line felt the effects in short order. The Datron team clearly was a customer of the preceding team, and Datron had its own customer—the next team. In the main, Raymond handled relations with supplier and customer teams under the watchful eye of his own boss, the second-level manager.

Vertical linkages also were tight. All production-relevant information, such as feedback about performance or changes in production targets, came to the team through the first level of management—Raymond, in Datron's case. Raymond also arranged for whatever resources the team needed to accomplish its work. Pete Townsend, the production manager, closely monitored the production of the line as a whole and took immediate action (through second-level managers) whenever any team showed signs of getting the line into difficulty. Emerging production problems usually were caught quickly and dealt with decisively by senior production management.

Among the most salient aspects of the organizational context for the Datron team were the plant maintenance and engineering staffs. Maintenance and engineering were separate organizations at Borman and not under Pete's control. The maintenance organization was responsible for ensuring that the production equipment kept operating—and operating within the close tolerances required to achieve quality objectives. Engineering staff were responsible for finding ever-better manufacturing methods and for developing new production processes when product specifications changed.

Although maintenance and engineering personnel were in separate departments, they had the authority to stop the line when necessary to do their work. This sometimes disrupted the production process or aborted the team's strategy for meeting its production targets. For example, when a machine (such as an oven) malfunctioned or went out of tolerance, Datron team members were not allowed to adjust it (indeed, members did not know how to make such adjustments). Instead, the team stopped production work, called maintenance, and then waited for someone to arrive and make the repair. Or, when engineering wanted to test some innovation in the production process, an engineer could simply appear and inform the team that he needed to "run a test batch." Regular production then stopped while the tests were performed.

Typically, such disruptions were managed by Pete persuading his counterpart on the engineering side of the factory that production was at a critical stage and therefore the engineers should defer their work until the crisis had passed. Datron team members had essentially no involvement, and certainly no say, in such negotiations. Those who actually made the product took a back seat to support staff members in these situations.

A final feature of the organizational context that noticeably affected life and work in the team was the organizational reward system. Management gave annual merit pay increases to individuals for exceptional performance. The team advisor recommended such increases, and second-level management confirmed them. Senior managers neither explicitly encouraged nor discouraged team advisors from rewarding their teams. On his own initiative, Raymond did provide a few performance-contingent team rewards—such as movie tickets or an extended lunch. But, overall, the reward system of the organization did not explicitly recognize and reinforce excellent team performance. Some managers were concerned that Chiptronics' compensation practices, which focused exclusively on individual performance, might unintentionally undermine the new team initiative at the plant.

The above description of the Datron team's organizational context is based on observations during our first visit, when the teams were still relatively young and untested. At that time, the context placed numerous constraints on the ability of teams to do what needed to be done to achieve their production targets. Moreover, there was little active support for teams in developing their work and interpersonal capabilities other than that provided informally by team advisors. Teams were there to execute the work within the existing organization, nothing more.

Between our initial observations and our follow-up visit a year later, a number of significant changes were made in the organizational context, changes that provided more support for teamwork. These changes, discussed in the concluding section of this chapter, resulted in improved functioning and enhanced performance for many (but not all) teams—even though serious economic difficulties and layoffs occurred in the intervening year. Yet, as we will see, even the skeletal teams that were in place at the time of our initial observations yielded some notable advantages over the individually focused production design that previously had been in place.

Harvesting the Benefits of Production Teams

There was general agreement within Chiptronics that Pete Townsend achieved something with teams at Borman that had eluded other production managers in the corporation. Indeed, production numbers were so impressive that delegations from headquarters and other plants regularly visited Pete intent on learning his secrets. And when the corporation decided to build a new, state-of-the-art production facility, Pete and Susan Jenkins (the internal organization development consultant) were among the first to be consulted about the organizational design of that plant.

What was it about Pete's teams that was responsible for the productivity improvements? After all, not much had been changed from the traditional Chiptronics design. Individual team members still had their own tasks to do, and the teams themselves were far from self-managing. Members did not have the authority to make those decisions that would have the highest leverage on performance outcomes, and they had to call on others for solutions to most work-related problems. So why did productivity increase? And why, after the initial settling-in process, did team members so strongly prefer working in teams? Might it just be a result of the well-known Hawthorne effect—improvements that result not from the actual content of changes made but simply because a change *was* made and employees received much management attention in the process?

My conclusion is that the benefits of teamwork at Chiptronics were real rather than ephemeral. They persisted even when serious economic problems hit, and the changes made between our first and second visits further improved the functioning of most teams. Our research data point to four ways in which teams enhanced productivity: (1) decentralization of quality control mechanisms, (2) improved knowledge (and increased flexibility) from cross-training, (3) improved communication among production workers, and (4) higher employee morale.

Location of Quality Control Mechanisms

Prior to the installation of teams at Chiptronics, quality control was handled by a separate department, removed both geographically and organizationally from the production operation. By giving production teams the primary responsibility for inspection and quality control, three advantages were obtained. First, errors were discovered and reworked more quickly. Second, feedback to teams about their performance became clearer and more immediate—providing both direct knowledge of results and the data needed to correct the errors that were causing any problems encountered. Finally, quality control tasks were among the few for which team members had real collective responsibility. This helped members feel interdependent with one another and strengthened team boundaries which, in turn, facilitated the development and enforcement of group norms that supported productivity and error-free operations.

Cross-Training

The work teams at Borman provided a natural opportunity for cross-training among production workers, and management strongly encouraged such activities. Team members liked cross-training, in part because it created more chances to switch tasks among members—and job switching reduced boredom. Cross-training also increased both the team's total pool of knowledge and skill and its flexibility in dealing with special circumstances, such as a production bottleneck at one stage of the operation or the absence of one or more team members on a given day. Finally, the act of cross-training itself had two important outcomes: it strengthened relationships among team members and fostered work-related communication among them.

Communication

Production employees at Borman talked to each other more once teams were installed, and this helped in many ways. For one thing, it increased the quality of members' relationships—their understanding of and empathy for one another. Good relationships were, in some ways, like savings for a rainy day: when problems did occur, members had a reservoir of trust and respect on which to draw as they worked through the difficulties. Moreover, much of the talk was about the work itself. This, of course, helped members increase the depth and breadth of their understanding of the work—especially of how members' different tasks fit together.

In many teams, it turned out that the more socially skilled or verbal members of the group would speak to the team advisors on behalf of those who had language difficulties or limited social skills. Such proxy communication allowed certain members to receive attention to needs or problems that otherwise might have gone unnoticed. It also improved upward communication: team advisors had a more complete understanding of what was going on than they had had previously, and they often were able to correct small problems or deal with perceived inequities before they became major issues.

Downward communication also improved: when the team advisor or a senior manager spoke to the team, there were more ears listening, and members could talk afterward about what was said and what it meant. Again, more knowledgeable or verbal members frequently assisted those who did not understand or who had language difficulties in interpreting the meaning of communications from management. In all, the increased communication that came with the establishment of teams improved communication in all three directions: laterally within the team, upward to management, and downward from management. As a result, the likelihood of errors based on misunderstanding decreased.

Morale

In a nutshell, people *liked* working in teams better than they did working as individuals strung out along a lengthy production line. The teams at Borman increased both employees' social satisfaction at work and their feeling that they were personally contributing to something of broader significance. People became more involved in their work after teams were formed, and they reported greater commitment both to doing the work well and to helping their plant maintain its record of success within Chiptronics.

Tensions in Growing Production Teams

Three conditions are prerequisites for a production team. First, the physical technology must be structured so that *groups* can accomplish the work. Second, supervisors need to understand that their job is to manage teams, not just individuals. Third, both teams and supervisors need to have information about how and how well teams are performing.

These basic ingredients were present from the start at Borman, and they were sufficient to get the teams there off the ground. Yet at first the teams at Borman were skeletal: little beyond these prerequisites was in place to support them. As time passed, team members and managers began to feel some tensions—tensions that may be inevitable when teams perform production work. In closing this chapter, I discuss these tensions and how they were dealt with between our initial observations and our visit to the plant a year later. As we will see, supporting and sustaining teams is a real challenge in a setting where production pressure never lets up and where teams must continuously adapt to evolving production technologies and to fluctuations in customer demand.

Direction: Too Much Versus Too Little

Without a clear and engaging direction for a team, members are unlikely to pull together energetically toward common objectives (Hackman, 1986b). At Borman, Pete Townsend and his management colleagues provided insistent, nonnegotiable direction regarding production targets and core production processes but relatively little direction about how the teams themselves should operate. Neither team members nor their advisors were given a vision of what the teams should be or what they should become. Senior managers' statements about how teams should develop were nowhere near as detailed or compelling as were their instructions about production objectives and processes. As a result, team development activities always took a back seat to production imperatives. One reason for this, of course, was simply that production *was* the bottom line at Borman; without good numbers, the teams (and everything else, including the plant itself) would be at risk. But the other reason was that, initially, nobody really knew how the teams were supposed to develop or what they were supposed to become.

This changed in the year between our first and second visits. It had become clear that the teams were wallowing a bit because of the lack of direction. Pete, Susan, and the second-level managers embarked on an ambitious program to assess the strengths and weaknesses of the teams as performing units and then to use that assessment to clarify aspirations for the teams. As these data were processed, and as managers began to accommodate to the fact that they were leading teams rather than individuals, the realities of the situation became clearer and confusion about direction for the teams decreased. Pete's insistence about the overriding importance of production outcomes never diminished. But he supplemented his emphasis on production with more careful attention to, and greater investment in, providing direction for the production teams' development over time.

Team Authority: Manager-Led Versus Self-Managing

One of the key questions about the direction for teams at Borman had to do with the degree of authority they had—or ideally should have had—for managing their own work. Should teams merely execute the work under management's tactical and strategic direction? Or should they have as much responsibility as possible for managing their work—deciding themselves when and how to take action to correct problems or to improve performance?

Borman managers disagreed on these questions. Some thought the teams should be self-managing, and they pointed out that this would both increase team flexibility and reduce the work load on supervisors. Others felt the teams might move toward self-management someday—but not in the immediate future. Pete Townsend's view was clear: teams at Borman were manager-led and they should stay that way.

That was no problem in the early lives of the teams.

Members were used to being told what to do, and they generally were compliant. They objected far more to any ambiguity in instructions they received than to the fact that they *were* constantly being instructed. Only as a number of teams became increasingly competent in their work and more comfortable with the prospect of making work-related decisions did signs of tension appear. Specifically, some members resented having to call someone else for a diagnosis or repair anytime a problem came up. For many problems, team members knew that they had a better understanding of the difficulty, and better ideas about how to deal with it, than any outsider—no matter how many academic degrees he or she held.

Gradually, managers began to feel a modest degree of bottom-up pressure for increased team self-management. The management group was ambivalent about how to respond. Clearly, many of the teams were, in fact, capable of doing more, and contributing more, than they had so far—but there also were some clear and significant risks in letting them do so. As the year between our observations made abundantly clear, the external environment in the semiconductor industry was quite capricious and showed no signs of settling down. Responding to that environment sometimes required draconian action, such as laying off team members or drastically changing production targets on relatively short notice. Pete was concerned that increased team authority would compromise his ability to respond quickly to such external events. Besides, Pete *liked* the manager-led model better than the self-management model. The challenge, as he saw it, was to find ways to further develop and empower the production teams—but still keep authority for the truly important matters firmly in management's hands. Just how that might be accomplished was still under debate as we completed our second round of observations.

Supervision: Production Versus Team Focused

Team advisors at Borman had two sets of responsibilities, and they sometimes conflicted. On one hand, Pete held team advisors directly responsible for production outcomes. On the other, the advisors were supposed to develop and to build their teams. Given the greater clarity of direction about production goals and constraints than about team development, it is not surprising that team advisors gave precedence to the former whenever a production crisis developed. When I queried team advisors about why they did not spend more time developing their teams, they typically responded that there was not enough time in the day to do all they had to do and that production just had to come first.

It is difficult to manage a full set of supervisory responsibilities in a production environment and still have time to develop work teams. This is particularly true when the teams are still young, because they need more help at that stage and because the organization may not yet have learned that team development requires extra supervisory time and resources. When it became clear to Pete and his colleagues that the team advisors were not making much progress in developing their teams, they took some explicit steps to help things along.

For one thing, they invested considerable time and energy in a team advisor training program. The design of the program was based, in part, on the results of the team diagnosis mentioned above. Topics covered included team-building techniques, communication within teams, strategies for recognizing and rewarding team performance, and exploration of what being a team advisor actually entails. This training improved both the confidence and the skills of most who attended, and it resulted in greater consistency among advisors in how they led their teams. Some team advisors did continue to have problems and, after a time, they were replaced. Over time, there was a noticeable improvement in how team advisors at Borman balanced between team development work and straight production supervision.

Rewards: Individual Versus Team Focused

Initially, management at Borman provided rewards and recognition only to individual employees, never to teams. This was how they had always done things, and their practices were consistent with Chiptronics' corporate compensation policy. A tension developed as teams matured and members gradually realized that they were contributing more to the corporation than they had before—but that they were not getting more *back* from the corporation. The tension was exacerbated in some cases when an intact team had surmounted a major work challenge, yet rewards were provided only to certain individuals within it.

Pete Townsend was concerned about this problem, and arranged to have an organizational consultant and the Chiptronics corporate vice president for organization development in the same room with him at the same time. "It's real hard," he complained. "The teams feel that they should be rewarded for their contributions, but there is nothing I can do. All I have is the special merit increase program, and I can use that only for individuals." As if on cue, the consultant expressed alarm and dismay. This state of affairs, he said, surely would undermine the teams over the long term. There had to be *something* that could be done to reward teams. Pete shook his head and re-affirmed that it was not possible. At that point, also as if on cue, the vice president allowed that it might be possible to use funds earmarked for rewarding individual excellence to reward exceptional teams. By meeting's end, Pete had achieved what he apparently had arranged the meeting for in the first place—flexibility to reward team excellence within the individualistic corporate compensation policy.

Even so, the rewards Pete now had available were not large enough to be highly consequential for a team—especially after being divided up among members. He dealt with this problem by using the money to award evenings out—such as dinner and a show at a nearby city—for team members and their spouses. That was fine initially, but it did not permanently resolve the larger question about how gains achieved through the work of teams should be distributed among plant employees.

Technical Support: Team Versus Staff Control

At the time of our first observations, production teams were at the mercy of maintenance and engineering staffs. This situation created inefficiencies, such as nonproductive waiting time and occasional conflicts between the teams (who were intent on meeting their production targets) and technical support staff (who had quite different agendas).

Pete eventually decided to take on this problem. He did so very gradually, and with a gentleness that belied his gruff exterior, by nurturing personal relationships with his counterparts in the plant's maintenance and engineering departments. After about a year of careful work, he succeeded in negotiating a redefinition of the relationship between the production teams and technical support staff. Production, they agreed, was everybody's ultimate goal. Therefore, the support staff should do whatever they could to help the people who actually made the product—and certainly everyone should try to minimize disruptions to their work.

Consistent with this understanding, individual maintenance staff members were informally assigned to sets of specific teams and sometimes even became "adjunct" members of those teams. Staff members came to team meetings when they could and often taught members techniques for adjusting their equipment—techniques they previously had guarded jealously (even to the extent of standing in a position that made it impossible for team members to see what they were doing while they adjusted equipment). Thus, even though it was still necessary, on occasion, to stop production so engineers could run a test batch or try out a new process, now it was likely that the timing of such tests would be negotiated between the engineers and the team.

The redefinition of the relationship between production teams and the maintenance and engineering departments was one of the most difficult and wrenching changes made during our observations. The adjustment took a long time and stressed many of the affected individuals. But it also was, without question, one of the most important and constructive actions that Pete took to support his teams. These actions, like his negotiations with corporate managers about compensation policy, provide a vivid illustration of how important it is for team managers to exercise influence upward and outward in their organizations in order to create an organizational context that supports teams.

Change: Holding Still Versus Constantly Adapting

Things do not hold still in a production organization. One cannot get teams all designed and trained and then bring them on line—as can be done, for example, in cutting over from an old computer or telephone system to a new one. Nor can one run the new organization in parallel with the old one until all the wrinkles have been worked out—as can be done, for example, with a new accounting system. Instead, changes in an existing, technology-intensive production system must be accomplished in real time while the work goes on.

Some changes, of course, are welcomed by everyone. After things settled down, the changes in compensation arrangements at Chiptronics, and those involving the maintenance and engineering organizations, were agreeable to almost everyone involved. So were certain changes in team composition and in team advisor roles and staffing. Other changes, however, including some that were unavoidable, were destructive to the identity and integrity of the fledgling work teams. Moreover, these changes made it difficult for teams to become deeply enough rooted to deal competently with subsequent shocks and disturbances to the work system.

The Datron team provides a good case in point. With eight team members under Raymond's leadership, the team performed very well and was, in one member's words, "riding high." Even though there was little recognition of the team's accomplishments, and even though external factors over which members had no control sometimes disrupted its work, the team's capabilities as a performing unit were high and growing. Then, in the year between our first and second observations, came the economic downturn—and the associated layoffs, leadership changes, and changes in team composition. These shocks weakened the team substantially. They were exacerbated by the limited language capability of two new team members and by a new team advisor who gave the team less help with internal communications and less overt recognition than had Raymond. And various technical problems, associated with externally imposed alterations of the production process, negatively affected the team's productivity. At year's end, the Datron team was not the shining star it had been, and members' morale and commitment to their team suffered. As one said, "It's a lot easier to stand by the team when you know you are the best."

Developing and sustaining work teams in a production environment is a delicate balance. Change is inevitable. Indeed, in most traditional production organizations, significant alterations of traditional ways of doing things are required to create a context that supports effective teamwork. Yet the risks of change also are great. Our observations at Chiptronics suggest that the early stage of team development is a fragile time and that too many changes, or the wrong kinds of changes, can keep a team from ever becoming a robust, flexible performing unit. To manage the balance between change and stability early in the lives of work teams is, perhaps, the greatest challenge of all for the managers of teams in production organizations.

Notes

1. Fictitious names are used throughout this chapter, including that of the organization.
2. Richard Hackman and I jointly observed the Datron teams.
3. Such cross-training was more common prior to the economic downturn that resulted in layoffs at the plant. Before the layoffs, time pressure on the team was moderate. The layoffs resulted in smaller team size, an increase in time pressure, and a reduction of the amount of cross-training that occurred.

28

Summary:
Production Teams

Production teams take raw materials and transform them into products using tools, technology, and members' labor. As Eisenstat noted in the first chapter in this section, the same kind of thinking can be applied to the creation of production teams themselves. Indeed, his account of the Fairfield compressor team start-up takes precisely that view. The materials from which the company produced the team included a facility, pieces of technology (some already in place, some on order), individual team members and managers (with more to come), and the all-important audit checklist that specified in detail what the team was supposed to accomplish. An iterative transformation process based on these materials resulted in an intact, functioning work team, with members ready and able to work together to produce high-quality compressor parts. The compressor team was, quite literally, the product of a production process at Fairfield.

Ginnett's cockpit crew can be viewed in the same way. This team, too, needed to be produced—and produced quickly: the team had to be functioning within an hour or so after the people who would become team members arrived for work. These individuals, while highly skilled, never had worked together before. All the other materials needed to produce a team were, however, already in place. The airline made sure of that because many new crews started up each day and it was important to everyone—crew members, managers, and customers—that the process unfold as smoothly and efficiently as possible. There was a facility (including a briefing room), a fully equipped and checked aircraft (although not at the gate where it was supposed to be), and a bundle of organizational features which Ginnett refers to as the "shell." The shell included everything from the company's objectives for crew performance, to preestablished roles (both within the crew and for others with whom the crew would interact—including flight attendants, maintenance staff, and air traffic controllers), to standard procedures for operating the technology. Because so much was already in place when individual crew members arrived, the captain, whose responsibility it was to "produce" the crew, had a relatively easy task. The transformation process occurred quickly: by the time members left the briefing room to head for the aircraft, individuals had become an intact team, ready to use technology and member labor to produce *its* product—transporting customers from one place to another.

The Datron team studied by Abramis was closer to the usual image of a production team. Although relatively new, this team was in place and working, day in and day out, adding layers to large numbers of semiconductor chips. Yet the Datron team was, in some ways, less fully formed than either the compressor team or the cockpit crew. The compressor team, for example, had started with few raw materials, but members engaged in intense, full-time work to develop the team as a performing unit. The transformation process for the cockpit crew, although it took very little time, also resulted in a full-fledged team—largely because the complement of available raw materials was so complete and appropriate, and because individual crew members had already been through the cookie-cutter team formation process many times before.

The Datron team was different. The raw materials available when that team formed included individuals who had no experience working in teams and whose skills were relevant to only one part of the work the team would do; a production facility and technology that had been designed for use by individuals rather than by teams; and a production schedule that had little slack for team development activities. It is not surprising, therefore, that the transformation process for the Datron team was incomplete—that even as the team was producing chips, work continued on producing the team itself. Indeed, as we completed our research, it was unclear what the team eventually would become. Some people at Chiptronics argued that it should evolve into a self-managing performing unit with considerable autonomy; they aspired to a team that would be similar to the compressor team in many ways. Others, including the production manager, were not at all sure that was a good idea. What *was* clear was that the organizational "shell" at Chiptronics needed to be realigned to provide the Datron team (and others like it at the plant) with performance conditions that supported teamwork rather than individual production. Accomplishing that realignment, as well as continuing with team and team leader development activities, was the focus of managers' attention when the research ended.

Problematic Products

Let us explore a bit further the "product" term in the "materials-transformation-product" sequence of creating production teams. What would be the properties of an ideal team, one that would accomplish *its* production work consistently well?

Traditional wisdom, rooted in the scientific management school of thought, suggests that production tasks should be analyzed in detail and then work and organizational designs "set" to optimize production. There is, in this way of thinking, one best way to produce any given product. Management's role is to conduct the analytical studies needed to determine what that way is, to design the work and the organization accordingly, and then to select, motivate, and supervise production workers so they follow the optimum production process closely and competently. The workers merely execute the work, leaving decision making and other matters requiring judgment to managers or staff professionals such as engineers.

Production organizations designed in accord with these

views rarely use teams; indeed, teams are incompatible with the philosophy of scientific management. The comparative advantage of a team is not in simple execution of the work. It is, instead, in a team's flexibility, adaptability, diversity (for example, in member knowledge, skill, and experience), and capability to learn and change over time. These qualities increasingly are sought in industries where change is the rule rather than the exception, and where competitive pressures are such that the ideas and judgment of production workers, as well as their efforts, are needed for success in the marketplace. These were, in fact, the aspirations of those responsible for organizational design at the Fairfield Components Plant and, to a somewhat less ambitious extent, at Chiptronics. And these are the values that generally are espoused for the behavior of airline cockpit crews—despite the considerable pressure for standardization of cockpit procedures and the pervasively individualistic culture of flying.

The individualistic orientation that characterizes aviation is common in production organizations: it is one part of the legacy of scientific management, it has turned out to be surprisingly strong and persistent, and it is one reason there is more talk than action about teams in manufacturing organizations. But there is more to the story than that. The imperatives of production technology and the symbolism of smoothly functioning machines also impede the development and use of teams in production organizations.

Production technology, by and large, is designed to be operated by a person, not by a team. When plants are laid out, the "natural" thing to do is to array the machinery in a long line, with materials coming in one end and products going out the other. This layout, of course, is an immediate and significant obstacle to team performance, especially if the distances are great or the noise is loud. One organization, committed to using teams for production work despite major technological obstacles, went so far as to equip each member with a wireless walkie-talkie and headset. Team members, who worked at individual stations arrayed down a long and noisy production line, were able to communicate with one another despite the fact that they could not hear (or, in some cases, even see) one another.

Real technological obstacles, such as machine design and plant layout, are reinforced by the symbolism of machinery. We want the machines on which we depend, whether a dishwasher at home or a metal stamping machine at work, to be predictable and reliable and to require a minimum of maintenance. This ethic runs deep in production organizations and, not surprisingly, tends to be applied to people as well as machinery. The production organization, like production machinery, ideally should be predictable, reliable, and maintenance free.

Such thinking does not lead one to teams as the design option of choice. Teams, when they work, are flexible, adaptive, and capable of collective learning.[1] These are different values, reflecting a different ethic about what a production organization should be. To the extent that the thinking of production system designers and managers about people and organizations mirrors the way they think about machines and technology, they are not likely to choose teams as the basic performing unit in their organizations.

Transformation Tensions

Even when teams are installed in production organizations, it can be a significant challenge to transform them into full-fledged, mature social systems capable of realizing their full potential as task-performing units. The transformation process is, of course, key to the effectiveness of any team, not just teams that produce things. As we have seen throughout this book, it takes expertise, hard work, and time to design, lead, and support teamwork.

The transformation (or group development) process can be especially daunting for production teams because such teams tend to develop and sustain an "inward" orientation. They focus on whatever it is members are producing to a considerably greater extent than on transactions with outsiders.[2] Paradoxically, it appears that a team's *external* transactions may both spur and fuel its *internal* development. Interactions with outsiders present problems and opportunities whose resolution can help a team clarify its own identity, elaborate its norms, and refine its performance strategies. Without such interactions, a team may be unable to keep pushing forward its own development as a performing unit.[3]

Why do production teams tend to have an inward orientation? One reason is that the nature of the work itself pulls members in. There is, after all, a product to be produced, and that product takes shape within the boundaries of the group. Members' attention and motivation focus on making the product, and once it is made it is done. Members may feel (or even be told by their managers) that what happens to the product thereafter is someone else's concern. Moreover, production teams often are insulated from others by their organizational location—for example, in a separate facility far removed from customers, from users, and sometimes from the rest of the organization as well. Finally, if a team looks outward there is always a possibility that members might see something that would require internal change. Because change invariably is anxiety arousing, members may find it more comfortable to keep their attention focused inside, on the team and on its product. Together, these factors can significantly reduce members' felt need or desire to deal with outsiders. While there is evidence (for example, Hackman & Oldham, 1980) that this tendency can be reduced by establishing direct contact between a production team and the people who purchase or use its product, such practices are the exception rather than the rule in production organizations.

The more production teams are allowed, or encouraged, to become islands unto themselves, the less likely they are to develop into full-fledged, mature performing units. It is ironic that attempts by team managers to "protect" production teams from outside involvement and interference—attempts intended to give teams ample room to develop—may run a significant risk of having the opposite effect.

Conclusion

For all their potential, and for all the public attention they have been receiving in recent years, teams continue to occupy an uneasy place within production organizations. In this summary chapter, we have attempted to identify some of the reasons teams have not spread throughout industry as the obviously best way to accomplish production work.

The potential advantages of teams for production work are considerable. Moreover, as both the audit checklist at Fairfield and the shell surrounding the airline cockpit crews illustrate, the process by which production teams themselves are produced can be at least partly prespecified. The designers of such teams must realize, however, that they are *not* producing a set of standardized individual worker "parts" whose interactions can be predicted and choreographed in advance. Instead, production teams are complex human systems whose distinctive advantage is their capability to reconcile change and adaptability on one hand with efficiency and reliability on the other. To the extent that designers embrace a machine model for the production of production teams, they are unlikely to reap the very benefits to which they aspire—benefits that well-designed and well-led work teams are, in fact, capable of providing.

Notes

1. Paradoxically, we have seen in this section that it is precisely the capability of teams to adapt to the unexpected that increases the reliability of the production process itself.
2. This was true at least for the production teams we studied, as compared with other teams in this book. In general, other types of teams had significantly more direct contact with clients, customers, or audiences than did production teams. Moreover, our informal review of other production teams, ones we did not explicitly study, suggests that the phenomenon we observed does have some generality.
3. The proposed relationship between the extent of a team's external transactions and its rate of internal development is merely a hypothesis. Although the experiences of the teams in this chapter are consistent with what we would expect (that is, the compressor team had both the most involvement with outsiders and the greatest development as a team, while the Datron team had the fewest external transactions and the most gradual rate of development), the hypothesis awaits systematic test.

Conclusion

```
╡╤╚╗╔╤╚╗╔╤╚╗╔╤╚╗╔╤╚╗╔╤╚╗╔╤╚╗╔╤╚╗╔╤╚╗
```

Creating More Effective
Work Groups in Organizations

Each work group we studied was, in some ways, like *all* other work groups in organizations. Certain features, it appears, are found in every group that performs work in an organization. Each group was, in other ways, like *some* other groups—as seen in the summary chapters for each section, where we explored the commonalities among groups of each type. And each group was, in still other ways, like *no* other group, a unique entity unto itself with its own special problems, opportunities, and ways of operating.

It is no surprise that the groups had features in common. We made sure of that by the way we defined our domain—we studied only groups that were real social systems, that had tasks to perform, and that operated in organizational contexts. This meant that all groups studied would share a need to address certain kinds of issues. Moreover, our orienting framework (sketched in the introduction to the book) increased the chances that we would "discover" dynamics having to do with group structure, group-context relationships, and process-oriented leadership.

Yet some crosscutting themes and issues that we had not anticipated also emerged. These issues did not derive directly from the way we defined our domain, nor were they anticipated by our orienting framework. In the section to follow, we highlight a few of the most salient of these themes. Then we turn to those issues that groups had in common with *some* other groups—that is, the special risks and opportunities that characterize each of the seven types of teams we studied.

We close the chapter and the book by reviewing our findings from an explicitly normative perspective. In that section, we identify five trip wires over which a number of our teams stumbled and fell. As will be seen, each of the trip wires also suggests something that those who create and lead work groups in organizations can do to increase the prospects for group success.

Crosscutting Themes

Time and Rhythm. Temporal phenomena were everywhere in the groups we studied, and they significantly affected what happened within them. Among the most powerful temporal features we observed were time limits and deadlines. For one type of group, the task forces that Gersick and Davis-Sacks studied, deadlines were definitional: to be a task force is to have one. Time limits turned out to be a powerful organizing force for these groups. The time available guided the pace of their work, and the reorienting transition that occurred in most of these groups occurred right at the midpoint of their lives. Similar phenomena also were present in other types of groups—such as the pacing of Eisenstat's compressor team to meet the target date for starting up the production line and the constant attention of Ginnett's cockpit crews to achieving on-time departures.

When deadlines were absent, fuzzy, or constantly changing, groups invariably encountered problems. Davis-Sacks's credit team, for example, suffered from its clients' tendency to change their minds about when they needed the team's reports. And her tracking team, which was pacing itself nicely in preparation for the start of the congressional hearings, fell apart completely (and understandably) the moment members learned that the hearings would not be held as scheduled. Finally, although Cohen's hospital top management team performed very well when members knew they had to be ready for reaccreditation review by a certain date, the group found it hard to keep up a head of steam once it had successfully passed that hurdle—even though it then had the opportunity to develop and implement new programs that could greatly have strengthened the hospital and improved its services.

Even groups whose work did not involve fixed deadlines often had standard cycles of activity that repeated over time. These cycles, like time limits, structured and paced groups' work. The activities of the prison staff Perkins and Abramis studied, for example, were paced more by the regular schedule of "teamming" sessions with inmates than by any other aspect of that team's work. The same phenomenon was present in Denison's airline maintenance control team: each maintenance problem the team encountered set off a work cycle. Here, however, the cycles were not predictable. Members never knew (and could not influence) when a new cycle would begin. Moreover, they had to manage repeating short cycles concurrently with longer-cycle project work. The athletic teams also had cycles within cycles—cycles of games, of seasons, and (for Wood's professional hockey players) of entire careers.

Groups that had regular cycles of activity tended to develop a characteristic rhythm to their work—a rhythm that, over time, became part of each team's special character. The rhythm of Butterworth's string quartet, for example, was steady and unhurried, while Kahn's basketball team repeatedly alternated between extended "down" periods (between games) and bursts of intense activity (during games). Saavedra's beer sales and delivery teams had yet another rhythm: each day involved constant, steady, physical work in the field, followed by time "back home" to relax and to enjoy the companionship of teammates.

In sum, temporal phenomena—time limits, cycles, and rhythms—not only affected how groups went about their work, but also shaped group climate and the quality of members' experiences. To overlook these phenomena would be to risk missing some of the most significant dynamics of groups that work.

Self-Fueling Spirals. We found considerable evidence to support the dictum that, over time, the rich get richer and the poor get poorer. Groups that somehow got onto a good track tended to perform ever better as time passed, while those that got into difficulty found that their problems compounded over time. A positive example is Ginnett's cockpit crew: it got off to a good start and, as members gained experience with one another and handled some challenging in-flight problems, the crew became increasingly competent as a performing unit. Cohen's corporate restructuring team showed the opposite pattern. Once it began to deteriorate (around the midpoint of its life) the rate of deterioration accelerated until the group finally came apart entirely.

Both pairs of customer service teams (Saavedra's two beer sales and delivery teams, and Cohen and Denison's two teams of flight attendants) split: one team in each pair showed continuous improvement over time, while the other did not. Of Kahn's two athletic teams, the basketball team continuously improved while the baseball team became less and less able to operate as a group as the season wore on.

What sets such spirals in motion? Our evidence suggests a two-factor hypothesis. One factor is the quality of the group's initial design. The other is the occurrence of positive or negative events that trigger the spiral. When a poorly designed team encounters events that set members back, a negative spiral tends to develop; when a well-designed team encounters reinforcing events, a positive spiral can be set in motion. Especially noticeable triggers, in our groups, were those that occurred early in the groups' lives and those that originated in their relations with their external environments.

The flight attendants illustrate the power of early events. The more successful team was given a challenging task (opening a new station) early in its life, and members experienced success and reinforcement in accomplishing that task. The other team had to contend with the early termination of one of its members and never fully recovered from that event. Friedman's two theater teams showed a similar pattern. The initial structure of both teams included both positive and negative design features, but the cast of *Cinderella* quickly got onto a positive track—apparently because of the initial excitement and challenging aspirations communicated by the director, who had written the play and had high hopes for it. The other cast not only did not have a good "launch," but it also had to deal with the early resignation of two cast members. This team never got settled; it was plagued by commitment and coordination problems throughout its life.

The beer sales and delivery teams show how the external environment can nudge a team onto a favorable or unfavorable track. One of the teams happened to have a sales region where standard company procedures worked fine; the other team's region required deviation from company policies to ensure good sales. Senior management did not recognize the environmental differences, and management's attributions about the relative competence and loyalty of the two teams eventually became self-fulfilling.

Attributions and labels are potent, and they can sustain both positive and negative spirals. Once a team is labeled (or labels itself) as either "good" or "bad," it can be very difficult to alter how people perceive it. Moreover, "good" teams tend to be reinforced by others and receive interesting work opportunities, thereby adding credence to the view (of members as well as outsiders) that the team is competent and potent. "Bad" teams, however, receive little praise and may be given less challenging assignments—because managers have little confidence in the group's capabilities. Eventually, members may accept the validity of their label and stop trying to perform well.

For these reasons, a negative spiral can be very hard to break once it has become established. Indeed, the actions most likely to reverse one are the least likely to be taken. Managers often cannot resist the temptation to intervene directly in the process of a group in trouble—in hopes of helping members solve their problems and get back on a good track. Unfortunately, such action can confirm members' worst fears about the group and thereby have an effect opposite to the one intended. A less obvious but probably more potent intervention strategy would be for managers to take initiatives to improve the structure of the group, the supportiveness of its organizational context, or the behavior of those in the group's external environment who are creating problems for the team. Then, once the group is in good shape organizationally, the team could be given work likely to result in a success experience. This two-stage intervention just might reverse the direction of the team's spiral and, eventually, alter how the group is perceived and labeled.

Authority. Like temporal phenomena, authority dynamics pervaded the groups we studied. Every group had to deal with authority issues of one kind or another. Four such issues were particularly salient to us and consequential for the teams: (1) the amount of authority a group has to manage its own affairs, (2) the stability of the authority structure, (3) the timing of interventions by authority figures, and (4) the substantive focus of those interventions.

The amount of authority held by the work groups we studied varied widely. Some had virtually none; they merely executed work that other people designed, monitored, and managed. Following Hackman (1986b), we refer to these as *manager-led teams*. Examples include Kahn's baseball team, Davis-Sacks's credit team, and Abramis's semiconductor manufacturing team (although the semiconductor team did have limited authority for managing some aspects of its work). Members of other teams had virtually unlimited authority: they chose their own goals, selected new members, and managed as well as executed work of their own design. Examples of such teams, which are called *self-governing teams*, include Butterworth's string quartet and Kahn's basketball team. Most common in our sample were *self-managing teams*, which fell between these two extremes: they had significant responsibility for managing their own work, but others usually made decisions about goals, team structure, and organizational supports.

It is not surprising that self-governing teams are relatively rare in work organizations. If every group in an organization were to set its own direction, design its own task, and arrange for its own organizational supports, it would be very difficult to achieve well-coordinated collective action in the organization as a whole. Manager-led teams also were rare in our sample. We find this reassuring since many of the benefits of using teams to accomplish work derive directly from members' authority to manage their own affairs in response to changing circumstances. Manager-led groups, in which members merely execute work under relatively direct and continuous management control, do not exploit the potential benefits of teamwork.

If a team is used at all, it surely makes sense to start it off with at least enough authority for members to manage their own work processes. Then, as the team matures and gains competence, the scope of its authority can be increased. Except in special circumstances, however, the authority of even mature work teams in organizations will be limited. In organizational work, a point at which the need for organization-wide consistency exceeds the value of team self-determination is inevitable.

A stable authority structure is extremely important. In our sample, the teams that had to contend with significant or frequent leadership changes invariably encountered problems. Eisenstat's top management group, for example, never fully recovered from the abrupt change in plant managers that occurred early in its life. In Shaw's mental health hospital, the constant flow-through of medical interns and residents (who, when present, had authority that exceeded their expertise and experience) kept the treatment teams chronically off balance and in some measure of disarray. Denison and Sutton's operating room nurses also experienced difficulty with their authority structure. While their head nurse remained in her role, the surgeons under whose authority members worked in the operating suite changed from operation to operation. The nurses not only had to manage relations within their own group, but they also needed to accommodate continuously to different surgeons' styles and expectations.

Also consequential for the groups we studied was the timing of interventions by authority figures. Clearly, the best time for authoritative intervention is at the beginning of a group's life. Our findings leave little room for doubt about the long-term effects of what happens at team start-up, and they affirm the potency of leader behaviors that occur at that time. These effects were perhaps most visible in Ginnett's cockpit crew, but they were present in virtually every team whose creation we observed. Interventions that occur at a natural breakpoint in the work (especially at the midpoint of the lifespan of time-bounded teams) also can be helpful in many instances. Examples include interventions by the instructor in Gersick's two student groups and by the chairman of the bank where her product development team worked (notably, the initiative for this encounter came from the team itself). When, however, an authority figure intervenes while a team is in the midst of planning or executing its work, the effects may not be constructive. This occurred both in Eisenstat's systems development group (when the plant manager revised the group's goals after the work was already well under way) and in Davis-Sacks's credit team (when high-level officials sought to change the specifications of the reports the team was writing even as they were being prepared). Both teams experienced problems getting back on track after receiving these interventions.

The substantive focus of interventions by authority figures also is consequential for work groups. Problems inevitably develop when interventions address matters that are properly the concern of the group itself. This is seen in Cohen's corporate restructuring team and in Kahn's baseball team. In both cases, external authorities (the chairman for the corporate team and the coach for the baseball team) intervened directly into team processes, making decisions about individual members and team performance strategy—decisions that undermined members' felt responsibility for outcomes. Motivation and commitment dipped in both teams, with predictable and unfortunate consequences for subsequent team process and performance.

Because most work teams do have the authority to monitor and manage their own performance processes, it generally is a good idea for managers to respect that authority once they are confident that a group has accepted it. Subsequent managerial interventions, then, would focus on those matters for which management has retained authority—matters such as the direction of the group, its structure, and the contextual support it receives. This is what the production manager in Abramis's semiconductor manufacturing plant did: rather than meddle with internal team dynamics, he exercised influence with managerial colleagues responsible for compensation policy, machine maintenance, and engineering support to increase the resources and support available to the teams he had created. Unfortunately, this manager's behavior was exceptional in our sample. More commonly, managers took a laissez-faire stance toward their teams, letting them proceed on their own until problems developed. Then they sometimes intervened directly into internal group processes—typically with little success and occasionally making things worse rather than better.

Work Content. Although our orienting framework sensitized us to the content of teams' work, we focused mainly on the degree to which team tasks were motivationally engaging. As we carried out the research, we came upon another aspect of the work content—one we were not looking for but that was impossible to ignore. For want of a better term, we refer to it as the *stuff* with which the groups worked. Top management teams, for example, dealt constantly with power and influence. Task forces worked with ideas and plans. Support teams traded in expertise—about computer systems for one team, airplanes for another, and economics for the third. Performing teams played: the athletic teams played games, the repertory theater company put on plays, and the string quartet played music. Human service teams dealt with people and, perhaps more significantly, with emotions and never-ending tensions around control. Customer service teams, of course, dealt with customers—and typically spent more time with them than with co-workers in their own organizations. Production teams, on the other hand, generally spent more time working with technology than with people.

Can there be any doubt that the stuff a team works with significantly affects the character of group life? Compare, for example, a group that spends its time playing games with one that seeks to cure or rehabilitate clients. Or a group that does economic analyses with one that fixes airplanes. Or one that sets strategic directions for an organization with another that delivers beer to bars or adds layers to silicon wafers. Surely the content of a group's work significantly shapes both the emotional lives of members and the interactions that take place among them.

Over time, the values of group members appear to become increasingly aligned with the materials a group works with. The process can begin even before the group forms, as individuals choose to join a particular group partly because they value the content of its work. Then, as the team goes about its business, members' continuing involvement with that content reinforces their prior attraction to it. Eventually, members may routinely construe (or even redefine) objective reality in terms of the special "stuff" with which they customarily work.

Both positive and negative outcomes can result from this process. On the positive side, the team should gradually achieve greater internal coherence as a social system: the materials they work with, the content of group interaction, and the values of group members should fit together increasingly well over time. As this happens, communication and coordination within the group should become easier to manage, and members may come to feel that the group provides them with a quite comfortable social home within the organization.

The team may also develop the collective equivalent of tunnel vision, however, and lose sight of the larger picture into which its work fits. In a top management team, for example, members risk becoming so focused on organizational politics that they neglect their real work—managing the organization (see, for example, Zaleznik, 1989). In a human service team, managing emotionality and control may become so important that the team risks neglecting the needs of patients. In an athletic team, play may spill over from the court or field and become the team's dominant style of interaction even in noncompetitive settings—where it sometimes may be inappropriate. Production teams may become so engaged with their technology that the people who use their products drop from members' attention, whereas customer service teams may become so involved with clients' needs that they neglect those of the parent organization.

We did not begin our research with any special interest in the substantive content of the materials with which teams work.[1] But we end our study convinced that there is much to learn about work groups by attending carefully to these materials and to their effects on both individual members and team dynamics.

Risks and Opportunities

Each type of team we studied has both some characteristic risks and some special opportunities. These features, which extend beyond the differences in work content discussed above, are summarized in Table 2.

Table 2. Special Risks and Opportunities for Work Teams.

	Risks	*Opportunities*
Top Management Teams	Underbounded; absence of organizational context	Self-designing; influence over key organizational conditions
Task Forces	Team and work both new	Clear purpose and deadline
Professional Support Groups	Dependency on others for work	Using and honing professional expertise
Performing Groups	Skimpy organizational supports	Play that is fueled by competition and/or audiences
Human Service Teams	Emotional drain; struggle for control	Inherent significance of helping people
Customer Service Teams	Loss of involvement with parent organization	Bridging between parent organization and its customers
Production Teams	Retreat into technology; insulation from end users	Continuity of work; ability to hone both the team design and the product

One special risk for *top management teams* derives precisely from their being perched atop organizations. The top management teams we studied clearly suffered from the absence of a supportive organizational context. What few supports they did enjoy were either created by themselves or provided by the chairman or president of the organization. Moreover, top management teams tended to have loose boundaries: membership sometimes was unclear, and meetings often started late, ran long, and wandered from topic to topic. That these teams did not provide a model of effective work teams in their organizations is surprising since members were always organizational veterans with much experience working in teams.

The special opportunity top management teams enjoy, of course, is that members have the power to design themselves as they see fit—should they choose to do so. Except for the most senior manager in the organization, there is no one to tell members what they can and cannot do or to withhold from them the supports and resources they need. These team members collectively control virtually all of the organizational conditions required for team effectiveness. So the potential for a top management team to be effective is very great indeed.

Why is this considerable potential not more fully exploited? It is significant, we believe, that the main responsibility of each team member typically is in his or her own functional area and that membership in the top management team is an extra activity for everyone—with the possible exception of the chairman or president. If he or she also views the team as just one of many competing demands, then it may be that *nobody* is paying much attention to building and supporting the team as a performing unit. Even though members may give great care and attention to teams they create in their own units, individually and collectively they often neglect what is probably the most important team of all.

The special hurdles of *task forces* derive from their being created to accomplish a finite piece of work that normal organizational procedures cannot readily handle. The team task almost always is novel, and members often are working together for the first time ever. If they are unable to structure adequately the unfamiliar work or to develop quickly the capability to work interdependently, problems are likely to develop. The compensating advantages for task forces are their typically clear and specific objectives and their status as temporary, time-limited entities. As we have seen, clear objectives and deadlines can both motivate and structure members' interaction—and can therefore increase the chance that members will be able to overcome the difficulties that derive from the unfamiliarity of the task and the other members.

The characteristic problem that *professional support groups* face is waiting for others, typically line managers in their organizations, to call for their services. This puts them in a dependent, reactive stance, which, over time, can erode morale and even diminish a team's capability to respond vigorously and professionally when its services *are* called for. On the other hand, professional support teams have the opportunity in their work to exercise and hone members' special expertise. Typically, support team members value such opportunities highly. Indeed, these opportunities can provide the fuel that keeps members working and learning even when they find their relations with their clients unpredictable and troubling.

The *performing groups* we studied all had skimpy support from their organizational contexts. Indeed, two of these groups— the basketball team and the string quartet—operated so independently that it was hard even to discern their organizational context. Although this precluded any possibility that these groups would receive meaningful support from their organizations, it also protected them from the possibility that an unsupportive parent organization would actively undermine team performance—a problem that the other performing groups in our sample (the repertory theater company, the baseball team, and especially the hockey team) did face to some extent. In fact, the most salient and helpful features of performing groups' contexts are located outside the organization: audiences and, for athletic teams, competitors. These external groups are powerful sources of energy for performing groups, and relations with them direct and intensify the play that is at the core of the teams' work.

The major risk for *human service teams* derives directly from the nature of their work: caring for and controlling the behavior of other people. This kind of work is emotionally taxing, and the struggle to remain in control of one's emotions (and of one's clients) can take a real toll on teams and their members. Human service teams continuously balance between two opposing risks. The primary risk is burnout; the alternative risk is that burnout will be avoided by objectifying the team's clients, which inevitably results in poorer quality service to them. The compensating opportunity for human service teams is the other side of the same coin: the clients of the team's work are other human beings who are genuinely in need of the teams' ministrations. This makes the work inherently significant and motivating and can provide a good point of departure for building a strong, competent human service team.

Customer service teams operate on the boundary between the parent organization and its customers, which is simultaneously their biggest risk and their biggest opportunity. The downside is that a team can lose its involvement with and commitment to the parent organization—that it may "go native" with customers and fail to meet legitimate organizational expectations. On the other hand, such a team is in an excellent position to serve as the primary link for the exchange of information between the organization and its environment. Being on the front line can be both challenging and engaging, but it requires that the team task be broader than simply selling the organization's products or providing its services. A well-designed task for a customer service team might also give the team major responsibility for the management of customer relations—including monitoring changes in customer needs or preferences and keeping customers informed about and involved with contemplated product or service innovations.

Finally, *production teams* risk becoming insulated and isolated by excessive involvement in the technology that is so central to their work. Because of their focus on technology and the products they use technology to produce, such teams may come to see both end users and other organization members more as disruptions than as clients and co-workers. To the extent that this happens, the effectiveness of a production team surely will suffer. A special opportunity for production teams derives from the fact that members typically work together, and with the same equipment, for an extended period of time. This gives these teams the chance to refine their work, and even the design of the team itself, as members gain experience with the work and with each other. A well-designed and well-led production team can, over time, become highly competent—as long as it appropriately manages the risks of isolation and insulation.

In sum, we discovered some distinctive risks and opportunities for each of the seven types of teams we studied. Managers who create teams, leaders who work with them, and team members who serve in them can take actions to minimize these risks and exploit these opportunities. The findings briefly summarized above (and explored in detail in the individual chapters of the book) may be of some use to managers, leaders, and members in highlighting issues they should watch for in their own teams and organizations.

Trip Wires in Designing and Leading Work Groups

In the course of our research, we identified a number of mistakes that designers and leaders of work groups sometimes make. In this concluding section, we describe the five most common of these mistakes and speculate about what might be done to lessen the chances that work teams will fall victim to them.

Trip Wire #1:   *Call the performing unit a team but really manage members as individuals.*

One way to set up work is to assign specific responsibilities to specific individuals and then choreograph individuals' activities so their products coalesce into a team product. A contrasting strategy is to assign a group responsibility and accountability for an entire piece of work and let members decide among themselves how they will proceed to accomplish the work. While either of these strategies can be effective, a choice must be made between them. A mixed model, in which people are *told* they are a team but are *treated* as individual performers with their own specific jobs to do, sends mixed signals to members, is likely to confuse everyone, and, in the long run, probably is untenable.

We did not observe work designed in strict accord with the individualistic strategy—we were, after all, studying work *teams.* Some teams we studied, however, barely met our criterion for being a group (see the introduction). This was the case early in the life of Abramis's semiconductor manufacturing team.

Over time, however, this set of people moved from merely being labeled a team to actually functioning as one. As the team developed, the production manager gave members increased latitude for self-management and took initiatives to develop organizational support and reinforcement for team activities. Eventually, members came to accept their collective responsibility for work outcomes. Davis-Sacks's credit team also was barely a group, but for a different reason. Here, the intent of the senior manager who created the group was for it to be a full-fledged, self-managing team. The team leader, however, subverted the manager's intent by using an insistent hub-and-spokes strategy in running the team. The signals sent by the senior manager and the team leader were in conflict, and it is not surprising that significant problems developed both among members and between them and the team leader.

Another way to trip is to install a full-fledged team in an organization in which either managerial behavior or organizational systems are strongly individualistic in orientation. Cohen's restructuring team, for example, operated moderately well early in its life (when the stance of the chief executive officer toward the team was what he called "benign neglect"), but it encountered serious internal problems once the CEO began to work directly and privately with individual team members on issues relevant to the team task. Wood's professional hockey team suffered from individualistic organizational systems over which its leader (the coach) had little influence. Specifically, the reward and career mobility systems of the parent organization assessed individual performance rather than team performance, and personnel decisions of great consequence for team members were based on those assessments. Even though members were interdependent in their work (competing with other teams), they were in competition with one another in their careers. This tension created difficulties for the team that defied all the coach's attempted remedies.

To reap the benefits of teamwork, one must actually build a team. Calling a set of people a team or exhorting them to work together is insufficient. Instead, explicit action must be taken to establish the team's boundaries, to define the task as one for which members are collectively responsible and accountable, and to give members the authority to manage both their internal processes and the team's relations with external entities such as clients and co-workers. Once this is done, management behavior and organizational systems gradually can be changed as necessary to support teamwork.

In some organizations, creating strong work teams may be next to impossible. The airline industry in which Ginnett's cockpit crew operated, for example, has a decidedly individualistic culture. Pilots bid for trips, positions, and aircraft as individuals, and bidding results depend strictly on seniority. Moreover, crew composition changes from trip to trip as individuals go off to training, take vacations, or begin new bidding cycles. The airline in which Ginnett's crew worked was relatively rare in civil aviation in that captains were required to conduct a briefing to build their teams before beginning work. It is more common for members to meet for the first time in the cockpit, where they may not even have time for proper introductions before starting to fly together. Even though the advantages of teamwork in the cockpit are widely recognized in the airline industry, the culture of that industry still emphasizes individual rather than team aspects of cockpit work.

The manager of the semiconductor plant that Abramis studied had a problem in supporting teamwork that originated entirely outside the organization. The market for the plant's products fluctuated widely and often unpredictably, and management constantly had to adjust team size in response to changes in demand. A team would just get settled when new members would be added or existing members furloughed. These changes significantly destabilized the teams and made it impossible for members to build and refine their teams over time. As our research was ending, the manager was experimenting with the idea of a core team whose members would, in effect, have tenure in the organization—that is, they would be protected from furlough. In exchange for their improved job security, core team members would accept responsibility both for maintaining their team's continuity and for managing the process when other individuals joined or left the team. Although we cannot say how this idea worked, it does provide one interesting way to use teams to do work even in uncertain and frequently changing circumstances.

Trip Wire #2:   *Fall off the authority balance beam.*

The exercise of authority creates anxiety, especially when one must balance between assigning a team authority for some parts of the work and withholding it for other parts. Because both managers and team members tend to be uncomfortable in such situations, they may collude to "clarify" them. Sometimes the result is the assignment of virtually all authority to the team—which can result in anarchy or a team that heads off in an inappropriate direction. Other times, managers retain virtually all authority, dictating work procedures in detail to team members and, in the process, losing many of the advantages that can accrue from teamwork. In both cases, the anxieties that accompany a mixed model are reduced, but at significant cost to team effectiveness. In our research, we saw the managers in Kahn's baseball team and Davis-Sacks's credit team holding authority too tightly. Conversely, the manager of Eisenstat's Fairfield Components Plant and the director of one of the two plays that Friedman studied (*Gold for the Queen*) exercised too little authority. The balance appeared to be about right in Eisenstat's compressor team start-up and in Perkins and Abramis's federal prison staff team.

To achieve a good balance of managerial and team authority is difficult. Moreover, merely deciding how much authority will be assigned to the group and how much will be retained by management is insufficient. Equally important are the domains of authority that are assigned and retained. Our findings suggest that managers should be unapologetic and insistent about exercising their authority about *direction*—the end states the team is to pursue—and about *outer limit constraints* on team behavior—the things the team must always do or never do. At the same time, managers should assign to the team full authority for the *means* by which it accomplishes its work—and then do whatever they can to ensure that team members understand

and accept their responsibility and accountability for deciding how they will execute the work.

Indeed, effective team functioning may be impossible unless someone exercises authority about direction. Contrary to traditional wisdom about participative management, to authoritatively set a clear, engaging direction for a team is to empower, not depower, it. Having a clear direction helps align team efforts with the objectives of the parent organization, provides members with a criterion to use in selecting its performance strategies, and generates and sustains energy within the team. When direction is absent or unclear, members may wallow in uncertainty about just what they should be doing and may even have difficulty generating the motivation to do much of anything.

For most work teams in organizations, someone in the management structure holds authority for questions of direction. Sometimes, however, a team has the opportunity to set its own direction. In our sample, this was true for the string quartet and, to a lesser extent, for the top management teams. When a team has such authority, members should take the trouble to specify the team's direction quite explicitly. As numerous worker-owned cooperatives have discovered, just having the authority for self-direction is not very helpful; teams must actually *use* their authority if they are to realize its constructive potential—and this sometimes turns out to be difficult for members of a cooperative to bring themselves to do. Ultimately, *who* holds the authority to set direction for a work team is less important than that *some* person or group has, and exercises, that authority.

Few managerial behaviors are more consequential for the long-term well-being of teams than those that address the partitioning of authority between managers and teams. It takes skill to accomplish this well, and it is a skill that has emotional and behavioral as well as cognitive components. Just knowing the rules for partitioning authority is insufficient; one also needs some practice in applying those rules in situations where anxieties, including one's own, are likely to be high. Especially challenging for managers are the early stages in the life of a group (when managers often are tempted to give away too much authority) and when the going gets rough (when the temptation is to take authority back too soon). The management of authority relations with task-performing groups is indeed much like walking a balance beam, and our evidence suggests that it takes a good measure of knowledge, skill, and perseverance to keep from falling off.

Trip Wire #3: *Assemble a large group of people, tell them in general terms what needs to be accomplished, and let them "work out the details."*

Traditional, individually focused designs for work often are plagued by constraining structures that have been built up over the years to monitor and control employee behavior. When groups are used to perform work, such structures tend to be viewed as unnecessary bureaucratic impediments to team functioning. Thus, just as managers sometimes (and mistakenly) attempt to empower groups by relinquishing all authority to them, so do some attempt to get rid of the dysfunctional features of existing organizational structures simply by taking down all the structures they can. Apparently, the hope is that removing structures will release groups and enable members to work together creatively and effectively.

Managers who hold this view often wind up providing teams with less structure than they actually need. Tasks are defined only in vague, general terms. Group composition is unclear or fluid. The limits of the group's authority are kept deliberately fuzzy. The expectation, in the words of one manager, is that "the team will work out the details." The unstated assumption is that there is some magic in group interaction process and that by working together members will evolve any structures that the team actually needs.

It is a false hope; there is no such magic. Indeed, our findings suggest the opposite: groups that have appropriate structures tend to develop healthy internal processes, whereas groups with insufficient or inappropriate structures tend to have process problems. Worse, coaching and process consultation are unlikely to resolve these problems, precisely because they are rooted in the team structure. For members to learn how to interact well within a flawed or underspecified structure is to swim upstream against a very strong current.

Our findings, consistent with the orienting framework with which we began the research, suggest that an enabling structure for a work team has three components. First is a well-designed team task that engages and sustains member motivation. Special attention should be given to the inherent meaningfulness of the work, to the amount of autonomy members have in executing it, and to the degree to which carrying it out generates direct feedback about results. Second is a well-composed group—one that is as small as possible (given the work to be done), that has clear boundaries, that includes members with adequate task and interpersonal skills, and that has a good mix of members—people who are neither so similar to one another that they are like peas in a pod nor so different that they have trouble working together. Third is clear and explicit specification of the extent and limits of the team's authority and accountability. Group members who have a history of working in traditional, individually focused work systems may not automatically assume that such authority is theirs; indeed, they may presume the opposite. Therefore, it may take some repetition and persuasion before members accept that it is their right, and their obligation, constantly to monitor the environment, to forecast changes that may require a group response, and to actively plan and revise the team's performance strategies.

The structures of some teams we studied fit well with these guidelines—for example, those of Davis-Sacks's tracking team (before its work was terminated) and Cohen and Denison's three-person flight attendant team. Also appropriate were the structures created by the three teams that were responsible for their own design: Kahn's basketball team, Butterworth's string quartet, and Gersick's bankers. Less satisfactory were the structures of Shaw's mental health teams and Davis-Sacks's credit team. As we would expect, these last two teams experienced more difficulties with their internal processes than did the others. The key question about structure, then, turns out not to be how much structure a team has. In fact, all teams need structural supports. The question, instead, is about the *kind* of structure: does it enable and support collective work, or does it make teamwork more difficult and frustrating than it need be?

Trip Wire #4: *Specify challenging team objectives, but skimp on organizational supports.*

Even if a work team has clear, engaging direction and an enabling structure, its performance can go sour—or, at least, it can fall below the group's potential—if the team is not well supported. Teams in high-commitment organizations (Walton, 1985) fall victim to this trip wire when they are given "stretch" objectives but not the wherewithal to accomplish them; high initial enthusiasm soon changes into disillusionment. The costs of inadequate organizational support are evident in several of our teams, ranging from Cohen's corporate restructuring group to Wood's professional hockey team. In contrast, the benefits of good support from the surrounding organization are clearly visible in Gersick's bank product development team.

If the full potential of work teams is to be realized, organizational structures and systems must actively support competent teamwork. The key supports, as specified in our orienting framework and elaborated by our findings, include: (1) a reward system that recognizes and reinforces excellent team (not merely individual) performance, (2) an educational system that provides teams, at their initiative, whatever training and technical consultation they may need to supplement members' own knowledge and expertise, (3) an information system that makes available to the team the data and forecasts members need to proactively manage their work, and (4) the mundane material resources—equipment, tools, space, money, staff, or whatever—that teams need to execute their tasks.

It is no small undertaking to provide these supports to teams, especially in organizations designed to support work by individuals. Corporate compensation policy, for example, may make no provision for team bonuses and, indeed, may explicitly prohibit them. Human resource departments may be primed to identify individuals' training needs and provide first-rate courses to fill those needs, but training in team skills may not be available at all. Existing performance appraisal systems, which may be state-of-the-art for measuring individual contributions, are likely to be wholly inappropriate for assessing and rewarding work done by teams. Information and control systems may provide managers with the data they need to monitor and control work processes, but they may be neither available nor appropriate for use by work teams. Finally, the material resources required for the work may have been prespecified by those who originally designed it, and there may be no procedure in place for a team to secure the special configuration of resources it needs to execute the particular performance strategy it has developed.

To align existing organizational systems with the needs of teams often requires managers to exercise power and influence upward and laterally in the organization. And, as the production manager at Abramis's semiconductor plant and the head of Friedman's theater company discovered, one's managerial colleagues may not welcome suggestions to revise the systems that they have developed and with which they are comfortable or to release resources for use by teams—resources that others in the organization also seek. An organization set up to provide teams with full support for their work is noticeably different from one whose systems and policies are intended to support and control individual work, and many managers may find the prospect of changing to a group-oriented organization both unsettling and perhaps even vaguely revolutionary.

It is hard to provide good organizational support for task-performing teams, but generally it is worth the trouble. The potential of a well-directed, well-structured, well-supported team is tremendous. Moreover, to stumble over the organizational support trip wire is, perhaps, the saddest of all team failures. When a group is both excited about its work and all set up to execute it superbly, it is especially shattering to fail merely because the organizational supports required cannot be obtained. It is like being all dressed up and ready to go to the prom only to have the car break down en route.

Trip Wire #5: Assume that members already have all the competence they need to work well as a team.

Once a team is launched and operating under its own steam, managers sometimes assume their work is done. As we have seen, there are indeed some good reasons for giving a team ample room to go about its business in its own way: inappropriate or poorly timed managerial interventions impaired the work of more than one group described in this book. However, a strict hands-off managerial stance also can limit a team's effectiveness, particularly when members are not already skilled and experienced in teamwork.

Thus, it can be helpful for leaders and managers to provide some direct, hands-on coaching as members develop the skills they need to work well in a team and as teams learn how to operate as task-performing units. There is no one best way to accomplish this, nor, despite volumes of research on the topic, is there any one leadership style that is optimal for coaching and helping work teams. The leaders of the teams in this book, for example, had very different styles. Some were energetic and free with advice and counsel, others were laid-back and soft-spoken, and still others were eclectic—doing whatever they could to help group members invent their own solutions to team problems. Coaching a group, like teaching a class, is done best when the leader exploits his or her own personality and style to get the lesson across. An active, energetic leader is likely to behave actively and energetically with his or her team, while a person who is generally soft-spoken and relaxed will tend to use that style. We would not have it any other way: when a leader tries to adopt a coaching style that is at variance with his or her personal style, leadership effectiveness inevitably suffers.

While we have a decidedly agnostic stance regarding leadership style, our findings point to three other leadership issues for which there are some specific right and wrong directions. One has to do with the timing of leader interventions. It is clear that groups are far more open and responsive to such interventions at certain times in their lives than they are at others. Favorable times for intervention include when a group is first launched, when it reaches a natural break in its work, and when it has completed its product or reached the end of a performance period. When a group has its collective head buried in the actual execution of the work, on the other hand, is a decidedly bad time for intervention.

A second implication of our findings is that coaching activities are unlikely to have lasting benefit if a team's performance situation is unfavorable. If members have little idea what they are supposed to be doing, if the team has been set up poorly, or if the surrounding organization undermines rather than fosters work by teams, then a leader would be better advised to address these problems rather than spend time on process consultations intended to help members work together well in what is a fundamentally untenable performance situation.

Finally, our findings affirm that whatever occurs when a team is created—when members first meet and begin to come to terms with one another and the work they will do—has enduring effects. For this reason, one of the most powerful and constructive interventions a leader can make is to help a team get off to a good start. Because start-up is rarely a crisis time, both time and energy usually are available to help a team become established and start functioning as a task-performing unit. If this is done, then the chances improve that the team will have reserves available to apply to a crisis when and if one does occur. If it is not, performance may still be satisfactory as long as the team is not seriously tested. But when all of the team's resources are required to meet a significant work challenge—such as completing a task on time despite serious and unavoidable last-minute problems—the long-term costs of a poor launch may, at last, become evident.

The role of a team leader or manager, then, involves three kinds of activities: (1) creating favorable performance conditions for the team, either on one's own authority or by exercising influence upward or laterally with managerial colleagues, (2) building and maintaining the team as a performing unit, and (3) coaching and helping the team in real time.

If a leader focuses on these activities, he or she will need to have little concern about the five trip wires discussed above. The team will be an intact performing unit that perceives itself as such (and that others deal with as such) rather than an aggregation of individual workers. It will have a clear, authoritative, and engaging direction for its work. The structure of the team—its task, composition, and authority—will promote rather than impede good performance. The organizational context will provide support and reinforcement for excellence through policies and systems explicitly designed to support team work. And ample, expert coaching will be available to the team at those times when members need and are ready to receive it.

It takes both work and skill on the part of leaders and managers to put these conditions into place and to keep them there. In our view, the payoff is more than worth the required investment. Indeed, our findings suggest that when the conditions specified above are present, the chances are good that a group will perform its work well—and, in the process, build the competence of the team as a performing unit and contribute positively to the personal well-being of team members.

Note

1. We should have been more alert to this phenomenon than we were, given that the substantive content of groups' tasks was found to affect performance in the project leader's very first study of group behavior (Hackman, 1968).

References

Alderfer, C. P. (1977). Group and intergroup relations. In J. R. Hackman & J. L. Suttle (Eds.), *Improving life at work.* Santa Monica, CA: Goodyear.

Bales, R. F., & Strodtbeck, F. L. (1951). Phases in group problem solving. *Journal of Abnormal and Social Psychology, 46,* 485–495.

Berg, D. N. (1985). Anxiety in research relationships. In D. N. Berg & K. K. Smith (Eds.), *Exploring clinical methods for social research.* Beverly Hills: Sage.

Bion, W. R. (1961). *Experiences in groups.* New York: Basic Books.

Canby, V. (3 April 1983). Some bright new talent commands attention. *New York Times.*

Cohen, S. G. (1988). *Group empowerment: Vision, goals, and efficacy.* Doctoral dissertation, Yale University.

Denison, D. R. (1985, August). *The growth and differentiation of People Express Airlines.* Paper presented at the annual meeting of the Academy of Management, San Diego.

Ekman, P., & Oster, H. (1979). Facial expression of emotion. *Annual Review of Psychology, 30,* 527–554.

Eldrege, N., & Gould, S. J. (1972). Punctuated equilibria: An alternative to phyletic gradualism. In T. J. Schopf (Ed.), *Models in paleobiology.* San Francisco: Freeman, Cooper & Co.

Freud, S. (1960). *Jokes and their relation to the unconscious.* (James Strachey, Trans.) New York: Norton. (Original work published 1905)

Gersick, C. G. (1983). *Life cycles of ad hoc task groups.* Technical report #3, Research Program on Group Effectiveness, Yale University School of Organization and Management.

Gersick, C. G. (1984). *The life cycles of ad hoc task groups: Time, transitions and learning in teams.* Unpublished doctoral dissertation, Yale University.

Gersick, C. G. (1988). Time and transition in work teams: Toward a new model of group development. *Academy of Management Journal, 31,* 9–41.

Ginnett, R. C. (1987). *First encounters of the close kind: The formation process of airline flight crews.* Doctoral dissertation, Yale University.

Hackman, J. R. (1968). Effects of task characteristics on group products. *Journal of Experimental Social Psychology, 4,* 162–187.

Hackman, J. R. (1984). The transition that hasn't happened. In J. Kimberly & R. Quinn (Eds.), *Managing organizational transitions.* Homewood, IL: Dow Jones–Irwin.

Hackman, J. R. (1986a). Group level issues in the design and training of cockpit crews. In H. H. Orlady & H. C. Foushee (Eds.), *Proceedings of the NASA/MAC Workshop on Cockpit Resource Management.* Moffett Field, CA: NASA-Ames Research Center.

Hackman, J. R. (1986b). The psychology of self-management in organizations. In M. S. Pallak & R. O. Perloff (Eds.), *Psychology and work: Productivity, change, and employment.* Washington, DC: American Psychological Association.

Hackman, J. R. (1987). The design of work teams. In J. W. Lorsch (Ed.), *Handbook of organizational behavior.* Englewood Cliffs, NJ: Prentice-Hall.

Hackman, J. R., & Morris, C. G. (1975). Group tasks, group interaction process, and group performance effectiveness: A review and proposed integration. In L. Berkowitz (Ed.), *Advances in experimental social psychology.* New York: Academic Press.

Hackman, J. R., & Oldham, G. R. (1980). *Work redesign.* Reading, MA: Addison-Wesley.

Hackman, J. R., & Walton, R. E. (1986). Leading groups in organizations. In P. S. Goodman (Ed.), *Designing effective work groups.* San Francisco: Jossey-Bass.

Hare, A. P. (1976). *Handbook of small group research* (2nd ed.). New York: Free Press.

Helmreich, R. L., Foushee, H. C., Benson, R., & Russini, R. (1986). Cockpit management attitudes: Exploring the attitude-performance linkage. *Aviation, Space and Environmental Medicine, 57,* 1198–1200.

Katz, D., & Kahn, R. L. (1978). *The social psychology of organizations* (2nd ed.). New York: Wiley.

Kidder, T. (1981). *The soul of a new machine.* New York: Avon.

Langley, S. (1974). *Theatre management in America.* New York: Drama Book Specialists.

Lawler, E. E. (1973). *Motivation in work organizations.* Monterey, CA: Brooks/Cole.

Leverett, J. (1985). Introduction. In S. Gray, *Swimming to Cambodia.* New York: Theatre Communications Group.

Lewin, K. (1936). *Principles of toplogical psychology.* New York: McGraw-Hill.

McGrath, J. E. (1984). *Groups: Interaction and performance.* Englewood Cliffs, NJ: Prentice-Hall.

Memmi, A. (1984). *Dependence.* Boston: Beacon Press.

Nemy, E. (30 May 1986). Broadway. *New York Times.*

Radcliffe-Brown, A. R. (1952). *Structure and function in primitive society.* New York: Free Press.

Rafaeli, A., & Sutton, R. I. (1987). Expression of emotion as part of the work role. *Academy of Management Review, 12,* 23–37.

Reimer, S. (23 December 1984). The airline that shook the industry. *New York Times Magazine.*

Roy, D. (1959). Banana time: Job satisfaction and informal interaction. *Human Organization, 18,* 158–168.

Shaw, R. (1985). *Mental health treatment teams.* Unpublished master's thesis, Yale University.

Spurr, D., Ehnis, H., & Feldkamp, J. (1981). A team approach to patient assignments. *American Operating Room Nurses Journal, 33,* 783–792.

Steinbeck, J. (1951). *The log from the Sea of Cortez.* New York: Viking.

Steiner, I. D. (1972). *Group process and productivity.* New York: Academic Press.

Survey Research Center (1976). *Interviewers' manual* (rev. ed.). Ann Arbor, MI: Institute for Social Research.

Tannenbaum, A. S. (1968). *Control in organizations.* New York: McGraw-Hill.

Tuckman, B. W. (1965). Developmental sequence in small groups. *Psychological Bulletin, 63,* 384–399.

Turan, K. (3 April 1983). Dennis Hopper, a survivor of the 60's, tries again. *New York Times.*

Van Maanen, J. (1986). Power in the bottle: Informal interaction and formal authority. In S. Srivastva & Associates, *Executive power: How executives influence people and organizations.* San Francisco: Jossey-Bass.

Vroom, V. H. (1964). *Work and motivation.* New York: Wiley.

Walton, R. E. (1985). From control to commitment: Transformation of workforce management strategies in the United States. In K. B. Clark, R. H. Hayes, & C. Lorenz (Eds.), *The uneasy alliance: Managing the productivity-technology dilemma.* Boston: Harvard Business School Press.

Wicker, A., Kirmeyer, S. L., Hanson, L., & Alexander, D. (1976). Effects of manning levels on subjective experiences, performance, and verbal interaction in groups. *Organizational Behavior and Human Performance, 17,* 251–274.

Zajonc, R. B. (1965). Social facilitation. *Science, 149,* 269–274.

Zaleznik, A. (1989, January–February). Real work. *Harvard Business Review.*

Index

509